THE BROKEN SPELL

THE BROKEN SPELL

A Cultural and Anthropological History of Preindustrial Europe

PIETER SPIERENBURG

 RUTGERS UNIVERSITY PRESS
New Brunswick

Library of Congress Cataloging-in-Publication Data

Spierenburg, Petrus Cornelis.
    [Verbroken betovering. English]
    The broken spell : a cultural and anthropological history of
preindustrial Europe / Pieter Spierenburg.
        p.   cm.
    Includes bibliographical references and index.
    ISBN 0-8135-1675-7 (cloth)   ISBN 0-8135-1676-5 (pbk.)
        1. Europe—Social life and customs.   2. Family—Europe—History.
    3. Attitude (Psychology)—Europe—History.   4. Privacy—Europe—
    History.   5. Body, Human—Social aspects.   I. Title.
    GT129.S68   1991
    391'.6—dc20   90-19386
                                                                    CIP

First published in Dutch as *De Verbroken Betovering:*
Mentaliteitsgeschiedenis van Preïndustrieel Europa by Verloren, Hilversum,
The Netherlands

Copyright © 1991 by Pieter Spierenburg
All Rights Reserved
Manufactured in the United States of America

To the memory of Norbert Elias,
who was my greatest teacher

CONTENTS

PREFACE

Past mentalities are the subject of this book. We learn about them from spectacular episodes like the impossible love of Giovanni and Lusanna in fifteenth-century Florence, the departure of Martin Guerre whose place was taken by a stranger in a French village in the sixteenth century, the great cat massacre by a group of Paris journeymen in the eighteenth century, and several related stories aptly told by their investigators. The ordinary aspects of daily life, however, have been studied by historians too and they equally form part of the history of mentalities. This book does not simply repeat the stories and analyses completed by other scholars. Its aim is to arrive at a synthesis. As it constructs an interpretative frame, it attempts to enhance our knowledge of world outlook and emotional life in earlier centuries.

Studying the thoughts and emotions of people in the past is not novel. Until recently, however, this effort was directed almost exclusively at the analysis of a few great minds and the scrutiny of a narrow range of themes belonging to official culture. The emphasis here is on new subjects which have received increasing attention in recent years. That is why the concept of "history of mentalities" (from the French mentalités) is used: to reflect a shift of focus from an investigation of purely intellectual developments to one which pays ample attention to psychological aspects and "unofficial" culture. It is a basic tenet of the history of mentalities that the entire personality structure of people in the past was different from what it is today.

The work which has been done so far largely has concentrated on preindustrial societies. This book, therefore, is restricted to the period that ends with the Industrial Revolution. Geographically, it is limited to Europe, but not every country can receive an exhaustive treatment. Much research has been performed in France and England, but there is also information from areas such as the Netherlands and Germany. In fact, we are dealing with developments which, to a large extent, characterized western Europe as a whole: west of the line Leningrad–Trieste, which is so dear to students of demography.

Since this is a work of synthesis, footnotes are not included. References are contained in the bibliography, ordered by chapter. Each title has been relegated to the subject with which it primarily deals. Sometimes, however, especially with themes in the field of family and community, titles have been used for more than one chapter. The bibliography has been split up nonetheless, so that the reader can see at once which is the literature relevant to a particular subject. Quotations of course are followed by a precise reference. Because only historical documents are cited verbatim, just the author reporting them is mentioned and the phrase "quoted by" left out.

This book is an English adaptation of a work originally published in Dutch. The effort of those who, by their critical comments, helped to shape the original edition should be noted here as well. My first gratitude is to the students who took the courses I gave at the department of history of Erasmus University Rotterdam from 1979 onward. They continually forced me to reformulate my thoughts and sometimes to change them. Rudolf Dekker and Herman Roodenburg read the entire Dutch version of the manuscript, while Herman Diederiks, Marijke Gijswijt-Hofstra, Florence Koorn, and Paul Schulten read one or more chapters. An essential contribution to the realization of this edition was made by Professor Herbert Rowen, who turned my rough draft into fluent English.

1 CHANGING EMOTIONS AND WORLD VIEWS

Some five centuries ago, according to the twentieth-century scholar Johan Huizinga, the daily events of life had sharper contours than today. Joy and sorrow, happiness and disaster were experienced directly and passionately, as only small children do nowadays. All the business of life, the beautiful and the ugly alike, was played out in public. The first edition of Huizinga's *Waning of the Middle Ages*, which dates from 1919, paid full attention to what he called "life forms," which we now describe as "mentalities" (after the French, *mentalités*). This focus was unusual at the time. Many colleagues, thinking that Huizinga was concerning himself with trivialities, chided him. At that time, a heavily political historiography was dominant. But it is no coincidence that Jan Romein, who introduced the concept of "theoretical history," was a student of Huizinga's. Romein looked at his former teacher with a mixture of criticism and admiration. He appreciated that Huizinga had offered him a keen insight into the mentality of preindustrial people.

Huizinga was the first scholar who studied the history of mentalities; he had no immediate successors. Comparable work was done only later and not at first by Dutch scholars. France was the first country where more than a few historians devoted themselves to subjects such as popular culture, sexuality, and death. The French school is usually associated with the journal *Annales*, founded in 1929 by Marc Bloch and Lucien Febvre. The *Annales* historians' predilection for mentalities, however, actually dates from the 1960s. Historians elsewhere, many of them inspired by the French, also began to investigate subjects relating to emotions and world outlooks. The English journal *Past and Present* regularly has contributions in this field. Currently, the history of mentalities shows a growing interest in Huizinga's homeland as well, as illustrated by the greater frequency of reprints of his classic *Waning of the Middle Ages*: five between October 1984 and April 1986 as compared to fifteen in the preceding sixty-five years.

Although we now have a huge amount of data at our disposal about the thoughts and feelings of people in the past, our knowledge lacks cohesion. To construct a general framework, we have to follow the example of the great historically oriented sociologists. Two authors, Norbert Elias, who published his major work in 1939 but only became generally known around 1970, and Max Weber, who was active at the beginning of this century, are the principal models. Elias in particular provides a theoretical frame of reference capable of accommodating varying findings from the history of mentalities. He shows how mental changes, as part of long-term developments, are mutually related. He also demonstrates their relationship with other developments in society, especially processes of state formation. His theory is based on empirical data which at times are surprisingly concrete. He analyzes the changing rules of conduct, for example, in etiquette books from the thirteenth to the nineteenth centuries, dealing with such things as table manners and the correct way of blowing one's nose. Elias concludes that human conduct has become more strictly regulated in the course of the period studied, first among a small elite and later among broader groups. Max Weber's work touches on a wide variety of themes. At the present time, his theories about changing world views are important. Weber claims that the world outlook of various groups had become less tinged with magic a few centuries already before the Industrial Revolution, and he investigates the role of world religions in this development. He also compares European developments with those in non-European societies.

This introductory chapter bridges the gap between Elias's and Weber's theoretical constructs on the one hand and the data collected by historians of mentalities on the other. Its outline follows from the combination of both. Mentality refers to world outlook, beliefs, and cultural customs as well as to personality, emotions, and attitudes. The subjects dealt with in this book are related to these aspects of life in particular. Studying them, we find that crucial changes have taken place in the realm of thought and feeling. The theoretical framework serves to describe and explain those changes systematically. During the preindustrial period Europe witnessed three large developments in the mental field which appear most fundamental: emotional life was attuned to a hierarchical rank order for a long time, but to a lesser degree toward the end of the preindustrial period; many aspects of life originally had a public character, but they gradually shifted from a public to a private sphere; perceptions of the cosmos and of human society became more impersonal, less tinged with magic and, ultimately, also less guided by religion.

Lastly, those developments must be linked to other social processes. People do not think and feel in a vacuum. Indeed, we are obligated to reconstruct their thoughts and feelings from the way these are expressed. This is a crucial point. By definition, whatever goes on inside human minds is unknown to historians. Even when someone voices an idea or an emotion, orally or in writing, this expression is indirect. Therefore, the historiography of inner life tells of concrete activities: drinking or praying, stealing or making love. Mentalities obviously are embedded in social life and mental changes are related to other forms of social change.

Personality and Hierarchy

Visible changes in human behavior are central to Elias's research and his theoretical reflection. They can be traced in etiquette books from the thirteenth century until the beginning of the nineteenth. Rules of conduct became stricter in the course of that period, notably with respect to bodily functions. From this Elias concludes that feeling and affect were given relatively free rein in the Middle Ages. People lived in extremes; emotions were scarcely channeled or repressed. In the course of the preindustrial period Europeans gradually developed a controlling force within their personalities. Self-control and the manipulation of emotions became stronger among elite groups in the early modern period, while this movement spread later to larger groups in society.

This development was not even or unilinear. Like every long-term process, its course was characterized by sudden accelerations, temporary interruptions, and counter-movements. It had no beginning either. There is never an absolute starting point to any development; it is always a matter of degree. Twelfth-century Europeans also regulated their conduct, but in another way. Even before A.D. 1000 certain monasteries, which were like small islands where a select group appeared to be capable of a relatively large measure of emotional control, were exceptions. It was only in the early modern period that larger groups adopted refined models of behavior.

Differences in conduct between various social strata occupy a central place in the analysis of forms of emotional control. The emergence of more refined codes of behavior began among elite groups. In the early modern period these were the court nobility and the upper bourgeoisie. Etiquette, civility and polite social intercourse were the hallmarks of courtly standards of conduct; virtue, thrift and industry those of their bourgeois counterparts. The bourgeois ethic, combined with aristocratic elements, formed the basis for nineteenth-century behavioral norms, which eventually influenced broader groups. This phenomenon is central to the history of mentalities. Mental changes can often be observed first among elite groups, while parallel changes take place among the majority of the population at a later time, usually in the industrial period. A comparable sequence is inherent in most of the subjects discussed in this book. The concealment of death, for example, manifested itself first among the aristocracy and the bourgeoisie. Members of the upper and middle classes became sensitive to the sight of public executions, while the rest of the population still was indifferent.

This "pioneer role" of elite groups may lead to a misunderstanding. Acknowledging it certainly does not imply an elitist view of our present culture or way of life. The social circumstances during the closing centuries of the preindustrial period merely facilitated the acquisition of a novel personality structure by European elites. In principle, every human being is capable of this development. Indeed, this personality structure became characteristic of broader groups, made possible by the changing circumstances in an industrial society. Some group differences remained of course.

This leads us to the relationship between hierarchy and emotions. The vast majority in, say, the sixteenth century were also required to control their behavior. Lower class people had to be reticent especially when confronted by persons from the elite. The latter could expect submissiveness and deference. Among themselves, peasants and artisans behaved differently. To a large extent the regulation of conduct was attuned to social distinctions. This held equally true among the elites internally. A subtle differentiation of ranks meant that everyone always had to take into account those with whom they were dealing. The adjustment of behavioral regulation to social distinctions may have become even stronger during the early modern period, because the elites withdrew from popular culture. Eventually, however, standards of conduct became more informal in some situations, although still channelled and controlled. We observe this, for example, with family life among the elites, where more personal and intimate relationships began to prevail toward the end of the preindustrial period. As social inequalities decreased further and power differences grew smaller in the industrial period, emotional life among the majority of the population was determined less by the social hierarchy. We can say that emotional life has been democratized over the last few centuries. These processes of democratization and informalization were accompanied by an increase in restraints upon emotions in social intercourse.

Another related development was the increase in people's capacity for identification. As the channelling force within their personalities became stronger, there was more room to reflect about the thoughts and feelings of others. Increasingly people recognized others as "somebody like me" and were capable of sharing their experiences. One of the results was that they treated fellow human beings more mercifully to a certain extent. To be sure, this form of identification was not extended equally to all fellow men and women. It was a question of widening horizons. Originally, only members of a restricted group—one's own—were considered as "somebody like me." Members of other social strata, occupational groups, nations, or races were hardly viewed as fellow humans. In the seventeenth century, for example, there was a form of mutual consideration among the elites. But nobles and bourgeois hardly cared about people from the lower classes, despite their many hardships. Although the hunger and cold they might suffer from in winter were not necessarily sources of amusement, neither was there talk of empathy. Physical punishment, meted out in public for some offense, was observed without comment.

From the second half of the eighteenth century, the ability to identify with others slowly extended across the borders of social strata. One of its expressions was that elites gradually became more sensitive to the suffering and violence often endured by people from the lower classes. They started to find the sight of punishment at the scaffold unpleasant. Slavery became controversial too. Even with respect to the suffering of animals a heightened sensitivity broke through. This increase in identification began in the preindustrial period, but it was continued in industrial society. Certainly, the horizons have not been widened as far as they can be. From a global perspective, today's measure of interhuman identification is still relatively low. Attitudes toward ethnic minorities in several countries remind us of this.

From Openness to Seclusion

The second general development in the field of mentalities is called privatization, and it is one of the central concepts of this book. Privatization refers to changes which can be observed at various levels. Through his analysis of books on manners, Elias was the first scholar to reconstruct the process. He usually speaks of human activities which gradually were hidden behind the scenes of social life. Those activities were varied, but many, in one way or another, had to do with the body. Examples of a relocation behind the scenes can be found in all five areas covered in etiquette books.

Bodily functions in a stricter sense of the term were among the first to disappear from public life. The magistrates of several late-medieval cities, those of Amsterdam for example, issued ordinances against urinating in the street. We do not know how conscientiously the inhabitants complied. Sixteenth-century etiquette books taught aristocrats to leave the company of others when they felt the need. Gradually toilets became a common feature of private homes and other buildings. In seventeenth-century Holland they were appropriately called "secret comforts." Next, the products of excretion also were banished from daily life. In the course of the eighteenth century, cloth manufacturers stopped using human urine, which until then had been a favorite bleaching agent. In the nineteenth century many urban residents opposed the introduction of a sewerage system because they were accustomed to selling their own feces as manure. This practice became a lost battle, since everything reminiscent of excretion including its odor was banished from public life. Alain Corbin describes the measures taken to this effect by the authorities at the end of the eighteenth and in the nineteenth century. Just as in other fields, the privatization of bodily functions is not absolute. Today, for example, the sight of a person leaving an Amsterdam pub and urinating into a canal is not uncommon.

The changes in meat carving offer an example of concealment with respect to table manners. At banquets of nobles and bourgeois, complete oxen and pigs used to be served at the table, and it was an honorable task for one of the guests to carve them into pieces fit for individual consumption. From the end of the seventeenth century the cook took care of this in the kitchen. Forms of concealment also characterized the changing norms with respect to spitting and nose-blowing. The history of sleeping habits, finally, features the transition from openness to seclusion quite clearly. Many homes had no separate sleeping rooms, and a good host shared his bed with a visitor. At the end of the seventeenth and in the eighteenth century, private bedrooms became more common. In our own time, retiring for the night has become such a self-evidently private matter that the expression "to sleep with" has a specifically sexual meaning.

Thus far we have drawn data from etiquette books. More recent studies have revealed analogous developments so that we may conclude that privatization was a process with wide ramifications. It is inherent in most of the subjects dealt with here. The disintegration of the communal life which nourished popular culture, for example, was a form of privatization. Well into the eighteenth century, the village or neighborhood community frequently intervened in the life of its members, endowing that life with a relatively public flavor. Courtship and marriage were among the things neighbors kept their eye on. Communal bonds lost their force around 1800. Developments with respect to family life closely paralleled these events. The nuclear family became domesticated, closing itself off from the environment to some extent. Among the lower classes this environment first of all meant the village or neighborhood; among the upper classes it was the peer group and the servants, among others. Sexuality too was surrounded by a relative openness for a long time. A process of concealment set in from the eighteenth century. In that case, clearly, behavior connected to the body disappeared from the public arena. That also applied to death. Dying, lying in state, burial, and cemeteries had a more public character than they have today. This changed from the sixteenth century, first slowly and later at a faster pace. Insanity too got its own secluded place. The first madhouses date from the fifteenth century, and their number increased in the course of the early modern period. In the nineteenth century psychiatry arose. In the area of violence and repression, finally, we observe an analogous development. For a long time, serious offenders were punished physically and publicly, but courts could resort to imprisonment from the end of the sixteenth century. After 1800 the prison became the most common penal option.

Privatization's three main characteristics are implied in these developments. The slogan, from openness to seclusion, reflects the process. Aspects of life and social activities, which are often but not always related to the body, disappear from the public arena to enclosed spaces. Second, it is a relatively long-term process. It does not take place simultaneously in every field and its first signs can be traced back to an early date. Privatization starts in the later Middle Ages with the concealment of bodily functions and the confinement of dangerous lunatics. An acceleration in the process of privatization is visible around 1800, partly preceding and partly coinciding with the transition to an industrial society. Between about 1750 and around 1850 the intimate nuclear family makes its appearance, and the old village and neighborhood communities disintegrate. The banishment of death in public dates from the middle of the eighteenth century. The transformation of repression, leading to the disappearance of public executions, among other things, takes place between about 1770 and 1870. Around 1800 the administrators of prisons and madhouses stop admitting curious visitors.

Third, one should realize that enclosed spaces, where various activities are hidden from public view, are themselves derivatives of the process of privatization. We can easily see this in the case of the confinement of delinquents and madmen. Before magistrates and private citizens adopted this policy, there were no empty prisons and lunatic asylums in the cities of Europe. The same conclusion applies at a more symbolic or ideological level. When passers-by stopped following a priest into the home of a dying person, it was not because they suddenly realized that this was an impropriety on the part of their ancestors, but because they became convinced that dying had to be confidential, watched only by intimates. A symbolic enclosed space, appearing around 1800 and still cherished by us today, is the private sphere. It arises especially in connection with the breakthrough of the domesticated nuclear family. More than in earlier times, people think that there is a part of their life which should be free from outside interference. Today, individuals even cultivate their own privacy vis-à-vis the people with whom they cohabitate.

The private sphere is less concrete and demarcated than the prison, a building that has unpleasant connotations. Thus, the enclosed spaces which arise in the course of the process of privatization differ in nature, depending on the area where the transition from openness to seclusion takes place. Enclosure can take the form of privacy but also the form of deprivation of liberty, of asylum, and of solitude. Those who restrict themselves to considering only the present may easily conclude that the barbed wire surrounding a state penitentiary and the hedge enclosing a suburban garden are unrelated. The connection can be demonstrated only by a historical analysis.

To prevent misunderstanding, two remarks must conclude the discussion of privatization. First, it should be restated that this is a process in the mental field. In other areas of social life a contrasting development in the direction of openness can be observed. This openness often is enforced by inferior groups as their power increases. The evolution of criminal law provides a good example. While the execution of the sentence moves behind closed doors, secrecy turns into publicity with trial proceedings. Citizens are allowed to watch the business of the authorities. Secondly, no seclusion is absolute. The notion of the private sphere, for example, is partly rooted in an illusion. Everyone is constantly confronted with models of how to behave at home; royalty and movie stars are not the only ones to suffer from occasional encroachments upon their privacy. Just like the rest of their behavior, people's actions within the private sphere are a part of that network of relationships which we call society.

The Disenchantment of the World

Max Weber introduced the concept of *Entzauberung der Welt*, usually rendered in English as "the disenchantment of the world." It has been adopted by numerous scholars and is also useful in the historiography of mentalities. Of course, Weber referred to the evolution of people's view of the world rather than any change in the natural environment itself. His concept implies that the world was once viewed as enchanted, which leads him to speak of a magic garden. In it there are romantic beings and positive forces such as fairy queens, satyrs, guardian angels, and good vibrations along with evil spirits, vampires, incredible snowmen, and devils. More precisely, according to the notion of the magic garden, the cosmos not only consists of humans and dead and living nature, but also of magical forces and supernatural beings, god(s) included. The disenchantment of the world is the process whereby the conception of the cosmos resembles the magic garden to an ever lesser extent. The word *lesser* implies that this garden has certainly not disappeared altogether from our minds.

We are dealing with two related themes: the marginalization of magical beliefs and explanations and the evolution of the supernatural imply first the emergence of a few world religions, while later religion slowly recedes from the center of social life. The direction the process takes has to do with both themes. Impersonal forces replace magical forces, and the borders of the supernatural recede. However, these two developments are not synchronous. In a simplified scheme, two stages can be distinguished. During the first, magical beliefs and customs are pushed back precisely because of the appearance of universal cults such as Christianity. They give rise to a world view rooted in the faith, while developing a systematic doctrine which sees the cosmos as a structured unity. Gods take the place of magical spirits. Within monotheistic religions all natural and supernatural events are ultimately traced back to the will and creation of one God. This relegates events into a system. In the second stage, however, supernatural events are increasingly denied instead of being systematized. The scientific-mathematical view of the world, as Weber calls it, emerges. As it breaks through, religion eventually occupies a more marginal position, a process we call secularization. This two-staged scheme is no more than a rough sketch. For one thing, magical beliefs were still widespread in society at a time when small groups of elites were already espousing a more impersonal and scientific image of the world. On the other hand, the earliest spurts in the direction of secularization antedate the scientific revolution by several centuries.

The first qualification needs little explanation. Magical rituals, distrusted or opposed by clerics in particular, continued to enjoy a wide popularity throughout the preindustrial period. Those rituals either served to ward off disasters or were connected to the afterlife. As to the latter, the beliefs of clerics and laymen were largely congruent since the later Middle Ages; but, with respect to the warding off of disasters, considerable antagonisms remained between both parties. In the eighteenth century, extra-ecclesiastical, "enlightened" groups took over the "struggle against superstition" from the clergy. In addition, they opposed a number of beliefs of the church.

Secularization is a dual process, observable at the mental level as well as at other levels of society. In the social sphere it relates to a decrease in the power and influence of the representatives of religion: church and clergy. In the mental sphere secularization concerns a diminishing of the religious content of world view and ideology. With respect to secularization, the preindustrial period can be divided into two phases. Before the beginning of the seventeenth century there was a balance of tension between secularizing tendencies and their opposites, increases in the influence of the clergy, or clericalization. An early example of the first is the emergence of an urban culture in the Middle Ages. Although pervasively Christian, it still contained a number of novel elements. But the tendencies toward clericalization were equally strong in that period, if not stronger. The influence of the clergy over lay-people's marriages and the ritual of death and burial notably increased. In the sixteenth century, too, there were movements of secularization alongside episodes of greater stress upon a religious interpretation of certain phenomena. The transformation of attitudes toward poverty, culminating in the establishment of prison-workhouses, reflected secularization in the social as well as the mental field.

Control over charity shifted from ecclesiastical to worldly authorities, and a religiously inspired view of poverty gave way to an approach toward public order. Conversely, the frequency of exorcisms increased in this period. The unusual behavior of a greater number of people was interpreted as the result of demonic possession. In the second half of the sixteenth and at the beginning of the seventeenth century, England, France, and Germany witnessed exorcisms, surrounded by vast publicity. Catholics and Puritans exploited exorcisms in an effort to bolster their propaganda against other denominations. In the course of the seventeenth century the tendencies toward secularization took the upper hand. Exorcisms became less frequent and, where they were still performed, they received no considerable publicity. An increasing number of people were inclined to interpret the behavior of those who might have been considered demoniacs in an earlier period as a symptom of insanity. The representatives of the church were obliged to adopt a defensive stance on various fronts.

The Social Context

To inquire into the social context of mental developments is to inquire into other related social developments. World views and emotional life are just as much a part of society as class conflicts, commercial networks, or technological discoveries are. Interdependencies in particular areas, such as those between changes in family life or the penal system on the one hand and the rise of states or economic processes on the other, are explained in the related chapters. Here, it suffices to sketch an encompassing framework. To introduce it, the traffic of our own time is contrasted with that in Europe around A.D. 1000.

A millennium ago society was feudal and stateless. There were roads connecting various places, but not many. Even the highways, sandy and hardly paved, were frequented by only an occasional traveler. The land surrounding the road was sometimes wild and sometimes cultivated for agricultural purposes. Within the space of a day the traveler passed the territories of several rulers. The potential risks were concrete, such as an attack by robbers or a warlord and his followers looking for booty. Travelers had to guard against these dangers and be prepared constantly to defend themselves with weapons. In such a society, the psychological brakes which prevented people from using violence were relatively insignificant, while their emotional life generally was more open and direct. Consider the roads in today's society, which contrast markedly with their early counterparts. Imagine an interstate highway in Europe where cars are speeding in both directions; in the fast-moving lanes Porsches catch up with Volkswagens. To the right, cars are leaving the road while others enter. The way in which one person imperils another has little to do with an armed attack. The greatest risk is someone's loss of self-control. In this network of traffic the security of most people is assured—since there are more survivors than casualties—as a result of the behavioral control the participants are capable of. But if a driver suddenly ignores a wrong-way sign, disaster might ensue.

The juxtaposition of two types of highways provides a model for the contrast between societies with a relatively low and a relatively high measure of existential security. The degree to which the security of every individual person is guaranteed is primarily a function of the level of state formation. Larger state units, within which a relative pacification was realized, appeared on the scene in Western Europe in the course of the preindustrial period. Violence and supreme rule were monopolized, which generally facilitated an increase of restraints upon the violent inclinations and the emotions of individual persons. As we will see, mental changes took place notably in the early modern period. The European system of states, with a number of large and middle-sized monarchies and a few patrician republics, was formed then. Eventually, this resulted to a certain extent in a society free from violence, except for the relations among states. Physical attack became less common in daily intercourse. People had to approach each other more cautiously, which required emotional restraint and a more subtle control of conduct. Early modern princely courts highlighted the interdependence of state formation and behavioral change. Novel and more refined models of conduct were first developed in the centers of the new states. In the prince's presence aristocrats had to behave courteously.

But the level of state formation was not the only determinant of the degree of existential security. The economic situation was crucial too, notably for the lower classes. Subsistence crises, which returned periodically and often caused a region's mortality rates to rise dramatically, constituted a permanent threat. From the seventeenth century on those "crises of the old type" became infrequent as a consequence of commercialization and a denser infrastructure. For large groups, however, life still remained precarious and many faced the threat of economic downfall. Next to starvation, sickness was a frequent cause of death. Recurrent plague epidemics ravaged Europe from the middle of the fourteenth until the eighteenth century. Besides, many other diseases were more lethal than they are today. Also with respect to these dangers, the upper classes were relatively privileged. They possessed the resources to flee from the plague and could afford to pay for medical help, although this was seldom effective. These considerations make it understandable why lower class people continued to live in extremes and only later became accustomed to new modes of controlling their conduct. From the sixteenth century they lived in relatively pacified states, but nonetheless they experienced a great existential insecurity.

Thus, differences in mentality between powerful and less powerful groups were especially great in the early modern period. Chapter 3 explains that this was the time when secular elites withdrew from popular culture. The aristocracy and bourgeoisie were the first, from the sixteenth century, to adopt new models of behavior. Eventually, this led to a conflict between the "civilized" culture of court and cities on one side and traditional popular culture on the other. The relative insecurity which was still a feature of lower-class existence also made them cling to magical beliefs and rituals for a longer time. Magic and faith in the supernatural served to ward off dangers and to make incomprehensible things comprehensible.

Two caveats conclude this introduction. It would be wrong if we conceived of preindustrial people, both from the populace and the elites, only in negative terms: as more emotional and less rational than we are. Things are not that simple. At a theoretical level, some changes in mentality which took a long time can be acknowledged. But the mentality of preindustrial people was rooted in their shared experiences and embedded in daily life. Their beliefs and their feelings were the cement of social relationships, and it is these which this book strives to elucidate. Then we may come to understand why people lived the way they did and to comprehend the dynamics of changing world views and emotional standards. The second caveat follows from the first. Mental changes can be listed under the rubric of a few long-term developments pointing in a particular direction. We are able to establish that direction, since we have the advantage of looking back over several centuries. However, in the daily reality of the past there were recurrent countertendencies and dead-end streets. The most conspicuous among these are dealt with here. Repeated warnings about the nonunilinear character of a long-term development would become rather monotonous. Nevertheless, the reader should be constantly aware of this.

FAMILY
AND COMMUNITY I

2 THE RULE OF THE FATHERS: Family Relations in an Agrarian World

Our personalities are shaped by the experience of growing up in the presence of parents, sisters and brothers and, later in life, by possibly sharing our thoughts with a partner and children. This holds true for all societies, no matter how different the lives their members live. The family, then, forms a good subject to begin with for the history of mentalities. The word appears in the titles of numerous publications, often in combination with other words such as marriage, children, women, household, sexuality, or inheritance. "History of the family" as a general term can refer to a number of related themes, all having to do with mentalities. Their connection is obvious. Research into the nature of married life leads to the question of the relationships between men and women in general; from the position of children we jump to the status of the young and the old and from accepted to illegitimate sexuality. Not every theme which can be associated with the family has to do with mentalities. Studies of women's labor or the subsistence strategies adopted by different households primarily belong to social or economic history. Demographic studies are taken into consideration here, but only in so far as they present data relevant to the mentalities approach. Attention is also paid to the interdependence of the developments under discussion with social and economic processes.

Historians have written so abundantly about family life that its treatment in this book comprises as much as two chapters. This chapter focuses on family structure and the broader social context in which it was embedded. Simultaneously, a few changes which took place at a fairly early date, putting family life in Europe on a particular track, are discussed. At the end, in chapter 8, our attention is directed to the ways in which relatives and family members treated each other. In that case, the emphasis is on the later preindustrial period and the transition to an industrial society. Here three themes are dealt with. The first section explains the main functions which families originally fulfilled and goes on to review the position of elite families in a society which was both agrarian and stateless, featuring the church as an influential force. The second section shifts the focus to the majority of peasant households and probes the demographic patterns prevalent in western Europe for conclusions relevant to mentalities. In the third section we are concerned with the influence exerted by Christian thought on conceptions of love, marriage, and sexuality.

A Challenge to the Power of Families

At any given time families are a part of the network of human relationships which we call society. They are social groups, just as classes, estates, or religious sects are. However, in past societies, the fate of individual families was more intricately interwoven with that of the other social groups referred to. Of course family life varies with the social stratum under consideration, but there is more. Classes and estates themselves are determined to a large extent by kinship ties. While elite groups basically consist of networks of families, those at the other end, slaves for example, know no family life of their own since they belong to their lord's household. In order to elucidate this problem, we may consider a simple scheme which contrasts the functions of families in the twentieth century with their counterparts in an agrarian society such as that prevailing in Europe around A.D. 1000.

From the House to the Nuclear Family

The essential functions of families in agrarian societies are related to what may be called the transfer between generations. Within the framework of the family it is assured that generations of people live together and survive and that, in due course, the next generation will take the place of the preceding one. First of all, this is realized by producing legitimate offspring. Only children born from a "true union," as distinct from a possible second-class marriage or concubinage, count as such. They alone are raised as true members of the family and acquire all the rights this membership entails. Thus, the primary function of familial groups consists of legitimate reproduction and socialization. Duby stresses this function's link with the dominance of men over women. Marriage creates fatherhood. The ordering of society into families adds a second line of descent to the maternal one, which alone is biologically evident.

Families are also held together by economic ties. Whereas, in our own time, cohabitating groups merely constitute an economic unit to the extent that they are consuming goods together, their counterparts in agrarian societies also produce goods together. Hence, they are economic entities in a fuller sense of the word. A farm is at the same time a household and vice versa. Family groups act as units of production and consumption. A third function, finally, is inheritance. The inclusion of this factor makes the importance attached to the legitimacy of reproduction understandable, since only "true-born" children are entitled to a full portion. Inheritance concerns material things such as land, farmsteads, furniture, or money and immaterial ones such as status or political power. They may be termed property and positions, respectively. The significance of inheritance, and hence that of one's affiliation to a particular family, obviously increases as the position is higher and the property more considerable. The distinction between legitimacy and illegitimacy should not be taken in any absolute sense. In the Germanic tradition, for example, it was customary for a man, in addition to his true wife, to have one or a few concubines, recognized by the community. The children from these second-class spouses were not 100 percent true-born, but they might still receive a small portion of the inheritance.

The functions of families in agrarian societies cluster in the social and economic realms. They never lacked a representation in the mental sphere, however. In the first place, every event crucial to social intercourse was accompanied by ritual; this was a characteristic of preindustrial Europe as well as many other societies. It was certainly true for the conclusion of marriage. A wedding was, as a matter of course, a public, ceremonial and conspicuous event in which nearly every act had a predetermined symbolic meaning. Second, the sexual aspect was crucial. Since producing legitimate heirs was the most important goal of marriage, that institution stressed reproductive behavior. By celebrating their union, two people embarked upon a sexual partnership. Since the generation of new life was felt to belong to a mysterious sphere, marriage as a whole belonged in it too; it partook of the sacred. To be sure, this sacred dimension did not automatically bring the involvement of priests with it, as we will see.

Up to now, words such as family and marriage have been prevalent, but they cannot be used satisfactorily to denote a group of people living together. The original meaning of the Latin *familia* is "all persons subject to paternal authority." Fathers themselves did not belong to their familia. The Greek and Latin words for house (*oikos* and *domus*), on the other hand, were frequently used in antiquity to refer to a cohabitating group. The house denoted both the building itself and everyone living in it, servants and slaves included. Preindustrial Europe knew this terminology too. The men of Montaillou, the fourteenth-century Pyrenean village made famous by Le Roy Ladurie, proudly spoke of their *ostal*, to refer to their own people as distinct from fellow villagers. Close by, in the Gévaudan region, it was *ousta*, also in the early modern period. In central Europe, variants of the word *Haus* were used in a similar vein. This kind of terminology would have been unthinkable in a society of nomads. Thus, it must have originated when the populations in question had become sedentary. Europe around A.D. 1000 was a sedentary society, but also a stateless one. The latter aspect is equally important to explain the tasks which families faced and the connotations of the word house. "House" did not primarily refer to the mutual bonds among a group of people, but to their shielded position vis-à-vis the outside world. The house was a fortress, sometimes literally. In a largely unpacified society, cohabitating groups often had to rely on their own strength for their defense. In addition, they engaged in violence if there was a feud. Of course one house would soon be defeated. Defensive actions as well as the initiatives in vendettas were usually coordinated within a larger kinship network. To conclude, families played a role in the regulation of social life. They exercised a form of rule.

One example, from fourteenth-century Ghent, may be cited to make this clear. Late medieval cities too witnessed numerous vendettas. To a certain extent, the magistrates attempted to curb these feuds, but often they condoned them, partly because their own position stemmed from membership in a family network and they largely shared the mentality of the contesting parties. A feud in Ghent opposed Pieter de Kersmakere and his kin against the brothers Van Riemeland. It began with the kidnapping of one of the latter. The others thought Pieter had done it, but, apparently, they failed to seize him. They did succeed, in 1360, in capturing one Jan de Kersmakere, whom they seriously maimed. This name, "candle maker," must have been fairly common. Too late, the unfortunate Jan claimed to be entirely unrelated to the alleged kidnapper. The magistrates thought it an excusable mistake. They proposed that the Van Riemeland brothers should pay an indemnity of eight pounds to their victim. The brothers only agreed if Jan would solemnly swear that he was indeed unrelated to Pieter de Kersmakere.

Still another element followed from the military and governing functions of the house: the affairs of kinship groups were handled by men, notably fathers. They were responsible for the behavior of women. Another example serves to illustrate this. The laws of Liutprand, king of the Lombards, were based on actual events. Liutprand had been informed that someone had taken a woman's clothes while she was bathing in a river. This woman had no other choice but to walk home in the nude, embarrassed by passers-by, who could not help staring. Anyone doing such a thing as stealing a woman's clothes, as the judgment had it, was to pay his *wergeld* (compensation for a vendetta). Had the perpetrator been seized by the woman's brother, husband, or kin, the king argued, he most certainly would have been attacked and possibly killed. Payment was preferable to starting a blood feud. This example is more illustrative still, if we read between the lines. The order in which the relatives are listed can hardly be a coincidence. Liutprand primarily had an unmarried woman in mind, whose father had already died. Such a woman had the largest room for initiatives of her own. Her father would not even have allowed her to go bathing without a chaperon, and hence, there is no talk of him. Unmarried women whose father was alive and most married women had less space for themselves. Their honor was protected within the framework of patriarchy.

Thus, we see that the tasks handled by the inhabitants of a house and the members of a kinship network were a function of the relative lack of state formation and economic differentiation in Europe around A.D. 1000. Consequently, the functions of families became different as circumstances changed. Economic developments and processes of state formation led to an erosion of the house as a social bastion. Without going into the details of these long-term processes, we can confine ourselves to noting the situation in the twentieth century. Governmental bodies have taken care of protection and have done away with the blood feud so that family groups no longer exercise a form of rule. As far as the economy is concerned, production is concentrated outside individual households and most people work for wages. Other social developments have led to the proliferation of schools and, more recently, to day care centers for the youngest children.

We can easily see how the changed social circumstances have made inroads on the original functions of family groups. Within our economic organization, production and consumption are largely separated: households are merely units of consumption. Partly as a result, the importance of inheritance has declined considerably. In most cases, a person's wealth stems from the proceeds of his or her own labor rather than from what he or she inherits. Social positions are seldom transferred automatically from father to son, although family connections still can be a boost to someone's career. Educational institutions and, for smaller groups, nurseries take care of socialization to a large extent. Although reproduction has basically kept its place within marriage, this is qualified by two factors. First, its quantitative importance for individual marriages has decreased as a result of birth control. Second, we were expressly discussing legitimate reproduction only. The distinction between children born in and out of wedlock was most significant precisely for inheritance. In a later period, when inheriting wealth was already less common, bastardy still meant stigmatization. This too has practically disappeared. Today it is no longer important for the legitimacy of reproduction whether it takes place within or outside marriage.

Nowadays, a majority of cohabitating groups consist of one or two parents with one or more children. To differentiate this unit from the larger body of relatives, we call it the nuclear family. Its character differs from the "house" of agrarian society as a result of the shifts in function discussed earlier. The bonds that keep its members together are primarily emotional and psychological. The advantage of having children, for example, is seen in terms of emotional satisfaction. According to a system of values which emerged in the eighteenth century, the nuclear family is a haven, shielding those within from the harsh world outside: again a fortress, but this time for protection against psychic dangers instead of physical attacks. In connection with broader changes in society, the evolution has been from the house to the nuclear family. Its significance will be analyzed in chapters 8 and 9.

The Incest Battle

Thus far, the role of the church has not been examined. Ecclesiastical interference with the problem of who was allowed to marry whom was a source of frequent disputes at first. Everything revolved around one theme: incest. To clarify this, we have to go back to the fourth century.

To the extent that extramarital sex is out of the picture, incest refers to the marriage of related persons just as much as to their sexual activities. The former aspect received primacy in ecclesiastical doctrine. Church leaders disapproved of a union if the partners were too closely related. This comes as no surprise, since such a disapproval is a feature of nearly every society. Its exceptional character lies in the fact that the prohibited degrees were extended almost endlessly, without any precedent to that effect. In the sixth century, marriages up to the third degree were forbidden; later, this became the fourth and, in the eleventh century, even the seventh degree. In addition, the prohibited degrees also came to apply to in-laws and spiritual relatives (those acquired through godparenthood). They even applied in cases of purely sexual "affinity": a man who had made love to a woman once could never marry her sister. To be sure, the church leaders' preoccupation with incest only began toward the end of the fourth century. The son and two daughters of Constantine, the first Christian emperor, had concluded a total of four marriages with full cousins. Such marriages were relatively common among the early Christians, and they had been permitted by Romans, Greeks, and the ancient Jews. The New Testament contains no single passage indicating their unlawfulness. The Northern peoples who adopted Christianity also accepted unions between full cousins. Nevertheless, popes, such as Gregory the Great, tried to force the extended rules of incest upon these nations. Thus, they insisted on prohibitions which ran counter to the customs of the population they had just converted, to the Roman heritage they drew from, and to the course suggested by their own sacred texts. Why?

To answer that question, Goody and Ross point to the opposition from church leaders to three other customs. They discouraged remarriage of widows, disapproved of adoption, and attacked concubinage. The common element in all these contested customs is their function as strategies of heirship. Without such strategies many families would be deprived of heirs; notably male ones, as many men perished at a young age in this society of warriors. A particular custom, the levirate, perfectly illustrates the concern for producing heirs. The levirate refers to the marriage of a younger man with his brother's widow. It was obligatory for, among others, the ancient Jews, but the newly promulgated ecclesiastical rules forbade it. The primary aim of marriages between cousins was to ensure that property remained within the wider kinship group. Concubinage acted as a strategy of heirship because the line separating true-born children from the others was never drawn sharply. When there was no full heir, a son born from a second-class marriage might be elevated to this status.

The effect of the practiced doctrines, therefore, was to deprive families of heirs. In cases of success, the largest profit went to the church itself. From the earliest times, Christian writers and dignitaries stressed the pious nature of gifts or bequests to ecclesiastical institutions. Especially for someone who lacked any heirs, this was an obvious road to salvation. In an agrarian society land was the most important form of capital. The church's landed property steadily increased in the course of the early Middle Ages, which would have been less likely without these doctrines. Of course the church also lost property: through pillage or other forms of unlawful appropriation; because noble families considered a convent or church on their land as a part of their domain; because goods belonging to a monastery were given away by abbots to their relatives; or, finally, when priests had heirs themselves. The latter habit seemed the least difficult to curb. The weapon was celibacy, which church leaders strived to enforce upon the clergy from the fourth century onward. It prevented ecclesiastical goods from getting into the hands of laymen through inheritance. Significantly, voices were raised against clerics who pretended to be legitimately married rather than those merely having a sexual relationship. Celibacy complemented the recommendation made to laymen to bequeath property to ecclesiastical institutions.

A few historians are critical of Goody's and Ross's theses. Some say that the church cannot possibly have adopted such a complicated and cynical strategy. That is of course true. There was no strategy at all, only a process by which the unconscious motive of gaining material advantage led every zealot time and again to emphasize the doctrines which also had that beneficial effect. The convergence of the four prescriptions precisely on this point remains a convincing proof. The church justified the acquisition of property with reference to its self-appointed task of caring for the poor, which is another reason not to attribute cynicism to the church. Mayke de Jong presents the most innovative criticism of Goody's thesis. She points to the custom of oblation: the offering of young children to a monastery as future monks, which became a common practice in this very period. It was profitable for the church, she argues, when families did have heirs, because the oblates took their portion with them, making it improbable that the church confronted strategies of heirship in other situations. For assessing this argument, it is crucial to know whether the oblates were younger brothers, and the sources usually fail to provide precisely that information. It is possible that if a couple already had several sons, an abbot would be quite content with a small portion, while simultaneously hoping that many other families would remain without heirs. In any case, material possessions always played a central role in the practice of oblation. Lay attitudes remained ambiguous. Some pious parents indeed presented their only child as an oblate to a monastery or gave a large part of their property to ecclesiastical institutions. There were also married men who actually profited from the incest rules. If a husband was fed up with his wife, hostile voices claimed, he could conduct an investigation into her ancestry, and thus, usually find a valid ground for having the marriage annulled by the church. On the other hand, many local nobles dominated ecclesiastical institutions. Well into the eleventh century, they could freely treat parish churches and convents as their own property.

In any case, the confrontation between the church and lay families was a permanent source of conflict from the early Middle Ages. This is crucial, because the course eventually taken by these conflicts led to changes in the character of family life. To clerics, the solidarity of kinship networks represented, more than anything else, the *world*, which they resented and needed at the same time. From the side of the world it was mainly the powerful who sustained the conflict. They had the greatest interest in strategies of heirship, while nobles were also keen on passing on the valiant ancestral blood in the male line. Hence, aristocratic men continued to repudiate wives who failed to bear a son, while great families were unable to accept the incest rules. Incest remained the principal point of dispute. Around A.D. 1000 it had become impossible for the French aristocracy to find marriage partners from among their equals who were not within the prohibited degrees in one way or the other. A stalemate resulted, opposing the king and a part of the nobility to the Pope and most of the bishops. In 1215 the range of prohibited degrees was again reduced to three. However, this moderated rule on incest still obstructed strategies of heirship and the existing conflict was prolonged.

Wedding Ceremonies

During the later Middle Ages, bishops, popes, and church councils sharpened their struggle on the marriage front. Ecclesiastical solemnization became the main issue. Clerical authors redefined marriage to become holy matrimony. Entering into the conjugal state was no longer merely sacred in a vague and general sense; it was a sacrament in the Catholic sense. It had to be sealed, therefore, by the participation of a priest. Originally wedding ceremonies had been purely secular affairs, just as marriage in general was of a mundane nature. The significance of the sacramentalization of marriage, which changed this, is easy to see. If priests succeeded in restricting the range of "true" marriages to those which they consecrated, then denial of clerical consent would prevent a legitimate union. This would enable the church to have a greater say in the question of who could marry whom and hence to increase its influence over the politics of families. In the later Middle Ages, the sacramentalization of marriage represented one of the most conspicuous countertendencies to the secularization which was slowly beginning in other fields.

With this new issue the church became involved more than ever before in a confrontation with patriarchy. Originally the decision of who would marry whom had largely been taken by fathers. The struggle against patriarchy was in no way a principled one. At other levels and in other circumstances, clergymen acknowledged the rule of fathers. When the Frankish bishops met in Paris in 829 to expound the church's matrimonial ethic again, the document they issued was directed exclusively at men, who alone were considered responsible for its implementation. The bishops put it plainly: laymen had to protect their women, who were generally known as weaker vessels, and to guard their virginity. If, at the end of the Middle Ages, patriarchy had become somewhat weakened, it was largely an unintended consequence of the struggle over marriages.

Entry into marriage had not always been a ceremonial event. Around 900, when private violence among the great was at its zenith in comparison with preceding centuries as well as later ones, young noblemen frequently abducted their future bride. To be sure, this was not the romantic elopement of later times. Using cunning, deceit, and violence, men from one family network took a woman, sometimes even a married one, from another network. This often started a vendetta between the two families. In other cases the abduction was a fake, which had been agreed upon secretly. This happened when a man wanted to rid himself of his wife or a father wished to spare himself the cost of a wedding. For whatever motive, abductions had become rare in France toward the end of the eleventh century. Concluding a marriage then meant concluding an alliance in a society which was still patriarchal and full of violence.

The developments with respect to wedding ceremonies have been studied in detail in Germany, which experienced private warfare for a longer time. Valuable information has been gathered from literary tales. These cannot always be trusted, but in the case of wedding proceedings they provide a realistic picture. In the twelfth century, Germany constituted an unpacified area to a still greater extent than France or England. Together with the sharp differences in rank between social strata, this determined the course of events at weddings in this period. Ecclesiastical bodies had hardly any influence upon the ceremony or the choice of partners. The conclusion of marriage was a purely secular happening, celebrated within the confines of the family without the participation of a priest. The kinship groups involved were accountable to no one precisely because they themselves were armed governing bodies. The principal function of a marriage was to bring together two such units in mutual alliance.

A few passages from the rhymed story by Sibote about "the taming of the recalcitrant woman" gives us a glimpse of the course of events. Sibote, a thirteenth-century Thuringian poet, wrote for an aristocratic audience. His theme was a literary cliché. A rich nobleman with a troublesome daughter, Kriemhilde, promises her hand to the first person willing to take her. The quick arrival of a suitor completes the literary motif. The sequel, however, contains obviously realistic elements, notably about making and sealing the marriage. In the first place, the suitor is not a farmer but a knight from the immediate surroundings, less wealthy than the father but young and strong. He visits his older neighbor in the company of some relatives and proposes to unite both families. To the knight this would mean social ascent, while the advantage for his intended father-in-law lies in the military prowess of the future son-in-law who, from now on, will also be at his disposal. Very quickly they reach agreement about Kriemhilde. A week later the bridegroom rides to the nobleman's castle alone, so that there is no chance that his arrival might be mistaken for an armed attack. Kriemhilde's father gives her as true wife to the knight. The latter takes his bride to his own castle, where the wedding is celebrated and the marriage consummated. The rest of the story is devoted to the means by which the knight succeeds in forcing his recalcitrant spouse into obedience.

This passage contains most elements of the type of wedding ceremony originally common among European elites. First, the conclusion of marriage is not confined to a specific moment. It is a process in which arrangements between both families, the handing over of the bride, the vows by the partners, the wedding celebration, and the sexual union are all a part. Second, as is evident from an analysis of a number of such stories, the ceremony varies according to the rank of the parties involved. Its course is different when, for example, a warrior from the entourage of a high nobleman sees his merits for his master rewarded with the hand of the latter's daughter, in whose castle he continues to live. In contrast to later times, there is no uniform ritual applicable in all circumstances. A third element is the ceremony's purely familial character. The presence of relatives and vassals as witnesses guarantees the marriage's validity, without any act of legitimation by a higher authority. This familial character also entails a strong dose of patriarchalism. Fathers play the leading role in the conclusion of marriage. A father is said to give his daughter to the bridegroom. The bride expresses her agreement in a few words, but, in her upbringing, she is so conditioned to her male environment that her consent is automatic. The bridegroom's vow primarily obliges him not to repudiate his wife. Next to the bride's father, the bridegroom plays a relatively independent role. Exceptions to this ritual, in which the bride has a rather autonomous role as well, always concern fatherless women, notably widows.

The three elements referred to disappeared in Germany during the later Middle Ages, largely as a consequence of interference by ecclesiastical bodies. This shows more than anything else, the church's determination to challenge the power of families and its eventual success. A wedding became a uniform ceremony, no longer reflecting status differences. It lost its character as a process: one ritual on one day constituted the marriage. This confinement to one day and the prominent involvement of priests were sealed by fixing church attendance at another date. Originally, the couple went to church after the first night of marriage, with the unspoken purpose of purifying the bride from the stains of defloration. Very gradually clergymen managed to make the couple agree to attend mass before the first night of marriage. In this way the divine service becomes the climax of the ceremony, with a priest taking over the leading role from the father. The priest brings the couple together, as it is now called. The consent of the bride has become more important and it evolves into the complement of the bridegroom's vow. The preceding family arrangements have been degraded to the level of betrothal. The church emphasizes that the partners' mutual consent alone makes a marriage, although it only becomes irrevocable with the first sexual contact.

The ideological battle fought by the church had its origins in the redefinition of marriage as a sacrament that was not fully valid without clerical involvement. As we assess its general social meaning, however, the power struggle with families looms large. The sacramentalization of the conjugal bond was not restricted to Germany. In France the most important step was already taken in the second half of the thirteenth century, when in the bishopric of Reims a priest joined the hands of the young couple. Comparable developments took place in northern Italian cities. When a marriage was made among Florentine patricians in the fourteenth and fifteenth centuries, the men from both families continued to have the strongest say, but the church increasingly was the place of the wedding ritual. Clergymen even tolerated the painters' unfavorable portrayal of Saint Joseph at his wedding with the Virgin (see chapter 8), so long as the event was situated in front of the church. For England, finally, we are well informed about the extension of clerical involvement. Originally only widows and other women without a guardian were not handed over by their father to a bridegroom. In such cases there was a sort of mediator, called *orator*, who acted as master of ceremony at the wedding. In the later Middle Ages clerics gladly played this role. They extended their influence in a few subsequent phases. At first, priests managed to acquire a monopoly on the role of orator. Next they transferred the ceremony to the church. From then on they were willing to give the kiss of peace, which reduced the tension and started the feast, only at the church. Finally, clergymen came to act as master of ceremony for all couples, whether or not the woman's father was alive. They acquired the crucial task of handing over the ring to the bridegroom, who put it on the bride's finger.

As has been said, processes of state formation had set all this in motion. Regional differences in the tempo of these processes accounted for chronological differences in the evolution of wedding ritual. As far as the legitimation of marriages was concerned, the interests of the church were interwoven with those of the rising states, but, nevertheless, there were conflicts between both parties. From the fourteenth century, secular authorities, too, occasionally attempted to acquire influence over weddings. Notably city governments have tried this. But eventually the secular authorities left the initiative to the church. Princes and urban patriciates tried to curb the power of noble families primarily by resistance to the blood feud. Increasing pacification deprived families of their armed power, which also made them less independent when confronted with demands on the part of the clergy. Increasing urbanization and geographic mobility weakened the rule of fathers as well. In the sixteenth century, church and state reached a modus vivendi. The churches were confirmed in their right to perform weddings, but the state took the main profit from their activities as offices of registration. Only in the Dutch Republic was it possible to choose a civil marriage.

The church had conducted its struggle against laity in general, but elite families, being models for the rest, had been its principal target. The thousand-year-old structural conflict, in which the state had joined the church at a later stage, was settled more or less around 1500. As a by-product of this long, drawn out combat, marriage had become individualized to a certain extent. The emphasis on an alliance between larger kinship groups was reduced, while a greater stress was laid on the start of two people's cohabitation and sexual partnership. The role of women had become a little less subordinate. Precisely at this point, to be sure, ecclesiastical and secular authorities issued measures to prevent individual freedom in the choice of partners from becoming too great. This conclusion is picked up again in chapter 8.

Peasant Families

In the preceding section the emphasis was on elite families. This was partly a consequence of the ever-present problem of the uneven distribution of the sources, but it was justified in this case because the elites took the main burden in the conflict with the ecclesiastical authorities. This section seeks to redress the balance to some extent. Demographic registers constitute the most important source for learning about the people's family life. In this case we are pushing the analysis somewhat further along in time than the previous section did, but we do not leave the domain of structural characteristics of the people of preindustrial Europe, mostly peasants, which is the main subject of this chapter.

The Making of the Household

The ancient Romans lacked a concept to denote the unit of husband, wife, and children. Still this primary group must have included the totality of residents in multiple dwellings, especially during the first and second centuries, which were noted for urbanization. Of course we cannot tell even approximately the number of such dwellings. Roman urbanization did not last, so we can concentrate on the agrarian world which succeeded it. In it kinship relations were entirely defined by relations of authority and production. Although a tiny minority of free farmers worked the land in groups of one or a few families, for the rest a dichotomy prevailed within society. Big and middling landowners had a farmstead and everyone working and living on it belonged to their group: relatives, servants, and slaves. We might call it a household, although a differentiated and sizeable household. On the opposite side were the slaves. Whether working the land or performing jobs in the house, they usually lived in barracks on their lord's farmstead. Slaves had neither a household nor recognized relatives. As members of their lord's familia, they could never marry officially. In the course of several centuries this situation changed, giving rise to the later western European household.

The change was caused by economic as well as ideological developments; more precisely by a shift in the availability of labor power and the arrival of Christianity. As long as the Roman Empire expanded, its numerous wars meant a constant supply of new slaves. On every estate there were too many rather than too few slaves, and large landowners tried to prevent them from reproducing. Inevitably, this attitude was reversed when supply stagnated. From then on landlords had an interest in the regulated reproduction of their servile work force and hence they began to encourage it. Furthermore, the scarcity of labor power resulted in a stronger position for the slaves; as a consequence lords became obliged to recognize the slaves' sexual bonds. A patron's recognition of such a bond primarily implied that other male slaves had to refrain from sexual activity with the woman in the new relationship. Thus the patriarchalism of the lords was imitated at a lower level.

At first Christianity did not basically change this system. Ecclesiastical dignitaries were aware of the economic necessity of unrestrained reproduction among slaves. When Caesarius, bishop of Arles in the sixth century, spoke about it, he did not seem bothered. As has been explained, in matters of marriage and sexuality among laymen, church leaders aimed their arrows primarily at the elites. The struggle over consecration at weddings had not broken out yet in Caesarius's time. Sometimes, though, priests were willing to marry unfree persons, whether called slaves or serfs, when their lord had refused to do so. Originally this counted as a special favor. Demyttenaere concludes that conciliar resolutions and other ecclesiastical texts well into the eighth century considered a marriage among slaves as less true and undissolvable than one among free persons. Eventually, however, Christian clergy began to think that even the sexuality and reproduction of those at the bottom of society should be legitimized by a conjugal bond.

The creation of the simple household must have taken place around this time. That follows from among other things the registration of living spaces on a few Bavarian domains in the years 820–821. Their serfs lived in separate households, the majority consisting only of parents and children. This is one of the oldest sources in which a statistical dominance of such nuclear households has been demonstrated. Comparable data, although somewhat more difficult to interpret, are drawn from the register of households on the manors of the abbey of St.-Germain-des-Prés near Paris in the same period. In quantitative terms, there is less information on the minority of free farmers in the preceding centuries. Some historians speculatively argue that the implicit shift in the living situation of unfree persons lay at the root of the so-called western European marriage pattern. This concept, dear to demographic researchers, primarily refers to a low frequency of complex households. During the early Middle Ages the position of bondsmen changed; from slaves living in barracks they became *servi casati* ("housed serfs"). This shift most probably had a dual cause. In the first place, the power of unfree persons had increased. In a juridical sense, slavery may be a strictly delineated category; in practice, however, there are degrees of bondage in many societies. Servi casati belonged to their lord, but they had a moral right to the soil they tilled. The second important factor was the influence of Christian theories, which increasingly advocated matrimony among bondsmen. Where slaves constituted conjugal units, it was eventually found most efficient for the manorial administration to place these couples in separate houses. Because of this, the majority of the agrarian population of Europe toward A.D. 1000 consisted of separate households.

This does not mean that servile families were henceforth to be considered as belonging to the same category, although at a lower level, of their lords. The servile households still belonged to the manor. They did not, of course, fulfill a military function, as kinship groups among the elite did. Contemporaries stressed this with their choice of words: a *casa* is merely a dwelling; military defense, including the protection of the *casati*, is within the province of the lord's *domus*. For the peasant population the creation of the household meant a first step on the road toward a greater independence of family life, but their ties to the great landowners remained strong. For a long time still, the rule of the fathers was the rule of the lords.

Surrogate Fathers and Emancipation

The rule of the fathers appears most clearly again in connection with marriage. The acquisition of a household by serfs did not automatically mean that they were free to marry whomever they chose. Well into the later Middle Ages landlords exerted a decisive influence over the marriages of peasants. They acted as surrogate fathers. Just as among the elite natural fathers created a conjugal bond by handing over their daughter to the groom, surrogate fathers did the same with their dependents. Lords often had the right to force their bondsmen into marriage. For example, according to the customary law of the abbey of Weitenau in Baden, which was codified in 1344, its secular bailiff had the authority to marry eighteen- or twenty-year-old male dependents to female dependents of fourteen. Where such coercion was not present, the lords had a voice at least in their serfs' choice of a partner. The obligation to take a husband or wife from one's own manor was tenaciously maintained. The economic interest of the landlords in all this is plain.

A part of their income derived from the contributions of serfs, who also had to perform manorial services. The continuity of economic production was fostered by the regulated continuity of the network of households which existed on a manor. Surrogate fatherhood was not confined to the agrarian world. The valets of nobles and, during an early phase, even the servants of urban merchants were also given in marriage by their masters.

Nevertheless, urbanization was one of the principal driving forces behind the decline of surrogate fatherhood. It was frequently stipulated in city charters that no outside lord had the right to force citizens to marry or, conversely, to forbid them to do so. In addition, cities offered more ample opportunities for an independent existence, which enabled servants and apprentices to withdraw from the control of their masters. Greater geographic mobility increased the marital freedom of citizens of low birth. These developments were felt in the countryside. Economic differentiation made the prospects for runaway serfs brighter and, if bondsmen were already entitled to a greater freedom of movement, they could threaten their lord with emigration to a town. Ultimately this obliged landlords to grant to their dependents the same privileges with respect to marriage as those enjoyed by urban citizens. Pressure from the church to transfer the supervision of wedding ritual among the lower classes as well from fathers to priests reinforced this tendency. In thirteenth-century England, for example, ecclesiastical and manorial courts were in permanent conflict over the boundaries of their authority. Representatives of the church stressed that everyone should have the freedom to marry whomever he or she wished. Yet, from time to time, they acquiesced when landlords made use of their ancient right to present a woman to a bridegroom. When a tenant married someone from outside the manor against the lord's will, he or she might be threatened with eviction or disinheritance. In England too, economic developments eroded such ancient rights.

Emancipation with respect to marriage formed an essential part of the general emancipation of the agrarian population of Western Europe in the later Middle Ages, which ultimately turned serfs into more or less free peasants. That movement reached westward to the Irish Sea and eastward to the Elbe river. In regions untouched by it, such as Poland in the eighteenth and Russia in the nineteenth century, landlords still exerted a considerable influence over the family structure of the peasant population.

Freedom versus Community Control

Next to the landlords and the church, in the later Middle Ages a third party appeared on the scene, who, if not actually creating a marriage, at least legitimized it: neighbors. They probably already were observers before ecclesiastical involvement in weddings spread to the agrarian population. As soon as the system of surrogate fathers had received its first blow, a more egalitarian form of control was a possibility. "Neighbors" should be understood to refer to the couple's immediate environment: fellow villagers or, in towns, residents of the same neighborhood. They may have included kinsmen, but most were merely members of the community. Community control was attuned to the popular procedure for concluding a marriage, which was also processual. The actual marital vows might very well have been exchanged in private, as demonstrated by examples from thirteenth-century England. Alexander Wrighte asked Isabel, daughter of Joan of Wisbech, if she was willing to become his wife, and she replied affirmatively. He promised to remain faithful to her and they joined hands. Alexander gave his bride a few presents. Witnesses to this ritual were not necessary; it was sufficient for the neighbors to know about it. Although they had not joined the two lovers, they assured that no one else would come between them after this and that the couple would eventually start to live together so that there was in fact a marriage. The community was not concerned about a specific moment when the marriage was considered to have begun officially, just as elite families had never worried about this matter.

Neighborly involvement was a notable feature of second marriages. The celebration of a second marriage never had been viewed as an entirely complete wedding; for one or both parties it certainly did not mean the first sexual encounter. If the man or the woman already boasted children, there could be no doubt about his virility or her fertility, so that ritual incantations were unnecessary. Priests withheld benediction from remarrying couples, which is demonstrated by the rules laid down by bishops and provincial councils in France and Italy from the twelfth to the seventeenth century. To be sure, in Venice (1418–1426) and Chartres (1689) this only applied when the woman was the remarrying partner. In Germany where originally a mass of purification after the first night of marriage was common, priests declined to perform it when the bride was a widow and hence had already been deflowered. Representatives of the church cast an especially suspicious eye upon a woman who was already past her menopause and still married for the second time. Evidently her reentry into the state of matrimony was not meant to put more children into the world.Nevertheless, ecclesiastical rules usually allowed remarriage. In addition, laymen from the village or neighborhood had a more concrete interest in viewing negatively a wedding which implied a second union for just one of the parties. Thinking that everyone should be satisfied after one period of marital bliss, they accused the "recidivist" of spoiling the marriage market. Since young men spoke out most loudly, this accusation was levelled especially against older widowers who robbed them of a young maiden.

To illustrate the neighbors' disapproval of second marriages, it is necessary to anticipate a theme which is discussed more elaborately in the next chapter: charivari. This is the generic term for various related rituals, all implying a form of ridicule, by which the neighbors punished someone who had broken one of the community's informal rules. The nature and meaning of charivari changed over the course of the centuries. In the oldest form, however, remarriage was central. Widowers were notably the targets of the earliest texts referring to charivari, which date from the fourteenth century. The ritual usually took the form of an unmelodious serenade with pots and pans, "rough music," while masks and fool's caps were worn. Such was the case in the early fourteenth-century *Roman de Fauvel*, the text in which the word, charivari, is first mentioned. During the night of his second marriage Fauvel, part horse and part man, was surprised by a loud noise from people beating on pots and pans and singing foolish songs. Later in that century, charivari also appeared in ecclesiastical sources and chronicles, all of them from France.

It is hardly coincidental that charivari is mentioned only from the beginning of the fourteenth century. That the custom had been well established before that date is improbable because in that case it certainly would have been alluded to in older ecclesiastical sources. It is equally important that the earliest references all came from France. Consequently, we may suppose that charivari originated in France toward the end of the thirteenth century. And it just so happened that France was the country in which the control of surrogate fathers over weddings among the agrarian population declined the fastest. This was paralleled by an increase in neighbors' influence; that is the key to unlocking the riddle of charivari's origins. To rebuke someone for his choice of a partner implies that there is someone to choose. The word, market, too implies this. As argued earlier, a marriage market relatively free from feudal restrictions was established around 1300, certainly in France and, a little later, elsewhere in Europe. However, a part of the influence exerted by landlords until that date fell into the hands of the local community. The neighbors made themselves heard through charivari, among other things. The question of whether or not landlords had been in the habit of discouraging remarriage is less important because it is unlikely that the community would have dared to oppose the lord's choice by way of a ritual.

Thus the emancipation of peasants with respect to marriage did not automatically make it an individual matter for them. The role of the community remained highly significant for a long period. Such was the case in the later Middle Ages with popular wedding ceremonies which at first sight look rather individual. A number of examples come from England. The majority of marital suits in church courts concerned the demand to validate an existing union and to have it confirmed in church. In such cases the aim was to acquire ecclesiastical legitimation for a marriage which, at least according to one of the partners, had already been concluded with worldly ritual. These secular rituals were usually of a simple nature and they were performed in widely varying places. From the suits we learn that marriages were concluded under an ash tree or an oak, in a field or garden or near a hedge, in the kitchen, in a little storehouse, a smithy, a tavern, on the king's highway and, finally, simply in bed. Yet it would be incorrect to suppose that such weddings involved only the couple. In those suits the plaintiff focused on the moment when vows were exchanged, "with words in the present tense" and unconditionally. That was the essential moment according to canon law. The church only recognized a marriage's validity if the partners had said something like "I, Jack, take you, Mary, for my wife" and vice versa. If Jack said "I will take you for my wife when I inherit my father's land," it was not valid. Nor was it valid when the marriage was conditional upon the woman's becoming pregnant, as John Wyk and Margaret Bele agreed upon when they tried. For their part laymen considered the exchange of vows merely as an episode in a process. A whole series of events enabled the community to legitimate marriage. The neighbors saw to it that the two lived under one roof, that they ate, slept, and went to mass together. This partnership of table and bed, plain to everyone, constituted the marriage.

That was the course of events when nothing went wrong. However, in the cases pleaded in church courts the crucial problem often lay precisely in the refusal of one of the parties, who denied the marital vow. The plaintiff then had to prove the existence of a conjugal bond. That neighbors acted as witnesses for either party underlines the importance of their role, but it is equally true that the cases in question reveal their failure. Supervision by neighbors became more problematic as geographic mobility increased. It was harder to keep track of the series of events creating a marriage when the partners came from different villages. In those cases the couple's own need for ecclesiastical solemnization increased, since, as neither a lord nor the community could legitimate a union, the church was the only institution left to do so. Exogamous unions therefore are likely to have been overrepresented in marital litigation. The figures obtained from another type of source in later medieval England, indemnities paid by women to their landlord in order to marry without his permission, are perhaps more representative. About a third of these women had pledged themselves to men who had not been born in the village. Another third paid the indemnity from their own pockets; this considerable minority consisted almost entirely of independent young women. Most of the latter spurned men from their own as well as from other manors, preferring freemen. These figures date from a period of transition when landlords no longer created a marriage but continued to draw a financial profit from their ancient rights. Later they would retreat entirely.

The Western European Marriage Pattern

The origins of what demographic historians call the western European marriage pattern go back to the developments just discussed. A model for beginning and maintaining a household is actually intended. Until the beginning of the nineteenth century, one pattern was dominant to the west of the line St. Petersburg–Trieste, although the Mediterranean regions in particular exhibited a few deviations. Some demographers therefore propose to replace the dichotomy between western and eastern Europe with a model with three or four patterns. Such refinements have little relevance to the history of mentalities. A brief sketch of the western European pattern, which is unique in comparison with all other preindustrial societies we are informed about, will suffice here.

Three main characteristics can be distinguished. The first was, in Mitterauer's words, a tendency to avoid the formation of households containing more than two generations. Nuclear households, without grandparents but also without married brothers or sisters of the couple, made up the overwhelming majority in most regions. Those households were the norm, even if we take into account that many persons never lived to become a grandfather or grandmother. The nuclear household was based on a few pillars, such as setting up separate homes. In the towns most newly wed couples left their parents' home; the daughters and younger sons of peasants did likewise. Sons of artisans only adopted their father's occupation when this was clearly advantageous to their career. Another pillar was the system of transfer. When they felt their strength decline, older farmers voluntarily retired in favor of their eldest son. The latter would wait for that moment to marry. The position of head of the household might also be transferred from a widow to a member of another family. If a man left no children or they were too young, his widow led the household. If she remarried, the management of farm or workshop went to her new husband. Membership in a guild too could be transferred in this way. A widow's eldest son, if present, then faced the prospect of waiting for his stepfather's retirement.

The second main characteristic directly follows from the first, notably from information about the time of marriage. To marry and to reach economic independence and, for the man, the position of head of a household were two sides of the same coin. Whoever could not achieve economic independence had to give up the thought of marrying. Many men remained bachelors all their life. The average age at first marriage in early modern western Europe is the statistical figure from which this can be concluded. It is considerably higher than in other preindustrial societies. In some Mediterranean regions this only held true for the bridegrooms, but elsewhere the age of the brides was almost equally high. We can roughly say that most women entering upon a first marriage were in their mid-twenties, while the men approached thirty. We should beware of the meaningless average, however. There is no reason to assume that the age in question was seen as particularly ideal. The figure does mean that it took some time, less for some and more for others, to reach economic independence.

The third main characteristic is the presence in households of life-cycle servants, as Laslett calls them. Germanic and Romance languages testify to their existence. They have various words which combine the meaning of "a man or woman growing up" with that of "someone who works for a master or boss." In English "maid" is an example. These words simultaneously refer to unmarried persons. Most servants, apprentices, and farm hands were adolescents. Their biological parents placed them with surrogate parents, who taught them a trade and of whose household they were a part. This system was based upon the cultural desirability of an exchange of youths as well as on economic necessity. The latter motive is the easiest one to observe. In some trades there was a great need for helpers; in others, they would count as unneeded consumers. The richer households absorbed more youths. The system of life-cycle servants was most widespread in England. On the farms of central Europe it was not uncommon for younger brothers and sisters of the new head of the household to continue their work after a transfer. In that case they had to remain unmarried. Thus, households could be quite sizeable, but they never contained more than one couple.

We may add a fourth main characteristic, which concerns women's labor, although it plays a lesser role in the tradition of demographic studies. For one thing, women worked on the farms alongside the men, performing the more strictly household tasks. Household and field were of course inseparable, but the house constituted the domain of the women and the field that of the men. That is certainly not unique for western Europe. The special feature is the relatively large number of women who were able to participate more or less independently in economic life. Those women were to be found primarily in the cities, although they were not absent from the countryside. On the annual lists of Ghent money lenders between 1361 and 1389 the percentage of women fluctuated between ten and forty. These businesses usually had been started with inherited property. In addition, women worked in occupations in the food and clothing sectors, important in the urban economy of fourteenth-century Ghent. In medieval and early modern England we encounter many female brewers and pubkeepers. Yet only a minority of such women were completely independent. The economic activities almost always took place within the framework of the household. Women performed them in or near the house and their commercial labor overlapped with their household tasks. They brewed their own beer, for example, and sold the surplus.

This is not the place to go into the many geographical and chronological variations, which receive ample attention in demographic studies. Those variations particularly concern the composition of the household. In some regions, such as southern France, more complex units indeed prevailed; other regions went through several cycles, with complex and simple households alternately predominating. Even small bordering areas could exhibit contrasting statistical patterns. At the end of the seventeenth century, two neighboring regions in Saxony respectively counted 90 percent nuclear households and 28 percent households with two grandparents, which is high in view of the life expectancy of the period. According to the custom of the first region, property was divided equally among the descendants, while in the second, one child inherited everything. The law of inheritance, then, played a crucial role in the statistical pattern of household types. Next to this, the economic system was important. Within the legal-economic structures individual families sought a way to survive and determined their strategy with this in mind. The relationships between the structure of the household on the one hand and the law of inheritance and the economic system on the other must have been known and self-evident to contemporaries. With respect to women's labor, finally, the picture is less clear when it comes to analyzing change. Some historians claim that the minority of women who participated independently in economic life steadily decreased from the later Middle Ages until the nineteenth century. However, we are still insufficiently informed about the exact course taken by this process.

For the history of mentalities, one conclusion from the demographic data is most essential: at least since the later Middle Ages western Europe was a less patriarchal society than most other preindustrial ones. That is the implication of its predominant household structure. Extended families, who were prevalent in eastern Europe for example, were always organized in a more hierarchic fashion, leading to a still stronger position of power for the fathers. Of course the difference was relative. In the nuclear households of western Europe too the man was the authority figure; only a widow could reach a relatively autonomous position. It is all too well-known that women very seldom occupied social positions which implied a form of rule. Women did not become bishops or bailiffs, although some boasted the career of reigning queen. Shifts in patriarchal relationships toward the end of the preindustrial period are discussed in chapter 8.

Love, Sex, and Christianity

The affective and sexual bonds among married and unmarried persons form the main subject of the final part of this book. It is briefly anticipated here as far as early developments and the influence of the coming of Christianity, the themes of this chapter, are concerned. For a better understanding of Christianity's role we have to return to Greek and Roman antiquity for a moment.

Penetration and Reproduction

Greeks and Romans knew no formal and elaborate system of norms regulating sexual life. This does not mean that everything was socially permissible. Custom, informal norms, and moralistic reflections influenced the behavior of those confronted with them. Just as among the tribes of northern Europe, the range of sexual activities open to an individual was largely determined by his or her position in society. We know very little of how the people of this period felt about sexuality. Greeks and Romans also saw it as belonging to the sphere of the mysterious, because it was linked to the creation of new life. Did men and women, as they committed the sexual act, have the idea that they were engaging in reproduction? We can only guess.

The most conspicuous difference between the norms of antiquity and those of later European societies is implied by the fact that the former put few restrictions in the way of sex between men. That is not to say that homosexuality was simply tolerated. The Greeks particularly praised the love of an adult man (approaching thirty) for an adolescent (of about fifteen). Foucault stresses that precisely this form of love was a problem for discussion: not in the sense that people wished to forbid it, but to the extent that philosophers permanently reflected on the most proper way in which it should be expressed. These philosophers made no claim to impose rules on anyone. They presented their ethic as an option to be considered by free persons should they desire to embellish their way of life. By taking the social hierarchy into consideration, we can extend Foucault's analysis further than he does. Classical Athens was a slave society. Those free persons to whom the philosophers directed their remarks were men from among the Athenian elite. They also had sex with their wives, concubines, and with male and female slaves. The boys they loved, however, also belonged to the class of distinguished freemen. That is why precisely those relationships were problematic. They involved equals, with the age difference an insufficient compensation. In all other cases referred to there was no equality whatsoever.

The ancients, then, always viewed sexuality from the perspective of a hierarchy. Social dominance and sexual dominance ran parallel. This attitude was also fostered by the image of penetration, which made a heavy impact on conceptions of sexuality. The people of antiquity could not conceive of it except in terms of the taker and the one taken. There hardly could be a greater contrast with our time. Nowadays sexual activities are considered problematic when they do not involve equals, while an orientation on the act itself is contested.

Christianity has been an ambivalent fellow traveller on the road from then to now. Christians did not approve of the love for boys; developments concerning homosexuality in preindustrial Europe are discussed in chapter 9. Ecclesiastical authors introduced a general distrust of sex. Virginity was seen as the ideal state for men and women. Only the necessity to reproduce could justify the sexual act. Marriage, Jerome claimed, is essentially bad, but it is acceptable because it leads to births and hence to the possibility of more people reaching heaven as virgins. Needless to say, Jerome's argument implied an acceptance of matrimony as a social institution, since the proclaimed goal could have been reached more efficiently in another way, with at least more men keeping their virginal state. The emphasis on penetration, finally, was handed down to the Christians by the ancients. Other forms of sexual conduct were seen as derivative or foreplay. Nevertheless, the moralists' attitude of general distrust made them disapprove of such conduct.

The resulting moral code of the church can be condensed into two commandments: first, sex ought to be completely in the service of reproduction; second, reproduction has to be confined to marriage. Starting from those commandments, church fathers and theologians worked out an elaborate system of logically derived rules: sex was permitted only between a man and a woman, only if they were married to each other, only if both were fertile—and even then they were not expected to enjoy it. Flandrin analyzes the refinements made in this system. Theologians rejected all kinds of possible and impossible positions as "unnatural," some of them with arguments completely eluding the twentieth-century scholar. Then there were particular days when the expression of marital love was forbidden. Penance books from the sixth to the eleventh centuries paid ample attention to them. The prohibited days either had to do with the Christian calendar (periods such as Lent and days of the week: Sunday, Friday, and sometimes still other days) or the woman's condition (such as menstruation and pregnancy). Flandrin presents his calculations for the years 750–753, according to the most severe rules. Those years respectively counted ninety-one, ninety-two, ninety-two, and ninety-three days when married couples were free to make love. Using his modern knowledge of the cycle of fertility, he contends that we might very well not all be here if all contemporaries had obeyed these rules strictly. In a later period, clerics mitigated the rules, so that their flock might be able to conform to them.

On the other hand, ecclesiastical theorists entered upon a course leading away from antiquity's hierarchical view of sexuality. The moral code of the church was a universal system of norms. It did not merely call upon free persons to refine their life style, which had been the aim of Greek reflection. The Christian system consisted of commandments and prohibitions to which everyone was bound in principle on penalty of being doomed. In theory, they did not discriminate between lords and slaves, nor between men and women. Where virginity was hailed as the ideal state for men and women, marriage was equally imperfect for both. It also brought equal duties for both partners. On the permitted days, sexual intercourse should indeed take place in the interest of reproduction. It was the marital duty which a husband owed to his wife, and she to him. With respect to the marital duty, most theologians argued, man and woman were equal. Both had a right to the other's body.

We should not overestimate the egalitarian tendency in Christian thought. In many other cases, ecclesiastical theorists cherished patriarchal views with regard to sex. What should we think of the fact that the prohibited positions included as a matter of course that of the woman on top? Ecclesiastical authors usually argued that equality with respect to marital duties was an exception to the norm. We may call their attitude ambivalent at best. This also applies to their judgment on sex between persons of unequal social status. Caesarius of Arles spoke against the double standard as well as against the lack of scruples demonstrated by upper-class men about their adventures with women of low birth. Nevertheless, penance books considered adultery of a man with a free woman a more serious offense than with his slave. The penalty was half way between the two if he promoted the slave to be his concubine.

Positive Sex

The church's ambivalence manifested itself in still another way: in situations where sexual imagery or even activity were positively valued. Monks and pious laymen in mystic trance sometimes had rather worldly visions of the Madonna. Her radiant beauty blinded them; to some she showed her breasts and a few were even allowed to touch them. This mystic tradition was not entirely compatible with moralist thought. The mystics spoke enthusiastically about kisses and embraces granted them in their spiritual relationship with God or the Holy Virgin. When common mortals did such things in reality, the moralists saw it as no more than foreplay to penetration, which continued to haunt them. It should be added that the moralists were unequivocally on the orthodox side, while the mystic tradition lingered on in the margins of official Christianity. A number of its representatives were suspected of heresy.

This concerned the imagination. Real sexual behavior, valued positively although involving persons not married to each other, was a feature of impotence suits. The evidence covers three different countries from the fourteenth century to the beginning of the eighteenth, which obliges us to transcend the chronological boundaries of this chapter for the sake of thematic unity. Three authors, Helmholz, Ruggiero, and Darmon, have unearthed it without apparently being aware of each other's findings. In canon law male impotence led to nullification of a marriage because it precluded reproduction. The earliest examples of an intriguing method for gathering evidence come from the records of York and Canterbury church courts in the fourteenth and fifteenth centuries. The judges called upon female jurors to excite the accused husband. Married women must have been among them, since one witness declared that "the rod of the said William was longer and bigger than her husband's rod ever was." William therefore passed the test with flying colors. It was different in the case of John, an older man married to a younger woman. One of the jurors gave the following testimony: "[She] exposed her naked breasts and rubbed the rod and testicles of the said John with her hands warmed at the fireplace. She embraced and kissed John many times and stirred him up to show his virility and potency as far as he could, admonishing him to prove himself a man as he should. And she says, diligently questioned about it, that, all the time, the said rod was scarcely three inches long." This witness and six other female jurors did not hide their resentment of the shattered union: "After [this witness] had finished, the women unanimously cursed him because he had dared to take a youthful woman for his wife, cheating her as he was unable to serve and please her sufficiently" (Helmholz: 89).

In other cases there was no talk of sexual activities by female jurors. In the course of a suit in Venice in the 1470s, the accused, a certain Niccolò, visited a local brothel in the company of a priest and a clerk. Niccolò managed to perform the sexual act with two different prostitutes, showing the result to the priest, who testified in court to his success. In early modern France, finally, the husband in distress might be required to show an erection to doctors or midwives. Occasionally the clerical judges found it necessary that the accused and the plaintiff both present definite proof. As late as 1677 a Parisian crowd gathered in front of the house where on the court's order the marquis of Langey had to make love to his wife in the presence of experts. At the door, the marquis expressed his confidence in the outcome, "as if he was already inside," a spectator wrote. But his wife's defiant posture and the curiosity of the old midwives, who frequently peeped through the bed's curtains, prevented him from succeeding.

The embarrassing tests to be passed by husbands justly or unjustly accused of impotence can hardly be considered a form of persecution. The procedure in question was civil, not criminal. Rather, these suits contributed to the curtailment of a strictly patriarchal view of sexuality. In fact, a complaint about impotence offered women an opportunity to get rid of a husband. The nullification of such unions followed from two ecclesiastical theories: that of reproduction as the sole aim of marriage and that of the mutuality of marital duties. Impotent husbands could not live up to their duty.

Love Within and Outside Marriage

What kind of links existed between sex and love, according to contemporaries in early preindustrial Europe? How heavy were marital duties? From this early period, there is only some indirect evidence. In classical Athens, Demosthenes declared that female companions (hetairai) were for pleasure, lovers for daily attention, and wives for producing true-born offspring and guarding the hearth. That did not necessarily mean that wives were unable to fulfill the other functions as well. Demosthenes's dictum is important first of all for its introduction of the middle category: a relationship based on affection, unaffected by considerations of status, property, or family alliance. A number of men from the Germanic elites and their concubines also must have enjoyed an affective partnership. In the early Middle Ages, the primary goal of such a relationship was to provide second-class heirs, but sometimes a slave was raised to the status of a concubine. In such cases there must have been an affective bond. The resulting question is whether at that time love was expected to blossom mainly outside marriage.

Church leaders opposed concubinage, as we have seen. They wished to restrict legitimate unions to monogamous marriage. Through their intervention the original distinction between true-born and second-class children was redefined as between the legitimate and the illegitimate. Rejecting extramarital relationships altogether, clerics were hardly in a position to recognize them as valid sources of sexual affection. However, they also knew that in reality this affection alone seldom led to marriage. When Peter Lombard, bishop of Paris in the twelfth century, attacked arranged marriages, he wrote: "Marriage is concluded by the mutual consent of the partners, even if it is love which has caused it." Admittedly, the bishop may have had a sudden infatuation in mind. This does not preclude that he considered affection desirable in conjugal life.

The best-known text which explicitly proclaims the incompatibility of love and marriage is the late twelfth-century "treatise on love" by Andrew the Chaplain. This author, although a cleric as his name tells us, voiced the opinions of his worldly environment: the entourage of countess Marie of Champagne to which he belonged. In the final part he retracts his earlier theses as contrary to the church's doctrines. In one of the imaginary dialogues, which make up the first two parts, the countess is asked whether love can exist between two spouses. She replies:

> We say and affirm in a straightforward fashion that love cannot manifest its power between two spouses, for those who love are attracted to each other voluntarily and without any necessity. Spouses, however, are obliged to comply with their mutual desires and the one cannot refuse anything, whatever it is, to the other. . . . Therefore, according to that argument, we proclaim what the prescription of love teaches us, namely that no conjugal situation allows one to receive the crown of love, unless bonds from outside marriage have been added in the womb of the militia of love (Pernoud: 119).

It is remarkable that the ecclesiastical conception of marital duties returns here. The involuntary character of duties is seen as incompatible with true love. Andrew the Chaplain's theses are compatible with a view of sexuality which confines the expression of love to the relationships of noblemen with their concubines or mistresses. Still, it is heavily debated whether the treatise's denial of conjugal love was representative for the opinion of the period's secular elites. Other literary works proclaimed the desirability of getting married in case of love, unless the obstacles were too formidable. Some historians argue that clandestine marriages, frequently referred to in the later Middle Ages, sprang from a need for romantic secrecy. However, the term, "clandestine marriage," originated from ecclesiastical law and it referred to a failure to publish the banns in church. In reality, those unions were far from secret. The rule that only the future partners' mutual consent made a marriage did of course offer an opportunity to evade the arrangements of one's relatives, and some used it to that effect. Peter Lombard's remark makes that point. Literary authors depicted it as a trick by low-born men to seduce higher class women into marriage. This motif implies that women were considered receptive to romantic feelings, while men sought the "true," material advantages of marriage.

These questions concern the emotions at the moment of marrying. They do not tell us much about a possible affection during conjugal life. An anonymous treatise, named Postquam after its first word and frequently copied from the thirteenth to the fifteenth centuries, perfectly illustrates the clerical idea of the experience of conjugal sexuality. It only deals with men's sexual desires. According to the treatise, there can be four reasons for a man to make love to his wife. The first is to beget offspring, a very laudable motive. The second reason, compliance with the marital duty, is honorable too. In less covert terms, this can only mean that he does it to satisfy her desires. The third reason is to avoid immoderateness (*incontinentia*). This should probably be read as: when he actually wants to make love to another woman. The anonymous author is ambivalent: this motive can be honorable, but it can also imply a venial sin. The fourth reason, a desire for sex, is always wrong. To determine the extent of its sinfulness, desire has to be qualified. When conjugal love is involved, the act is a venial sin. A man commits a mortal sin when his libido is so strong that he cannot tell whether he is having sex with his wife or another woman. According to the treatise, then, the extent of sexual desire is inversely related to the measure of conjugal love. The author does expect love in marriage, but he assumes the incompatibility of the conjugal bond and sexual excitement. In fact, he elaborates on an old theme. Jerome already charged the man who loved his wife too much with adultery, and many Christian authors repeated this. Why shouldn't we conclude, then, that one thing was found self-evident by clerics: the strongest love is the one enjoyed in furtive moments with mistresses and concubines.

Next to this, clerics worked out a model for the ideal form of conjugal love, which had to be more serene. Kelly calls it the mystical code because it was based on the writings of the mystics. The kisses and embraces they experienced in a spiritual trance returned in realistic descriptions of the desired form of conjugal love. The authors concerned did not treat these expressions of love as foreplay but as an aim by itself. They seldom referred to orgasmic pleasure. From the marginality of the mystic tradition we may infer that originally the serene model did not belong to the ideological mainstream. From the later Middle Ages, however, clerics increasingly held it up to the laymen.

3 THE SILENT MAJORITY: Popular Culture and Life in Villages and Neighborhoods

$\mathbf{W}$e started with a particular theme that dealt with all social groups; now we will look at the realm of thought and feeling as a whole, but only for a specific group. Although that group forms the majority of the population, it is labelled silent, because it has left relatively few traces. Those who attempt to discover its tracks, nonetheless, frequently use the term, popular culture, which is difficult to define. We must introduce this concept here, however, because it is a common analytical tool for understanding a number of related themes within the study of past mentalities. Peter Burke identifies these themes through their opposites: classical culture, kept alive in the schools and universities of medieval Europe; the tradition of scholastic philosophy and theology; a few cultural movements in the early modern period, notably the Renaissance, the scientific revolution, and the Enlightenment. Next, he turns away from those traditions and looks at what is left: mystery plays and farces, broadsheets and chapbooks, folktales, pious images, decorated marriage-chests and, most of all, the great festivals such as carnival and midsummer.

In summing up, Burke emphasizes directly visible forms of culture. Muchembled, on the other hand, deals mainly with rituals, beliefs, and experience. Both authors refuse to consider the series of opposites previously described that provide the concept of popular culture with a preliminary demarcation. First, the concept of popular culture is based on an acknowledgment that various forms of culture commonly have been the domain of a minority. For example, the scientific revolution passed unnoticed by most inhabitants of villages and neighborhoods. Those inhabitants had their own beliefs, and the concept of popular culture refers to those beliefs. Second, for a long time historians have paid uneven attention to the culture of the minority. The study of popular culture strives to redress that balance. Of course, if certain themes, such as festivals and folktales, have been neglected by historians, this does not necessarily mean that these subjects constitute a unity. However, we can see their relationship as we review the empirical data.

Although these considerations do not prescribe an outline, the material in this chapter follows one: the first section elaborates the problems created by the concept of popular culture. Next, conceptions about the cosmos (in the second section) and the image of social relations (in the third) are dealt with. The last section attempts to link the preceding two and to penetrate the very essence of the silent majority's mentalité. Various changes at the end of the preindustrial period and the eventual decline of ancient popular culture are discussed in chapter 9.

The Lesser Tradition

There are two ways to determine which ideas and customs should be counted as popular culture. We may start with culture itself, attributing every expression to either one of its domains. Alternatively, we may focus on distinct social groups and investigate the differences in their customs and their view of the world. The first course is easier, since historians can rely on their own judgment. For example, they decide that in many societies culture can be divided into a "great" and a "little" tradition. Burke does this, following the anthropologist Redfield. (Although we adopt their notions, we call the traditions "greater" and "lesser.") Or historians adopt a formula analogous to Bakhtin's: in a number of societies, the official culture, which is just serious, is confronted by an unofficial one which combines seriousness and the trivial. Burke's and Bakhtin's models put us on the right track. If we restrict ourselves to reviewing the evidence on the seventeenth and eighteenth centuries for a moment, we can easily see which customs and beliefs belong to one sector of culture or the other. Carnival, for example, is deadly serious to some participants, just a game to others, and a little bit of both to most people. Hence, carnival belongs to the lesser tradition. By contrast, Newton's theories or the etiquette at Versailles, even though few contemporaries master them, are taken seriously by all.

They belong to the greater tradition. The greater tradition carries more prestige; hence, its name. For seventeenth and eighteenth-century Europe, it is a viable enterprise to distinguish the greater from the lesser tradition in this way. Having done that, we are to trace the roots of the various elements of which the lesser is made up. It is by no means self-evident that these elements were equally "unofficial" in an earlier period. To the contrary, the migration of ideas and customs from the official to the unofficial sphere, and possibly back again, is one of the most interesting problems for research.

Elites and the People

Are popular culture and the lesser tradition one and the same, however? That question leads us to the second line of demarcation. We may simply ask who are the people and who are the elites, but the answer is far from simple. The concept of popular culture is tied to its counterpart, elite culture. Thus, we are distinguishing two broad social groups, the elite and the non-elite. To denote the latter by a positive term, we may call them the populace or the people. This simplified dichotomy is useful for research purposes; in historical reality there is a richer variety of social groups. The difficulty with the model lies in the ambiguity of the concept of elite. An elite is a small group which has more of something than the rest: more power, more prestige, more schooling, more money, or a combination of these. The problem is that these things are not always correlated. Historians who speak of elite culture usually have two things in mind. For one, the elite means the learned: those who have enjoyed a measure of education. Included are priests and ministers, even though they were often of humble status by other criteria. Viewed from this angle, elite culture is more or less the same as learned culture. From another perspective, the elite means "those ranking highest in social stratification": aristocrats, patricians, and rich bourgeois. However, the aristocracy certainly was not learned at first, and it remained uninvolved in the major intellectual and scientific movements. From the second perspective, then, elite culture is primarily the culture of the powerful.

Yet it would be incorrect to claim that, because of the ambiguity of their counterparts, lesser tradition and popular culture are unrelated. The less powerful and the unlearned are largely overlapping groups. It is only the line that divides them from the elites which has to be drawn differently each time, depending on the particular custom or belief studied.

The distinction between elite and popular culture can be explained in still another way. The greater tradition literally was less accessible. It was cherished in palaces and universities, in patrician homes and court buildings. The common people had no access to this world (except, in the latter case, as delinquents). Peasants and artisans did not read Latin, nor were they versed in courtly etiquette. The lesser tradition, on the other hand, had a more public character; many could participate. This public nature can also be taken literally. It was the openness of the street and the field, or, in the cold northern regions, the tavern and the common barn. In other words, popular culture had strong links with the village or neighborhood. The places where the greater tradition was fostered were national or even international centers. By contrast, the lesser tradition was locally based; numerous local communities together made up the people. Popular culture was the culture of those local communities: villages in the countryside and neighborhoods in the towns. For a long time, villages and neighborhoods were relatively isolated and left to themselves. First of all, this isolation should be considered literally, from a geographic point of view. Villages in particular were like small islands, far from the large centers and from each other. Second, local communities stood apart in a social sense. They constituted separate worlds, to which the aristocracy and the bourgeoisie, although not entirely excluded, did not really belong either. Social isolation also characterized urban neighborhoods. Thus, the lesser tradition is the culture of local communities, which explains many of its features. Of course, the lesser tradition's local base and the relative isolation of village and neighborhood communities do not preclude that the preindustrial popular cultures of Europe had characteristics in common.

Interactions   Simple models rarely reflect reality. The one just outlined has two main shortcomings: it suggests too rigid a separation of the lesser from the greater tradition, and it is insufficiently attuned to changes over time. Let us try to eliminate these shortcomings.

To remove the first, we have to tolerate the second for a moment. We are considering a limited period, ranging approximately from the end of the sixteenth century to the middle of the eighteenth. Cultural items belonging to the greater or the lesser tradition are easily classifiable. Village and neighborhood communities have not yet lost their distinctness and cohesion. Rich bourgeois keep a certain distance from neighborhood life, aristocrats from common farmers, and clergymen from parishioners who are not always noted for purity of doctrine or conduct. Nevertheless, the lesser tradition is public. Just as the courts and patrician mansions are inaccessible to the people, so the marketplace and the tavern are accessible to the elite. Indeed, the latter actually participate in various events of the lesser tradition. In Romans in the south of France at the end of the sixteenth century, for example, rich citizens as well as artisans created "kingdoms" during carnival time. One kingdom used a partridge as its symbol, another a rooster, the third a sheep. Carnival involved the whole town and every peasant from its surroundings. That held equally true for Italian and southern German cities. There are other examples which show that the elite were no strangers to the lesser tradition. The upper classes of Spain, the king included, were fervent supporters of bull-fighting; clowns were welcome at princely courts and in taverns; priests sprinkled their sermons with popular tales. Art objects made by craftsmen are listed in the inventories of noble homes. Some rich bourgeois owned a voluminous collection of chapbooks, which they may not have gathered purely for purposes of study.

It is possible of course that those bourgeois read the books out of a detached interest in folklore. Merchants and gentry may have partici-pated in feasts to increase their own popularity without really enjoy-ing themselves. However, there is sufficient reason to assume that many from among the elite appreciated these things and shared expe-riences with the populace. Thus, the lesser tradition was upheld by both the elites and the people. For the people, however, the lesser tra-dition was the only one in which they actively participated, while for the elites it meant a secondary experience. This observation quali-fies the distinction between elite and popular culture, but it does not oblige us to reject it. Rendered in technical terms, the popular classes were monocultural and the elite bicultural. Popular culture is that culture which was central to the people and supplementary to the elite. The lesser tradition was also more serious to the people but more of a game to the elite.

We qualify the model still further when we speak of lesser traditions in the plural. Preindustrial popular culture was certainly not homoge-neous or uniform. Its degree of homogeneity of course depends on the range of application various authors give to the concept. Muchembled situates "traditional" popular culture in the agrarian regions of fif-teenth- and sixteenth-century France. Whoever considers the culture of the countryside as the only popular culture and urban traditions as absolute derivatives will observe a greater homogeneity. The exis-tence of an urban popular culture is particularly assumed here which makes the distinction between town and countryside one of the most important differentiations within the lesser tradition. The annual cycle of festivals, for example, was connected to the seasonal rhythm to a much greater extent in agrarian regions. In towns, traditional group rivalry was stronger. The inhabitants of two urban neighborhoods had even more opportunities to engage in mutual fights with each other than those of two neighboring villages. In the cities also there were rivalries between occupational groups or, as in eighteenth-century Amsterdam, fights between Christians and Jews.

Also, we should take into account regional differentiation. Although many customs could be found all over Europe, their details might vary from region to region or from country to country. For example, English adolescents were not organized into formal youth societies as those of the Continent. Festive behavior in the cold Scandinavian winter was less exuberant than in the South; the midsummer festival, when the sun did not set, formed the climax of the annual cycle in the northern regions. Still another important difference is between the settled and the roving population. Vagabonds had their own way of life and were largely excluded from the culture of villages and neighborhoods. Using a well-known sociological concept, we can call the variants within the lesser tradition subcultures. As long as the differences among subcultures are less than the difference between the lesser tradition as a whole and the greater it is justified to speak of a separate popular culture.

The third correction of the model follows from acknowledging that the greater and lesser traditions were open to each other. That also introduces a time perspective. Over time, elements from one tradition migrated to the other and vice versa, or, from a hierarchical viewpoint, went from high to low and from low to high. The latter was the case with certain popular notions about the afterlife, which were included in theology in the form of the doctrine of purgatory in the twelfth century. In a later period, popular dances and songs were stylized to become courtly music and dance, and fairy tales were adapted for the upper classes. For example, the English ballad "Greensleeves" with its melody adapted by a composer, was a favorite at Elizabeth I's court. It continued to belong to both traditions. Almost a century later, in 1661, Samuel Pepys heard Admiral Mountague sing a humorous ballad about the fall of the Puritan regime which used the melody of "Greensleeves." Downward migration occurred with the romances of chivalry, originally meant for and listened to in noble castles, but appreciated only by the populace after 1500. Other examples include the imitation of courtly forms of civility by non-aristocrats and, at the end of the eighteenth century, the reception of enlightened ideas among groups of artisans. Thus, there was interaction between elite and popular culture. It appears, though, that the elements migrating downward were more fundamental. They seem to have more substance, while those migrating upward have to do with form.

We must say, finally, that the lesser tradition cannot be equated with popular culture in every period. As said before, this is true mainly for the period from the end of the sixteenth to the middle of the eighteenth century. Looking at an earlier period, we find more often that elite persons not only participated in festivals and youthful societies but that they acted in a leading role. A writer such as Rabelais freely played with "popular" humor, which he did not consider "unofficial."

Much of what was urban popular culture in the seventeenth century belonged to a shared world of experience by the entire citizenry in the later Middle Ages. Patricians sat in the first row and acted in vernacular plays. The greater tradition for that period should be restricted to Latin culture, but the undignified songs, *carmina burana*, were also composed in Latin. Maybe we should contrast the unlearned nobility, along with burghers and peasants, to the clergy, but then we have a problem. The feast of fools, which was characteristics for the lesser tradition around 1500, had an ecclesiastical origin. Belief in magic, finally, which various authors consider typical of popular culture, was widespread also among the clergy for a long time.

All this draws us to a conclusion about the phases of cultural change in preindustrial Europe. At the beginning, we do not find two separate traditions. Cultural differences between groups are real, but all forms of culture are equally "official." This continues into the sixteenth century. It is the greater tradition which breaks away from the original common culture. Before the sixteenth century this greater tradition has an embryonic presence in the form of scholastic philosophy and refinements in conduct at territorial courts. In the early modern period it becomes more pronounced, turning the original culture's residue into an unofficial, lesser tradition. Increasingly the elites take only the greater tradition seriously. During the eighteenth century they even distance themselves from its counterpart. The elites withdraw from popular culture and, hence, stop being bicultural. Only then, preindustrial popular culture is a culture of the people alone; but simultaneously, though not necessarily because of this, it starts to decline.

The Cosmos and the Rhythm of Life

To say that "the people are superstitious" would not have been un-common for a nineteenth-century bourgeois. Many might have ar-gued, for example, that success is the result of one's own efforts and cannot be forced by good-luck charms. The word, superstition, im-plies a judgment. It connotes the user's intellectual superiority, since few people consider themselves superstitious. Those who label oth-ers in this way belong to different cultures. This brings us back to the distinction between greater and lesser tradition. The development of a greater tradition in Europe ran parallel to a "disenchantment of the world" in Max Weber's sense. Popular culture stuck to a magical world view for a longer time. In this area too, it was the greater tradition which broke loose from a common culture. Originally all social groups shared a magical view of the world, although its contents might differ with the group under scrutiny.

Variants of Popular Beliefs

The magical beliefs and conceptions of the populace often concerned the practical and daily realities of life (and death, as we will see in chapter 5). One example is the problem of recovering lost or stolen ob-jects. Astrologers or clairvoyants might offer help, but the owners could also try a magical formula themselves. The options of self-help and the consultation of a magical specialist were also open in cases of the more serious problem of preventing and curing diseases and ail-ments. Reciting the Lord's Prayer and carrying an amulet or the caul (a part of the amniotic sac) might help, as many French people thought around 1500. Other activities were to be avoided. To prevent an ail-ment of the eye, one never should urinate between two houses or to-ward the sun. Urinating against a convent led to kidney stones or a stroke. Other customs dealt with the precariousness of love and hap-piness. Cats were considered good for both. A cheated wife could win back her husband's love if she hid her cat with its feet tied and smeared with butter in a barrel for two days, feeding it only bread soaked in her urine. The fireplace also had a special relationship with good and bad luck. If a girl remained seated while watching the fire being put out, she would not marry that year. These examples still come from fifteenth and sixteenth-century France, which makes it imperative to add at least one from another time and place. The scene is the southern German village of Beutelsbach in 1796. When hoof-and-mouth disease broke out in the region, the villagers buried their common bull alive at a crossroad just outside the inhabited area. Two or three men carried the struggling animal to its grave, and a dozen others immediately threw sand and stones into the hole to prevent it from escaping. The magical power of this ritual served to protect the remaining cattle from succumbing to the disease.

There are many more examples. Folklorists have recorded lists of comparable beliefs well into the twentieth century, although in more remote regions. The state of historical research does not permit an analysis of regional variation or phases of change in preindustrial Europe. The most systematic study in this respect is that by Keith Thomas. He observes a decline of magic in England in the course of the early modern period. Muchembled presents a broad characterization of the "magical universe," as experienced by most Europeans in the sixteenth century. He speaks of an animistic view of the world. Humans, animals, and things were linked by all kinds of living forces. Within that network of forces, people tried to maintain a certain quality of life and death. Knowledge about effective remedies, helpful rituals, and activities to avoid was cherished and handed down by women in particular. An anthology of French popular beliefs was called "the gospel of the distaffs." The human body had contact with the magical universe notably through its lower parts, a theme which is also central to Bakhtin's work. This world of magic is obviously related to the subject of witchcraft, which will be dealt with in the next chapter.

Although it was a mental construct, the magical universe had a material base too. We learn this from Piero Camporesi's work about the effects of permanent hunger on the very poor. To soothe empty stomachs, herbs, seeds, and opiates were added to the little bread that was eaten. To fall asleep, children were given a poppy drink. Adults, however, suffered from sleeplessness caused by the "uppers" among hallucinogenic substances and exacerbated by the fear of vampires or werewolves. Thus, the day and the night were intermingled, and the transition between dreaming and waking became vague. Mothers and grandmothers, instead of village sorceresses, evoked this enchanted world. In Florence the preacher Savonarola complained about bread baked from cannabis seeds, which made people drunk. The seventeenth-century physician Ovidio Montalbani, on the other hand, praised the poppy as an excellent antidote to hunger. It is quite possible that preindustrial Europe counted more opiate addicts than today's world.

A few popular beliefs deserve special attention because they are linked to other themes in popular culture or the history of mentalities as a whole. A very intriguing set of ideas concerns a group of wandering spirits. This belief was actually a cluster of related myths, which differed according to region and over time. The common element in all variants was the notion of a group of creatures who lacked a fixed residence and were not living people. The present state of research allows us to distinguish two main variants: the wild horde and the comic troop. The first can be subdivided into a popular and a Christian version. In the popular version, the wild horde essentially consisted of the dead who could not find rest, since they had died prematurely through violence or in another way. They were doomed to wander forever. As is appropriate for spirits, they usually transported themselves through the air. References to this wandering army date back to before A.D. 1000. The spirits were frequently led by a female figure, alternately called Holda, Perchta, Diana, or Herodias. The leader could also be male. Such is the case in the earliest text which mentions the Christian version, Ordericus Vitalis's history of Normandy, written at the end of the eleventh century. Ordericus relates how the priest Gauchelin passed through a deserted area on his return from a visit to a sick parishioner one night in 1091:

A giant man, carrying an enormous club, caught up with him. He waved it above the priest's head, saying "stop, go no further." Stiffened from fear, the priest stood still, leaning on his stick. But the club-carrying giant did not part from him and waited, without doing anything to him, for the passing of the army. Look, an immense host of warriors passed him on foot. On their necks and backs they carried poultry, all kind of kitchen utensils and other equipment, while they wore clothes resembling those usually worn by robbers. . . . Then a host of armed porters followed, whom the said giant suddenly joined. They carried about fifty coffins. . . . On each coffin a human person was seated, as small as a dwarf but with a big head. . . . Next, two Ethiopians dragged a rack with them. A lamentable person, loudly screaming from pain, was tied to the rack. A creepy devil, who was sitting there too, pressed fiery spurs into his loins and his back, which made the blood stream. Gauchelin clearly recognized the tortured man as the murderer of the priest Stephen (Driesen: 25; paraphrase).

And it continues for a while. The priest killer is followed by scores of other sinners: people who were well known during their lifetime and whose evil deeds had remained unnoticed. The knight Landric of Orbec, for example, acting as a judge in civil suits, had accepted a large sum of money from numerous parties in exchange for a favorable judgment. The conspicuous presence of sinners in the wild horde identifies this passage from Ordericus Vitalis as a Christian version. The dead are not merely the miserable, possibly innocent, whom fate alone has doomed to remain without rest. They are the guilty, bound for punishment. This image fits into the ideological development which would lead to the belief in purgatory a century later.

When the army passed, Gauchelin had yelled, "This must be the *familia Herlechini*, Herlekine's suite, that I have heard so much about." The leadership of Herlekine (Harlequin) was not necessarily characteristic of the Christian version of the wild horde, but it does introduce the second main variant. The poultry and kitchen utensils carried by his followers are essential. The familia Herlechini frequently turns up in the literature of the later Middle Ages, increasingly in a humorous context. Pots and pans and various types of animals remain its constant attributes. This comic troop also appears in vernacular plays. In "The Game under the Foliage" by Adan de le Hale, first played in Arras in 1262, Herlekine's people are jesting at the back of the stage. One of them advances to the front and plays his part all along. He calls himself Fool-eater because those who are afraid of him and fly are fools. As a comic troop, the familia Herlechini still remains associated with the Christian version of the wild horde. Herlekine's people are jesters and devils at the same time; the grin on their faces is a devil's grimace. Their hilarious walk follows from the fact that they normally move through the air and are unaccustomed to a stage floor. As devils, they appear at the same time in religious plays. Then they ascend from hell, which is situated under the stage and covered by a *chape de Herlequin:* a curtain with the giant portrait of a devil showing his bare teeth. These two main variants were related to each other.

Another group of creatures were certainly no spirits, which means we are confronted with a new cluster of popular beliefs. This creature was called the wild man or woodman. He was hairy, went naked, and hid in dark forests. He was halfway between a man and an animal. Wild men were the opposite of civilized people; they were unrestrained, violent, and sexually insatiable. Wild women are mentioned too, but not very often. The belief in wild men was widespread until the eighteenth century. Stories were told about people who had caught one. The hunt for a wild man and his possible trial and execution after his capture appeared as a motif in popular plays. As a rule, wild men were sharply distinguished from the spirits of the wandering army, whether as demons or not. Thomas Aquinas argued that the wild man, who merely acted upon his passion, was not as dangerous as demonic seducers.

We cannot draw a clear line between popular and elite culture with respect to wild men. Scholars such as Linnaeus believed in their existence. That applied equally to giants. They were seldom absent from festive processions of urban citizens, whether in the form of puppets carried on a cart or moved by persons hiding in them. Such was the case in Flanders and England. Well into the eighteenth century many clerics were convinced that giants really existed, not the least because they were mentioned in the Bible. The little creatures still familiar to us from fairy tales, finally, whatever their names in various European languages, were just as real for large numbers of people. The Scottish populace believed that if a child was not baptized quickly enough, the fairies would try to take it and put another in its place. Family and neighbors often held a wake until baptism had been accomplished.

Christianity and Popular Devotion

Strictly speaking, many of the beliefs just discussed were not quite compatible with official Christian faith. Any learned monk consulted about it would have replied that God alone protected people from disease, or punished them with it, so that it did not matter whether or not one urinated toward the sun. Ecclesiastical doctrine acknowledged numerous supernatural phenomena and events, but an attempt was made to integrate them into a system. Max Weber's theory of an original contribution by world religions to the process of disenchantment has been discussed in chapter 1. Medieval scholastic philosophy was a relatively rational doctrine. Official theology tried to establish a connection between supernatural and magical phenomena by tracing their origins to one God, or to the devil, whose power ultimately, only derived from God's permission. This process of rationalization set in very gradually. Also in the religious realm, the greater tradition developed as an offshoot from a common culture of devotion. The majority held on to a more magical and less systematic religiosity, which became a popular one. The elaboration of a learned theology in the Middle Ages and the struggle against unorthodox popular beliefs and practices in the early modern period are both a part of the process of disenchantment of the world. This process did not proceed in a unilinear fashion. From the twelfth century the authors of saints' lives and other pious tales included more miraculous events into their stories than had been customary until then. That is evidenced by the Golden Legend, a collection of tales about saints gathered and rewritten in the second half of the thirteenth century by the Dominican Jacopo da Voragine.

The crucial change took place in the sixteenth century. Protestants, soon followed by Catholics, started to delineate the boundaries of official religion more rigorously. What was left was called superstition, and superstition was essentially pagan. Before the sixteenth century, church leaders had been accustomed to adopt a more lenient attitude, even though they also considered certain notions as pagan. Still, that period witnessed tensions between official and unofficial traditions. As large parts of Europe were converted to Christianity after a learned theology had been fully developed, its details were not immediately clear to everyone. We may ask ourselves what it meant to a ninth-century Saxon to proclaim himself a Christian—probably no more than the acknowledgment that the foreign God of a conquering nation was henceforth his God too. His daily habits and his view of the world must have been scarcely affected by it. All European nations were in this position at different moments in time. In daily life, Christian doctrine did not overcome the Germanic or Greco-Roman world of images. Both were intermingled instead. During most of the Middle Ages clerics remained vigilant, watching for allegedly pagan customs and beliefs.

Thus, the confrontation between surviving heathen traditions and the pure Christian faith caused tensions between church leaders and the flocks entrusted to their care from the start. At least from the tenth century, for example, bishops ordered parish priests to discourage the belief in the wild horde, which they labelled as pagan. However, until the sixteenth century the tensions were not acute. The world view of ordinary priests was close to that of the populace. When confronted with customs and beliefs considered dubious, church leaders and learned theologians did not always push their opposition to them. They tried instead to transform those traditions, integrating them into the faith.

The Christian version of the wild horde is an example of such integration. One of its earliest hallmarks is the veneration of saints' relics, originating from a need for a more concrete form of devotion. For the majority, the cult of saints had a strongly magical character. The devout populace credited relics with a special power. Oaths sworn on these sacred objects were often taken more seriously than those sworn on the Bible. Many pilgrims visiting a saint's grave thought that he himself cured their disease. Theologians justified popular custom with the argument that miracles were actually performed by God through the intercession of that particular saint, just as the intercession of a vassal with his lord might benefit the former's client. The development of the doctrine of purgatory also was a reaction to unorthodox beliefs. This doctrine brought popular and Christian notions of the afterlife nearer to each other, as we will see in chapter 5. It is well known, finally, that Christmas originated as a heathen winter festival. The feast survived, but with a changed content.

The survival of pagan traditions has prompted some authors to state that the majority of the population in the Middle Ages were not really Christian. This proposition, however, implies that the historian passes judgment as to what is Christian and what is not. Even today there is no agreement about this. Whoever calls himself a Christian should be termed one by historians. When the process of conversion had been completed, practically all Europeans unconditionally considered themselves as such. The magical universe was integrated into the teachings of the church, broadly understood, and into the reality of ecclesiastical institutions. That explains prescriptions such as "beware of urinating against a monastery." Intentionally, popular devotion was just as Christian as the matins and lauds of pious monks. Spiritual leaders might be concerned from time to time, but certainly in the period before the sixteenth century, they too considered the majority of the population as being within the bosom of the church. From their point of view, only a minority of heretical groups were expelled from it, and the attention of the defenders of the pure faith was primarily directed at those dissidents. Most heretical ideas, however, sprang from learned culture.

And yet the degree of integration between official doctrine and popular religion should not be overestimated. First, in some cases the people integrated Christian faith into the magical universe in ways completely unacceptable to church leaders. The images of saints, for example, were sometimes molested by the local population. The populace not only worshiped the saints, but they also held them responsible for their failures. That happened, for example, in thirteenth-century Normandy. When the summer was too cold or the harvest damaged by thunderstorms, the peasants took the images of the Holy Virgin and the patron saints from the parish churches to insult and flog them. Where a patron was not subjected to such humiliating treatment, his very identity might be rejected by church leaders. Thus, about the same time a visiting inquisitor in the bishopric of Lyon expressed his distrust in the cult of Saint Guinefort because he had never heard of this saint. But he was really shocked when he heard that the object of worship was a dog. The local population took Guinefort for a protector of the life of the newly born, although he could be harsh in doing so. A legend about a greyhound who had defended a baby against a snake during the parents' absence was the origin of this cult. People in the Lyon region still remembered it in the nineteenth century.

The second caveat refers to beliefs rather than practices. Occasionally, ideas surfaced which were so remote from ecclesiastical doctrine that clerics unconditionally condemned them as heresies. It is difficult to determine whether these had pagan origins. The ideas of radical sects in seventeenth-century England can be traced back to late medieval popular traditions. The Family of the Mount claimed: "Heaven is when people laugh and are merry; hell is sorrow, misery and pain." Some even denied the existence of God and the devil; others denied the immortality of the soul or the resurrection of Christ. Such opinions remained exceptional, however. Besides, many popular radicals were anticlerical rather than un-Christian, and it is not possible to call their ideas magical. They belonged to a minority tradition, characterized by a heavy dose of soberness and realism.

A popular dissident made famous by Carlo Ginzburg was called Domenico Scandella, better known as Menocchio. This miller from the small town of Montereale in Friuli at the end of the sixteenth century astonished his inquisitors with ideas they found quite bizarre. Menocchio's beliefs were a typical product of interaction between popular and elite culture. This miller was literate and had done a great deal of reading. His interpretation of a text, and his selective memorizing of passages were guided, however, by preconceived notions. These notions were probably derived from popular traditions of dissent. For example, many contemporary Italians saw Saint Joseph as a cuckold (See Chapter 8.) and Menocchio's poor view of Mary, denying her virginity, was in line with this. He thought that a passage from an Italian adaptation of the Golden Legend confirmed his views. Jacopo da Voragine had related how, at the Virgin's funeral, a pagan priest had tried to desecrate the coffin, had been punished for it with great pain, and in the end was obliged to acknowledge the glory of the mother of God. Menocchio only remembered the desecration, which he took as a confirmation of Mary's infamy. His notion of the generation of the cosmos from a process of fermentation, the way cheese originates from milk, is curious too. This mass of rotten cheese was the earth, where worms, being angels at the same time, appeared as the first creatures. Ginzburg relates the cheese to ancient rituals of fertility. His compatriot Camporesi presents an interpretation of the worms. The populace, plagued by hunger and illness, had a particular fear of intestinal worms. These were viewed as an incarnation of spirits, usually devils but sometimes angels. Menocchio's opinions, like those of the English radicals, were strongly rooted in anticlericalism. He considered the church, with its huge landed property, as the greatest oppressor of the people.

As has been said, clerics conducted an increasingly fierce struggle against various popular customs and ideas from the sixteenth century on. This struggle lay at the base of the repression of popular culture that set in later, so that it will be discussed in the final chapter. To be sure, the protagonists of the Reformation and Counter Reformation were not hostile to the lesser tradition as a whole. Luther's followers especially put a number of popular motifs to propaganda use. Their adversaries were ridiculed according to traditional popular practices. Engravings pictured Catholic writers in animal form or the pope and his cardinals on the gallows. The association with feces was also a favorite: once literally, when the authors of a libel against Luther had it returned to them, "illustrated" with dung. This propaganda was based on worldly themes rather than religious feelings. Its spokesmen used familiar cultural codes to convey a novel religious message.

The Rhythm of the Seasons

The succession of seasons determined most people's experience of the cosmos. The annual rhythm concealed the secrets of fertility and infertility, touching upon a mystery which was central to the life of the community. The change of seasons was felt most intensely in agrarian regions because the pace of work was finely attuned to it. But the contrast between town and countryside was less than it may seem at first. Urban residents also lived with the calendar. As Julio Caro Baroja formulates it, the rhythm of the seasons was also an "order of passions": an oscillation between pleasure and seriousness, youth and old age, love and desertion, exuberance and contemplation, life and death. Artisans in the cities were familiar with alternating periods of scarcity and abundance. The rhythm of festive joy and humble poverty was one they knew all too well.

The annual cycle of festivals synchronized the life rhythm of all members of the community. Festive rituals, drawn from a rich repertoire with regional variations, often revolved around the problem of fertility. Bachelors usually took care of the organizational tasks, but the whole community participated in a feast. The exact dates varied locally, but the principle of the festive calendar was more or less universal. One particular area, early modern Spain, may be taken as an example, with an emphasis on the agrarian world. Feasts were concentrated in two periods of the year, winter and summer. The winter began with Advent, a time for labor. Villagers performed the last activities before the inevitable breakthrough of the cold. It was a period of soberness; only an occasional wedding took place. Christmas started two weeks of joy until Epiphany. The people sang, recited poems, and amused themselves. The day of the Innocents and that of the Holy Family fell within this period too. Festivities actually continued until Fat Tuesday, the last day of carnival and the climax of the annual cycle. Next, Lent was a time for contemplation. People ate just one meal a day, and wandering preachers found a receptive climate. Lent coincided with the first inspection of the vineyards and the pressing of olives. Passion plays were performed and processions held during the Good Week. In Valladolid the whores participated while their pimps watched to prevent them from being converted.

The summer rhythm began with Easter. Spring broke through and many marriages were concluded. The May celebrations followed, including the election of the May queen. June witnessed the zenith of exuberance: Saint John's night (24 June), also midsummer festival, although the church favored Sacrament's Day with its religious processions as a rival. Then the actual summer set in, and people worked the land or left to assist with the *mesta*, the cattle drive to the northern markets. In the cities it was time for the construction of houses and the organization of commercial fairs. This period of work culminated into the harvest and the vintage. There were a few festivals in between, though: Santiago, the patron saint of Spain (25 July), the Ascension (15 August), and the Birth of the Virgin (8 September). Just before Advent there might be local celebrations on different days, especially when the harvest had been abundant.

A comparable cycle could be found all over Europe, including Protestant regions, where the demise of the cult of saints did not necessarily put a stop to the celebration. Admittedly, Protestant regions eventually witnessed fewer festivals. Notably, the Reformation meant the end of carnival, although not immediately, since during its first decades the populace of Germany and Switzerland celebrated antipapist carnivals. Protestant feasts generally retained carnivalesque elements. Because those elements are related to the theme of the world upside down, they are discussed further in the last section. One aspect of carnival still deserves attention here. The end of the celebration was sealed by the death and the burial or cremation of lord Carnival himself, often preceded by his trial and condemnation. On Fat Tuesday toward midnight the participants burned a puppet that represented him or beheaded a pig in his place. Lent could be personified too, as Carnival's staunch opponent. The combat between Carnival and Lent appeared as a motif in thirteenth-century literature and it was sometimes performed as a play during the feast itself from the fifteenth century onward. The contesting parties were often represented, respectively, as a fat man and an old skinny woman, but there was also a variant with two male figures. Writers associated Carnival with meat and game, Lent with fish and vegetables. In general, the scene was different according to the social context. In medieval texts it was common for Carnival to win the combat, whereupon he magnanimously conceded forty days of rule to his beaten opponent. After 1500, obviously in Catholic regions, Lent was always the victor.

This motif forms another example of accommodation between Christian doctrine and popular rituals. It appeared at the same time in the thirteenth century as the celebration of carnival itself. Unlike other festivals, carnival had no place on the official Christian calendar. Despite this, it obtained a semiofficial position through the connection with Lent. The motif of the combat linked them. The scene was a symbolic representation of the contrast between two periods of the year, which simultaneously were two periods on the church's calendar. Looked at from this angle, carnival meant rejoicing over the coming of Christ, starting with Christmas and culminating on Fat Tuesday. It was succeeded by forty days of atonement and reflection, until the renewed joy over Christ's resurrection. Thus, the order of passions inherent in the change of the seasons became identical to the Christian order of passions.

Historians of popular culture find it more exciting to write about carnival than about Lent. Still this sober period also stirred up popular imagination, although rather in the form of irony. Cynics knew that not everyone fasted conscientiously. The consumption of fish was permitted in any case, as emphasized by popular writers in sixteenth-century England. John Taylor relates how his hero, Jack-a-Lent, continues to have a good time after carnival, treating himself to various sorts of fish with sauces, salads, fruit, almonds, spices, and drink. Thomas Nashe thinks that Lent was invented to make the rich butchers play the second fiddle for a while and to encourage the fish sellers. During Lent the butchers travelled to buy oxen and calves, while their wives were cheating on them.

Community Life

Through the festive cycle, the village or neighborhood community orchestrated the life rhythm of its members. The leading role in feasts was often played by youth societies. Youth is associated with the rhythm of life in still another way. Viewed from a long-term perspective, that rhythm is the succession of life stages. With respect to them, communal involvement was equally intense. The community accompanied the life of its members from the cradle to the grave, which was one of the major expressions of mutual solidarity. When a woman was pregnant, other women showed their empathy and visited her when she gave birth. A wedding was celebrated by the entire village or neighborhood. When a person died, neighbors held a wake and they all appeared at the funeral. Various other chapters treat these subjects in greater detail.

Anthropologists use the concept of *rites de passage*: rituals taking place at the moment of transition to a new stage of life. The wedding ceremony is one of them, the transition to adolescence another. Everywhere youths were recognizable as a group, although they were not always organized formally. France especially had formal societies of young people. In the Poitiers region they were called *bachelleries*; the boys were called *bacheliers* and the girls, *bachelières* or *bachelettes*. In most places, to be sure, only the boys were organized. Although the word *bachelier* did not originally mean 'bachelor,' a person's marriage usually ended his membership. Older bachelors probably withdrew from the societies, but there is no information about this. The age of admittance varied according to region. Near Poitiers most members were in their twenties. These societies had the status of corporations and they could act as such in court until the eighteenth century. In villages their leaders were often youths from the richer families. The bachelors took a stand against similar societies from a neighboring village if there was a feud. Sometimes they fought the married men.

A custom at the crossroads of popular culture and family life is the gathering of a group of villagers in a barn. The French spoke of *veillées*, Germans of *Spinnstuben*. The neighbors spent winter evenings together working and socializing. At French veillées the women sewed or mended clothes while the men repaired tools. Sometimes, however, these gatherings were open only to women, who had no access to the male domain of the *cabaret*. For bachelors, winter evenings offered an opportunity to socialize. Young men visited young women who might be working in a barn. As their name tells us, Spinnstuben originally housed only women, but later they were known mainly for meetings between boys and girls.

Since the cities had no equivalents for these barns, the phenomenon was restricted to the countryside. But there was another source of solidarity in the cities, which was usually lacking in the countryside. The work community, whether or not in the form of a guild, had an importance equal to that of the neighborhood community. The occupational group, with feasts and rituals of its own, constituted an obvious frame of reference to its members. Workmates often went out together at night.

The major frames of reference for Chavatte, a worsted weaver in Lille at the end of the seventeenth century, were, in this order: the Catholic faith, his trade, the city of Lille. Precisely because they had no occupation, vagabonds remained outside the community. People on the move, in town or countryside, were obviously unable to share in the experience of the settled population. In England though, some vagabonds roamed from one local fair to another. One group of vagrants, traveling artists, played a role in popular culture nonetheless. The settled population loved to listen to their songs or to watch their dancing bears. For their part, the magistrates watched them with suspicion. In the Netherlands these performers were treated as wanderers, in Germany as infamous persons, with whom physical contact should always be avoided.

The exclusion, to a large extent, of the nonsettled population warns us against a too idyllic picture of community life. In villages and neighborhoods almost everyone knew each other, and lived close to one another. This created a form of mutual solidarity, but at times it could just as well lead to fierce tensions. Sabean emphasizes that the word, community, refers to shared experiences as well as shared conflicts. In the German villages he studied he found numerous examples of intense hatred, jealousy, frustration, and fear felt by one inhabitant toward the other. Whoever received bread from a neighboring woman threw a piece to the chickens first to find out whether it was poisoned. For England, Gillis reaches a similar conclusion. Rituals served to ease the anxiety and uncertainty which were immanent in conflicts and tensions. This also applied to the wedding ceremony. Every marriage meant a redistribution of status and economic resources within the community, which might lead internal conflicts to change their course. At weddings as well as funerals fights were not uncommon. Being collective events, both were suitable occasions to settle old scores. Fist fights during weddings were also reported from the Poitiers region. The less idyllic aspect of community life is reflected in the practice of charivari, with which the next section opens.

Folklore and Hierarchy

If preindustrial popular culture were viewed only from the angle of the magical universe, a number of essential elements would remain hidden. There were numerous concrete practices and activities which, in one way or another, reflected the social order and the people's perception of it. Peasants and artisans listened to stories which commented on daily reality or allowed them to escape it. They drew on ancient traditions to confront those in authority, or simply to comfort themselves. They enforced informal norms of their own. Let us start with these norms and return to charivari. Then we will analyze types of folktales from which we can learn about the popular view of the social hierarchy that encompassed village and neighborhood communities. Finally, the question of whether popular culture and protest were intimately related will be raised.

Charivari

As already explained, local communities not only were known for solidarity but also for conflicts. At times the community's concern for the personal life of its members took the form of meddlesomeness. Neighbors saw to it that a person's life course conformed to their norms and undertook action in case of deviation. Gossip was the primary and mildest type of reaction. Permanent gossip caused severe damage to someone's reputation, with all kind of unpleasant consequences. Alternatively, neighbors might react to behavior they disapproved of in a more concrete way, namely with the rituals and customs of charivari. In the previous chapter charivari was defined as a form of ridicule for breaking community norms. Form and content of the ritual varied according to region, and they were also subject to change. Let us start with a few general characteristics, valid in different periods, and continue with a brief discussion of change. Under the rubric of general characteristics, we may consider the ritual, the performers, and the victims.

The origins of the word, charivari, are unknown. Variants of it were first used in central and southern France, from where the word spread to northern Spain. Most regions, however, retained their own nomenclature, which might also vary with the ritual's content. Italians spoke of *mattinata* or *scampanata*, Castilians of *cencerrada*. In Bavaria it was *haberfeldtreiben*. In other German-speaking regions the people made *katzenmusik*, which became *ketelmuziek* in Dutch. In Flanders it was *scharminkelen*. The English, finally, spoke of skimmington, rough music, or riding the stang. Without systematic research, a volume devoted to the subject lists sixty-two different names from southern, western, and central Europe. Historians have adopted the word, charivari, as the international generic term.

The ritual's content varied, but it always implied a form of ridicule. Many Dutchmen still remember the procession with the dung-cart, customary in the village of Staphorst until recently. The victims usually got off without physical injury, although they could be given a relatively harsh treatment. But extreme types of popular justice, such as lynching, are not included into the category of charivari. The donkey ride and the serenade with unmelodious music are the two major forms of the ritual. In the first case, the performers put the victim backwards on a donkey, which was led through the streets. In England it might be a horse. The company wore masks or fool's caps, but in Italy they were not so dressed. In the second variant, the performers made noise with pots, pans, and lids under someone's window or as a married couple left the church. The donkey ride could also be accompanied by this kind of noise. That is why various authors consider the production of loud noises as the essence of charivari. A few anthropologists refer to every form of collective noise making, as observed, for example, in New Guinea during an eclipse of the moon, as a charivari. The context and meaning of these rituals, however, are entirely different from those of preindustrial Europe. A victim, for example, is lacking. The ritual of ridicule might deal such a serious blow to someone's reputation that the events led to homicide.

Charivari's performers were usually youths, members of the society of bachelors. That was the case in the Poitiers region. In England, however, and in a number of French cities from the sixteenth century, all age groups were involved. At a Bavarian charivari at the end of the nineteenth century, thirty-two out of ninety-seven participants were in their thirties; the mean age was twenty-nine. But everywhere only men were involved. In theory, it was the community which meted out a punishment, with the performers implicitly claiming to represent collective opinion. Recent observations from Staphorst suggest a course of events which might very well have been familiar throughout preindustrial Europe. The young men of Staphorst took care of the ritual punishment, but they had been urged on by repeated remarks, only slightly disguised, from the older people. Such a course of events does not necessarily mean that everybody agreed with the instigators and the performers. Consensus as well as conflict could be expressed in charivari. There might not be any discussion about the very existence of the ritual, but its applicability in individual cases was a source of disagreement at times.

The events leading to a charivari determined who was the victim. The norms upheld by the community were almost always related to marriage. We already saw that remarriage could trigger the ritual. When the couple left church, the bachelors treated them to rough music, or they did so in the morning before the service. The youths were especially eager when an old widower took a young woman for his bride, or, which happened less frequently, when a young man married an older woman. Large age differences at a first wedding or a wedding of a girl with a boy from another village often led to charivari too. Sometimes the bridegroom could make his assailants stop by offering drinks or money, or he could buy them off in advance. Dutch placards from the seventeenth century speak of drinking money, forcibly received by "licentious persons" at weddings. In such cases, the participants cannot have acted from a serious indignation which they felt had to be expressed at all cost. A couple's refusal to pay, however, could lead to a quarrel. In 1660, in the French village of Saint-Marcel, the bachelors seized the furniture of an unwilling couple and sold it to acquire the money they claimed they were entitled to. It was different in the Italian town of Modena at the beginning of the sixteenth century. Neighbors and relatives approached the bridegroom in advance and offered for a sum of money to "defend" the couple against uninvited gusts on their wedding day. If the bridegroom was unwilling to pay, they threatened to produce a disturbance themselves. If he did, they used the money to drink to the couple's health; they treated them to a melodious serenade and chased away the youths who might still come to make rough music.

When the couple had been married, the neighbors kept an eye on conjugal life. If they found something wrong, they might take action. In a number of towns and regions those guilty of extramarital sex were the target, especially when they already were unpopular. Alternatively, the cheated husband was mocked. That could happen in England, where men suspected of homosexual practices were also potential victims. The most characteristic victim, however, was the man who allowed his wife to dominate him in the affairs of the household, especially to beat him. The English word, skimmington, comes from the skimming ladle which women used to make cheese if not for hitting their husbands on the head. The dominated husband was put on a donkey, since the donkey ride was the most appropriate form of the ritual in such a case. When the performers did not manage to get hold of their henpecked victim, one of them rode the animal in his place loudly exclaiming, "It is not for my deed but for my neighbor's." The ritual could also be enacted as a part of carnival. In Lyon in 1566 it was made into a large-scale enterprise. During a festival, seven moving platforms appeared, carrying actors who represented husbands identified by street and occupation. They had their beards pulled, were beaten with pans and spoons, and kicked between the legs. In this case, the ridicule consisted of an imitation of the offensive behavior. Such a mock play was performed as a charivari more often not only in France, but in England as well.

However, charivari did not unambiguously serve to bolster patriarchal authority. The attitude of the community's male members to that authority was somewhat ambivalent. This became clear, for example, in May, the month of women. No man was allowed to beat his wife then, and whoever did could become the victim of charivari in his turn. In such a case the woman was protected. That held true even more when the victim was a man who, although beating his wife according to patriarchal custom, did so excessively. Charivaris for that reason have been reported from, among others, seventeenth-century Geneva. Thus, the neighbors' view of an orderly household implied that the man was the boss but refrained from abusing his authority.

The changes in the meaning of charivari deserve to be investigated more thoroughly. In the early medieval legend of Merlin we already encounter a charivari-like episode. Since he had started to live as a wild man in the woods, Merlin had consented that his wife, Gwendoloena, take another husband. On the wedding night, however, he came to the bride's home with a herd of deer who produced a loud noise. The previous chapter mentioned that the word, charivari, appeared for the first time in the fourteenth-century *Roman de Fauvel*. Seeing that the performers were dressed up and masked and singing foolish songs, Fauvel credited Herlekine's followers with the rough music which disturbed him. Thus, the performers of charivari were associated with the familia Herlechini. Because of this, Ginzburg thinks that, originally, they represented the wild horde. Supposedly, they wanted to frighten the couple who had spoiled the marriage market by invoking the spirits of their common ancestors. This interpretation should certainly be qualified. In the fourteenth century, the familia Herlechini no longer appeared exclusively in the shape of the wild horde. They could also act as a comic troop. And indeed, the rough music to which Fauvel was subjected, was largely meant as a joke. In seventeenth-century England, Ingram argues, the participants equally viewed the ritual as a pleasant game. Thus, charivari may have had a not entirely serious, an "unofficial" character from its inception.

The previous chapter also listed a number of reasons why people saw a second marriage as less true than a first one. That attitude can be considered a sufficient explanation for the reaction from the neighbors. Nevertheless, several authors have tried to find one particular reason why neighbors mocked the couple. The question of the marriage market must have played a role, since large age differences at a first marriage were an occasion for charivari too. But this is not a sufficient explanation for two reasons. First, especially in Italy, charivaris were often organized when a widower took a widow for his bride. Such a couple hardly could be charged with spoiling the market. Second, the ritual originally belonged to the world of the elites as well. That is confirmed by the participation of Charles VI of France in a charivari aimed at a lady of the court who remarried in 1389. In such cases, perhaps, the performers voiced the anger or jealousy of the deceased first partner. Also, in the cities of the early modern period, one incident was no blow to the marriage market. Charivari at a second marriage probably became a tradition just in the end, which was maintained because of its venerability and out of a need for amusement. At the same time, the populace got the idea to apply the ritual in other dubious situations, such as that of the wife's dominance. Eventually, the range of infractions which might provoke its enactment became broader, until it included such things as adultery and sodomy.

Popular Tales

Before we scrutinize the social hierarchy to reveal the people's views of it, the popular narrative tradition should be described. It consisted of folktales and printed booklets, songs and plays. There were escapist and realistic stories next to technical treatises offering useful information. Finally, we have a few autobiographies of artisans.

Popular culture had oral roots, since writing forms the nucleus of a greater tradition. Chivalric romances were recited from memory long before someone got the idea to write them down. That also applies to the ballads and songs of the troubadours. In the early modern period, when the nobility no longer lived in castles and participated in the greater tradition, the populace still had its folktales and myths which were handed down orally. Songs belonged to an oral culture in a double sense, since not only the text remained unwritten but the music as well. That allowed every singer to make variations to the melody. The oral tradition of preindustrial Europe remains unknown to us. We know only about texts which have been written down later, such as the ancient British ballads collected by Francis Child in the nineteenth century. Folktales were recorded at an earlier date, around 1550 for example by Straparola in Italy and by Timoneda in Spain. At the end of the seventeenth century the Frenchman Charles Perrault, a learned writer well versed in classical literature, published his "Tales of Mother Goose." However, this relatively early recording is no guarantee of a true rendering of popular tradition. We know that Perrault wrote for an aristocratic audience who had become somewhat estranged from popular culture, cherishing an idealized view of romantic country life. He embellished the stories he heard, adding some elements and dropping others. A more accurate picture of the tales, as they were told in France in the seventeenth and eighteenth centuries, can be gained from the work of recording undertaken by folklorists a little over a hundred years ago.

Two examples illustrate the problems with the source material, while simultaneously testifying to the existence of interaction, also in this field, between the greater and the lesser tradition. The first has the familia Herlechini as a point of departure. We have seen them appear on stage as a company of comedians in late-medieval popular theater. Herlekine became a joker par excellence equally so for writers from among the elite. Hence, it was not a big step for the author writing for an Italian company in Paris to introduce the comical figure, Harlequin, in a play first performed in 1593 (In the Parisian dialect, the "e" changed into an "a" before an "r"). Throughout the seventeenth century this Harlequin remained a favorite character in the *comédie italienne* of the French capital. At the same time the *commedia dell'arte*, a popular form of theater with professional players but based on improvisation, flowered in Italy. A number of standard types figured there, and Arlequino became one of them only after 1700. Thus, he boasted a return to the lesser tradition in a renewed shape and in a different country. Finally, he became a puppet and withdrew into a children's world.

The second example begins with Charles Perrault. As explained, he adapted and beautified the oral tradition to cater to the tastes of his readers. He changed "Little Red Riding Hood" from a tale meant to frighten into one with a happy ending. Her red hood itself, viewed as a symbol for menstrual blood by twentieth-century psychoanalysts which made them unjustly attribute a preoccupation with sexual taboos to peasants from the Ancien Régime, had been invented by Perrault. In its new, published version the tale became known among French Huguenots, some of whom had fled to Germany around 1700. It was passed on, still with the red hood, by generations of Huguenots, until in the nineteenth century, it reached Jeanette Hassenpflug. Hassenpflug, whose father was neither a Huguenot nor an immigrant, became one of the main sources for the brothers Grimm. They included "Little Red Riding Hood" into their collection as a genuine German folktale, after which it eventually gained world-wide popularity.

As soon as something has been printed, historians can at least read it. Although they are certain now about content, the problem of interpretation becomes more considerable. In a similar vein as those authors who argue that the people's ancient traditions were only present in pure form in the countryside, some historians consider the emergence of a printed popular literature as an attack on those very traditions. Supposedly, this literature formed part of a pseudopopular culture, which in reality represented elite values. It mainly consists of chapbooks and broadsheets, preserved in great quantities since the seventeenth century. Other historians see them as specimens of a flowering popular culture. Because of their low price, they argue, almost everyone could afford them, while in the seventeenth and eighteenth centuries, many more people were able to read. Although this literature seldom reveals any degree of rebelliousness, it does not praise the existing social order either. In any case, its success points at a need for books among the popular classes. It is improbable that the publishers selected themes which were incongruent with the public's demand. For that reason, the literature of chapbooks and pamphlets is counted as popular culture for the time being.

Research into the popular literature of the seventeenth and eighteenth centuries has been done mainly in France and England. Because French chapbooks usually had a plain blue cover, they are collectively known as the *bibliothèque bleue*. The first publishers resided at Troyes, and Mandrou analyzes the works from that company which have been preserved. Unrestrained by censorship, the publishers were completely free in their choice of subject. They indeed based it on public demand, about which they were informed by merchants and hawkers. Then they ordered their own journeymen, typesetters, or other servants to write the books, which appeared anonymously. Mandrou divides the works into five main categories: mythology and the marvelous world of fairies; works about nature and the cosmos; religious and pious tracts; novels, farces, and worldly songs; works about "society," that is, occupations, games, education, and history. With the help of Mandrou's categories, Spufford undertakes a quantitative comparison of France and England. She uses the collection gathered by Samuel Pepys, famous for his diaries in the 1680s. In both countries the third and fourth categories were represented in the largest proportions. The most conspicuous differences are to be found with the first two. Works about nature made up 17 percent of the total in France and 27 percent in England. This was largely caused by a greater number of almanacs in the latter country. The marvelous world, finally, good for 11 percent in the bibliothèque bleue, remains under 1 percent in Pepys's collection. Apparently, the

English had no taste for fairy-stories, although they did believe in them.

Was the content of this literature really received by craftsmen and peasants? There is only indirect evidence, some of it contained in the works themselves. English authors expressly said they were writing for a lower class audience, presenting their stories as based on the experience of persons from that class. Some books were aimed at specific groups: those from town or the country, men or women, occupational groups such as weavers, innkeepers, or domestic servants. Although some upper class French possessed copies from the bibliothèque bleue, in public they depreciated them as a superficial recreation for the despised common people. French peasants must have enjoyed these stories in particular during the veillée, when a literate villager read them aloud to the others present.

As a special genre of popular literature, almanacs have also been studied in France and England. Technically speaking, an almanac was just a calendar of the astronomical events of the coming year, and as such it dates back to antiquity. Printed almanacs were published in various European countries already before 1500. In the early modern period they belonged to popular literature. Next to the movements of the stars, the almanac contained practical information such as the dates of fairs, the condition and location of highways, and medical and agricultural tips. Knowledge of the phases of the moon too was more relevant then, than now, since there was no public lighting outside the larger towns. The main difference between English and French almanacs lay in the former's orientation on the religious and political controversies of the mid-seventeenth century. They were full of prophesies about the triumph of one's own party and the defeat of one's adversaries. French prophesies, usually announced as a pleasant diversion, were more innocent. Another difference was implied by the existence of special almanacs for women in England. The first was composed in 1658 by Sarah Jinner. She came up with famous representatives of her sex, such as the legendary pope Joan, to prove the intellectual capabilities of women.

The Social Order

How then did the popular classes view their own position, that of higher social strata, and the social order in general? Ideally, the answer should come from representatives of the people themselves. This is not entirely impossible, since a few autobiographies of artisans in the seventeenth and eighteenth centuries have been preserved. Two

French-speaking authors, the worsted weaver Pierre-Ignace Chavatte from Lille and the Parisian glazier Jacques-Louis Ménétra, contrasted markedly. Chavatte was a pious Catholic, but Louis XIV, who had just conquered Lille, did not have his sympathy. Ménétra was anticlerical and less pious in his many sexual adventures, but before the Revolution which he witnessed at an old age, he did not betray any political involvement. The authors resembled each other in so far as both were strongly oriented toward their occupational group. Of course we do not know how typical the two autobiographers were.

A systematic knowledge of the perception of the social order can be gathered by a detour. The way the social world was valued can be deduced from the typecasting of various characters in popular literature. Burke looks for the heroes and villains among them and his analysis can be supplemented with Capp's study of English almanacs.

Burke distinguishes four hero types: the saint or martyr, the ruler, the warrior, and the outlaw. Hero types are those who are the principal character of a work and who receive an unconditionally positive appraisal. These four types can be found almost throughout Europe. The saint was often depicted in a heroic posture, such as John the Baptist roaming through the desert and feeding himself with locusts and wild honey. Protestants glorified the martyrs they remembered from religious wars. The ruler preferably was a great conqueror such as Alexander or Charlemagne. Or it was Salomo as the prototype of the wise judge. The warrior type as a favorite theme descended from the nobility to the common people. Medieval *chansons de geste*, like "The Four Sons of Aymon," were retold in the bibliothèque bleue and often reprinted. At a time when the aristocracy was no longer a race of warriors, the knight still was a popular hero. Hearing about the outlaw, we immediately think of Robin Hood. The populace cherished his myth well into the nineteenth century, although bandits who stole from the rich to give to the poor have never existed in reality.

In between the heroes and villains were the personages receiving a neutral typecasting. Usually they were not principal characters. The most common neutral persons were in fact the peasants and craftsmen themselves, who formed the majority of readers and listeners. They usually appeared as accessories, good willing but never central to the plot. It may also be clear that women are absent from Burke's hero types. Yet there were heroines, such as the female sailors and soldiers in men's clothes, whose life story was recorded, or the English "female highwaymen." Representatives of the middle class too are seldom to be found among the heroes; only occasionally, the adventurous entrepreneur appears on the scene. Merchants were often depicted as usurers; tax collectors or farmers were always extortioners. This brings us to the villains. They also included the lustful, fat monk or the priest who demanded money for every service. Finally, various kinds of outsiders, Turks and Jews for example, were consistently cast as villains. In many stories the traitor Judas was the prototype of the wicked Jew.

The next step is to extrapolate from the characters in the stories to the social groups in the real world to whom these characters ought to be reckoned. In this way, it might be concluded that the representatives of religion were viewed ambivalently. They appear among the heroes as well as the villains. Of course the readers are likely to have imagined the hypocrites and frauds as belonging to the opposite denomination. The English almanacs suggest this with their attacks on religious adversaries. Kings were seen as benevolent father figures by the populace of early modern Europe. The king could do no harm; trouble was blamed on his evil advisors. That explains why the ruler could figure as a hero. Two exceptions, the Pharaoh and Herod, were too far removed from daily reality. The warrior type refers to the aristocracy. Aristocratic landlords, like the king, lived far away. Hence, the populace could imagine them as good men; at best they had a bad steward. On this point, English almanacs were a little more realistic. Next to the ever benevolent kings, they came up with a number of landlords who oppressed their tenants, but this was often accompanied by the prophecy of a decrease in their cruelty. Additionally, the almanacs complained about greedy grain traders, which is in line with the picture derived from chapbooks. Artisans and peasants surely had daily contacts with merchants and tax gatherers. They particularly hated the latter. It is less clear what we should think of the outlaw as a hero. Common criminals were certainly not viewed positively by the majority. In some cases though, successful band leaders were discontented noblemen. Must we conclude that the outlaw type referred to the nobility? In any case, the Robin Hood myth reflected a modest amount of displeasure with existing social relationships.

The self-image of peasants and craftsmen can be called neutral, analogous to the place they occupy in the stories. There is no hint of a "class consciousness" in the form of self-elevation. At best there are individual Cinderellas, but the majority's collective fate is one of resignation. The almanacs espouse a comparable view. Capp defines their social ideal as conservative paternalism: a hierarchy is a good thing but it entails a moral obligation for those at the top. The poor have to accept their fate, but the rich and mighty ought to give charity, offer protection, and provide a good example. In their view of outsiders, finally, English almanacs comply with popular literature generally. Foreigners and ethnic minorities, the Dutch, for example, but especially the Irish, bear the brunt of resentment. The Irish are called "stinking savages;" at a lunar eclipse, the moon is said to be ashamed to watch them. The ethnocentric personality, identified by twentieth-century investigators, may have been quite common in preindustrial Europe.

And yet the attitude that emerged from chapbooks and almanacs cannot be equated simply with the people's view. We should subject the oral tradition to a comparable analysis. This hardly has been done so far, but Darnton's study of the tales told by French peasants in the seventeenth and eighteenth centuries forms a beginning. Compared to printed narrative, these stories have a more realistic flavor. They continually impart the idea that one should be clever in this rotten world. They often exhibit a preoccupation with food, and they always reflect the hardships of peasant life. In addition, they do not always embrace the paternalistic view of the royal figure. Thus, in the story of the peasant son Benoit, the hero manages to marry a princess, after he has beaten both the king and the queen on their bare buttocks through a ruse. Perhaps, bibliothèque bleue, almanacs, and oral tradition each reflect a different angle of the people's view of the social order. Alternatively, they may represent different subgroups among the populace.

Popular Culture and Protest

The only direct road left to reconstruct the people's view of the social order leads us to the study of actual social protest. We may inquire into the presence of typical elements from popular culture at the level of symbols, for example. This is a promising course. The attributes of charivari or the rituals of festivals were a permanent feature of preindustrial protest. During carnival urban magistrates might be mocked, partly out of discontent with their policies. Or a magistrate was subjected to charivari by proxy, officially because he beat his wife in May, but also because he was corrupt. Cross dressing played a major role in social protest. In France as well as England there were riots in which men in women's clothes participated or whose leader had a female nickname. The movement of resistance against deforestation and enclosures in Wiltshire in the second quarter of the seventeenth century combined the elements of charivari, cross dressing, and popular sports. Its protagonists wore women's clothes and called themselves Lady Skimmington. The local leader in Newland carried a stoolball club, normally used in the village's favorite pastime.

In these cases, either the ritual was secondary to the revolt, or, when the ritual came first, public order had not been seriously disturbed. This is different when a festive gathering forms the occasion for a riot. Many examples date from the sixteenth century, the period of religious antagonisms, and the seventeenth century, the period of the great tax revolts. Armed parades of citizens were a customary feature of urban festivities in those days. This caused the tensions, which were already present, to explode readily. In the countryside feast and protest were also linked, and this remained so for still a longer time. In most cases the feast just got out of hand without anyone's having expected an uproar. When the riot had been planned in advance, we should speak of the feast as a pretense.

One of the earliest examples dates from before the Reformation. During the Berne carnival of 1513 peasants from the immediate area pillaged the city. This had indeed been planned in advance. In Cambrai in the 1560s the feast of fools was the occasion for political protest. People wearing jesters' costumes demanded the retreat of Granvelle, Philip II's main advisor in the Netherlands. Planning and spontaneity both were a feature of the events in the small town of Romans, to the South of Lyon, in 1579–1580. The tensions between artisans and rich citizens, between peasants from the surroundings and big landowners, between Huguenots and Catholics reached their zenith during the carnival periods of both years. They culminated in a petty civil war at Mardi-gras of 1580. In the seventeenth century, tax revolts often began with a feast or a game, as in Dijon in 1630. Around the same time, English local communities used a football match as a cover for a protest against enclosures. In the eighteenth century those games were the occasion for food riots. By then, the link between festive and rebellious behavior manifested itself in Germany too. The miners of Freiberg in Saxony were accustomed to celebrate the Magdalen feast on July 22. Following conflicts with their superiors in 1737–1738, the twenty-second day of July henceforth counted as a day of combat. Interestingly, the miners thought that their feast dated back to 1681, when the electress Magdalena Sybilla had celebrated her name day in Freiberg, while in fact it can be traced back at least to 1500. In England the connection between popular culture and protest remained strong well into the period of industrialization, although in the country's periphery. The last traditional food disturbances took place in 1867 in Cornwall and Devon as a part of the festivities of Guy Fawkes day (5 November).

Bercé explains both the ritual elements in riots and the latter's origins in festive gatherings in terms of "natural derivation." We need not suppose that the people wished to defend their culture or to underline ancient rights. They simply fell back on familiar means of expression, sanctioned by custom. Burke, meanwhile, argues that popular culture and protest eventually came together. Simultaneously with the increasing repression of several popular customs, artisans and peasants are supposed to have acquired a heightened political consciousness, at least in England, the Netherlands, and Scandinavia. This resulted in a politicization of popular culture. In France, in the nineteenth century, this had gone so far that charivaris primarily had a political significance. Villagers made rough music under the window of a representative of the established order, for example. In nineteenth-century Bavaria, too, charivaris sometimes had a political bearing. Still, the problems of popular culture and hierarchy have not been solved yet. They return in the next section.

The World Upside Down

If we allow ourselves to imagine what the world upside down would be like today, it might be this: each year on a fixed date a student is allowed to act as the head of his or her university; he or she presides over the meeting of the board of governors and orders the administrators to sing their memos in a reversed order. The teachers, dressed in clothing of the opposite sex, parade the campus and debate the value of soap operas. Hilariously and seriously at the same time, everybody ends their tasks. Comparable things happened in Europe until the sixteenth century. The world upside down was such a crucial motif within the lesser tradition and it was linked up, directly or indirectly, with so many expressions of popular culture, that it deserves a separate section.

The Comic Renewal

To begin with, the work of the Russian literary scholar, Mikhail Bakhtin, provides a key. It must be accompanied by a warning though. Bakhtin primarily bases his study on the work of the French sixteenth-century writer Rabelais, who certainly cannot be included as a member of the populace. He was of bourgeois origin, had studied at a university, and was familiar with the Greco-Roman heritage. He adorned his "popular" stories with classical elements. But, no doubt Rabelais was equally familiar with the lesser tradition. As explained, in the sixteenth century it had not become separated yet from the greater. Rabelais's work cannot be understood without a knowledge of the lesser tradition and, in its turn, it presents us with new insights into that tradition.

According to Bakhtin—and his compatriot Vladimir Propp agrees with him on this—laughter was central to ancient popular culture. Humor, then, was the primary element in the Rabelaisian world. But it was not simply that. The popular humor of preindustrial Europe, although of a carnivalesque nature, also had a deeper meaning. It was far from being just negative; simultaneously it brought regeneration and renewal. In the lesser tradition, satire was interwoven with serious business and with life generally. We already saw that Herlekine's suite could play a serious as well as a comical role.

The regenerating power of popular humor was connected with the human body and its functions, especially the lower parts, An association with the body and the material world served to debase highly esteemed things. By celebrating the feast of Saint Sausage, also a phallic symbol, the participants mocked the cult of saints, but simultaneously they confirmed and rejuvenated it. A week later they celebrated the feast of Saint John, full of inner conviction. Despite the phallic symbol, bodily processes occupied a more prominent place than sex. Popular humor loved the realm of urine and excrement, and it had a preference for strange grimaces, defiant bodily postures, and chaotic scenes. In his treatise on laughter of 1579 Laurent Joubert wrote that everyone thought it funny when somebody accidentally bared their "shameful parts" or buttocks. If a bystander suddenly touched the bare buttocks with a hot iron, people fell into fits of laughter, provided the injury was negligible. Certain animals, notably the donkey, were associated with the body's lower parts. It is no coincidence that the words for donkey and the behind, have a common origin in several languages.

To swallow and to excrete were equally interesting. Next to the regenerative humor and the private parts, was a love of food and drink, the third element. We have seen that kitchen utensils and poultry were carried in comic processions. Copious meals, a favorite motif in popular tales, were a part of festive reality too. Sometimes they were associated with the function of debasement. The heroes of several stories played with their enemies by eating a copious meal while the latter were tortured. Eighteenth-century bandits occasionally did that to their victims. In a number of cases, eating was explicitly linked to a topsyturvy world. In the medieval story about Aucassin and Nicolette, the queen went to battle while the king stayed home and gave birth to children. The war was fought with cheese, baked apples, and mushrooms.

The last element, the neutralization of anxiety, is more abstract. One of the functions of the comical forms and the debasing effect was to conquer or at least control several sorts of fear. The ultimate fear was to be sent to hell. It is not surprising, therefore, that popular culture could conceive of hell in a humorous fashion. The underworld was frequently represented in sixteenth-century carnival plays. Rabelais pictures hell as a place where earthly accounts are settled. Whoever had not yet suffered from syphilis on earth, got it there. Those powerful during their lifetime were servants in hell, and poor wretches, notably poor philosophers, ruled there. Diogenes beat Alexander the Great for not having correctly patched his breeches. This is truly a world upside down.

In this way, even the devil could become a comedian. The demonic grimace of Herlekine's people in late-medieval popular theater also served to neutralize the fear of the prince of evil. In mystery plays too devils are malicious and ridiculous at the same time. Although clumsily, they continually try to thwart the history of salvation. Dispelled from heaven, Lucifer says: "From fear of fire I fart loudly." When he returns to earth one day in search of damned souls, Saint Peter quickly descends into hell. The heavenly porter plays dice with a professional gambler, whom Lucifer had appointed as a temporary supervisor, and he wins back a number of souls. After the Annunciation the parliament of demons convenes, confusedly discussing the meaning of this event. Everything undertaken by the devils is a hopeless failure. That is in line with Christian doctrine which teaches that Satan will ultimately bow down. There were successful demons too. In some places, in the fifteenth and sixteenth centuries, it was customary for the actors, who were to play the demonic roles, to travel through the town and its surroundings in their devil's costume a few days before the performance. They were permitted to act in conformity with their evil role. Thus, they extorted money from the peasants, which they were not expected to do. In Chaumont the devils, instead of the priests who did so elsewhere, welcomed the Palm Sunday procession as it approached the town from outside. Before opening the gate, they threw fireworks from the walls on the faithful. This is a topsyturvy world too.

Folly. The events at Chaumont suggest that the humor and rituals of reversal from the lesser tradition were not confined to the world of laymen. To the contrary, the earliest texts referring to comparable phenomena in preindustrial Europe are ecclesiastical. Medieval clerics were allowed to amuse themselves at Christmas and Easter by singing songs and telling jokes. They loved to read Cyprian's Supper, a parody on Holy Scripture. This text originated in the early Middle Ages; in 877 Pope John VIII wrote a rhymed version. At Easter priests also might tell comical stories from the pulpit to the faithful. Sometimes they danced in church with laymen or even with nuns.

All these rituals did not involve role reversal. That happened for the first time in episcopal cities in the twelfth century. Its chapters admitted scores of youths who received some schooling and were ordained as subdeacons. These subdeacons had their own annual feast, where folly was again on top. They danced during mass, ate sausages on the altar, and sang obscene songs. After mass, some of them naked, they crossed the streets. In Evreux a shroud was laid on the church's choir on the day of the subdeacons, with a bottle of wine in the middle and four at the sides. In the fifteenth century the participants in this ritual claimed that it had been instituted by a canon who had died two hundred years previously, Guillaume de la Bouteille. Next to folly, there was another element to the feast of the subdeacons. The young clerics played the part of the authority over the respectable canons. They took their choir seats and recited a false service; some canons were beaten into obedience. The subdeacons justified this with an appeal to the Bible. They knew that Jesus had said "let the children come unto me" and "the first will be the last." The importance of role reversal for the participants in this ritual emerges plainly from efforts to control it, which have been made from the beginning. Around 1200 the subdeacons of Sens promised their bishop to stop the celebration, if only they were allowed on that day to confront their superiors with another biblical verse five times: "Deposuit potentes de sede et exaltavit humiles" ("He has cast the mighty from their throne and elevated the humble").

The feast of the subdeacons evolved into the feast of fools. Folly and the reversal of hierarchic relationships spread from the chapter and the cathedral to the rest of the town, until they were well established everywhere. First, it came to rituals which were still performed in church, but with a considerable lay participation. The ass mass, for example, was meant to glorify the poor. Officially, this service was held in commemoration of the faithful animal who had taken Jesus and his parents to Egypt to escape from Herod's persecution. A canon or a prelate led the donkey into the church with great ceremony. On its back the donkey carried a young woman with a baby in her arms. The liturgy was suited to the occasion, praising the animal's noble character. At the end the priest said "ia" three times and the audience replied similarly. This was a form of reversal, as the donkey, normally a symbol of lowness and associated with ridicule, became an object of veneration.

During the later Middle Ages the laity in towns and villages celebrated their own festive days, dominated by the combination of folly and topsyturviness. Details varied, but the common element was always that one of the humble was acclaimed as the ruler of the town or village for a day. In several places this feast continued to be celebrated into the seventeenth century. The humble person who became ruler could take various shapes, depending on the locality. Two shapes, however, prevailed: the child or youth on the one side and the fool or crazy person on the other. In Spain, for example, a boy was elected as *obispillo* (child bishop) and obeyed by clergy and laity. Elsewhere the inhabitants chose a child abbot. It is not such a big step from a ruling child to a king of fools, because innocence and foolishness are each other's complements. Someone acting as a fool or jester, rather than a really mad person, usually may have been elected prince or abbot. The term, feast of fools, can be adopted as the generic name for those celebrations; the day when it took place varied with the locality. The child bishop often exercised his rule on the day of the Innocents (28 December), but that was not the case everywhere. Folly belonged to the chain of winter festivals, starting with Christmas and ending with the coming of Lent. The two main characters stood for the two major aspects: the fool for satirical enjoyment and the child for inferiority turned into authority for a day.

Carnival.   Evidently, folly also belonged to carnival. Before the fifteenth century, however, that festival was one of the less prominent in the winter cycle. It only became more pronounced as the feast of fools started to decline under the influence of opposition from the church hierarchy. Celebrations such as the day of the subdeacons had always met with opposition, but more so from the end of the fifteenth century. Secular authorities began to have second thoughts too. In the sixteenth century they kept a low profile rather than playing the inferiors, so that the reversal was not complete. The last feasts of fools with rituals of reversal, already devoid of obscene elements, took place at the beginning of the seventeenth century.

As an intermediate stage between feasts of reversal and carnival, folly was institutionalized in societies. In the sixteenth century, the place of the fool or the child ruling for one day had often been taken by companies whose hilarious activities were spread over the year. They were called joyous or foolish companies or they had fantastic names such as "the abbey of misrule." Sometimes they were confined to a specific occupation. The social life of journeymen typesetters, for example, was channelled into the brotherhood of the misprint. More often the joyous companies overlapped with the already existing youth societies. Each of the three neighborhoods of Clermont had its "kingdom"; those of great foolishness, good time, and the moon. Youth societies were also prominent in carnival.

Carnival became the popular festival par excellence in the early modern period. Or rather, we should speak of carnivalesque feasts, since carnival proper disappeared in Protestant regions. Its characteristics returned in other popular festivities, such as local wakes and fairs in England. A carnivalesque atmosphere implied jest, making fun of everybody and everything, exuberance with a fine layer of seriousness. Carnivalesque festivals were a form of the world upside down but no longer in the direct sense of a reversal of the existing social hierarchy. Carnival's reversal belonged to the realm of symbols: folly, as an abstract principle, reigned temporarily, instead of the wisdom that did so for the rest of the year.

A focus on the body, as in popular humor, was still prevalent. Carnivalesque feasts revolved around eating, making love, and fighting. On regular days this behavior was subject to increasing concealment and regulation, especially among the elites. Thus, carnival was a sort of free time as opposed to the self control required during the rest of the year. The three elements belonged together, which again serves as a warning against a too idyllic notion of preindustrial popular culture. Making love and eating might seem innocent, but carnival was also a time when latent conflicts surfaced or new ones were even created. The neighbors publicized scandals and mocked the conduct of some among them. People insulted passers-by, and they stole or destroyed property. The English might act more innocently. Young men speedily slid down the roof from the chimney, taking tiles with them. Animals had a difficult time all over Europe. The participants chased dogs, roosters, or another animal depending on its symbolic meaning. It is understandable that in spite of carnival's atmosphere not everyone was amused, so that fights were endemic. Carnival time in France, until the sixteenth century and in some regions into the seventeenth, meant freedom from judicial prosecution, which also offered an opportunity for personal satisfaction. In seventeenth-century Rome carnival excesses were punished. The delinquent had to stand under the gallows in front of the joyful crowd while the rope was pulled very gently three times.

Related to the carnivalesque was the Land of Cockaigne. Depictions of this earthly paradise in popular literature were most frequent in the sixteenth and seventeenth centuries, especially in Flanders, Italy, Germany, and France. In the Land of Cockaigne one does not have to work for a living. There is plenty of food and drink and a lot of gold. The people often make love and they feast day and night, but war is unknown there. Hence, the three elements of carnival have been reduced to two peaceful ones. Additionally, the fountain of rejuvenation stands, sprinkling its visitors with eternal youth. But the road to this fantastic land is a hard one, except for the poor and oppressed. That reminds us again of the world upside down. Some historians interpret Cockaigne as a materialistic utopia or a nonreligious earthly paradise. For that reason, it is far removed from the feast of fools, which had an ecclesiastical origin.

Cities in the Air

Thus, the world upside down lost its sharper sides in the early modern period. Its presence in carnival was merely symbolic; in the motif of Cockaigne it had been reduced to a utopia. The actual reversal of existing hierarchical relationships disappeared, but simultaneously it returned in prints. There we see, for example, the poor giving alms to the rich, the servant commanding her master, or the child teaching the doctors (again a biblical theme). Power relations between men and animals become topsyturvy too: the horse nails hoofs to the smith and the sheep shaves the herdsman. It is the same among the animals themselves: the mice catch the cat and the hen sits on the rooster. With some reversals among people, such as the blind man leading the seer, the hierarchical aspect is less pronounced. Finally, there are several forms of physical reversal: ships on the land, cities in the air, or a horse galloping backwards, steered by its rider at the tail. These motifs appear on broadsheets, separately as well as in combination. We find a comparable representation of the world upside down in elite culture. One of Andrea Alciati's emblems, published in 1531, pictures the exchange of Cupid's and Death's arrows, which had crossed accidentally when both slept in the same inn. A poem underneath tells how old men fall in love and youths are on the verge of dying. The latter beg for a re-reversal.

No doubt, the favorite theme on engravings was the reversal of roles between men and women. We see a man with a baby on his lap, while his wife smokes a pipe and relaxes. Women command men and besiege castles. The reversal of sex roles was a widespread theme in the visual arts and literature in general. From Greek mythology we know about the nation of the Amazons. In preindustrial Europe the dominant wife, whose husband ran the risk of such an unpleasant humiliation, was often portrayed on prints. Painters resorted to symbolic or mythological representations, such as Breugel's *Mad Maggie* or *Phyllis Riding Aristotle* by Hans Baldung Grien. The turning of sex roles was also the only exception, although a minor one, to the disappearance of rituals of reversal in the early modern period. It actually happened, but in a playful fashion. During carnivalesque festivals men were dressed in women's clothes and sometimes women wore men's clothes. Cross dressing, described previously, became a characteristic element of popular culture in the early modern period. On engravings though, pipe-smoking wives and baby-carrying husbands wore their own clothes, since it was impossible to visualize the reversal otherwise. Finally, the obligatory consideration of women in May might lead to a form of reversal. Temporarily freed from the threat of being beaten, some wives profited from it and experienced independence for a while.

The Eternal Hierarchy

The motif of the world upside down is more general and older than European culture. Several African nations know rituals in which man–woman relations are turned. The Romans had the saturnalia, feast days when masters served their slaves. Thus, the reversals of hierarchical relationships in Europe were not unique. What was their meaning?

Some authors argue that the world upside down was a source of inspiration for a possible rejection of the social order. Heers claims that the rituals of the ass mass and the day of the subdeacons reminded church leaders of an anti-hierarchical tradition which, although belonging to Christianity, had become submerged. In a secular context, Bakhtin presents a comparable argument. The world upside down was reminiscent of a primitive equality which had once reigned. The rituals remained threatening to those in power, but they had no choice but to condone them. There are indeed examples of a connection between the world upside down and revolutionary traditions. As early as the fourth century, it was the rebellious sect of Circumcellions whose members obliged masters, instead of their slaves, to draw carts and to move treadmills. During the conflict-ridden carnival of Romans a reversed pricelist of food items was published, on which hay and rotten herring were expensive and turkey with cinnamon and fat veal cost almost nothing. Popular leaders during the English Revolution prophesied that the poor would live in the homes of the rich, while their adversaries charged them with turning the world on its head.

But the opposite, drawing a conservative lesson from the world upside down, happened too. This could be done by stressing the eventual return to normal. We might also ask ourselves whether the broadsheets' apparent equalization of a reversal of hierarchic relations with cities in the air meant that both things were viewed as equally impossible in reality. A number of authors, therefore, embrace a type of theory contrary to the previous one. Thus, Russell sees a catharsis produced in the audience by the devil's comic role in plays and rituals. Laughter at the devil and his weird grimaces relieved one's conscience, which ultimately led to a reconfirmation of the faith. Also with respect to the secular order, rituals of reversal can be viewed as a form of encapsulation, a reconfirmation of the existing social relationships. Hierarchy became acceptable because the frustration it caused was reduced at times.

Although mutually incompatible, these theories about the world upside down are helpful to solve the problem, left over from the previous section, of popular culture and the social order. The relationships between the two were probably more complex than that acknowledged in a simple scheme of confirmation or denial of the existing order. The view of society which emerged from chapbooks, almanacs, and peasants' tales was not uniform. Neither may the world upside down have been uniform. A clear sign of ambivalence is the nonreversal which accompanied the world upside down.

A crucial element in the celebration of the feast of fools at Saint-Etienne during the later Middle Ages deserves our attention. The participants were divided into four groups, representing the town's four parishes. The company who belonged to the parish of the cathedral elected a pope of fools, while their fellows of Saint John had to accept an archbishop; those of Saint Magdalen a bishop; and those of Saint Paul a cardinal of fools. When they met, the latter trio had to throw themselves to the ground for the pope and receive his benediction. Thus, among the parishes, the existing hierarchy was upheld. That provides a key. Reversal or not, the constant element was the hierarchy as such. The people of preindustrial Europe could not imagine the world in any other way than always having a top and a bottom.

At a microlevel this argument is valid too. The difference between a tolerated and an unacceptable reversal is plain. It was a question of honor for men to respect the principle of May as the month of women. But it was intolerable if a woman beat her husband, certainly in other months. The accepted reversal was temporary and of a ritual nature. In addition, it was seldom complete. Like sixteenth-century burgomasters and village aldermen who kept a low profile during the feast of fools, husbands did not rule in May but they refused to be dominated. A permanent challenge of patriarchal authority was unthinkable, as attested by the charivaris aimed at henpecked husbands. Again the constant element is the hierarchy, present in the ritual reversal as well as in the breach of norms which was flooded with ridicule.

The rituals of the world upside down suggest that the populace thought it not quite self-evident that the seats of power were taken by those who sat there and not by others. But the principle of a hierarchy as such was found self-evident. Tensions between social classes were an unmistakable reality in preindustrial Europe. The revolts which actually broke out, with elements from popular culture, give evidence of that reality. However, most people could only imagine a reversal, no leveling. There was no egalitarian ideology behind preindustrial riots; at best there was a notion of paternalistic justice. The world upside down is: the fool says what to do; the layman blesses the bishop; the poor live in the homes of the rich. Twentieth-century ideas about an equal distribution of resources were unknown. The world upside down still is a hierarchy.

4 THE PERSECUTION OF WITCHES: A Drama Featuring the Community, the Authorities, and Women

The previous chapter advised us not to conceive of a too idyllic idea of life in villages and town neighborhoods. Besides providing shelter, they fostered conflicts. More than anything else these were reflected in accusations of sorcery. Those who distrusted their neighbors called them evil and accused them of witchcraft. Cases of witchcraft were not limited to villages and neighborhoods but came before judges, rulers, and bishops. They had an obvious bearing on family life, since the principal victims were women. The topic of witch persecutions is therefore situated at the intersection of the subjects discussed in the two previous chapters. Yet its ramifications are wider. The collective delusion that reigned for two centuries after a long and gradual evolution, resulted from changes in religious experience and a heightened fear of Christianity's adversaries.

Consequently, doctrines of witchcraft and the trials based on them constitute a subject central to the history of mentalities. The study of this doctrine provides new insights into the structure of thought and feeling among preindustrial people. The first section of this chapter deals with the prehistory of witchcraft and its subsequent formation and contents. The patterns of persecution, such as trial procedures and variations in intensity, are reviewed in the second section. The third section discusses the problem in depth, paying attention to the role of women and the confrontation of popular and elite culture. The end of the witch persecutions will be treated in chapter 9 because it is directly related to the cultural changes that took place on the eve of the Industrial Revolution, the subject of that chapter.

A Background to the Witch Persecutions

From the middle of the fifteenth to the end of the seventeenth century many Europeans were convinced there existed a secret sect of devil worshippers—a conviction we call the doctrine of witchcraft. It had gradually surfaced in the preceding period, from about the end of the thirteenth century. The chronology of the witch persecutions is a function of this intellectual development. Large-scale witch hunts only took place between around 1480 and 1680; they were often interrupted and at no time occurred everywhere. They can be termed a unique episode for two reasons. First, witchcraft doctrine was confined to the period mentioned: it has to be distinguished from magical beliefs in general, which were widespread both before and after and are prevalent in many other societies. Second, witchcraft doctrine and the persecutions based on it were restricted to parts of Europe and a few overseas regions settled by Europeans, notably New England. The uniqueness of this episode, however, does not preclude locating it within a specific historical evolution.

Jews, Heretics, and the Devil

The basic idea of witchcraft doctrine has appeared often in history, including antiquity and in the very recent past. It embodies the notion of a clandestine club, operating within the larger society and threatening its very existence, whose members engage in all kind of inhuman practices. Briefly, it is an anti-society within society. This fantasy usually is linked to already existing groups. In the first century B.C. the Greeks of Alexandria attempted to compromise the Jews by spreading the story that they worshipped a God in the shape of a donkey. In the Greco-Roman world the primary victims were the early Christians, a bit of historical irony in the light of later centuries. Many pagan Romans believed that the Christians constituted a sect which indulged in ritual murder, cannibalism, and all conceivable kinds of sexual excesses. When Christianity itself became the dominant religion, the orthodox began to level almost identical accusations against their own adversaries: religious dissidents and non-Christians, especially Jews. The basic notion of the anti-society remained alive after the period of witch persecutions. Freemasons, with their mysterious lodges, constituted an ideal target for these suspicions. At the height of the Cold War, on each side domestic adherents of the other side were often represented as a dangerous, clandestine sect.

In the last variant the anti-society has become secularized. America and Russia each became for the other the agent of Satan's empire. The Christian image of the devil and the changes it underwent make up an important part of the developments leading to the witch persecutions. The church fathers elaborated the theology of the devil: Satan was the generator of evil and of unpleasant events. The Gods of the Romans became demons, Satan's subordinates. Satan and his demons ruled that part of the world that had not yet been converted to Christianity. But the early Christians were convinced that conversion would eventually be universal, for when confronted with a real believer, Satan would have no chance and he and his demons would have to bite the dust time and again. This was the belief of a young and combative church full of self-confidence. After A.D. 1000, however, the situation changed. The obsession with Satan and his works gradually grew stronger. The representation of the devil and his subordinate demons in the visual arts became more and more monstrous. In literary depictions their power increased. Richalmus, abbot of Schöntal in the second half of the thirteenth century, blamed the devil for all evil inclinations of humans, no matter how petty. The devil was behind whatever went wrong in the monastery. If Richalmus had to cough during meditation or fell asleep over his holy books, it was the work of demons.

Long before the inception of witchcraft trials, the obsession with the devil led to bloody persecutions. Concern for the purity of the Christian faith increased in the course of the eleventh century and attitudes toward outsiders hardened. Inside Europe the Jews were the first victims. A relative tolerance toward them had originally prevailed. Especially from the sixth to the tenth century, their position was more favorable than ever since. Representatives of both religions freely debated each other, and Jews propagated their religion among the Germanic nations without disturbance. In the eleventh century, however, many Christians began to identify Jews with the adherents of Islam, both being infidels. During the first Crusade, which was officially aimed at the Moslems, fanatical priests incited the amassing soldiery to mass murder Jews. Urban craftsmen joined them enthusiastically. During the following centuries, the situation of the Jews became increasingly precarious. Sometimes formal trials were held at which the wildest accusations were leveled against the Jews, such as poisoning wells during the plague epidemic of 1346–1350. In a sense, these trials prefigured the witch persecutions of a later period.

Intellectual developments ran parallel. From the twelfth century on the stereotypical image of the anti-society was applied to the Jews with full force. The Dominicans and Franciscans in particular, monastic orders founded at the beginning of the thirteenth century, participated in the doctrinal attack on Judaism. The Jews, it was said, were not only responsible for the death of the Messiah, but strived to repeat the murder of Christ over and over again. To prevent it, ecclesiastical law required them to remain indoors on Good Friday. In order to reenact the killing of Christ, they were supposed to try to seize consecrated hosts, into which they drove nails or knives. They did not spare Jesus's flocks either. At secret conventions, according to their accusers, they committed ritual murder, in particular sacrificing Christian children. In addition, the blood of Christians reputedly served as a medicine to cure a number of diseases and ailments to which only Jews were susceptible. Paradoxically, they were also accused of needing hosts and other sacred objects for ritual healing. Since Jews were considered impure, even their men menstruated. Last of all, they were proficient in the art of magic.

Shortly after the deterioration of the Jews' position set in, religious dissidents within the Christian church began to be treated in the same way. Orthodox clergy had always combated heresy, but the intensity of their struggle increased from the twelfth century. Organized repression, supported by the secular authorities, arose with burning of heretics at the stake. Again, these persecutions can be seen as a prefiguration of the later witch burnings. An intellectual component was not lacking. Heretics were viewed as subhuman; they held indescribable orgies and ate babies. Although the perception and accusations against heretics resembled those against the Jews, they were baptized Christians whose ideas deviated from orthodox doctrine. Their recruitment was an even greater success for Satan. Thus, the belief in the demonic inspiration of heresy reinforced the fear of the master of evil. The next step was the belief in the existence of a sect having devil worship as its primary aim.

The Witchcraft Doctrine

Information about the content of witchcraft doctrine can be gathered from two types of sources: treatises expounding the doctrine and the records of witch trials. Obviously a treatise was always more elaborate than a single list of denunciations. Although one or more of the ingredients which can be said to belong to witchcraft doctrine might be absent in individual trials, it is still possible to tell what were the recurrent elements. Combining the analyses of Cohn and Schormann, we can distinguish five ingredients: sorcery, the demonic pact, sex with the devil, sect-building, and assemblies. Taken separately, these items were not new. The novelty lay in their combination. In the course of the fourteenth and fifteenth centuries the five elements were united to become a coherent doctrine. Some of its ingredients actually had been popular beliefs, but witchcraft doctrine as a system was a creation of clerical and secular elites. This creation is another example of interaction between the greater and the lesser tradition. The five ingredients are discussed in about the same order as they appeared on the scene as parts of the system.

Before the thirteenth century sorcery was hardly viewed as a threat to Christianity. As far as it received attention from ecclesiastical authors, they gave equal treatment to white magic, applied to beneficial ends, as to black magic. The practitioners of sorcery usually considered themselves good Christians. Magical formulas often consisted of sacred words, and manuals of sorcery explained that only the truly faithful could master the art. Around 1300 the representatives of the church began to display an increased interest in sorcery. Their attention shifted to black magic, stressing its un-Christian character. Secular authorities looked at the problem of sorcery from another angle, the legal concept of malefice, defined as the infliction of harm on persons or their property by occult means. The emphasis in this definition lies just as much on the harm done as in the occult. When a child died as a result of a spell cast over it, it was treated as murder, no less than if someone knocked out a neighbor's brains. Consequently both acts were equally punishable. Already by the early Middle Ages, malefice was officially listed as an offense, although there were as yet few trials. When ecclesiastical authors adopted the concept, it acquired novel connotations.

As a separate item, the demonic pact was also quite older than witchcraft doctrine. The legendary figure of Theophilus rose to a high position in the church hierarchy with the help of Satan, who took his soul in return. Theophilus's monstrous contract was not a source of collective anxiety, however. Whoever sold his soul to the devil ultimately himself suffered the most. Such a doomed individual made a suitably bad example to hold up to others inclined to prefer earthly vanities to eternal salvation. However, in the course of the fourteenth century, worry increased. The contract with the devil was associated with malefice. According to the clergy, magical powers could not but derive from the devil and demonic magic was by definition harmful. In this line of thought, the harm lay in the means used rather than in the ends pursued. White magicians had always considered themselves as the masters of demons. Yet some manuals claimed that slaughtering an animal might entice demons when they were slow to appear. This could be viewed as an offering, in which case the roles were reversed and the demon became the sorcerer's master.

The notion of sexual contact between humans and extraterrestrial beings was cherished by the ancient Greeks, among others. In Christian Europe it originally belonged to the domain of popular beliefs. But Thomas Aquinas explained that demons loved to make nocturnal trips and he thought them capable of begetting children. This was accomplished in two phases. The demon set out in the shape of a woman who lay with a man, and then in the shape of a male passed on the collected sperm to a human female. Sex with the devil was first listed among the accusations in a criminal case, the political trial against Lady Alice Kyteler in Kilkenny, Ireland, in 1325. At the height of the witch persecutions the sexual aspect was prominent in the accusations leveled in particular at women. Nevertheless, in theory Satan offered his body to his male followers too, since it was not hard for him to adopt all conceivable forms.

The three ingredients discussed up to now basically led to a belief in individual scions of evil. That conviction did not give rise to great anxiety. But the notion of sex with the devil fitted perfectly with the image already present of heretics and their orgies. This introduced the fourth ingredient. Individual allies of the devil were transformed into a society of worshippers, who strove to win new recruits. Witchcraft was associated with heresy, which had already been conveniently demonized. The notion of a sect of witches-heretics appeared at the beginning of the fifteenth century. The devil endowed the members of this sect with the power of harmful magic. Witchcraft doctrine was almost complete.

The fifth ingredient, assemblage, is notably important because it involved the participants' means of transport to their meeting places. The belief that witches could fly constituted the final building-block of witchcraft doctrine, which it entered in the course of the fifteenth century. If the participants had to go to the meetings on foot, these could not be represented either as frequent or as sizeable. Thus, to add the element of flying meant crossing a crucial threshold which made the sect of witches many times more dangerous. The fact that the intellectual elite crossed this threshold supports the contention that the rise of witchcraft doctrine implied a partial increment in irrationality. Popular lore was a source of supply for the fifth ingredient. It originated especially from the notions of the wandering army (See Chapter 3) and the *stryx* from Mediterranean tradition, who also flew by night. Those beliefs, which had been around for centuries, were suddenly used now for the construction of the image of the night-flying witch.

Thus, witchcraft doctrine was completed around 1450 with the notion of the witch's sabbath. They assembled from afar for cannibalistic banquets and orgies. The devil instructed his followers and new recruits were initiated. His flock knelt before him and kissed his behind while he took the shape of a goat. The ceremony was a ritual reversal of Christian worship, just as each event at the witch's sabbath meant a reversal of society's positive values. For anti-Christian and antisocial were largely considered synonymous well into the seventeenth century. This reversal, to be sure, was unrelated to the idea of the world upside down that was so central to the lesser tradition. It did not take place in an atmosphere of folly, and it had no existence outside the imagination of contemporaries.

Did Witches Really Exist?

For a deeper analysis of the fantasies of contemporaries, we have to define our terms more strictly. The description of witchcraft doctrine presented here can be considered as an ideal type, in Max Weber's usage. During the actual persecutions one or more elements might be missing, while others received greater emphasis. In Scotland, for example, the witch's sabbath played an insignificant role, but that should not prevent us from speaking of witchcraft. Contemporary theoreticians did not always pay equal attention to the five ingredients, but almost all considered the demonic pact as the essence of witchcraft. Indeed, at the height of the persecutions the alliance with Satan frequently appeared among the accusations.

Yet, trials for malefice alone continued to be held. In that case, we cannot speak of witchcraft. It is useful, therefore, to maintain a distinction between witchcraft and sorcery. We may meet sorcery as an ingredient of witchcraft but it stood by itself. As has been explained, belief in magic was more universal, chronologically and geographically, than the doctrine of witches. Sorcery might have useful as well as harmful results, obliging us to distinguish white from black magic. The difference between them lies in the sorcerer's intentions; the means used are the same. An individual person might do wrong or good, depending on his or her inclinations at a particular moment. The distinction between witchcraft and sorcery is an analytical one. Contemporary names varied widely, so that in each instance modern investigators have to establish with which of the two they are dealing. Trials for malefice alone, as far as they were conducted during the period of the witch persecutions, will also receive attention.

Further, it is necessary to distinguish witchcraft from sorcery because the reality of the latter practice cannot be doubted. For one thing there were learned sorcerers as the existence of manuals of magic implies. In the later Middle Ages a number of philosophers were attracted to the theory of natural magic, which originated in antiquity. It is probable that there were even more people practicing sorcery in villages and neighborhoods. They stuck nails into a doll, hoping that the person it represented would die, concocted love potions, or spat in the water to make it rain. Some earned money with magical healing or tracking down stolen property. Others had the reputation of being evil sorcerers, and a number must have considered themselves sorcerers. One or two persons may even have considered themselves witches. But this tells us nothing about the latter's existence. It only means that, once it had been established, witchcraft doctrine could have a strongly suggestible effect upon certain unstable persons.

The question of witchcraft's reality may sound strange, but it is pertinent. Nobody today, of course, is expected to believe in nocturnal trips on broomsticks and almost all clergy will deny the reality of the demonic pact. It is not the supernatural details which we have to consider. Bizarre notions may contain a kernel of truth. Those who do not subscribe to the Catholic faith, still acknowledge that the Pope exists. In the case of witchcraft, the question is: Was there really a network of secret, anti-Christian societies, whose members were persecuted as witches and were thought capable of a variety of physically impossible deeds?

Concrete evidence for this is lacking. The writings of the persecutors cannot be considered as such, any more than the Nazis' claims about a Jewish conspiracy proved that Jews actually harbored such secret plans. Eyewitness accounts of a witch's sabbath by nonparticipants have not been found either, which leaves us with the confessions of those prosecuted. There is sufficient reason to assume that all these confessions were made under torture and were not based on any reality. Almost all recent investigators are convinced of this, arguing that a secret witch's society never existed. The opposite has been claimed by only a few nonspecialists, among whom the British Egyptologist Margaret Murray, whose publications date from the 1920s, is the best known. What was termed devil worship by the authorities, she argues, was in fact an ancient fertility cult, surviving from pre-Christian times. Supposedly this cult became threatening to Christian authorities only at the end of the Middle Ages, whereupon they fiercely repressed it. That would explain why witch persecutions appeared as late as they did.

Murray's theory is implausible, however, and built on quicksand. It is highly unlikely that church leaders would have been prepared to tolerate a rival cult until the fifteenth century. Furthermore, Murray consciously manipulated her own sources. She claims that a number of witches' confessions depicted quite a normal and cozy sabbath meeting. Norman Cohn, who consulted these sources anew, found that they actually contain passages in which people flew through the air and changed into animals; passages which Murray had purposely left out of her quotations. Cohn's position is as inescapable as it is true: stories containing plainly impossible elements cannot be accepted as evidence for natural events on any point. A few theories related to Murray's are also discredited by Cohn.

With the help of a unique collection of documents from the Spanish Basque country, Gustav Henningsen has dealt an additional blow to the thesis of the witch sect's reality. At the beginning of the seventeenth century, persecution was rampant in the French part of the Basque country. The flow of accusations crossed the border to the Spanish side. In Spain such matters were handled by the Inquisition, which made for two peculiar circumstances with respect to prosecution. First, suspects showing repentance usually escaped with a warning. Consequently, they were rewarded for confessing, in harsh contrast to the proceedings elsewhere. Second, the tribunal recorded every story, even the smallest details, so that we have at our disposal bountiful information.

In 1609 an inquisitor travelled through a number of villages, recording hundreds of confessions—cases that were left alone for a while. The records contain the most detailed and "realistic" descriptions ever discovered about the witch's sabbath and the structure of the witch sect. The court even collected twenty-two jars with ointments and powders. Nevertheless all the confessions turned out to be unfounded and made from fear. The cases' uniqueness lies in the fact that the modern investigator does not need to put the confessions to a test, since this had already been done in 1611. In that year a second inquisitor, Alonso de Salazar Frías, visited all the suspects anew. He had them repeat their stories and indicate the spot of the witch's sabbath. Each time the declarations from the purported participants turned out to contradict each other, so they eventually withdrew them. Two women told the inquisitor that they had fabricated the witch's ointment themselves, taking their chances with pork fat, water, and soot. The parish priest had threatened to burn them at the stake if they did not come up with something. Salazar Frías, who afterwards wrote a voluminous report for the supreme council of the Inquisition at Madrid concluding that witchcraft did not exist, demonstrated that even the most realistic depiction of witchcraft lacked a kernel of truth. That must be all the more true for the confessions extorted from all other European witches.

So witches never have existed. The persecutions between 1480 and 1680 were not aimed at a real sect, of whatever nature. Witchcraft doctrine should be termed a collective delusion. It is another question to identify the range of social groups who shared this delusion. Besides, the observation of witchcraft's unreality does not preclude the existence of common characteristics among those persecuted. These problems have to be handled next.

Patterns of Persecution

This section examines various details which should provide us with a clearer picture of the persecutions. We will attempt to answer questions such as where, when, for how long, how intensive, and in what way. Subsequent themes include the beginnings of persecution, geographic differences in intensity, and the various forms of legal procedure. Finally, this section distinguishes four patterns of persecution.

The Beginnings

It is impossible to establish a definite starting point of the persecutions for two reasons. First, they consisted of formal criminal cases, judged by secular or ecclesiastical courts. Related offenses such as malefice and heresy had been tried for a long time. The witch trials were an offshoot of this tradition of prosecution, so that there was no official, legal beginning. The second reason lies in the gradual formation of witchcraft doctrine, making it difficult to distinguish sorcery from witchcraft in fifteenth-century criminal justice. In the course of some individual trials, and in other centuries as well, the focus of the accusation sometimes shifted from sorcery to witchcraft.

In any case, before persecution could start on a more than occasional basis, two necessary preconditions had to be met. In the first place, witchcraft doctrine, or at least some of its tenets, had to be widely known. This may seem obvious, but it is crucial that the mere belief in sorcery would probably not have led to mass persecutions. The collective anxiety inherent in the notion of a devil worshipping sect, on the other hand, repeatedly found an outlet in an actual hunt for witches. The second precondition for the appearance of mass persecution concerned the procedure in criminal cases. Two procedural changes made it easier to prosecute malefice or witchcraft. The first was the abolition of the so-called talion. This was the principle that a plaintiff unable to state his case convincingly received the very penalty which the accused would have got had he been found guilty. As long as this was customary, accusations of malefice were understandably scarce. In 1451, for example, a resident of Bamberg was denounced as a sorceress in the town court by a Strasbourg citizen. The Bamberg magistrates judged the woman to be innocent and had her accuser drowned in the river Ill. Most of the early witch trials, however, were conducted by the Inquisition, according to a procedure which did not include the talion. Later, when witchcraft cases were usually handled by secular courts, the talion had disappeared for good. The second crucial change, the introduction of torture, had also taken place by then. Torture enabled judges to compel the accused to name their accomplices more readily; this increased the chance of mass trials.

The first precondition formed part of the evolution leading to the witch persecutions. The second was an external precondition. Its fulfillment primarily depended on juridical changes, which in turn were a function of processes of state formation and urbanization. Its contribution to the inception of the witch persecutions was merely coincidental. When the two preconditions had been met, a permanent wave of trials did not automatically ensue. The intensity of the persecutions varied strongly, according to time and place. The situation which came into being at the end of the fifteenth century might be termed "structural ripeness." The existence of witchcraft doctrine and the availability of the legal facilities made society ripe for widespread persecution. For two centuries large parts of Europe were structurally ripe for the appearance of mass witch trials. Some regions, however, never experienced them and even the core areas knew periods of tranquillity.

Witchcraft doctrine first surfaced in its complete form around 1450, during a series of heresy trials in Switzerland, Savoy, and the French Pyrenees. The inquisitors spoke of a new sect. Local circumstances may have contributed to the start of the persecutions in precisely those places. The fact that they were all mountainous regions has no special meaning. At about the same time a series of witchcraft trials were conducted in Arras in the southern Netherlands. As said before, the actual beginnings should be situated in the 1480s, when trials proliferated over large regions for the first time. Two inquisitors, Sprenger and Krämer (or Institoris), were active in Germany. They persuaded Pope Innocent VIII to issue a bull against witchcraft in 1484, which they included as an appendix to their work *Malleus Maleficarum* (*The Witches' Hammer*), published two years later.

The "first European witch hunt" lasted about forty years. Originally parts of France and Germany were involved. Shortly after 1500 it reached the Basque country, northern Italy and, a little later, central Italy. From around 1520 to 1560 a period of tranquillity followed, when the coming of the Reformation seemed to divert the attention of all Europeans. After 1560 the persecutions flared up again, reaching a climax toward the end of the century. The beginning of the "second European witch hunt" may be fixed at about 1580, while the end, depending on the region one has in mind, came around 1610, 1630, 1650, or 1680.

Books expounding witchcraft doctrine published after 1500 failed to add essentially new elements. The genre is called demonology. Whereas fifteenth-century demonologies were written by inquisitors, famous laymen, such as the lawyer Jean Bodin and the Scottish king, James VI, carried the banner later. Their most remarkable feature is the strong drive toward intellectual conformity. Opponents of the persecutions, like Johannes Wier who published his *De Prestigiis Daemonum* (*On the Performance of Demons*) in 1563, were few in number. They stood the danger of themselves being called witches. Bodin, directing his *Démonomanie* of 1580 primarily against Wier's book, explicitly denounced him as one. This mechanism is typical of great persecutions; it was also present in the American "witch hunt" led by Senator Joseph McCarthy. A document drawn up in 1629 for use in the courts of Nassau-Siegen in Germany mentions fourteen categories of suspects. The twelfth consists of those persons who "defend the art of sorcery or witchcraft or take it to be a fantasy or dream work, thinking that this art should remain unpunished and seriously persevering in that opinion" (Schormann, 1981: 47). This is a perfect illustration of witchcraft doctrine's firm grip on people's minds.

The Intensity of the Persecutions

The historian of today is only satisfied by hard figures. Unfortunately, they cannot be supplied. There are two reasons why the exact magnitude of the persecutions is unknown. First, much research in local archives has yet to be done; it may either bring new trials to light or dismiss previous high estimates, based on unreliable sources, as myths. Second, a considerable amount of documentation is no longer extant. The records of some courts have been lost, while those of others are full of gaps. Numbers referred to in chronicles or by judges who took pride in having completely eradicated the devilish sect in their territory are of course less reliable. The second reason also implies that we will never know the true magnitude. In any case, the high numbers once suggested are almost certainly wrong. Historians around 1900, who were fond of exaggerating the contrast between the superstition and cruelty of an earlier age and the progress made in their own time, thought that more than a million witches had died at the stake. A little later, this was carefully reduced to some hundreds of thousands. But every recent investigator thinks rather of some tens of thousands.

It has been estimated, for example, that in all of England a mere two thousand trials were conducted from the middle of the sixteenth century to the beginning of the eighteenth. Elsewhere, on the other hand, the total number of trials might indeed rise high. Those executed numbered 970 in the Swiss canton of Vaud alone between 1581 and 1620 and 3,229 in southwestern Germany between 1561 and 1670. An estimate for the whole of Germany is made possible by the trial excerpts collected from 1935 to 1944 upon the initiative of no one other than Heinrich Himmler. The collection consists of 3,621 dossiers with a total of about 30,000 accused; 3,052 dossiers concern Germany, the only country researched thoroughly. But the investigators also included older trials for sorcery. We can estimate the number of those accused of witchcraft in Germany at around twenty thousand. Because Germany was the core area of the persecutions, it is probably sufficient to double this figure to arrive at the European total. And we may have to reduce it again by half to estimate the total number of those executed. In a preindustrial context, twenty thousand victims is still a considerable toll.

The persecutions were certainly not equally intense everywhere in Europe. Some areas were not affected at all, simply because witchcraft doctrine never reached them. This was the case in the world of Orthodox Christianity, which apart from Russia, was largely ruled by the Turks in this period. Nor did witchcraft doctrine spread to southern Italy, most of the Iberian peninsula, and Ireland. Persecutions in northern Spain practically stopped around 1610, partly as a result of Salazar Frías's report. In the northern Netherlands persecutions of any magnitude hardly have taken place. Witchcraft doctrine had little influence in England, but sorcery trials were continuously conducted there in the sixteenth and seventeenth centuries. Some peripheral areas were only affected by witchcraft doctrine at a later time. In Sweden and her colony, Finland, persecutions started in the 1660s, continuing until the end of the century. In Poland the zenith was not reached until the eighteenth century. Among the core areas of witch hunting were the Alpine regions, the German states, France, the southern Netherlands, Scotland, and parts of Scandinavia.

Also within individual core countries, regions with high and low intensity of persecution can be distinguished. In Scotland the lowlands were principally involved. The *Parlement* of Paris, exercising appeal jurisdiction over two-thirds of France, considerably reduced the number of convictions by the early seventeenth century. The most intense witch hunts raged in the surrounding border regions. The German (Holy Roman) Empire had a zone with a relatively low number of witch trials, extending from the lower Rhineland around Cleves over the great plains to the Northeast. In that area only Mecklenburg experienced many trials. All other states and small territories, with the exception of Bavaria, belonged to the core area. But even this is a rough division. The intensity varied from each town to another and from one village to the next. It might be just a half day's walk from a place where witches were regularly burned at the stake for over a century, to another where the fire was never lit. Such a situation prevailed in large parts of Europe.

The geography of witchcraft trials reveals no particular pattern, in the sense that the core and the peripheral areas contrasted with respect to other social variables as well. Because of their beginnings in the Alps and Pyrenees, it has been imagined that the trials were mainly confined to the mountains. That is only partially so. Conspicuous exceptions in the German Empire were Mecklenburg in the plains and Bavaria at the Alpine edge. Persecutions hardly reached the Scottish Highlands. Nor does the town-countryside dimension take us much further. Muchembled suggests that witchcraft was especially at home in villages. This may be true for France, but in southern Germany Imperial and episcopal towns conducted many trials, while the capital's surroundings were strongly involved in the Scottish witch hunt. In the Netherlands the cities likewise contributed their share. From a detailed quantitative analysis of Jutland in Denmark it can be concluded that the relative numbers of trials in urban and rural areas were matched.

Ethnic contrasts were sometimes reflected in the persecutions, but ambiguously. The *Parlement* of Bordeaux led the witch hunt in the Basque-speaking border region of France. Pierre de Lancre, the trial judge, returned home convinced that all Basques were witches. In Finland, on the other hand, most trials were conducted in the Swedish-speaking regions, but people born there and immigrants from the mother country were affected to an unequal extent. In Scotland the population of the tranquil Highlands spoke Celtic. We may add to these European observations the fact that in New England American Indians never faced charges of witchcraft. Consequently there is no reason to view the persecutions as an attack upon ethnic minorities. Unequivocal relationships with state formation or economic developments cannot be demonstrated either. Processes of state formation sometimes did affect the intensity of persecution, but in two contrasting ways. The great German panics took hold of the smaller territories in particular, while centralization led to a decline of prosecution in the jurisdiction of the Parisian Parlement. In Scotland and Luxemburg, on the other hand, centralization served to bolster the number of trials.

At a microlevel, Kamber is able to provide an explanation for differences in intensity. Witchcraft trials in the Swiss canton of Vaud were concentrated in the parts where grain and wine were cultivated and as a result villages were more populous and closer to each other. He explains this concentration in the following way: in the "crowded" villages pasturage entailed special problems. Although the mountain slopes, the less populous parts with fewer trials, witnessed grazing conflicts too, these usually brought entire villages into conflict. In the grain and wine regions there were conflicts among villagers. Because cattle formed the favorite target of sorcerers, these internal conflicts regularly led to charges of malefice. Hence, Kamber's thesis presupposes that the Vaud witch trials had their starting point within local communities and that prosecution began with one or a few sorcery trials, transformed into witchcraft trials through the intervention of the court, after which accomplices were tracked down. The next section deals with these problems in greater detail.

To contemporaries, at the height of the persecutions, religious antagonisms represented the most fundamental division in Europe. During the first phase from 1480 to 1520, a Catholic church was still unified. When persecution flared up again toward the end of the sixteenth century, the Reformation had definitively put an end to the unified church. Along with a number of smaller sects and the church of England, Europe henceforth had three international religions: Lutheranism, Calvinism, and reformed Catholicism.

A quick look at the map of Europe forces us to abandon the idea that one of these three in particular fostered the witch hunt. There is no correlation between the distribution of religions and the intensity of the witch persecutions. All three religions were rooted in both the core and the peripheral areas. Lutheranism was based in German territories which were very deeply involved as well as in Sweden and Finland where almost no witch trials happened until the end of the seventeenth century. The Catholic southern Netherlands were among the core areas, while in Spain, where its sovereign resided, the Inquisition was utterly passive. Calvinism was well established in Scotland when the witch hunt broke out there. Geneva, its mother city, conducted a number of trials but judged rather mildly compared to neighboring cantons. The Dutch Republic, where Calvinism became the dominant religion, took almost no part in the witch hunt.

A few studies have dealt with this problem at a microlevel. In the Jura region all three religions were represented, but Monter discovered no significant differences between the various territories. For southwestern Germany Midelfort did find a difference. Trials in Catholic localities outnumbered those in Protestant areas, while the former also had more executions per series of trials. However, this difference was only visible after 1600 and it was contingent upon a special circumstance. Theologians at the Protestant university of Tübingen held opinions which led to mildness in the witch hunt. Although these opinions originated before the Reformation, Catholics after 1600 tended to consider them Lutheran. This is the only example known so far of a correlation between religion and intensity of prosecution, and there is a specific explanation for it. Consequently we have no ground for the supposition that any religion in particular fostered witch hunting.

There is still another way in which confessional divisions might have reinforced the persecutions at their height. Protestants might have seen the devil at work mainly among Catholics, and vice versa. Religious minorities led a precarious existence in many territories. Trevor-Roper claims that the reemergence of witchcraft persecution after 1560 grew out of an intensified hunt for religious dissidents. Suspects who could not be charged with clearly deviant beliefs were accused of witchcraft instead and sacrificed as scapegoats in the struggle of religions. Their clandestine services were easily interpreted as demonic sabbaths. Walinski-Kiehl, testing Trevor-Roper's thesis for the bishopric of Bamberg, concluded that it has to be rejected. The witch hunt was not primarily aimed at those parts of the bishopric where Protestant minorities were concentrated. Furthermore, a prominent witch hunter explicitly stated that the devil's allies were rather to be found among the Catholics, since Satan, already possessing the souls of Protestants, had no need to recruit them. Dutch research makes the thesis more unlikely still. Numerous specialists in countermagic were active in the Republic, who often resorted to Catholic-like ritual in order to lift a spell. Yet the Protestant authorities initiated few witchcraft trials.

Thus, religious antagonisms do not explain differences in the intensity of witchcraft persecution any more than other social distinctions. The causes of these fluctuations remain in the dark.

Trial Procedures

The importance of legal procedure has already been stressed. To the extent that it facilitated obtaining a confession and, still more important, naming accomplices, the chances for mass witch persecutions increased. Even at its height, the pattern of persecution was influenced by the legal context. This is therefore an area in which differences in intensity can be partly explained, but only to raise new questions in turn.

First let us consider legislation. In the sixteenth century new penal codes were promulgated in various countries, but they seldom referred to the full witchcraft doctrine. One of the legal texts most often cited is the ordinance issued by Philip II for the southern Netherlands in 1592, supposedly drawn up by the demonologist Martin del Rio. Yet it mentions the demonic pact only in passing and the witch's sabbath not at all. It mainly lists concrete practices, such as sorcery, fortune telling, making astrological predictions, and causing illness. Armed with this ordinance, the judges could arrest anyone even a little deviant, but they were not expressly instructed to pursue a devilish sect. The German Carolina code, promulgated in 1532 during the pause between the first and second European witch hunts, only lists malefice as a punishable offense. Nonetheless numerous courts in the Empire later based their witchcraft sentences upon this law of Charles V. It is no surprise that English criminal law was also confined to malefice; but this was also the case in Scotland. Thus, codes and ordinances often served as the official legitimation for the punishment of witchcraft, but by themselves they never initiated a hunt.

Although ecclesiastical tribunals had started the witch persecutions in the fifteenth century, at their height these were mainly a matter for the regular secular courts. Only in Spain and Italy did the

Inquisition manage to maintain a virtual monopoly of prosecution. The tribunals of the Inquisition in early modern Spain and Italy were quite unlike their medieval predecessors. Trials were conducted at a slow pace with attention to detail; torture was seldom applied, and leading questions were avoided. The primary goal of the Inquisition was not punishment of the guilty but the return of sinners and those in error to the bosom of the church. The institution maintained this principle when confronted with witchcraft. Only those whose guilt was considered proved and who persisted in denying the charges were handed over to the secular authorities to be burned. A person who confessed and repented had to undergo a public humiliation and wear a penitential garment for a time. This is an additional explanation for the low number of executions in Spain, since the Inquisition was very hesitant to accept proof against those who denied the accusations. Everywhere else it was highly dangerous for a suspect to confess.

Secular justice, by contrast, sought to determine guilt and arrive at a judgment. Sometimes the trial began with the complaint of a wronged party. That was always the case in England, since the magistrates were not allowed to initiate a prosecution by themselves. Nor did English courts apply torture; a jury pronounced the verdict. This was one reason why serial trials were practically unknown in England. On the Continent an individual plaintiff too might start a procedure, but it happened more often that, following rumors, the authorities arrested and accused one or more persons. The pattern of mass persecutions is dealt with later. For an individual suspect the trial began with a denunciation in the form of rumors or expressed by someone who had already confessed to witchcraft. An accusation by several persons was necessary for an arrest; those arrested were taken into custody. The interrogation was the first step in a series of efforts to prove the suspect's guilt. The judges might inquire into relations with the devil, concrete acts of sorcery, or both. Witnesses could also be heard in this phase. Villagers might tell of the damage they had suffered; accomplices might give a few more details.

If the suspect persisted in her denials although the judges thought the indications of guilt were sufficiently strong, she was usually put to the rack. Torture was normal in such situations in trials for burglary, robbery, or homicide. In witchcraft trials, however, a few more devices for arriving at the truth were customary, which were never used for other offenses. The water ordeal is well known. Ordeals had become obsolete as early as the thirteenth century, but their application was revived in some regions during the witch persecutions. The water test did not mean, as is sometimes believed, that an "innocent" person was drowned. The executioner held a rope tied around the person's waist, with which he pulled the victim out of the water after she had sunk. Another peculiar means of proof was the devil's mark, which Satan imprinted on the body of his followers to seal the pact. When pricked at this spot, a witch did not feel pain, nor did she lose blood.

Leading questions, whether or not asked under torture, prompted numerous suspects to invent wondrous stories of participation in the witch's sabbath, listing every ingredient of witchcraft doctrine. Confession led to a condemnation. In some regions, such as northwestern Germany, it was customary to base the sentence on the advice of academic lawyers. After the judgment the magistrates might ask for the names of accomplices, often under threat of renewed torture. A suspect who managed to persist in denial was not always simply released. If the judges still harbored serious doubts, they condemned the suspect to a lighter punishment. That is why a considerable number of trials ended with banishment. The age of the accused was another factor affecting the severity of the judgment. Young children were usually not condemned to death. According to the estimates of recent historians, about 50 percent of those tried during the witch persecutions suffered capital punishment. But the percentage varied strongly with the jurisdiction.

Like the penalties, the details of procedure varied with the region. The pattern of persecution was affected by whether or not certain legal rules were respected. The most skeptical lawyers only found a condemnation justified when the *corpus delicti* had turned up: a written pact, better still when countersigned by Satan himself. This precondition would have made the level of condemnations infinitely low, but no court took such an extreme position. Nevertheless, the Parlement of Paris soon tightened the rules of evidence to such an extent that the number of executions within its domain remained relatively low. Magistrates in the Jura region refused to give credence to accusations leveled at children, or even confessions by them, and they were hesitant to apply torture. Elsewhere the judges had fewer scruples in this respect. Schormann cites the example of the small town of Arensburg in the county of Schaumburg-Lippe, where the procedure had become routine. The judges assumed the women committed to jail there were guilty from the start. Their bad reputation had been confirmed in a number of solemn declarations, and several witches who had already confessed had accused them. Hence they only had to be tortured until they admitted to being witches themselves. When that had been accomplished, the magistrates had them locked up in their cells and went to dinner, knowing that the university at Rinteln would determine the judgment.

Thus, the nature of legal procedure affected the intensity of the witch hunt. Where procedural rules were more strict, fewer victims were counted. Nonetheless, in the discussion of the intensity of persecution, this factor has not been proposed as a possible explanation. This is because the differences in trial procedure need an explanation in turn. They were not simply the consequence of accidental differences in legal tradition but were part of a broader variation in the intellectual field. In case of witchcraft trials, courts usually ignored the clauses which offered the suspect some protection. But in some places the magistrates were more radical in this respect than in others. Witchcraft was considered an exceptional offense, precluding the observance of all normal legal rules. At the hunt's peak, special tribunals with full powers were instituted in several places, for example in Bamberg in 1627. The problem remains: why was the fear of the devil and his troop so great during the witch persecutions that courts were prepared to push aside the rules of procedure which were customary in other cases, and why was their readiness greater in some regions than in others? This is a question of mentalité.

Waves and Still Waters

From the preceding discussion conclusions can be drawn about the patterns of persecution for witchcraft and harmful sorcery in Europe during the period 1480–1680. The present state of research allows us to distinguish four patterns: fragmented, isolated but steady, small panics, and great panics. The last two types usually occurred in combination with either one of the first two.

The fragmented pattern of course was at home in those areas which escaped from an intensive witch hunt, such as Sweden before 1660 or most provinces of the northern Netherlands before the end of the sixteenth century. Trials were a rare occurrence in these regions during these periods. They were conducted very occasionally in some jurisdictions, without any regularity as to when and where exactly they happened. An incidental accusation had led to such a trial. The schout (prosecutor) and schepenen (magistrates) of Amsterdam, for example, are known to have been active in this matter only three times, first in 1542. In 1555 a woman and her two daughters were burned, and another woman in 1564. Two years later the magistrates suppressed rumors of witchcraft. In Gelderland a small number of trials, spread out chronologically and geographically, were conducted during the sixteenth century. Few serial trials are known from the northern Netherlands at all. Larger outbursts occurred a few times in the province of Groningen during the second half of the sixteenth century and once in the province of Utrecht in the 1590s. Throughout the Dutch Republic the witch persecutions came to a stop by around 1610. Belief in the devilish sect had never been very widespread; most sentences just referred to concrete acts of malefice. The small number of those persecuted may have been related to the near absence of interest in large-scale meetings of witches. Several historians claim that a preoccupation with the witch's sabbath, more than anything else, caused trials to proliferate, since the judges were inclined to ask repeatedly for the names of accomplices. Scotland, however, where interest in the witch's sabbath was almost lacking and mass persecutions still took place, forms a counterexample. In the northern Netherlands, in any case, the witch's sabbath was relatively unimportant even during the 1590s. The Dutch meetings were just minor orgies, where a few witches danced in the shape of cats, with their forefeet joined, on a dike or at a market square.

The second type, the isolated-steady pattern, was especially characteristic for England. The near absence of the notions of the witch's sabbath and the demonic pact implied that the judges had no incentive to inquire into possible accomplices. The legal system required that each time an individual plaintiff accused someone of one or more malefices, he had been its victim. The accusation was usually leveled at one person, which explains the isolated character of the trials. The existence of laws against sorcery and the tradition of indictments for this offense still facilitated a steady flow of trials. In the county of Essex, with about one hundred thousand inhabitants, trials averaged a little over three per year between 1560 and 1680. More than 50 percent, to be sure, ended with a verdict of not guilty. Only in 1645 did two witch hunters manage to set up a special tribunal and to introduce demonological conceptions. Nineteen women were then hanged in a small part of Essex. The English pattern was transplanted in the seventeenth century to Puritan New England. There too it was confronted with one exception, involving the same number of casualties: in Salem in 1692.

Small panics were characteristic for those regions where witchcraft doctrine was influential, at least among the magistrates, but courts clung to relatively strict procedural rules. The Jura forms an example. Normally, the number of those condemned simultaneously remained below ten. For a small community this still meant being completely overtaken by the witch hunt. Outside the years of panic, isolated trials might be conducted. The northern German town of Kiel exhibited an identical pattern. In 1578 the local court had eight women burned. In 1638–1639 they numbered nine. The last small panic occurred in 1666–1668, involving six persons, three of whom were found not guilty. Outside those years, over the entire period 1530–1676, only ten persons were accused. In the last year the only man died at the stake.

Southern and central Germany formed the classic area of great panics. Wherever they flared up, victims were counted by the dozens, sometimes over a hundred. In the bishopric of Bamberg between 1626 and 1630 at least 468 persons were arrested, 278 of whom are known to have been sentenced to death. In Oppenau, a place with about 650 inhabitants, fifty persons were burned within nine months in 1631 and another 170 formally accused. Such panics were of course restricted in number. They alternated with periods when a fragmented or an isolated pattern prevailed.

Those huge panics must have cast a shroud of permanent collective anxiety over an entire community. Everyone was afraid of the witches as well as of the accusers. In this climate of fear and suspicion more than one inhabitant may have taken his or her own life. As far as we know, the population remained largely passive in the face of the terror inherent to the situation. A twentieth-century observer is inclined to ask whether there was any talk at all of resistance. Just one example can be found in the literature. The incident took place in Paderborn at the time of the panic of 1628–1631. The prosecution of witchcraft in Paderborn was entirely in the hands of one person: the academic lawyer Kaspar Reinhard, who, as trial judge, must have taken an unusually tough stand even for that time. A few inhabitants, afraid of being arrested and executed themselves, conspired to kill him. Their activities ultimately brought them little advantage, although their wish not to take their last breath at the stake was realized. The conspirators shot Reinhard while he was dining with the magistrates. The witch hunter was just seriously injured, but a clerk and the court's messenger were hit and died. The attackers were caught and found guilty of murder. They were broken on the wheel, their dead bodies burned.

In individual instances of mass persecution a particular pattern was often also manifest, for the first time in the *vauderie* of Arras in 1459. The course it took forms a micromodel, or ideal type, for any mass persecution: an accidental beginning with one or two accusations— spread of the accusations—transfer of the case to fanatical prosecutors—a spiral of trials, condemnations and new accusations—involvement of high-ranking persons—a stop to the series of trials—rehabilitation of the victims. This last phase happened in Arras thirty years later. Practically none of the later European victims enjoyed such posthumous satisfaction. The spiral especially was characteristic of mass witchcraft persecutions. The involvement of more and more persons, even magistrates at times, caused the stereotype of the witch as primarily an elder, poor woman to break down. The resulting crisis of confidence among the judges led them to put a stop to the persecutions. This pattern has been demonstrated for southwestern Germany and the bishopric of Bamberg.

A number of great panics were confined to one place. Others came in waves. Some of these swelled to international proportions, storming over parts of Europe like a hurricane. Schormann, from whom the word "wave" has been borrowed, identifies three German ones, which dragged large parts of the Empire into the hunt around 1590, 1630, and around 1660. The middle wave, most heavily concentrated in time, took about five years and included the largest panic witnessed by Bamberg as well as southwestern Germany. The first wave took about ten years and the third about fifteen. Probably the first was the most international, rolling over large parts of the Empire and its peripheral areas, such as Switzerland and Lorraine. The 1590s reached a climax in Luxemburg and the Cambrésis, possibly in the whole of the southern Netherlands and at least in Utrecht and Groningen in the northern Netherlands. The wave of the 1590s even extended to Scotland.

Next to the crisis of confidence, other factors could stop a massive witch hunt. Sometimes the reason was very trivial: lack of money. The baron of Vierves in Luxemburg, for example, ruined himself in a series of trials that lasted for several years. According to the claims of earlier historians, witchcraft trials were very profitable for the magistrates, notably because of confiscations which served as a powerful incentive to initiate them. All recent historians, however, have established that witchcraft trials cost money rather than producing a profit. Besides lack of money, the threat of war might diminish the enthusiasm of the prosecutors. In the canton of Vaud the number of trials declined rapidly during years of military crisis. When actual war broke out in a particular region, the witch hunt usually came to a complete stop. During the Thirty Years War this was the case in Luxemburg and southern Germany. In the latter region, notably, the Swedes undermined the hunt.

Instigators and Victims

Modern investigators have understandably presumed that an answer to the question of the identity of the witches would provide a key for explaining the persecutions. Were the persecutors aiming at specific groups, consciously or, more likely, unconsciously? A related question concerns the leading persons who took the initiative. Who persecuted whom? At present, clues to an explanation are sought in two directions in particular: the unequal distribution of the victims between the sexes, and the contrast between elite and popular culture. The use of the word, victim, is by no means self-evident. As a rule, the person who has suffered from a crime is called the victim. Contemporaries might denote the farmer whose cow was bewitched as one, or the whole community of the faithful, suffering from the God-provoking presence of Satan's allies. Only during great panics, experienced as a form of terror, would they have viewed some of those arrested as victims. But, even then it is likely that they thought in terms of abuse in the sense that too many people were accused of a crime, which was certainly real. In short, our notion of the witches as victims is actually an anachronism. It is adhered to here, nevertheless, because it is such a commonplace.

Women as Witches

The primary answer to the question, who were the witches, must be: mostly women. The figures are clear as can be seen from the percentages of women accused of witchcraft in selected regions:

Bishopric of Basel (1571–1670)	95
Essex (1560–1675)	92
County of Namur (1509–1646)	92
Jutland (1612–1637)	90
Cambrésis (1371–1783)	82
Southwestern Germany (1562–1684)	82
Eastern Bothnia (Finland) (1665–1684)	78
Duchy of Luxemburg (1509–1687)	76
Bishopric of Bamberg (1595–1680)	74
Canton of Vaud (1581–1620)	66

Within the larger areas the percentages often varied by jurisdiction. The figures for Basel and Vaud, representing the maximum and the minimum within the Jura, have been included for that reason. In the region as a whole the average was about 80 percent. A few authors mention somewhat less precise figures. According to Larner, the percentage of women in Scotland approached that of the Jura and southwestern Germany, while in Norway too there was talk of about 80 percent. These figures concern the accused, but we can easily substitute "victims," since, once arrested, men and women had an equal chance of receiving the death penalty. In Luxemburg women made up 75 percent of those executed as compared to 76 percent of those accused. It is a hard fact that four out of five victims of the European witch persecutions were women. Next, age was a crucial factor. Although a considerable number of younger women, mostly daughters of witches, died at the stake, the majority were relatively aged. (We have to realize that in those times the physical symptoms of old age were visible from the menopause.) All authors agree on this, as they do on the fact that most of the accused were poor. Thus, the stereotypical witch was the elderly poor woman.

Our next inquiry is into the origins of this stereotype. Because sorcery was one of the ingredients of witchcraft doctrine, it is logical to look in that direction. All Indo-European nations have associated women and magic, not only white but also and especially black magic. Greeks and Romans saw the sorceress as an old woman practicing love magic; for herself, blinded by an improper passion, or for the benefit of a third party for a fee. In more gruesome stories she killed children because she needed their entrails. The Germanic nations also linked women and magic. In the Edda only women practiced it. They were either old and ugly or young and seductive and, hence, pernicious. During the European Middle Ages this association was not exclusive. Male thunderstorm-makers, for example, roamed around then, extorting money form the peasants and promising not to demonstrate their powers as long as they were paid. But sorcery at the village level largely remained women's work. This age-old stereotype of the sorceress must have influenced the popular image of the witch in the sixteenth and seventeenth centuries.

We cannot, however, simply ascribe the witch stereotype to the people. There was an equally age-old association of women with evil among the intellectual elite. The majority of Greek philosophers as well as the early Christian writers considered women as second-class beings. During the Middle Ages this antifeminine tradition was kept alive especially by ecclesiastical authors; examples are many. The religious movements stemming from the Reformation adopted the negative image. It is not surprising, then, that the demonologists integrated it into their system. As its title suggests, the *Malleus Maleficarum* was most outspoken in this. Because women are the weaker vessel, Sprenger and Krämer argued, it is quite natural that they are particularly vulnerable to the devil's temptations. Later authors added to this that the share of women among the accused proved their perniciousness.

Thus, the image of the witch as primarily a woman was alive among broad groups in society. According to some authors, this explains the unequal sex ratio. Larner posits that the machinery of justice looked for the perpetrators of violence and murder among men and for bewitchment or poisoning among women. During the sixteenth century courts were increasingly inclined to start procedures generally against women. Yves Castan sees the initiative as coming from below, but he arrives at a comparable conclusion. Every child in preindustrial Languedoc learned at an early age how to insult someone: a man as a thief, a woman as a whore. If the woman was too old for this label, she was called a witch. These affronts were more threatening to the extent that they were based on a person's actual reputation in the village or neighborhood. The community only resorted to justice when they wished to get rid of unwanted persons. The neighbors accused unwanted men of theft and unwanted women of witchcraft, as long as these were offenses. Besides, women controlled the gossip circuit. When one was arrested, other female suspects were easily named; for, both sexes shared the stereotype.

Larner's and Castan's argument suggests a rather close relationship between the prevalent stereotype of the witch and the sex ratio among the victims. That leads us to inquire whether this ratio was maintained during mass hunts. The great panics in the south of Germany resulted in an erosion of the stereotype. At a certain moment the witch was no longer a poor woman but a rich man, a burgomaster of Bamberg for example. Notably in southwestern Germany this trend implied an increase in the male's share among the accused. Midelfort explains this as follows: at the beginning, persons who were already reputed witches were accused. Next, the judges put pressure on them to name others. Since more than one accusation was needed for an arrest, it is understandable that eventually better known persons, such as merchants or innkeepers, ran increased risk. However, an increase in the male's share during great panics has not been demonstrated elsewhere. In eastern Bothnia the percentage of men declined to 15 percent in serial trials. In the Cambrésis it was also lower as the period witnessed more cases. Scotland, finally, perfectly contrasted with southwestern Germany, even though it witnessed similar panics. The percentage of men declined from 20–27 in the tranquil periods to 11–12 during panics. Larner's explanation is therefore the mirror image of

Midelfort's: during the great panics there was a shortage of persons who had long been suspected of witchcraft. New suspects, therefore, were primarily sought from among those who met the stereotype. To conclude, the study of large-scale witch hunts cannot yet solve the problem under discussion.

A particular thesis blames the sex ratio of the victims on accusations leveled at folk healers. There was a tradition of practical medical help by women, notably with midwifery, in the local communities of preindustrial Europe. These "wise women" certainly constituted a risk group. In the first place, the line dividing medicine from sorcery was rather fluid. Some women also applied magical healing methods or practiced countermagic when they thought that an illness had been caused by harmful sorcery. The ups and downs of success in this profession constituted the second risk factor. A stillborn child or the failure of an herbal recipe to prevent the death of a sick person might be held against the wise woman, causing her to be considered a witch. The demonologists, finally, especially distrusted midwives. According to the *Malleus Maleficarum*, many of them were witches, who were accustomed to present infants to the devil before they could be baptized.

Apart from these risk factors, it is sometimes suggested that professional physicians consciously deflected accusations of witchcraft to wise women. This thesis is totally unfounded. First, village healers were not competitors of academically trained physicians, whom the villagers could not afford. It is true that the tradition of female medicine was strong enough for a number of late-medieval women to become learned doctors. Male physicians at the universities attacked them as early as the fourteenth and fifteenth centuries, when witchcraft doctrine did not yet play a role. And the overall offensive of academic doctors was primarily directed at male quacks. Measures specifically aimed at the supervision of midwives, by contrast, date from a later period; French authorities began to be concerned about them only in the eighteenth century. The rivalry between learned medical men and nonacademic doctors, then, has nothing to do with the witch persecutions. To the contrary, physicians had a reputation of looking for natural causes first, where others sensed the smell of witchcraft. Johannes Wier was a physician too. Even though wise women constituted a risk group and may have been overrepresented among the victims of the persecutions, Horsley's supposition that they were a majority among the accused is based merely on a number of Swiss trials from the period 1450–1550. Other research does not confirm his thesis.

Thus far our search has been restricted to an explanation for the real overrepresentation of women among the accused. It is another question whether the witch persecutions were aimed at the female sex as such. Twenty percent of men is still a conspicuous minority. Larner formulates that witchcraft was sex-related but not sex-specific. Nevertheless, she argues, it is worthwhile to inquire whether the sex-relatedness of witchcraft can explain the appearance of the persecutions as such. Feminist oriented works usually presume a close relationship between the two. The persecutions are viewed as an expression of patriarchal anxieties or feelings of hatred. Such a theory can be made plausible only in two ways. The first possibility is to demonstrate an increase in the hatred of women at the end of the fifteenth century. If we want to avoid a circuitous argument, the witch persecutions themselves cannot serve as proof for this. The second possibility is to refer to concrete demographic changes which might have stirred up a fear of women.

Using the first strategy, some authors do come near to a circuitous argument. To them, the antifeminine nature of the *Malleus Maleficarum* is a sufficient reason to speak of an increase in hatred of women in general. The publication of that work, it is presumed, triggered the persecutions. However, the book appeared in 1486, shortly after the first peak in witchcraft trials in the years 1480–1485. Furthermore, it contained an incomplete description of witchcraft doctrine. The witch's sabbath was mentioned hardly at all, even though the oldest demonological treatises from the middle of the fifteenth century had informed their readers quite thoroughly about it. A general increase in misogyny around 1500 has not been demonstrated so far. (The evidence in chapters 2 and 8 makes this rather unlikely.) The antifeminine cultural tradition is at least two thousand years older than witchcraft doctrine, and it is difficult to accept that this tradition would suddenly have led to witch persecutions between 1480 and 1680. Significantly, when Sprenger and Krämer discussed the inferiority of women, they were not looking for support from earlier authors, as they had with other subjects. For them the point was simply self-evident.

The second strategy is equally problematic. A few authors assume that the witch persecutions reflected changes in family structure or the pattern of marriage. The most common argument is that a rise in the average age at marriage or another demographic shift caused the number of solitary women to increase. In a patriarchal society this abnormal situation would have provoked an anxiety that was translated into an obsession with witchcraft. This theory is largely based on assumptions, since hard demographic data are almost totally lacking.

The earliest figures on the average age at marriage, covering a larger area, date from the second quarter of the sixteenth century, after the first European witch hunt. It is also doubtful whether the persecutions hit primarily solitary women. Midelfort does observe this for southwestern Germany but only during the opening phase of the great panics. In his study of the Jura, Monter speaks of "a-typical women" in general. Later studies fail to confirm the thesis of an attack on solitary females. Larner establishes that about half of the Scottish witches whose marital status is known had a husband at the moment of arrest. The others were mostly widows. In so far as the persecutions were concentrated on elderly women, it is understandable that widows were overrepresented. In Denmark and Norway even widows were scarce. The overwhelming majority of witches there consisted of married women, which was also the case on the other side of the ocean, in New England.

The conclusion is clear: the appearance of the witch persecutions cannot be explained in terms of changing relationships between men and women. We must look for other explanations. The unequal sex ratio among the accused was brought about through the interaction of elite and popular conceptions. At the level of villages and neighborhoods the concept of witch was interpreted as sorceress: primarily a woman. The demonologists adopted this view and linked it to familiar notions of the weakness and inferiority of women. In this way the stereotype of the witch came into being. For women it was a fateful by-product of the persecutions; a consequence of the course they adopted, intellectually and in practice.

Popular Culture and the Elites

The concept of popular culture has been treated extensively in chapter 3, where it is linked to local traditions. Several historians hope to explain the appearance of the witch persecutions by the interaction of local traditions, the aspirations of elite groups, and more impersonal long-term developments. Let us first consider the intellectual component.

There can be little doubt that witchcraft doctrine originated in elite culture. The demonologies were learned works. The elites must also have been more intensely afraid of Satan, since the people's anxieties were eased by the association of devils with laughter. Because the intellectual foundation of the persecutions was a matter for the elites, a number of historians claim that most other people were uninformed about witchcraft doctrine. The learned beliefs presumably existed unnoticed by peasants and artisans, who only knew the sorceresses and sorcerers with whom they had always lived. In certain regions, to be sure, assemblies were part of the repertoire of popular beliefs. Such was the case in the Basque country and in Sweden, where the "blue hill" in the North was the traditional meeting ground of sorcerers. But the demonic pact seldom belonged to this repertoire. The question, then, is whether the people continued to believe in sorcery alone, unaffected by elite ideas, throughout the period of the persecutions.

Historians who answer affirmatively claim that peasants and artisans interpreted learned concepts in familiar terms. If an inquisitor or a secular zealot came to a village or a neighborhood to inquire into the presence of witches, the inhabitants named those persons who had an air of harmful sorcery about them. The evidence for this thesis is not entirely convincing. Kieckhefer comes up with a few dozen trials in which the initial charges, according to him, reflected popular beliefs. The emphasis lay on sorcery, while the demonic pact and devil worship were absent. Those trials, however, date from the fifteenth century, when witchcraft doctrine was not yet widespread among the elite. English villagers, in any case, did not know and remained uninformed about the pact and the witch's sabbath. But that too is not surprising, since these notions remained unfamiliar to all groups in that country. It would be more significant if popular beliefs in Germany in the first half of the seventeenth century had been restricted to sorcery. This is questionable. Schormann stresses that priests and ministers preached witchcraft doctrine from the pulpit. The executions, at which the sentences were read aloud with the confessions, presented another occasion to familiarize the people with the notions of alliance with the devil and the witch's sabbath. We can only guess to what extent the message was taken to heart. A preliminary conclusion about popular beliefs might be this: before and after the period of the persecutions the population of villages and neighborhoods believed in sorcery and had a magical view of the world in general. During the period of the persecutions, when there was talk of witchcraft, they primarily thought of harmful sorcery. At the peak, however, the notion of a devil-worshipping sect must have played a role too.

Although the populace often took witches to be sorceresses and sorcerers, this does not mean that the initiative to prosecute exclusively originated from above. It is the implicit or explicit opinion of several authors that witch persecutions were in line with the policies of secular and clerical authorities, so that they must be considered the instigators. There is hardly any concrete evidence for this thesis. To the contrary, Ankarloo concludes that the Swedish panic of the 1670s resulted from strong pressure from the populace upon a reluctant central government. Examples of a local community asking for witchcraft trials are known from Germany as well. In 1589 the people of Elz submitted a petition to their overlord in Trier. It began with a request for a delay in the payment of taxes, since the harvest had been destroyed by a hailstorm. But the hailstones had been so unusually big that they must have been the work of sorceresses. Hence the petition concluded with a request to punish the guilty ones, who were said to be well known. The Elector should order local courts to prosecute. If not, the drafters of the petition claimed they had no other choice but to move with their women and children and to leave everything behind. The Elector did not give an order to the courts, despite the fact that prosecution was going on elsewhere in the territory. In a few other known instances, however, the lord reacted positively to this kind of supplication.

In areas where the notions of witch's sabbath and demonic pact had little influence and trials revolved around concrete acts of malefice, prosecution was not initiated from above. Accusations in England often resulted from a specific mechanism, which was common in Denmark too. Projection played a crucial part. As a rule, the accusers were somewhat richer than the victims, who were frequently dependent on charity. When a fellow villager denied alms to a poor woman, he might feel guilty later. Then, he projected his guilt onto the woman by imagining her to be a sorceress. If a child fell ill, or a cow died shortly afterwards, that supposition was confirmed. In such cases, then, criminal trials were a direct result of tensions within the community.

Macfarlane and a few others theorize from these observations. The breakthrough of capitalism and economic individualism in sixteenth-century England, they argue, undermined the cohesion of village communities. A more individualistic ethic was incompatible with traditional charity, which caused the tensions leading to these cases of projection. If this analysis holds true for the Continent as well, it might explain why witchcraft trials proliferated in the sixteenth and seventeenth centuries. A new attitude with respect to poverty indeed came to prevail in this period (See chapter 7.), but traditional charity was not completely eroded. Besides, the witches prosecuted outside England seldom belonged to the marginal population. Although they were mostly poor, they were within the bounds of the community. They might have a bad reputation, but they were not pariahs. In this they clearly differed from the persecuted Jews in an earlier age. Tensions and conflicts were endemic to local communities. By the eighteenth century such conflicts still found an outlet in accusations of sorcery without resulting in criminal trials. In all likelihood, a comparable situation prevailed in the Middle Ages. Even if the tensions inside local communities had increased at the beginning of the early modern period, this cannot explain the witch persecutions. It is only because the judicial machinery could be readily involved, which had other causes, that local conflicts could take such a dramatic turn.

Although Muchembled also focuses his explanation around changes within local communities, in his view the initiative to prosecute originated from above. He situates witchcraft trials at the crossroads of two long-term developments: the civilization offensive against traditional popular culture, and the socio-economic evolution leading to a more complex stratification in the countryside. When witches faced charges of sexual intercourse with the devil, he argues, this should be seen as a condemnation of extramarital sexuality in general. The newly rich in the countryside are said to have supported the offensive of religious and secular authorities by directing accusations of witchcraft against local deviants. Occasionally, Muchembled goes so far as to claim that the witch persecutions were aimed against the people's magical world view.

The difficulty with these explanations lies in chronology. The attack on popular culture was not launched that early. Muchembled himself traces its origins to the second half of the sixteenth century, which at least precludes an explanation for the first European witch hunt of 1480–1520. The role attributed to the sexual motif is not free of ambiguity either. An unbridled promiscuity had been one of the standard charges thrown in the face of religious dissidents for ages. Admittedly the notion of sex with the devil was new, but precisely on this point the chronology of events is incompatible with Muchembled's thesis. The claim that the witch persecutions were directed against the people's magical world view is quite the reverse of what actually happened. The formation of witchcraft doctrine meant an increase in the magical content of the elites' world view. The notion of sexual contact between humans and supernatural beings and that of nocturnal trips, as we know, had been foreign to the elite world for a long time. A text originating in the tenth century, known as the Canon Episcopi, condemned such popular beliefs. Priests, it says, must explain to women who imagined that they had flown with the wandering army that it was all an illusion. It was a pagan superstition, since humans are unable to fly. At the beginning of the fifteenth century, however, clerical and lay intellectuals themselves started to believe in those nightly trips and the demonologists took them for real. Are we to think that the elites adopted popular conceptions they had discarded earlier, with a view on attacking popular culture?

Ginzburg, finally, has another theory, in which popular culture is equally central. According to him, the conception of the witch's sabbath was a travesty of an older cluster of beliefs concerning sorcery and fertility rituals, although not of a secret cult as claimed by Murray. He developed his thesis from the evidence on the so-called *benandanti*. The peasant population of Friuli thought that persons born with a caul had special gifts and that their mission was to use these to protect the community from harmful sorcerers. Whoever had been born with a caul indeed believed in their obligation to do good: be a *benandante*. He or she dreamed of waging battle against sorcerers at night, together with a host of comrades. If the sorcerers won, the harvest would fail that year; if they were beaten, abundance would come to the community. The fighters were convinced of the reality and the collective nature of their nocturnal experiences. When some of them were questioned by the Venetian inquisition at the end of the sixteenth century, they said so, emphasizing their noble intentions. But the inquisitors had never heard of benandanti, so they thought they were dealing with witches. In the course of a series of trials in the first half of the seventeenth century the inquisitors managed to impose their view upon the populace. Ultimately, benandanti themselves confessed to being sorcerers or witches, while their community was convinced of their evil intentions.

The problem is to what extent we can generalize from these findings. The benandanti make a fascinating story but, except for a partly comparable case in Livonia at the end of the seventeenth century, it is unique. It simply looks like a regional variant to the sort of beliefs which were building blocks for witchcraft doctrine elsewhere. Nonetheless, Ginzburg thinks he is on to something bigger than that, what was once a coherent system of collective representation throughout agrarian Europe. He calls the system "pre-sabbatical," because it is supposed to have been the substratum upon which the elites later based witchcraft doctrine. The demonological system was a compromise between learned and popular beliefs. But as much as we try, witchcraft doctrine cannot possibly be termed a compromise. It is absolutely unclear which points of view were reconciled by it.

The information gathered and the analyses offered by various investigators with respect to the relationships between witchcraft trials, popular culture, and the position of women increase our understanding of the mechanisms that played a part in the persecutions. But they fail to add up to a plausible theory of why the witch persecutions happened at all. Plausible explanations have been proposed for their decline, which is dealt with in chapter 9.

THE VICISSITUDES
OF THE BODY

5 THE BODY IN DECAY: Certainty and Uncertainty in the Experience of Death

"Nothing is more certain than the fact that we shall die and nothing is more uncertain than the moment when." This was the favorite opening phrase for French seventeenth-century notaries when they drew up a will and surely they were not the first to formulate it. This cliché introduces the story of the experience of death in preindustrial Europe. Take the first observation: death is an inescapable biological reality, but it does not present a problem for any other species. In the course of their evolution only humans have learned to conclude, from continually watching other people die, that they themselves and their loved ones will die too. In every society known to us, therefore, attitudes toward death are a crucial feature characteristic of that society. In addition to the certainty that they would die, nearly all contemporaries were convinced of something else: existence did not end with death. Conceptions about the hereafter, together with the changes these ideas underwent played a leading role in reflection upon death. But the notion of the hereafter also leads us to the other side of the coin: for all believers, there was a fundamental uncertainty about their fate upon death. And finally, there was the capriciousness of the duration of life on earth, referred to in the second part of our cliché. Death took its toll at unexpected moments, even more then than now. Material existence was insecure, not only because of a lack of control over nature but also as a consequence of social relationships. The experience of death balanced between certainty and uncertainty. Death has always been problematic, but the shifts in the balance, or the ways to handle the problem, provide an insight in the mentality of the age under scrutiny.

The concept of "experience of death" may need some explanation. It seems that nothing about death can be experienced, but on further consideration, this is not quite true. First, we can study how individual people sense the coming of death and prepare for it. Second, it should be realized that death is embedded in a social context. Besides death, this chapter also deals with the consolation of the survivors, the attitudes in one's immediate community toward dying, and the image of death and the dead among various social groups. A few topics are not included here because they fit better into subsequent chapters. Violent death at the hands of murderers or hangmen forms an important part of chapter 7. Suicide is treated in connection with the discussion of insanity. Attention is paid to infant mortality within the framework of parent-child relationships. What remains can be subsumed under the heading of the natural death of adults.

In this field, Philippe Ariès has made the most admirable effort at synthesis. However, his chronological scheme covering fifteen centuries has been interpreted differently by various commentators. Let us adapt it for our purposes. Ariés, like most other specialists, holds that a radical change in the experience of death took place in the course of the eighteenth century. Until then, a few fundamental characteristics had enjoyed a continuity of more than a thousand years. This long millennium still witnessed some changes, especially during the last centuries preceding the great shift. This leads us to the order of our analysis in this chapter. The first section discusses the fundamental characteristics which retained their validity nearly throughout the preindustrial period, tracing the history of the experience of death from about 500 to around 1300. The next section treats several of the new elements visible between the fourteenth and seventeenth centuries. The radical change in the course of the eighteenth century forms the subject of the last section, which closes with the question of explanations.

The Long Breath

This section deals with a few fundamental characteristics of the experience of death, which remained unchanged from about 500, or maybe even earlier, until the beginning of the eighteenth century. Next, it pays attention to another central theme: visions of the hereafter and life after death.

Two Models: The Saint and the Knight

Let us start with two models: two ideal images of the good death as they were presented to people at the beginning of our period. The first is the dying process in saints' lives from the fifth and sixth centuries. The second, of a somewhat later date, is culled from the feudal romances of chivalry. In both cases we are dealing with natural death. Saints from the first three Christian centuries were usually martyrs, but afterwards the proportion of those who died in their beds increased. Knights regularly fell in battle but often died a few days after the fight from their wounds, while some even reached old age. Those knights of course were all men. Among the holy people whose life was written down there was one woman, Saint Radegonde.

The tale of holy death is not concentrated on the moment itself but comprises the last days as a whole. It begins with the illness, to which only a scrap of the account is devoted. The saint does not have to endure painful agony. The biographers are concerned less with a biological passage than with a religious and mystical transition. The struggle against Satan, which later was to become the central motif, does not yet figure in that transition. The battle against demonic temptations had been skillfully fought by the saint during his lifetime, and his death is the moment of ultimate triumph. That moment does not come as a surprise. In almost all *vitae* the tale of the last days opens with the theme of foresight. The saint informs his disciples and friends that he will pass away. The *vita Martini* says: "Thus, Martin knew about his death long before and declared to his brethren that the decomposition of his body was nigh" (Sutto: 189). Consequently, the saints have the opportunity to say farewell to their loved ones, which sometimes amounts to a true sermon. Many prayers are said as well, but no special role was reserved for a priest in this period. At the moment when the saint draws his last breath, he has turned his face toward heaven or toward the East. Then his soul embarks upon the journey to heaven, a glorious journey, for there is no chance that the soul of a holy person ends up in some other place. This triumph is described in three different ways: the soul is a small child, accompanied to heaven by angels; the soul is a little bird flying to heaven; the soul is a fiery light reaching heaven in a straight line. In all cases music and singing can be heard from the highest. After this scene the climax has passed. Few words are devoted to the care of the body, and the funeral is only interesting when it forms the occasion for miraculous cures. One element, finally, seems to contradict the Christian and holy character of this death: mourning. Although orthodox writers stress their preference for singing psalms when someone has passed away, lamentations are prominent in the vitae. Women play their traditional part in this and sometimes they look like professional mourners.

There are resemblances as well as differences in the model of knightly death. It is composed of passages from the *chanson de Roland*, the tales of the Round Table, and the poems about Tristan. The knight too knows that the end is near. He feels his life force diminish and informs his companions that he has just a few days left. The ritual starts on the last day. The knight lays down his armor and proceeds to lie in bed or on the ground when he is out in the field. He crosses his arms over his chest, turns his head to the East, and starts to pray. Next, he recollects the memory of persons and things dear to him and reviews his life. Roland, for example, thought of the lands he had conquered, his beloved France, his ancestors, and Charlemagne, his lord and educator. After these reminiscences the knight directs himself to his comrades. He asks them forgiveness for whatever wrong he may have done them, says farewell, and recommends them to God. Sometimes he requests to be buried at a particular spot. Then he recommends his soul to God, prays again, and dies. Immediately afterwards those present burst out into ritual moaning and teeth-grinding. For the rest, the course of events has been rather simple and self-evident.

Several elements in these models are important for our discussion. They demonstrate respectively the religious and the relatively unproblematic character of death. The motif of foresight, figuring in both models, is essential too. But we should never forget that they are ideal images. Ariès incorrectly takes the case of the knight for an entirely realistic description. To the contrary, no fear of death was expected from these valiant warriors, and the story is embellished with this in mind. In a similar vein, the saint was supposed to rejoice in joining his creator. Up to today saints have always been commemorated not on their earthly birthday but on the day they died, when they were "born into heaven."

Burial: The Origins of the Churchyard

After those ideal images of dying scenes we return to solid ground with a discussion of burial. The word, burial, can be used as the general term for the disposal of the body, since methods known in other cultures, such as cremation, were not customary in preindustrial Europe. But we should adhere to a distinction between churchyard, in its literal meaning, and the more general term of cemetery. That has to be explained.

A fundamental shift in the attitudes toward cemeteries and burial took place around 500. That was the principal reason to choose that year as our point of departure. Pagan Romans feared the dead and kept their bodies at a distance. In the urbanized Roman Empire cemeteries were situated outside inhabited areas. The inhabitants especially wanted to prevent the dead from returning to trouble the living. A change in the location of cemeteries marked the shift. It did not coincide with the spread of Christianity. The first Christians were buried next to their pagan townspeople, and when Christianity had become the dominant religion, graveyards remained outside the walls. Very quickly the desire to be buried in the vicinity of a saint became common. The grave of a famous martyr was a place of worship and a church was often built around it. When the cult persisted, it led to the construction of more buildings, so that these places eventually lay within the town's orbit. That gave rise to a conflict. Burial next to a saint or in the church where his bones rested henceforth meant a burial within the inhabited area, which was formally prohibited. The legend of Saint Vaast, a bishop of Arras who died in 540, illustrates the conflict's solution. When the bearers arrived to carry his bier outside town as required, the body felt so heavy that it could not be lifted. The canons saw this as a sign from God and Saint Vaast was buried in his own cathedral instead. The interpretation of the sign reveals a strong desire to bury the bishop in the church. The divine hint made it possible to ignore earthly laws, which were subsequently abolished. To be buried henceforth meant: to rest with the saints or at least in consecrated ground; therefore in one's own village or within the walls of one's own town. The churchyard had come into being.

The chronology of this shift is important for two reasons. First, it can be concluded that burial inside the walls was characteristic for preindustrial Europe, but not for every preindustrial society. The Romans were buried outside the walls. Second, the new custom did not coincide with the coming of Christianity. The early Christians conformed to Roman practice. The origins of the churchyard were rooted in the cult of saints. The Christianization of the population must have had an effect though, even though delayed. The graves of various heroes of pagan antiquity were places of worship too, in spite of the greater anxiety. This dedication to deceased "heroes" acquired a greater intensity in the early Christian period. With the emergence of the cult of saints, concentrated on relics, a special meaning was attached to the body. Ultimately, this gave rise to a specific familiarity with and a closeness to the places where the bodies of saints and the faithful in general rested.

Familiarity with cemeteries continued to be prevalent until the eighteenth century, so that it is one of the fundamental characteristics of the experience of death in this long period. Ariès speaks of an intermingling between the living and the dead. First, this remark has to be taken literally. Just as clerics sometimes travelled with the relics of saints, now and then the bones of ordinary believers might lie in the open. To make room for new graves, the old were dug up and the bones collected into charnel houses. Although these were often situated in the vaults of the church or chapel, they were accessible to the public. Not subterranean at all were the *ossuaria*: galleries along the walls of the churchyard where skulls and bones were placed in a decorative fashion. A visitor also might stumble upon graves which were not quite closed or reopened and see a body halfway in the process of decomposition. This was not at all a problem to the faithful. As long as the bones remained within the sacred ground, there were no complaints.

A second manifestation of familiarity with cemeteries was the use of the churchyard for secondary purposes. The church and its garden formed the center of social life in a village or parish. For a long time they were also sanctuaries where the secular authorities had to refrain from exercising their power. Inside, the dead as well as the living rested in peace. When the churchyard ceased to be a sanctuary, it maintained the character of a meeting place. Religious ceremonies for which the church itself was too small, such as large-scale processions or sermons with a wider audience, usually took place in the churchyard. Worldly activities were performed there too. Merchants came to negotiate their business and small traders had stalls to sell their goods. Agreements between villagers or neighbors, drawn up by a notary, were read aloud on Sundays after mass. Sometimes the communal oven or bakery was in the churchyard. People went there for a chat and occasionally it was the scene of a feast with songs and dances. It was a favorite spot for prostitutes too. During all these activities no one seems to have been troubled by the sight of graves and charnels and the smell of corpses.

A third and last manifestation of familiarity with cemeteries lay in the great interest shown by the living in the spot where their mortal remains would later come to rest. Those who had a higher status or more money, could count on a grave nearer to the sacred nucleus. An obvious hierarchy of prestige can be deduced from late medieval sources. The best and consequently the most expensive site was beneath the church's choir, close to the altar where the priest said mass. The chapel of the Holy Virgin, where her image stood, was second best. The images of other saints also lent prestige to the location of the grave, but they were somewhat less in demand. In a later period a spot right under the crucifix or beneath the family bench were favorite locations. This all refers to a burial within the church itself. A respected and wealthy parishioner only accepted a place in the yard when there was no other possibility. Usually this space had nothing but anonymous mass graves; the habit of marking individual graves originated in the early modern period. A voluntary choice for a place in the churchyard was an act of special humility. Christian doctrine, to be sure, recommended humility to everyone. The official position of the church has always been that a burial in the building itself ought to be an exception, reserved to bishops, very holy persons, and a few laymen such as the lord of the parish.

Acceptance of Death

Along with familiarity with cemeteries, a familiarity with dying prevailed. This is the second of the fundamental characteristics, or rather both can be combined into "familiarity with death." We must not view this familiarity in a too idyllic sense. It has already been mentioned that Ariès attributes too much realism to the romances of chivalry. He thinks that most people in this period thought of their own death with resignation, knowing no fear. He calls this "tamed death." Both Chaunu and Elias criticize him on this point. The first claims to know sufficient examples of anxiety from literature to be able to conclude that many people did not accept the end of their own life. He does concede that a relative indifference toward dying in general prevailed. Thus, tamed death primarily refers to the experience with the death of others, among whom the loved ones must not be included. Chaunu speaks of a "social familiarity." People assented to and accepted death as a social phenomenon, as a reality repeatedly observed in their environment.

Three more specific manifestations of familiarity with dying can be noted. The first is its ritual character, which is also manifest in the model of the knight. Although this was an ideal image, we can be certain that rituals played an important role in reality too. The next section discusses how the ritual of dying grew into an art in the seventeenth century. Ceremonies and ritual behavior generally, with various social events, were more prominent in preindustrial Europe than they are today. The dying ritual was one way to come to grips with the problem of death and thereby to neutralize it. This function of neutralization is also comprehended in the conception of death as a kind of sleep. Even today that idea persists in expressions like "may he rest in peace." The conception of death as sleep was linked to the idea of the nearness of the dead. The deceased ancestors of one's own village slept in the vicinity and sometimes it was possible to conjure up their spirit or to make contact with them. These notions had a pre-Christian origin, but Christian ideas corresponded with them at least until the twelfth century. The deceased embarked upon a long period of rest, waiting for the resurrection of the body and the last judgment. During this period their souls slept in the bosom of Abraham. Only very holy persons reached heaven in a straight line, and to be committed to hell directly was the fate of only a small number of very serious sinners. That was the opinion of Augustine, among others. Although he scornfully declared that he did not know where the bosom of Abraham might be, he confirmed that the souls of the deceased rested at a secret place while waiting for the last judgment.

The last manifestation of familiarity with dying, foresight, is the most intriguing one. It meant that people could prepare themselves for death. The idea that death sends a warning was not simply a question of magical beliefs: quite a few people must have been able to sense their approaching end through a routine observation of the daily facts of life. But this ability should not be exaggerated; it cannot be established how many people correctly knew of their passing in advance by this method. Certainly, foresight was desirable. We know this, because numerous sources reveal that the opposite, unforeseen or sudden death, was considered as horrible or even shameful well into the eighteenth century. Nothing better illustrates the contrast between reflections about death then and now. Today it is the wish of many, when their end has to come, that it do so unexpectedly and without pain, preferably when they are asleep. Before the eighteenth century this was a dreadful thought. Sudden death knows neither ritual nor witnesses, and it is just as infamous as that of a hanged person or a vagabond found along the road (although an execution, as explained in chapter 7, certainly is a public and ceremonial event). In all probability, a sudden death is a sign of God's anger.

Indeed, the importance attached to foresight and the infamy of sudden death also have a religious component. This becomes clear when we consider Luther's demise in 1546. The great reformer appears to have died while asleep, but the sources are unequivocal. Whatever was the case, the rumor went "that Luther had been found dead in his bed," without having had the opportunity to say farewell to his loyal followers. They thought it necessary to contradict these rumors or at least to give them a finer shade of meaning. Cölius explained that his teacher had been properly ready for death. He had incessantly thought about it during his last year, referring to it in sermons, conversation, and writing. This defense failed to impress his Catholic adversaries, who claimed that the devil had taken him away. In 1568 it was even said for the first time that Luther had hanged himself. The eagerness with which this theme was exploited for religious propaganda reveals the idea behind it: whoever dies suddenly is unprepared for a Christian death and hence is probably doomed. The populace understood this argument very well, but it did not belong to official theology. As late as 1701 the Lutheran minister Haas attacked it. Some people are just summoned by God at once, he stated.

The last of the fundamental characteristics is death's public character. For a long time, dying took place openly. This held true first of all for the unnatural or uncommon deaths which receive less emphasis at the present time: execution; perishing in battle or pillage; the slow death of the poor in hospitals; mass mortality during epidemics (more about this in the next section). But openness equally characterized natural death. The dying ritual ought to take place in the presence of family and friends. This was another reason why it was dreadful to die suddenly, since it left them no time to assemble. A crowd around the deceased was common in higher as well as lower circles. In villages and neighborhoods this was one more task for the community. Relatives and neighbors went to the home of the dying person to say good-bye and to be present at the ceremony. In larger cities it was even customary for passers-by to join a priest, as he carried the *viaticum* (the host for the last Communion), and accompany him into the house of the dying person. Villagers and neighbors watched over the body lying in state. It is unlikely that strangers went into the house at the death of an aristocrat or a bourgeois, but all who lived there, domestic servants included, were present at the moment of death. The death of Françoise de Montespan, former mistress of Louis XIV, in 1707 provides an example. In his memoirs Saint-Simon relates how afraid she was of dying alone. She lay in her bed with the bed curtains open so that she could see the room full of burning candles. A few women watched over her in order to call upon the others in time. Every two minutes she shook them awake: "You should chat or eat or no matter what, but not doze off." But on May 27 Madame de Montespan felt she would really die and her anxiety was gone. She had all her servants, even the lowest, called to her bed and asked their forgiveness. She spent her last moments in the midst of this gathering, thinking of eternity and contemplating her sinful state but yet consoled by confidence in God's mercy.

Several authors relate the fundamental characteristics, openness and social familiarity, to the demographic realities of the age. This is not the place to present series of mortality figures; what matters is that people died in widely varying stages of life, so that an individual, long before he might reach old age, was more frequently and intensely confronted with the death of those he knew than is the case today. Death was omnipresent. Still, we should beware of a circuitous argument. To a large extent, the omnipresence of death was a result of its public character. The equanimity with which death was approached and represented was primarily a manifestation of a particular mentality, and it was linked to the openness also prevailing in other spheres.

The Magic Universe

Let us put the fundamental characteristics in a still broader cultural context. Two elements are picked from that context subsequently: death's ties to the magic universe and the conceptions of the hereafter.

Chapter 3 discussed how the cluster of magical beliefs and customs which belonged to the lesser tradition had the function of ordering and giving meaning to the entire cosmos. Death found a place inside this cosmic awareness as well. In the magic universe a deceased's fate could be either of two opposites. No doubt the majority of the dead were just asleep: a popular notion which was in line with official Christian doctrine for a long time. No rest was granted, according to magical beliefs, to those who had died prematurely. Murder, a fatal accident, execution, or being slain by an enemy meant that one's spirit was doomed to roam. Nocturnal travelers in classical Greece took a detour to avoid a cemetery for fear of the prematurely dead who haunted the vicinity of their graves. At the site of a battle at night the Greeks often saw a phalanx of ghosts. In preindustrial Europe the unquiet dead took the shape of the wandering army, already discussed. The idea that some of the dead continue to roam around among the living was familiar to Christian writers too, but they were inclined to attribute this activity not to the prematurely dead but to sinners, whose souls haunted the places where they had committed their evil deeds.

A second magical belief concerned the possibility of contact between the dead and the living. This could be mediated by special persons who had the gift of communicating with the world of the dead, as the Friulian benandanti had. Female benandanti were capable of seeing how one's grandmother or brother fared in the beyond, undoubtedly meeting a deeply felt need of the relatives. Even in our time some people attempt to establish such contact through a medium. It requires no special gift to see a dead person when he temporarily returns among the living of his own accord. In early preindustrial Europe this happened frequently. By definition, ghosts were distinct from the wandering army; they interrupted their sleep for a short while, usually to give a warning to those to whom they appeared. This magical belief also was shared by clerical authors for a long time. Bishop Thietmar of Merseburg (about 1000) even considered such ghosts as proof of the afterlife; he expounded the argument to the infidel Slavs. Before him Gregory the Great told how the body of a notorious sinner, who had managed to obtain a burial in the cathedral by bribing the bishop, desecrated the church. One of the martyrs who rested there appeared to the bishop at night, demanding the removal of "this stinking flesh" within thirty days. The bishop refused and, when a month had passed, he himself died.

A few concrete practices make up the third example of death's link with the magic universe. These practices usually encountered quick opposition from church leaders. In a future discussion we will see how clerics in the later Middle Ages attempted to push aside the mourning chant as a funeral rite. Gifts like meat, cheese, bread, fruit, or cakes to bodies lying in state were considered pagan as well. Provincial councils in France issued prohibitions of such customs as late as the sixteenth century. A remarkable phenomenon is the viaticum. Pagan Romans used this word for the coin laid under the deceased's tongue to pay for the journey to the underworld. Christian Romans maintained the custom but placed a host under the tongue instead. This is again an example of an integration of Christian rites into the magic universe. But church leaders did not accept the custom. It was proper when a person who was still alive received the communion at his deathbed, but it was a pagan superstition if presented after he had passed away. Local councils between 400 and 600 forbade putting the host into the mouth of the dead or laying it in the grave. In the later Middle Ages presenting the communion to the dying became a regular rite and the host, significantly, retained the name of viaticum.

Finally, attention has to be paid to another theme also discussed in chapter 3. We saw how, within preindustrial popular culture, various forms of fear could be neutralized by humor and merriment. This was also the case with respect to death. The anxiety raised by the demise of a member of the village or neighborhood community was smothered in merry rituals. Among some non-Western nations and with us today mirth sets in after the funeral, but in preindustrial Europe the wake was the principal scene of joy and play. Often the community's adolescents watched over the body lying in state. They danced, played cards, performed a pantomime or had a mock fight in which one of them "died." And there was constant drinking; what was drunk depended on the custom of the country. In England, where wakes remained customary into the seventeenth century, those watching sometimes played a game in which they beat each other's bare buttocks. As a rule clerics disapproved of the wake. Around 900 Regino of Prüm condemned watchers who danced, jumped, drank, or sang filthy songs.

These customs should in no way be seen as showing a lack of respect for the dead. The disgusted clerics may have treated them as such, but to the participants they were meaningful, neutralizing their subconscious fears. The wake's ritual character was incompatible with degeneration into mockery or cynicism. Note that the corpse itself was left in peace. When the rule was infringed, such lack of respect was condemned. Klaas Slot, a resident of Haarlem, shocked those present when he tried to pour beer into the mouth of his own dead mother. When Klaas was arrested in 1613 for a tavern brawl, this deed, "going against all honor and human fear," was added to the charges against him.

The Hereafter

Although the dying persons we have met up to now acted as pious Christians, the priest remained in the background even at the deathbed of saints. There was little talk of an image of the afterlife. This is one reason why Ariès thinks that "tamed death" was rooted in pre-Christian times. The acceptance of death presumably went back to the Stone Age, while prayers and pious wishes were "natural" acts rather than imposed rites. This statement should be qualified. Certainly Christianity is more than just the clergy, and religion is more than Christianity alone. In all preindustrial societies, from the Andes to the Yellow River, religious feelings and conceptions were prevalent. An image of the hereafter formed an essential part of all those creeds. Several authors even consider this the principal function of religion. The problem of every individual's mortality is solved by promising the faithful a life after death. Whether or not this is indeed the primary function of religion, it is undeniable that conceptions of the hereafter must have considerably influenced the experience of death. The prevalent familiarity with death was also a consequence of the firm belief in an existence prolonged after one's earthly life. The views of this existence changed over time.

In this connection, two medieval developments are important: the clericalization of the dying process and the emergence of the theological doctrine of purgatory. The Christian aspect of the experience of death from the fifth century cannot be doubted. The attitudes toward burial unambiguously testify to it. But originally clerics played a subordinate role in the ceremony of dying. Priests offered absolution for one's sins, but otherwise remained in the background. This was plain in the two ideal models. Worldly rituals, such as excessive lamenting and expressions of grief, were more prominent than ecclesiastical ceremonies. Professional mourners were sometimes hired for them. In medieval England the relatives viewed this as the essential ritual rather than the actual interment. When the burial finally came, the mourners usually had left for home. In the course of the twelfth and thirteenth centuries, however, the clergy's passivity disappeared so that the ceremony acquired a more ecclesiastical character. Priests prayed at the deathbed and provided the sick person with the sacrament of extreme unction. Often the deceased lay in state in the church. A priest also now conducted the funeral, in which the obsequies or requiem mass became the essential part. Those who wished could obtain a solemn obsequies at which the *Dies Irae*, composed in this period, was sung. Thus the position of clerics as exclusive mediators between God and the people was reinforced. They were particularly intent on mediating at the crucial moment of transition from earthly life to eternity.

The other development took place in the same period. The concept of purgatory as a distinct locality in the hereafter appeared in theological writing in the twelfth century. The elaboration of this doctrine has various implications, but it is only those relevant to the experience of death which concern us here. In many cultures a dualistic image of the hereafter prevails. Two worlds are usually distinguished there, the one somber and full of torments, the other a comfortable environment. The Romans contrasted the Hades with the Elysian fields and the Germanic tribes knew Valhalla along with a dark underworld where the goddess Hel reigned. The quality of one's earthly life almost always determined in which of the two spheres of the hereafter one would end. The Germanic Valhalla was especially reserved for heroes slain in battle. During the first millennium of its existence Christianity too knew a dualistic system. The good went to heaven and the bad to hell;

essentially, there was nothing else. Heaven was less connected to warfare than in other religions, although as a rule a martyr's death earned the sufferer a free ticket to eternal bliss. Since death in a crusade was considered equal to martyrdom, the crusaders' heaven came near to the Valhalla of Germanic warriors, while the crusade became the equivalent of the enemy's holy war.

The early Christian dualism had two important aspects. First, the assignment to heaven or hell was irrevocable. As soon as one was doomed or chosen, no power whatsoever could alter this; any border-crossing from one sphere of the hereafter to another was precluded. This irrevocable decision, however, was usually postponed; this was the second important aspect. Early Christian theologians put an emphasis on the Last Judgment. After the Second Coming, at the end of time, all bodies were to rise again and the just would be separated from the sinners by God all at the same time. Some holy people possibly entered heaven directly after death and a few very heavy sinners were flung into hell immediately, but these were exceptions. The majority of the faithful had to wait a while. In the intervening period, as pictured by writers and in the visual arts, their souls rested in the *refrigerium* or in the bosom of Abraham.

In Le Goff's analysis a few intermediate stations mark the road to the emergence of purgatory. The custom of praying for the dead arose as early as the third century, but it was not linked to the image of a place where this prayer could be effective. The introduction of the celebration of All Soul's Day, November 2, in the eleventh century was another station. In the second half of the twelfth century, then, the notion of purgatory as a distinct, third sphere in the hereafter made its appearance. It served to chastise the souls of those who were not doomed but did not yet deserve heaven. As a consequence of this theological shift, the two aspects of the dualistic system were no longer valid. The Last Judgment admittedly was not discarded by theologians, but it received less emphasis. The preliminary balance sheet, drawn up directly after one's demise, became more important. At that moment, God determined who sinned so heavily that they were cast into hell at once, who were the lesser sinners spending a term in purgatory before they deserved heaven, and how long this period lasted. In the second place, the degree of irrevocability of a stay in one of the spheres of the hereafter had become smaller. When they had paid their penalty in purgatory, souls crossed the border to heaven. More important still, God's sentence with respect to the term of a stay in purgatory was not irrevocable. The living were able to influence it as they prayed for an alleviation of punishment. That was the crucial

The gallows-field of Amsterdam.
Drawing by G. Lamberks, c. 1790. (Gemeentearchief Amsterdam)

Top left: Burial of the bull at Beutelsbach, 1796.
(Württemberg Landesstelle für Volkeskunde, Stuttgart)

Flying witches transformed into animals.
(From Ulrich Molitor's demonology, 1489)

Bottom left: Adultery.
From *The Ship of Fools* by Sebastian Brant, Basel, 1494)

The replica at Heemstede of Rousseau's tomb.
(Drawing by F. A. Milatz, 1804)

consequence of the theology of purgatory for the experience of death. Those left behind could do something for the deceased.

The notion of purgatory was developed by learned theologians. But the shift it testified to was the product of interaction between popular and elite culture. Praying for the dead had been a regular activity of common believers long before the twelfth century. The intermediate stations just mentioned were partly a reflection of the populace's vague ideas about a world of the dead, whether or not it was a place of purification by fire. The official theological conception had to be disseminated among lay people in turn. Ariès claims that a concern for the souls in purgatory was not implanted in the minds of the faithful until the seventeenth century, but this is probably true only for a few peripheral areas. At the beginning of that century, for example, the Bretons identified the figure of death with the devil, saying that only heaven or hell awaited people after their earthly life. For other French regions Le Goff and Chiffoleau demonstrate that a concern for the souls in purgatory can be found among broad groups as early as the fourteenth century. The new theological image of the hereafter did not simply imply a greater conformity to popular conceptions of death. The idea of death as a sort of sleep was a hallmark of popular culture and was incompatible with the shift from last to first judgment. The deceased have few chances to sleep in the tripartite hereafter; in purgatory their souls are tormented. It cannot be a coincidence that the figure of Abraham practically disappears from the visual arts after 1300. The thesis of conformity is valid to the extent that families and communities imagined a close tie linking them to their own dead. The intercession of the living for the benefit of the souls in purgatory cemented that tie.

Purgatory's influence upon the prevalent familiarity with death must have been ambiguous too. On the one hand, it made death more problematic. Instead of sinking into an eternal sleep, dying persons now faced an immediate judgment whose outcome was uncertain. On the other hand, the deceased now had to be outrageous sinners to go to hell, while they could count on the help of their loved ones in purgatory. That may have made dying easier. The clergy, finally, was endowed with still more power by purgatory. The prayer of a monk or a chaplain was more effective than a laic's to get a soul out of that place. Knowing this, the relatives sought clerical assistance, which often involved payments. The influence of the clergy upon God's punishing hand was soon considered to be very large indeed. In 1300 Pope Boniface VIII promulgated the first indulgence for all pilgrims to Rome that year, including those whose fate it was to perish on their way. It meant that the pope could decree of his own authority that a soul was to leave purgatory. Within two centuries indulgences had become extremely common. This merchandizing of the hereafter was one of the practices which caused Luther to turn against Rome. The Protestants would abolish purgatory again.

Around A.D. 1300 an experience of death characterized by familiarity and openness still prevailed. In addition, this experience was strongly interwoven with a religious view of the world. The main reason for not including the religious aspect among the fundamental characteristics is that it continued to be prominent in the industrial period.

Exuberance, Fear, and Resignation

Various developments put their mark on the experience of death from the fourteenth to the beginning of the eighteenth century. In this period the fundamental characteristics discussed in the previous section retained their validity. Although some changes can be viewed as an encroachment upon them, others made them appear more pronounced. In the midst of the age the experience of death was split into Protestant and Catholic versions.

The Black Death

This period opened with plague. The history of mentalities knows few examples of a short-term event with far-reaching and persistent consequences but this is one. The name Black Death was not conferred by contemporaries, but for centuries it has been the common term to denote the first of the great epidemics ravaging Europe after a relatively tranquil period of about six hundred years. Plague broke out in 1346 among the troops of a Mongol prince besieging the port town of Caffa in the Crimea. It forced him to withdraw, but not before the infection had passed the city gates. From Caffa the disease quickly followed commercial routes to the Mediterranean and northern Europe. In 1347 it reached Messina and Marseille; in 1348 Venice, Barcelona, and Paris; the next year Vienna, Utrecht, and London; in 1350 Copenhagen and Stockholm. Then it was over. A few towns and regions were spared, in others some 60 to 70 percent of the population perished. Specialists estimate that the Black Death took the life of a third of the population of Europe as a whole. It struck not only massively but also quickly. Infection with the plague led to death within a few days, sometimes within a few hours, after the first symptoms appeared. Once a person was infected, the chances of survival were almost zero.

The Black Death had repercussions everywhere, including the economic sphere, but we must restrict ourselves to the mental consequences. The appearance of the flagellants was one of the most remarkable reactions. Believers who voluntarily subjected themselves to a flogging for pious motives had been seen before, but the "brotherhood of the cross," founded in 1348, perfected this into a method. The majority of the brethren came from Germany and the Netherlands, but they travelled through much of Europe. The movement based itself on a letter, delivered at Jerusalem by an angel in 1343, in which God declared that he would visit plague upon humankind as a punishment for its sins. To placate God the brethren went from town to town in a long row of two by two. The master and two lieutenants marched ahead, followed by the ordinary crew and, finally, a number of women (who were not allowed to take part in the ceremony, however). They wore dark clothes with red crosses at the front and back and on their caps. During their march they kept silent, except for singing an occasional hymn. When they reached a town or village, they usually went to the market square where they threw themselves to the ground. First, the master beat several sinners who were adulterers and perjurers or who had broken the brotherhood's rules. Then came the climax. The brethren flogged themselves with leather whips into which sharp iron pins were set. They rhythmically beat their back and chests, repeatedly threw themselves to the ground, and went into a deeper trance as the blood flowed more copiously. Meanwhile they called upon everyone to do penance for their sins, imploring God's mercy. Some flagellants collapsed. The audience, assembled in large numbers, wept or encouraged the brethren to chastise themselves more intensely still.

The flagellant movement fell victim to its success. Although uncertainty remains as to the actual beliefs of the brethren, it is unmistakable that they very quickly ceased to consider themselves merely humble penitents but acted as a band of pure and chosen people. At the end of 1349 when they attacked the church hierarchy the pope condemned them as heretics. Since the plague was also fading, the movement disappeared like snow under the sun. The flagellants are a perfect illustration of the mentality of the age. Religion was expressed more exuberantly than it is today and was integrated into daily experience; a mentality we can still meet in some Islamic countries. The ambivalence with regard to death and violence is remarkable too. On the one hand, epidemic mortality caused intense weeping and teeth-grinding, while the conclusion that it was God's punishment for the sins of humankind was taken for granted. On the other hand, this idea led some people to actions that led to suffering or even death, amid the approval of a majority of the population. It was a life in extremes.

Understandably, the plague of 1346–1350 affected the experience of death. No familiarity was possible during those years. Mortality's massiveness made the indifference toward the death of others disappear, while as everybody realized they had a good chance of being infected themselves individual anxieties grew more intense. We have come upon a major exception to the fundamental characteristics discussed in the previous section. Although the omnipresence of death was related to the social familiarity with it, the relationship was reversed as mortality figures rose too high. Lebrun states that a mortality of 5 to 6 percent in a year constituted the critical level above which acquiescence gave way to collective anxiety. That level, to be sure, was regularly reached before the years 1346–1350. Next to epidemics, famines were a second cause of possible mass mortality. Subsistence crises of the "ancient type," as economic historians call them, ravaged Europe from time out of memory until the seventeenth century. Collective anxiety prevailed in both situations; during epidemics, however, it was more acute and widespread, if only because everyone, rich and poor, was in danger.

Reactions to the coming of the plague varied. In a world of insufficient medical knowledge most people felt powerless. Many fled their town in panic in the hope that at some remote spot the danger would pass them by. When rumors about the coming of the plague were heard in Angers in 1626 and again in 1631, the magistrates quit the affairs of government, merchants left their goods, and mendicant monks fled their monasteries. Another type of reaction, probably among those who possessed too little to take refuge in a rural estate but still had something to spend, sprang from the thought of "it's all over anyway." In the face of death these people indulged in feasts and drinking orgies; a scene magnificently represented in Werner Herzog's film *Nosferatu*. The opposite attitude was manifested by those who, like the flagellants but mostly in a less fanatical manner, stressed humility and expiation. A threatening type of reaction, finally, was the search for scapegoats. Even before the Black Death lepers were sometimes suspected of a deliberate desire to infect the healthy out of jealousy. In a later period, the belief that a group of conspirators, called *en-graisseurs*, spread an extract of the plague substance was widespread, notably in Savoy and the Genevan area. During the years 1346–1350 the Jews in particular were thought to be guilty and a number of them died at the stake.

Not all reactions resulted from powerlessness. In later centuries the authorities frequently tried to avert the spread of plague, especially through quarantine measures. Conflicts sometimes arose as a pragmatic mentality collided with a traditionally religious one. Cipolla describes one such conflict in the Tuscan village of Monte Lupo in 1630–1631, where one party put its trust in processions in order to placate God and the other in observance of the rules of quarantine. Among the clergy in seventeenth-century Italy, to be sure, there were also persons who favored a medical approach to the problem.

The Macabre

Skeletons, bones, and other realistic representations of death and the corpse became very common in the art of the fourteenth century. These motifs are collectively referred to as "the macabre," after the *danse macabre* or dance of death. A relationship with the coming of the plague is easily claimed, but there is disagreement about its precise nature. Macabre motifs appeared as early as the first half of the fourteenth century; the danse macabre was even prefigured in the thirteenth century in poems and on frescoes by the motif of a confrontation between the living and the dead. The emergence of the macabre may be related to the spread of the notion of purgatory. The original spelling was *macabree*, which seems to refer to the Maccabees of the Old Testament, whose prayers for the dead were taken as proof for the existence of purgatory. On the other hand, the word *macabree* was not linked to the death dance until the end of the fourteenth century. Most authors agree, therefore, that the plague of 1346–1350 at least had a catalytic effect on the breakthrough of the macabre. Those motifs became considerably more frequent after it.

The macabre reinforced the open and common nature of death. The theme's religious implications can be evaluated in two contrasting ways. For one thing, it expressed the view that the body is no more than a sack of filth which does not reveal its true nature until it is partly or entirely decomposed. On a fifteenth-century drawing the soul of a pilgrim who has just perished speaks to his corpse: "Mischievous body, which is so vile, stinking and dirty, meat for worms, where is your pride and your courage now?" On the other hand, the

macabre draws attention to the body and hence away from the hereafter and the fate of the soul, which is what really matters. The representation of a skeleton can be interpreted as a cry of sorrow over the
body's transitoriness. This sorrow was not entirely proper from a theological point of view, since the just would receive a glorified body after
the Last Judgment. When we follow this interpretation, the macabre
gave expression to the breakthrough of a more secular mentality.

The living also figure in the death dances as they did in the
thirteenth-century predecessors, but they are now doubles who accompany their own skeleton and whose presence only serves to represent its earthly state. The theme, then, is extremely earthly; the danse
macabre serves as a social satire. All social groups figure in the dance,
whose lesson is that death makes everyone equal again. Nobles will
lose their pride and magistrates their sternness, and usurers cannot
take with them the money they have extorted. As well as the split between rich and poor, humankind is divided along other lines. Death's
scythe hits the fat and skinny, the tall and the short, the sick, of course,
but also those apparently healthy. Death seizes grey-haired persons
but also couples in love and whores. Women participate in the dance
in Germany but not in France, although separate *danses macabres des
femmes* appear there after 1500. After the Christians have passed, a
Jew or a Turk is sometimes represented at the end of the procession. To
conclude, the danse macabre is not about death but about society on
earth. It is significant nonetheless that death could become a favorite
theme for satire. In the eighteenth century the elites no longer appreciated it, so that the dances then belonged only to popular culture.
French nobles and priests showed their resentment of these "Gothic
prints" after 1750.

The death dance is not the only macabre motif. The lifeless body
appears in the visual arts in various forms and situations. Originally,
the semidecomposed corpse was represented most frequently; its place
was taken later by the "dry skeleton." The macabre figured especially in
tomb architecture and allegorical painting. Allegories pointed to the
contrast between beauty and decay, for example, as in Hans Baldung
Grien's *Death and the Young Maiden*. A still more frequent motif was
the triumph of death, painted by Breugel and others. This motif is quite
threatening compared to the danse macabre. Death carries arms and
drives a chariot drawn by oxen. He rages like a blind man, sparing no
one, and his route is marked by every possible form of dying. The personification of death was especially popular in Italy, where the danse
macabre hardly spread. In Italian literature, however, the theme of the
decomposition of the body was prominent. Thus, the various macabre

motifs reflect geographic differences, but the mentality expressed in the macabre was shared by most Europeans.

The Art of Dying

From dying in the arts we come to the art of dying. This does not refer primarily to a splendid performance, although seventeenth-century spectators at the deathbed could appreciate it, but to the technique of passing away in a dignified and Christian fashion. This technique could be learned during one's lifetime from a genre of books usually called by the Latin name of *ars moriendi*. The *artes moriendi* appeared after the middle of the fifteenth century, its chronology unrelated to any change in the reflections about death but simply following from the invention of the art of printing. One art stimulated the other. The earliest representatives of the genre in manuscript form date back to around 1400. Artes moriendi could be understood by everyone, including illiterates. In popular versions there were illustrations for each page of text.

These illustrations are as interesting as the written words. They picture the process of dying as a temptation at the moment when the devil has his last chance to gain the upper hand. With the assistance of a priest and his loved ones, the dying person fights a spiritual battle against Satan. Others continue this battle after the moment of passing. The standard representation of that moment shows the soul as a little man, leaving the body with the last breath. Angels and demons struggle for the soul, which is taken by the winners to purgatory or hell, as the case may be. Heaven of course is further away, but it can be reached eventually by way of purgatory. The latter place, therefore, was infrequently used by preachers to frighten their audience. Hell remained the most suitable subject in this respect. Several historians argue that it is incorrect to attribute the function of neutralizing the fear of death to religion, since clerics put the fear of damnation in its place. Sermons about hell, however, were aimed at the living. They served to restrain them from sinful acts, just as the executions ordered by the secular authorities were to deter them from committing crimes. The artes moriendi offered everyone an opportunity to learn how to prepare for death with reassurance.

The text of the artes moriendi usually concentrated on the approaching end, the ceremony proper, and the mistakes which might be made in both. The well prepared Christian, according to *The Book of the Craft of Dying* of 1490, looks forward to death as a friend:

To con to die is to have an heart and a soul every ready up to Godward, that when-that-ever death come, he may be found all ready; withouten any retraction receive him, as a man would receive his well-beloved and trusty friend and fellow, that he had long abideth and looked after.

Thus, the art of dying actually is the art of living. The artes moriendi essentially convey a simple religious message: Whoever lives well and follows God has no need to be afraid to die. This is the positive counterpart of the sermons about hell and damnation aimed at sinners. The message is so self-evident that the lesson can also be reversed, as in "The Tour of all Toures," originating from the same period:

Learn to die and thou shalt con to live, for there shall none con to live that hath not learned to die . . . . If thou wilt live freely learn to die wilfully.

These English examples are a representative illustration of the genre, which became widespread throughout Europe. For France, its popularity has been investigated quantitatively. When we consider the number of editions as a percentage of the total stock of religious literature, the artes moriendi had two peak periods: at the end of the fifteenth century and in the course of the seventeenth. In between, as far as religion was concerned, the French were occupied with questions of humanism and reform.

The Poor

At this point, it is worthwhile to pause and ask if we cling possibly too much to ideal images. The availability of a literature of consolation, as has been said, certainly did not prevent individual people from dreading the end of their life. But another problem calls for attention: what were the social groups in which the dying were able to arrange for a beautiful death according to the ideal formula? More research is needed to establish this, but there can be little doubt that burial and dying among the very poor were not quite so ceremonial and honorable, certainly not as the process of urbanization progressed. For one thing, the great plague epidemics proved this. The majority of poor victims were buried without further ado in a plague cemetery. The survivors kept their distance, justifying themselves with the thought that, since the plague was God's punishment, the victims must have had moral shortcomings.

However, the poor were also underprivileged in times of average mortality. We should rather speak of the poor and the suffering together, a group including in the first place executed criminals and suicides, whom it was forbidden to bury in sacred ground. German ordinances, from before as well as after the Reformation, ordered their interment outside the town "in some field." This measure applied not only to suicides and criminals but also to persons with an infamous occupation or status, such as skinners, street singers, bath keepers, executioners, and gypsies. Even young mothers who had died in childbirth might be included in this group. Their infamous departure from this world was called an ass's funeral, a term already used by Burkhard of Worms in the eleventh century. The ass's funeral remained customary until the seventeenth century; afterwards the authorities gradually adopted the practice of designating special cemeteries. In addition, the Germans had the funeral of the poor in sacred ground but paid by the charity board or the government. This too was considered less honorable, and anyone able to saved money for a decent burial. It was a persistent popular belief that those whose burials were paid from the poor box would return as ghosts. In France an infamous funeral was the fate of non-Catholics in particular if they were poor. When a vagabond had died, a priest was called to look for signs of Catholicity like a rosary or a pious booklet. If these could not be found, the unlucky one was buried in unconsecrated ground just to be sure, since otherwise his corpse might defile the churchyard. The poor in England, especially in the towns, could not always obtain a decent funeral either. In her book on the English situation Gittings notes still another category of the suffering: stillborn children. They were viewed as hardly human. A passage in the seventeenth-century oath of midwives obliged the jurors to see to it that stillborn children were interred at a quiet spot so that no dog could reach them.

The underprivileged position of the poor persisted until the end of the preindustrial period and even later. Richard Cobb has written a short book based on the reports about corpses found in the Seine during the years 1795–1801. It is called *Death in Paris*, possibly to remind us of Thomas Mann and Luchino Visconti, but the title is also identical to Chaunu's book which appeared at the same time. Cobb's dead were the social opposites of Chaunu's dead. They were suicides or victims of accidental drowning but first of all were poor. The bodies of the drowned from richer circles were regularly picked up by a relative for a paid funeral, which kept them out of the records. Many of the poor had lived in lodgings without a lock, with only a bed that was often rented to a night worker during the daytime. Sometimes people were pulled out of the Seine wearing three pairs of pants and several shirts in July. They simply had all their possessions with them. If no one else died without paying heed to the customary ceremonial, these "silent dead" did.

The infamous demise of the very poor was an encouragement to those who were just above that line, artisans and farm workers with a fixed residence, to do better themselves. There can be no doubt that the desire in particular for a well organized funeral was harbored by broad groups in society. One of the causes of the so-called Undertakers Revolt in Amsterdam in 1696 was the people's fear that a newly instituted tax would put a decent funeral outside the reach of the vast majority. Guild rules in Dutch cities usually included the obligation to comfort dying members and to be present at their funeral. Elsewhere, notably in the Romance countries, special brotherhoods were established to share the burden. In Provence and the Avignon region they existed as early as the twelfth century, but the greatest wave of foundations dates from the fourteenth century, another result of the Black Death. In France the members were called *agonisants* or *pénitents*. In addition to a financial aspect, these brotherhoods had a markedly religious character. When a member died in insolvency, his funeral was of course paid from the common box, but money was also furnished in order to have masses said for the salvation of his soul. In addition, everyone who joined made a vow to pray in church during a member's dying hour. The word, brotherhood, indicates that membership was restricted to men. In southern France women had the alternative of joining "third orders," lay societies associated with a monastic order, but boasting considerably fewer members than the pénitents. Among the latter, criminals could also be found. On the Spanish galley fleet a distinct brotherhood united the guards and the Christian oarsmen, to assure both groups of a decent burial.

The living poor had a special relationship to the funerals of the rich, at least in Catholic countries. Since the emergence of purgatory the opinion prevailed that the prayers and tears of the poor in particular softened the heart of God and, consequently, got a soul out of its place of punishment more quickly. They were, therefore, welcomed to the funeral procession. It also served the soul of the deceased well if he had reserved a portion of the heritage as a charitable gift to these poor people, which also served an as incentive for them to show up. In Paris they received five sous each or gifts in kind. The amounts given to the poor were often specified by testament. In Aix-en-Provence the percentage of testators who included such a clause increased from 26 to 45 in the second half of the sixteenth century. For Provence as a whole this percentage was still high at the beginning of the eighteenth century. Testators requested, for example, that the administrators of the hospital join the funeral procession together with the poor they cared for: all of them, or twelve in number like the apostles.

Baroque Death

This theme leads us back to the upper and middle classes. A few French historians gave the name of baroque death to the "classic" experience of death from the end of the sixteenth to the beginning of the eighteenth century, just preceding the first signs of concealment. This theme has been investigated most thoroughly in France, so that a warning is in order: baroque death may have been most typical of the French situation and, in any case, it was primarily at home in the Catholic parts of Europe. Many of its elements are directly related to purgatory. The general characteristics discussed in the previous section remained valid of course.

The word, baroque, comes from art history. It refers to a period when the visual arts were characterized by immense splendor, pompous ornaments, and external forms, as in Rubens's cherubim and the ostentatious splendor at the court of Louis XIV. In religious art, baroque forms were well suited to express the triumphal feeling of the Counter Reformation. With respect to death, then, the baroque meant exuberant and external piety, theatrical ceremonial and majestic funerals. Two themes are deserving of further discussion: burial and the concern for one's own salvation.

With respect to the latter theme in particular, testaments constitute the preferred source. This may seem strange. Is not a testament an economic document? Within early modern Catholicism, however, this was only partly true. Testaments were also pious documents in which a person settled all his affairs, material and immaterial, during his lifetime with a view on a well prepared departure for the hereafter. This function of the testament dates from the twelfth century when the clericalization of dying set in. Originally, priests often wrote down testaments, but from the sixteenth century this became the exclusive business of notaries.

Thus, taking care of one's own salvation began with the drawing up of a testament. The notary knew what was expected. He opened with the standard phrase about the certainty of death and the uncertainty of the moment when, which prompted the testator to settle his affairs. As the notary proceeded, other pious exclamations were inserted. In Chaunu's Parisian study these phrases are quantified, which proves that the sky is the limit for computerization even in the history of mentalities. The frequency of all nouns, adjectives, and verbs was calculated and tabulated, producing what looked like hitparades. In the period 1600–1650 *Dieu* leads the chart of the nouns with 560, followed by *Paradis* (436), and *Ame* (431). The top forty of the period 1650–1700 have the same chart leader, but the fast-rising *Fils* is second, having nearly caught up with *God*. Chaunu adorns these figures with interpretative comments, which we will leave for what they are.

In addition to pious exclamations, the testator took care of his own salvation more concretely. He indicated the charitable gifts he intended to make not only directly to the poor but also to religious and lay institutions. Those who had found a shelter in them were to pray for their benefactor. Next, the testator summed up various obligations to those staying behind: the number of masses to be said for the salvation of his soul after his death, the number of invitations for the funeral, and even the number of candles burning beside his bier. This concern was expressed likewise by testatrices; in Provence women even demanded 10 percent more masses. The connection of these requests with the belief in purgatory and the intercession of the living on behalf of the dead is plain. This intercession was literally contracted for.

The baroque form of the dying ritual can also be reconstructed from testaments, supplemented by *artes moriendi* and iconographic sources. The dying person lay in bed with the usual kin, servants, and passers-by assembled around him. He addressed himself to those present with an admonition, praising the solidarity and mutual love among Christian relatives. Sometimes he confessed his sins in front of everyone; in any case, the priest arrived to provide him with the last sacrament. He presented the host, saying, "Brother, accept the viaticum consisting of the body of our lord Jesus Christ, which will protect you from the evil foe and accompany you into eternal life." Next, he offered extreme unction, recited the passion of Christ and placed a crucifix before the dying person, who by then was half conscious. During all this, the physician discretely remained in the background; his presence merely confirmed that death was drawing near. Finally, the dying person was made to hold a blessed candle and breathed his last.

Baroque funerals were characterized by external splendor and ostentatiousness. It was for everyone to see. As has been explained, a decent funeral was valued among the lower classes too. A richer person, who could afford a more beautiful ceremony, was obliged to have one by his rank. In Anjou in 1700 there were seven rate groups for burial. In this respect, the adage that death makes everyone equal lost its credibility. Originally nobles and bourgeois hired town criers to announce the decease of a family member; in the course of the seventeenth century they were replaced by printed posters. Mourning letters were common from about 1600. Bells were tolled during the funeral and often the participants carried torches. The number of guests formed another indication of the deceased's rank. A minority of devout people, making up 12 percent in Provence, rejected all "earthly splendor and vanity" out of humility, but this is one more proof of their importance to the majority, who still found it prestigious to be buried in the church itself. In Paris in the period 1650–1700, 79 percent of the testators and 70 percent of the testatrices made this wish known. Lack of money was the usual reason to choose the churchyard. Not everybody may have been able to achieve their wish, but figures on funerals in other French cities at the end of the seventeenth century suggest that about one-third to slightly over half of all adults were buried in the church.

The baroque reached a climax after the funeral. Skillful craftsmen made splendid gravestones for the somewhat less wealthy, and artists built pompous tombs for the richest bourgeois and aristocrats. One aspect of baroque tomb sculpture is remarkable in particular: the unmistakably erotic style of certain death portraits, which we also encounter on paintings and sculptures showing pious women in mystic ecstasy. The work of Gianlorenzo Bernini is the model for this. Ariès attributes a special meaning to these forms of art. From the end of the sixteenth to the beginning of the nineteenth century he sees the rise of a kind of mystic union between love and death, between agony and orgasm. The works of De Sade, presumably, testified to this union, although at a less lofty level. All this looks rather speculative. It is undeniable, however, that the intermingling of eroticism and death constitutes a recurrent motif in the visual arts, reappearing in Romantic painting.

The Protestants

Because images of the hereafter affected the experience of death from the fourteenth to the eighteenth centuries to such a crucial extent, it is a matter of course that we pay separate attention to the social groups who adopted the Reformation after 1517. That year only forms a watershed from the point of view of the conquerors. The larger heretical groups of the Middle Ages were Protestants of a kind too, but they were ultimately vanquished. The Cathars of Montaillou, for example, had their own, deviant dying ceremonies. Taken generally, however, the experience of death in Montaillou was not very different from that among the orthodox. After 1517 the borderline separating Catholicism from Protestantism was largely geographical, so that we have to consider several countries separately. Baroque death did not entirely pass by Protestant countries, if only because some Protestant German princes had tombs built which are considered baroque by art historians. A splendid tomb was built for William the Silent, designed by Hendrik de Keizer at the request of the Estates General of the Netherlands in 1614. However, we may ask whether the Protestant experience of death was as exuberant as that of French Catholics. Two elements in the Reformation, the rejection of purgatory and the emphasis on simplicity and soberness, seem incompatible with the baroque experience of death. Historians should inquire whether they had that effect in reality, but few have done so yet.

The statements of the sixteenth-century reformers are quite clear on these points. Luther claimed that purgatory had been invented by the scholastics and that only heaven and hell existed; besides, good works were of no use to earn heaven. In the writings he and his followers devoted to dying, consolation consisted of invoking God's mercy. The earliest Evangelical chants treated death in a sober fashion; they only spoke about being prepared to die. Other possible themes, such as the consolation of the relatives, eternal peace, or praying for the deceased were absent, especially the prayers which might be viewed as papist. In England a legal prohibition against paying for masses for the deceased was issued as early 1529, hence before the break with Rome. In 1547 the Anglican church published an official condemnation of "the vain opinion of purgatory." Calvin too rejected purgatory, stating that God had determined in the distant past who would be doomed and who would partake of eternal life. The Puritans of England and New England added that the body was merely a worthless wrap, not even deserving a gravestone once the soul had left it.

Let us continue with funerals and churchyards, since more information is available about them. Calvinists of different persuasions originally received sober funerals. That holds true for the French Huguenots, who had churchyards of their own until 1685, and for the New England Puritans. The latter, however, did not cling to their soberness for long. Their funerals became more expensive and conspicuous, with church bells tolling, in the second half of the seventeenth century. In 1724 the Massachusetts authorities found it necessary to promulgate a law putting a ceiling on funeral expenses. In England too this expenditure rose in the very period when Puritans were most active, between 1580 and 1650. In that period the poor regularly flocked to aristocratic funerals; this custom only disappeared in the course of the seventeenth century. When Oliver Cromwell was buried in 1658, it was anything but a sober ceremony. Among the Anglicans common meals and the presentation of gifts continued to be valued as a part of the ceremony. Tomb sculpture with an erotic flavor could be found in England too. That was less common in the Dutch Republic, but it was compensated by other remarkable elements. The Reformation did not put a stop to burials in the church. The floor of St. Bavo at Haarlem, for example, consists of gravestones to this day. A modern visitor can observe the same practice in the Swedish town of Uppsala despite the fact that Scandinavia has become Lutheran. In Hamburg, which turned Lutheran too, the funerals of the rich in the seventeenth century matched those of the French, and status was equally important. Bells tolled, mourning clothes were worn, and the funeral procession was interminable. When burgomaster Schulte was buried in 1692, four hundred people attended. Conversely, magistrates as well as clergymen, doctors, and lawyers could be hired to act as mourners, giving extra prestige to the procession. Thus, where the poor participated in France, in Hamburg it was the rich. The overwhelming majority must have joined the procession just out of curiosity. In 1694 a chronicler remarked: "Many came to the funeral, because the weather was pleasant."

A preliminary conclusion can be drawn that practice was less sober than theory. A few other cases point to this too. Around 1600 the theme of the consolation of the relatives appeared in German Evangelical chants. Consolation also played a major role among the Huguenots. In the edifying works written for them it was assumed that others, but not the reader, would end up in hell. The most valuable information about the Protestant experience of death comes from one source only: printed funeral sermons and orations. This source is Evangelical Germany's equivalent to French testaments.

The tradition originated in the special circumstances surrounding Luther's demise. The funeral orations delivered by Melanchton and other intimates were published almost immediately, because they explained that their teacher had been well prepared for death. Such a publication was a novelty at the time, but the example of Luther's intimates was soon followed. After the death of numerous aristocrats and rich bourgeois, a funeral sermon or oration, or perhaps both, was published. There were two peak periods of the genre: the first two decades of the seventeenth century and the turn from the seventeenth to the eighteenth century. In their standard form those works had three parts: the Christian sermon, the biography of the deceased, and elegies composed by relatives and friends. The first two had often been said at the occasion of the funeral. When Tübingen professors were buried, for example, the sermon was first delivered by a minister in the main church, followed by a colleague's oration in the auditorium. A scheme of 1654 presents the standard content of the part dealing with the biography: birth, parents, studies, doctorate, marital status, children, offices, "a good Christian," sickness, Christian preparedness to die, blessed demise. The last days were as important as all the rest of the life story; the publications were often entitled "Oration about the Life and Death of the Departed."

Several historians refer to the tradition of funeral sermons as a Protestant continuation of the ars moriendi genre. They characterize the style as baroque. The tradition more or less filled the gap left by the disappearance of purgatory. As they proclaimed the exemplary nature of the life and death of the dear one, relatives and friends demonstrated that a further intercession by them, had it been possible, was nevertheless unnecessary. In this way they had done something for the deceased after all, while they possessed a concrete souvenir. It was the implicit assumption, of course, that there were no obstacles to the admittance of his soul into heaven. Sometimes this supposition was said aloud. The soul's entry into heavenly paradise was frequently compared to a marriage in which the soul played the part of the bride: the bridegroom welcomes her. She is beautifully dressed and wears splendid ornaments, while a wedding song can be heard. There is talk of heavenly desire and a sweet union. Thus, an erotic flavor again. Baroque death was certainly not unknown to Protestants.

The Beginnings of Concealment

The beginnings of concealment of death cannot be dated precisely. The relocation of cemeteries outside towns during the second half of the eighteenth century is the most concrete example of a transition. A few related developments can be observed earlier in this century and sometimes even in the seventeenth. In addition, concealment of death was a longer-term process, going through a phase of romanticization during the nineteenth century and assuming the form of denial in the middle of the twentieth. These were features of an industrial society, so that they need not concern us here. The beginnings of concealment can be illustrated with three examples: the decline of baroque piety in Catholic countries, the increasing intimacy of funerals, and the disappearance of the churchyard.

Decline of the Baroque

In France the statistical analysis of testaments amply demonstrates the retreat of baroque piety. Where the most extreme Provencal testators around 1700 preferred to demand masses for the salvation of their souls by the thousands, this number fell to the hundreds around 1720. The average per testator declined drastically after 1755 in towns as well as in the countryside. The same development took place with respect to charitable gifts to churches, monasteries, and hospitals and to the poor in general. In Anjou the shift came around 1760. After that pious gifts were still regularly listed in testaments, but the religious wording was lacking. In Paris those developments took place a little earlier. A considerable minority of Parisian testators did not demand masses at all as early as the first half of the seventeenth century. For the rest, there were strong parallels with the other French regions investigated.

We are essentially dealing not with a quantitative but with a qualitative change, which would be completed in the nineteenth century. The testament turned modern. Pious exclamations and other remarks and clauses of a sentimental natural eventually disappeared as well. This made the testament into the one we know: an act for the settlement of material affairs instead of a document aimed at the hereafter. Protestants had always used this type of testament, which explains why those documents have little value as sources for the study of the experience of death. Catholics now conformed to this movement. Vovelle and Lebrun think that it points to a waning influence of the clergy and of Christianity in general upon French society, but this is questionable. The explanation offered by Ariès appears more plausible. He links the transformation of the testament to the emergence of the closed, domesticated family in this very period. The testators, he argues, stopped committing personal and intimate matters to paper and instead verbally confided them to their next of kin. Henceforth they could count on family members. It should be added that this explanation is valid only for Catholic regions. The fact that Protestants had known a material testament for over two centuries can be ascribed to the abolition of purgatory.

It was precisely in France, however, that in the eighteenth century a minority rejected Christian dying ritual altogether. This was the age of Enlightenment, when deism emerged: the doctrine according to which God did not interfere with the world once it was created. Deists considered the Christian ceremony too somber despite all its words of consolation; it put too much emphasis on punishment of sin. Anticlericals loathed the power with which the ritual endowed priests at the precise moment when people were at their weakest. To La Mettrie and Rousseau the ideal way of dying was anything but a conscious process. It was better to pass away gently with a smile on one's face, like falling asleep after making love. La Mettrie, who had been an army surgeon, claimed he watched more than one soldier die in this way in the hospital.

Nonetheless the number of unbelievers who did not even tolerate a priest at their deathbed remained small. This was partly a consequence of the monopoly enjoyed by the Catholic church and upheld by the state in prerevolutionary France. Whoever refused to make a minimal gesture placating the clergy lost the right to an honorable funeral, which was unthinkable to almost everyone. Voltaire took great spiritual pains at his deathbed, so as to be entitled to such a funeral without denying what he stood for. A few radicals were more indifferent. Their anticlericalism was so strong that even during their last moments they delighted in ridiculing the church's ceremonial by making cynical jokes. Thus the marquis of Maugiron, hearing about the good shepherd, said he preferred shepherdesses who would kiss him into eternal sleep. Were those cynics unafraid of death? They could comfort themselves at least with the thought that their jokes would live on in the minds of posterity. The great philosophers also cherished the idea of generations of new readers who would provide them with a kind of pseudoeternal life. In the words of Diderot: "Posterity is to the philosopher what the next world is to the religious believer" (Macmanners: 168).

The Enlightenment and then Romanticism tended to privatize the dying scene. The presence of the family, in addition to a physician and a cleric, sufficed; servants and outsiders eventually disappeared from the dying room. This primarily happened with the elite. The decline of preindustrial popular culture and notably in this case of the various brotherhoods led to a decrease in the involvement of the village, neighborhood, and work community with death. In this way, death fell back upon family and kin also among the lower classes. Various family portraits around 1800 show a weeping father with young children and a single faithful servant, expressing their grief at the wife's bier. Of course the death of a young mother was an ideal theme for Romanticism, but these pictures also reflect the relative frequency of mortality among adults in the prime of life. The withdrawal of death into the family began before the great demographic changes set in. In the twentieth century the deceased have become primarily grandparents.

Funerals

Around 1700 a marked change can be observed in the organization of English royal funerals. The heraldic funeral, with over a thousand people participating in the procession, was common in the sixteenth and seventeenth centuries. Horses drew an open carriage with the coffin and a life-size effigy of the deceased monarch. During the obsequies the coffin stood under a giant canopy. In 1685 Charles II was the first to have a more sober funeral, but this was the result of special circumstances. The ancient ceremonial would be displayed once more in all its glory, however. When Queen Mary died from smallpox in 1695 at the age of thirty-one, her funeral may have been the most expensive one ever organized for an English sovereign; at least it had the longest procession. Among others, both houses of Parliament participated in mourning clothes. At William III's funeral in 1702 the procession was accompanied by three hundred torchbearers, but for the rest the proceedings were more sober. In the course of the eighteenth century ceremonial was restricted still further. In official descriptions the eighteenth-century royal funerals were called private, in contrast to those preceding.

Among the English aristocracy funerals had been made more intimate a little earlier yet. The heraldic funeral became less common during the seventeenth century; it became fashionable to organize the event at night for a restricted audience, but still with torches. The character of those nighttime funerals was sentimental rather than ritual. The waning influence of the heraldic forms was also related to the appearance of professional undertakers in the seventeenth century. The subsequent commercialization of death, although important, is a subject too little investigated. Nighttime funerals also became customary in parts of Germany in the second half of the seventeenth century. In eighteenth-century Hamburg the ceremony as a whole became less public. Although a long row of carriages still followed the bier, the guests sat shielded from the public, who were only passive spectators. In the Netherlands the funerals of Limburg aristocrats have been investigated. These also acquired a more intimate and less public character, but in a long drawn-out process from the end of the eighteenth until the beginning of the twentieth century. In France, finally, the poor eventually disappeared from the procession. Numerous Provençal testators in the second half of the eighteenth century declared their presence undesirable. Some continued to bequeath money to charitable institutions, but this was to buy them off, "to make them stay away with their poor." The trend with respect to funerals is undeniable: from theater to intimacy, from public to private.

Cemeteries

The changes in the character of cemeteries can be described quite clearly in terms of a sequence of phases. Most examples again come from France. In the first phase, the familiarity of cemeteries and the use of the churchyard for secondary purposes gradually gave way. Already from the sixteenth century, clergymen had combated the more profane activities in the church itself and in its yard. Gradually churchyards became more sober places. At the end of the seventeenth century, ecclesiastical authorities in Anjou and other regions insisted on the enclosure of churchyards so that stray cows and pigs could not make their way in. In the course of the eighteenth century the exhibition of skulls and bones in galleries inside the church went out of vogue. In tomb sculpture too the skeleton lost its attractiveness. In eighteenth-century England it was replaced by images of flying souls or cherubins. New England gravestones also became devoid of skulls. It has already been noted that eighteenth-century elites no longer appreciated the danses macabres. The intermingling of the living and the dead ended around 1750.

The second phase partly overlapped with the first. It appears from the studies of testaments that the number of people wishing to be interred in newly established cemeteries outside the towns increased in the course of the eighteenth century. Although those new grounds usually had a chapel, they did not belong to a parish church. Thus, the new cemeteries were not churchyards in a literal sense. In Paris immediately after 1700 a sizeable number of male testators omitted revealing their preferences which was the usual way of expressing agreement to a funeral outside town. Among Parisian women and among male and female testators in Provence the shift came at the middle of the century. To be buried outside town also became customary in Anjou then.

The third phase, also partly overlapping with the one preceding, began with protests against burial in churches. These protests, usually supported by hygienic arguments, were soon extended to the unhealthy conditions in the ancient urban churchyards. Remarkably, the first published rejection of burial in churches based on considerations about stench and health came from a member of the clergy. Father Porée's essay appeared in 1743. One of its arguments was that the nearness of the dead and the familiarity it gave rise to prevented a true commemoration of the deceased. To visit their graves outside town would be a great deal more moving. The campaign against churchyards was intensified in the 1760s. Its protagonists no longer displayed a sentimental attachment to these holy places. For the most part they came up with medical and scientific arguments, although they did not fail to point out that the ancients and the first Christians had buried their dead outside town.

The disappearance of the churchyard constituted the fourth phase. In many places the age-old cemeteries adjacent to parish churches were closed, usually on the orders of the municipal government. This movement set in in a few European countries in the 1770s. The change wrought by it was far from absolute; everywhere it affected the big cities in particular. In ordinary villages, where a smaller pile of bodies caused conditions to be less harmful to health, cemeteries often continued to be near parish churches. This holds true in the Netherlands, among other places, until today. The Dutch development in general was somewhat slower than the French. Protests of any significance against burial in the church proper were not heard until the last quarter of the eighteenth century. Burial inside a town was prohibited in the French period, but the new regime made it provisionally legal again in 1813. A royal decree of 1825 established a definitive obligation to bury the dead outside town.

In France a national edict putting restrictions on burials within the inhabited area was promulgated in 1776. During the following years the ancient churchyards were closed in a number of towns. The demolition of the churchyard of the Innocents in Paris in the 1780s provides a model. Hygienic conditions in it had deteriorated further in the eighteenth century because those living in adjacent houses were accustomed to throwing their garbage and feces from the windows into the churchyard. A sewerage ditch was of no use, since the trash often landed too far from the sides. We may wonder whether this points to familiarity or to a need to profane death. A monumental fountain was constructed at the site of the churchyard of the Innocents. We might suppose that the relocation of cemeteries was accepted, since a clause about burial in the church or its yard was absent in more and more testaments. The majority of testators in question, however, were from the middle and upper classes, like the reformers, among whom a change of mentality had indeed been under way. This is why French historians claim that the edict of 1776 sealed an evolution that had already taken place. But there are indications that the lower classes did not simply acquiesce to the change. The closing of churchyards sometimes led to popular protests. Local authorities in Anjou often obstructed the relocation of cemeteries outside the walls, but they were motivated primarily by financial considerations. In some towns in northern France, however, this relocation resulted in riots, with the populace denouncing the "banishment of the deceased."

The fifth and last phase logically followed from the previous one. A "natural" and pastoral environment became the ideal model for the new cemetery. This model did not become widespread until the nineteenth century but it was elaborated in the eighteenth. The movement had its roots in England in the form of memorial stones placed in the newly made landscape gardens. When the fashion of landscape gardens conquered France, the owners sometimes had their family tomb constructed in them. The grave of Jean-Jacques Rousseau, who died in 1778, became the symbol of the new mentality. It was situated on an island in a lake on the estate of the marquis de Girardin, one of his admirers. The island itself was Rousseau's monumental tomb: the man of nature in the landscape of nature, away from the town and especially away from the crowded chaos which had characterized the ancient churchyards for more than a thousand years. Yet Rousseau's grave was not quite natural. The island in the lake was artificial. Its builders had searched the area for picturesque pieces of rock, given them numbers, placed them on the island in a scenic pattern, and covered them with moss. Next, poplars were planted. The body of the dead Rousseau found its rest in a nature designed by the living.

This was not yet the limit of artificiality. Following the wave of admiration for Rousseau and the breakthrough of the Romantic experience of death, the last resting place of the great writer was copied even when no corpse was present. The Dutch writer Jacob van Lennep had a monument constructed on his splendid estate near Heemstede; it was called "Rousseau's tomb."

Explanations.   Several explanations for the eighteenth-century shift have been offered which are not necessarily incompatible. They can be related to a few long-term developments. In this case, the shift was linked to a particular phase of those developments.

The attack at the churchyards was motivated primarily by a concern for hygiene and unpolluted air. The piling up of corpses must indeed have been a source of infection. The spread of scenic cemeteries was halted between 1760 and 1780 because it was thought that trees would keep the winds from supplying fresh air. When it was discovered that trees produce oxygen, this concern came to an end. The episode illustrates that fear of disease coincided with irritation over stench. The smell of corpses, which had been tolerated as a matter of course for over a thousand years, was increasingly found offensive. It has been noted in chapter 1 that a campaign to banish all kind of foul smells from public life was begun at the end of the eighteenth century. The attack at the churchyards belonged to a movement with projects such as the design for a paved street with a sewerage system for toilets by Pierre Patte in 1769. Thus, the offensive originated in an increased sensitivity toward waste and stench.

But that is not the whole story. Why was the first battle launched against the odor of churchyards? Etlin argues that the campaign against churchyards was also rooted in a new religious mentality, which considered the presence of the dead incompatible with the dignity of the church. This argument is in line with the theses of Vovelle and Lebrun, who claim that a change in religious sensibilities with regard to burial and death in general took place. Vovelle in particular relates the decline of baroque piety largely to a process of what he calls de-Christianization. Chaunu rejects this thesis, arguing that for the majority of the people the more intimate experience of death in the nineteenth and twentieth centuries still had a strongly religious flavor. But we saw that an enlightened minority had rejected belief in the hereafter and repudiated ecclesiastical rites even before 1800. Among that group a more secularized mentality must have played a part.

Gittings argues differently. She puts emphasis on the gradual breakthrough of individualism as a factor for changes in the experience of death in the course of the seventeenth and eighteenth centuries. The beginnings of concealment of death were related to an increased awareness of the uniqueness of each individual. The stronger this awareness, the more painful it was to see such an irreplaceable person go. With varying accentuation, Ariès and Elias also consider individualization as an explanatory factor. In a similar vein, the process of increasing interhuman identification can be noted. Grief over the loss of irreplaceable ones was extra strong because it reminded a person of his own coming end. As a consequence of increasing identification even the death of strangers could give rise to this thought, making it more problematic. This weakened the social familiarity with death.

Finally, privatization should be drawn into the picture. Ariès's thesis that death withdrew to the closed, domesticated family, which was just on the rise around 1800, has already been mentioned. In a later work Vovelle appears to join him in this notion. Macmanners, however, stresses the link between developments in the realm of the family and the experience of death most consistently. The emergence of the closed family, also a manifestation of privatization, is discussed in the final chapter. The concealment of dying and grief within the bosom of the family established a link between two aspects of this long-term process which, for the rest, were far apart. Privatization is also reflected in the other trends mentioned. Cemeteries were first enclosed and then banished outside the inhabited area. The trend in burials was from public to private. Pictures of death became more elusive. Privatization was interwoven with the alternative long-term developments, which had an effect of their own. But privatization was the principal factor, which follows from chronology. The period 1750–1850 witnessed an acceleration of this process in various fields.

6 THE BODY ADRIFT: The Image of Madness and Attitudes Toward the Insane

In the previous chapter we saw how people handled a matter with which each would be confronted. Understandably this taught us something about the mentality of all groups concerned. It is equally interesting to inquire into the ways in which the majority dealt with relatively peripheral phenomena such as deviant behavior. This chapter treats those forms of deviant behavior which can be conceived of in terms of madness or insanity, mild as well as severe. An introductory section explains that the historian is principally interested in behavior which contemporaries themselves viewed as disturbed, and the changes in it. The second section discusses ideas about insanity. It attempts first to discover the beliefs of the learned and the populace, then discusses the representation of madness in literature, and concludes with changes in its image, shaped by a history of possession, suicide, and religious enthusiasm. The final section deals with the reactions to insanity in practice. Depending on the period, they consisted of the promotion of pilgrimages, whippings, and confinement in special institutions.

Madness Dissected

Two different terms, insanity and madness, are deliberately used here. This dualism highlights the fact that we are dealing with an ambiguous phenomenon. Words such as "mental illness," on the other hand, have been consciously avoided, since their utility for scholarship has been contested for several decades. Whoever attributes an eternal value to the categories of today's psychiatry can say without hesitation what research into past madness is all about. The investigator then pins psychiatric labels on the behavior of all kind of people from earlier ages, and possibly concludes with the question of whether contemporaries viewed it from the same angle. This is certainly an anachronistic procedure. The history of mentalities teaches us that the psychological characteristics of the people of our time are not automatically valid in preindustrial societies. Similarly, there is a difference between forms of conduct seen as abnormal in the past and those viewed as proper for psychiatric intervention now. So we have to discover what was considered "crazy" by preindustrial people and how they reacted to it.

That is easier said than done. Earlier generations used a whole series of words to denote deviant forms of behavior and character traits. How are we to decide which of those words can be assigned to the category of "madness?" We might incorrectly suppose that some concepts refer to forms of madness, while, conversely, we might fail to acknowledge this in the case of others. This difficulty can be removed by the application of the so-called retrospective method: from the knowledge of our own time we argue backwards. What is called "mental illness" or "psychic disturbance" today was often termed "insanity" in the previous century, when psychiatric hospitals were usually called lunatic asylums. In this way, we can go further back each time, inquiring into the concepts related to "insane" and "lunatic." Then we find out, for example, that the concept of "melancholy," which nowadays has romantic overtones, referred to a form of disturbance before 1800. Melancholy and madness are not identical. With the help of the retrospective method we have discovered a series of related concepts belonging to one particular sphere. Just outside that sphere is folly, as it came to the fore in popular customs and festivals. It fits better into the subject of chapter 3 in which it has been treated.

From the angle of the history of mentalities, the crucial questions are: what was the image of madness and what does it teach us about the prevailing image of mankind as a whole? What conduct was labelled as insane, and how did the environment react to it? Was the image or were the reactions subject to change, and how can we explain it?

A Background to the Research

In the 1960s and 1970s psychiatry began to be questioned and the ensuing discussion also inspired historians. The debate especially concerned the medical approach to insanity and treatment in closed institutions. Before 1960 maladjusted behavior was consistently viewed as sick and treated by medical specialists. Treatment frequently included forms of coercion. A movement usually called by the name of antipsychiatry opposed these customs.

The best-known representative of this school is Ronald Laing. He developed his ideas from working with people diagnosed as schizophrenic. Laing saw schizophrenia as a journey through another world, a period of moral cleansing, which might ultimately produce a deeper insight in life. The parallel with the LSD "trip," popular at the time he wrote, is unmistakable. Such a journey would only be hindered by efforts at therapy. When the state of schizophrenia turned out to be permanent, Laing saw the person in question as a dropout, someone who refused to participate any longer in a society that itself was rotten and insane. This view has a quasi-religious flavor. Laing referred to the journey and the process of being reborn as "metanoia," conversion. This meant that to a certain extent he drew on an older, less secularized image of madness.

This quasi-religious element is entirely absent from the work of Thomas Szasz. Not belonging to the antipsychiatrists, he published his principal work, *The Myth of Mental Illness*, before this movement appeared. Szasz's argument is simple but consistent: there is no such thing as mental illness, because the mind cannot be ill. There are just numerous forms of conduct, some of which we do not fully understand or value negatively. The medical model is a metaphor which cannot be granted the status of a scholarly concept. Szasz does not adopt a romantic approach to persons whom others call psychiatric patients. Forms of conduct commonly explained in terms of mental illness do exist, sometimes causing real problems. Consequently, Szasz criticizes Laing, reproaching him for the creation of a mirror image of traditional psychiatry: everything is still the same, but the values are reversed.

Szasz's most historical work is *The Manufacture of Madness*. In it he draws a comparison between the persecution of heretics and witches in preindustrial Europe and the diligent search for persons needing psychiatric treatment in America in the 1950s and 1960s. In both cases, he claims, we are dealing with negative reactions to deviant behavior and an excessive urge to track down this behavior.

Psychiatric patients are the scapegoats of today, just like the heretics and witches who were pushed into that role earlier. Hence, Szasz considers both groups as victims. Despite his power of imagination, his thesis meets a number of objections. For example, an analysis of attitudes toward madness in preindustrial Europe is lacking. Psychiatrists writing history pay attention to the witch persecutions as well. They think—very incorrectly, as appears from chapter 4—that the majority of victims were in fact the "mentally ill." In this view, witches are also compared to psychiatric patients, although these authors are positive about psychiatric treatment. Ironically, Szasz himself creates a mirror image. Where his counterparts see two categories of patients, he sees two categories of the persecuted. The evolution from the medieval image of insanity to the twentieth-century psychiatric model cannot be explained in this way.

In search of preindustrial madness, therefore, we have to find another guide. The debate concerning psychiatry can still serve as a point of departure. Trimbos identifies four characteristics of antipsychiatry: a repudiation of the illness-model; a rejection of institutional psychiatry, institutions being considered dumping grounds; criticism of psychiatry's function of social control; a positive, or at least not a negative, valuation of madness. From these four points an equal number of historical questions follow. Has the illness-model always been maintained? Were crazy people confined or left alone? Which social functions did the treatment of the insane fulfill? What was the image of madness, and did it change? The first and fourth questions have to do with ideas, perceptions, and the labelling of behavior. The second and third questions refer to the reactions to insanity and changing customs of treatment. Both perspectives are dealt with successively in the second and final sections.

One remark to conclude this section: an inquiry into the problem of whether or not certain forms of conduct were interpreted according to an illness-model reveals nothing about the possible cause of this conduct in individual persons. A few somatic diseases lead to behavior superficially resembling that of persons diagnosed as mentally ill. The last stage of syphilis is perhaps the most telling example. Some preindustrial people who were called insane by their fellows may actually have had a somatic defect. In all probability this was the case with one of the most notorious crazy persons in history: King George III of England. Macalpine and Hunter established that four living descendants of the king had a latent hereditary aberration called porphyria. In its rare manifest form porphyria leads to delirium-like attacks, which can be intense. George III was considered mad by his contemporaries; there was little knowledge of genetics at the time. The question of whether some of the insane of the past had indeed a biological defect, if it can be answered at all, is not relevant here. Our subject is madness as defined by contemporaries.

The Image of Madness

If we want to know what the image of madness was like, two questions need an answer: which type of conduct was viewed as crazy, and did contemporaries have recourse to an illness-model in order to interpret it? Since preindustrial Europeans were frequently inspired by theories from antiquity or passages from the Old Testament, these receive brief attention first.

Madness among the Greeks and in the Old Testament

Our information from antiquity is almost exclusively of a literary nature. Among the Greeks madness is present in the tragedies in particular. Their authors view almost every form of extreme passion in this light. They also describe hallucinations and delusions as the revenge of the Gods. More expressive forms of madness could have a supernatural cause too. In one of Euripides's works the Furies have struck Orestes with insanity because he has killed his mother. Orestes stares with cold, lifeless eyes; his hair is wild and he looks like a ghost. The most elaborate description of a madman can be found in Sophocles's Ajax. Madness takes hold of the hero when the Greek leaders refuse to grant him Achilles's armor. He mistakes sheep for his enemies and fights them. Finally, Ajax commits suicide.

Writers of comedy sometimes exploited the notion of insanity. In "The Wasps" by Aristophanes, an old man named Philocleon suffers from the lunacy of constantly wanting to judge others. He is obsessed with sitting on a jury and is always ready to go to court to impose sentences. Philocleon's son first tries to correct his habit by persuasion; then he immerses his father in water. His next attempt is to offer him the religious function of corybant; then he takes him to the temple of Asclepios. Finally, Philocleon is simply confined at home. Aristophanes invented this lunacy for satirical purposes, but the reactions mentioned apparently belonged to the ordinary repertoire.

Concepts related to insanity are also present in the Old Testament. When David took refuge with the Philistines, he pretended to be a madman. He let his spittle glide down his beard and scratched while in the town gates of Gath. The most notorious persons, considered lunatic at least by some, were the prophets. They led a peculiar life indeed, which made them respected and feared by some but despised by others. Besides, the prophets were involved in the political struggles of their time, which led their opponents to call them *meshugga*. The use of words like lunatic to insult someone is old indeed. When the idiom of madness is in vogue in a society, it may serve in the case of tensions between social groups to pin an incriminating label on one's adversaries. This happens in our time as well.

Did antiquity experience an illness-model? The insane Orestes referred to his nagging conscience as his illness and Menelaus retorted with "there are cures." Thus, the insanity itself was not called an illness. Hippocrates of Cos, however, the "father of medicine," was also interested in lunacy. According to Hippocrates, an excess of bile caused corruption of the brain. Hysteria was another invention of his. A woman's uterus (*hystera*) supposedly wandered occasionally within the body. This not only caused pain but also delusions, mania, and suicidal tendencies. Sex might be a good remedy or else the uterus could be lured back by herbs implanted in the vagina. It would be incorrect still to conclude that the Greeks had an illness-model. They believed instead in a constant interaction between mind and body, which also happened in sane people. In the second century A.D., Galen synthesized antiquity's views of this question. His work was to be influential until the seventeenth century.

Europe: Learned Beliefs

With Galen as our bridge from classical antiquity to preindustrial western Europe, we start with the beliefs of the learned. The Galenic system is based on the theory of bodily fluids. These fluids, or *humores*, are derived from the four elements of Greek natural philosophy: earth, water, air, and fire. Four basic conditions, coldness, wetness, drought, and heat, respectively, correspond to those elements. Next, each of those conditions has its *humor* in the human body. They are, respectively, black bile (originating from the spleen), slime (*phlegma*), blood, and yellow bile (*cholera*). A person's temperament is determined by the specific combination of bodily fluids. With his *humores* in the right balance, an individual has a sane mind in a healthy body. A disturbance of the balance leads to illness or insanity. Someone who has too much black bile (*melas cholos*) suffers from *melancholia*. In the seventeenth and eighteenth centuries this became the collective term to denote various forms of insanity. Robert Burton was the first to make it a collective term in his *The Anatomy of Melancholy* published in 1621.

In the course of the seventeenth and eighteenth centuries new theories appeared, competing with that of bodily fluids. They were not essentially different, however. According to some German authors, madness stood for a heating up of the brain as a consequence of fever or delirium. In England the hydraulic theory was developed following Harvey's discovery of the circulation of blood. By analogy, its adherents thought that the nerves were also fine veins containing a fluid. Disturbances in its circulation caused all kinds of mental troubles. Another English invention was the theory of vibration. It held the body to be an elastic entity, in which too much or too little tension led to forms of insanity. George Cheyne, who combined both theories, recommended a diet of milk and vegetables. He thought that the luxurious way of life of the English upper classes made them susceptible to spleen. This belief has moralistic overtones. Conversely, too great deviations from the norms of civilized conduct prevailing among the elites were also considered symptoms of insanity.

Again we may wonder whether scientific conceptions imply an illness-model. The answer might be: to a certain extent, but not as we understand it today. Just like their Greek counterparts, these theories presuppose a complete symbiosis between biological constitution and mental condition. We also acknowledge that the two are connected, as when we speak of psychosomatic pains, for example. But nowadays they are as a rule more strictly distinguished. The twentieth-century illness-model implies that mental disturbances are drawn into the medical sphere even in the absence of physical symptoms. At the same time, few people wonder what is the physical component of mental conditions that are found acceptable. By contrast, in the doctrine of bodily fluids, observations of physical processes on the one hand and mental conditions and corresponding behavior on the other were intricately interwoven. The interaction between mind and body was equally strong in normal and deviant persons. This theory offered a cluster of explanations for every human action, but the conclusion that a doctor was needed was rarely drawn.

A pure illness-model also implies that the insane person is free from guilt: insanity just happens to him. On this point earlier theoreticians were not consistent either, as we saw with Cheyne. More than once madness was drawn into the sphere of good and bad, in a religious or in a general moral sense. Burton for example, constantly speaks of sin in his work on melancholy. The conduct of some of those confined as insane in the eighteenth century was simultaneously condemned in moral terms. But this was a secondary approach. Where moral disapproval gained the upper hand, behavior was not defined in terms of insanity. The notion of diminished responsibility has always been connected to madness.

An obvious difference between today's beliefs and preindustrial theories, finally, is that the latter were embedded in a Christian context. Supernatural explanations intruded into the Galenic system. According to contemporaries, divine or demonic forces also affected human character and conduct. Taken strictly, the Christian tradition with its sharp distinction between the body on the one hand and the soul, including the mind, on the other, was incompatible with the theory of bodily fluids. But even religious authors were not always consistent on this point. The twelfth-century abbess Hildegard of Bingen, for example, mixed biological and supernatural notions in her description of mental conditions. The humanists followed Galen, but they left room for Christian as well as astrological explanations. In addition, a special sort of madness, taking the shape of possession, was caused by the devil; it is discussed later in the chapter. Biological and religious explanations were not viewed as mutually exclusive. Observers might ascribe a suicidal tendency to a disturbed balance of the *humores*, while simultaneously believing that the devil had taken hold of the afflicted person.

Thus, an illness-model was partially present in preindustrial Europe, to the extent that deviant mental conditions were also seen as unhealthy biological disturbances. But the context was so different from that in the twentieth century that we are dealing with quite another view of madness. The same will be observed as we study practice. The use of the concept of illness as a metaphor, finally, was imitated from antiquity too. In the sixth century, Boethius, imprisoned by Theodoric, king of the Ostrogoths, described his mental condition as a *morbus* or *aegritudo* (disease). *Philosophia* was his doctor, offering him consolation and thereby curing him. The fifteenth-century English poet Thomas Hoccleve described a period of his life during which he suffered from insomnia, feelings of worthlessness, and a longing for death. Staring into the mirror to search for its symptoms on his face, he wonders if insanity has struck him. Inspired by Boethius, Hoccleve refers to his condition of mental suffering as "sycknesse" and "disease." A divine "reason" has to liberate him from his sad state. Ultimately, this bout of melancholy is a period of moral cleansing, in which he has gained a deeper insight into life. Hence, Hoccleve's description of his insanity strongly resembles Laing's view of schizophrenia.

The Literary Representation

With Hoccleve we reach a new subject: the image of madness in literature. Hoccleve's work is probably autobiographical, but this is not certain. From the Renaissance onward madness is a recurrent theme in literature, and in it we are certainly not dealing with accurate descriptions of real life. Insanity is wielded as a literary instrument, either serving satirical purposes or functioning as a mirror held up to the audience. One of the most notorious madmen in literature is King Lear. The psychological typecasting of the king is the principal element of the drama, but simultaneously it conveys the message that madness hides a form of wisdom. In the crucial passage Lear declares that the vices and sins of the great are usually covered up. Hearing this, Gloucester's son Edgar exclaims, "Look, there is reason in madness." That becomes a recurrent theme in literature: because of a lack of restraint the madman easily makes statements implying a keen insight into society and the human condition. This madman, however, remains an intellectual; he is a dramatized construction of the writer. The majority of the insane, before Shakespeare's time as well as later, were not treated as wise men. Foucault wrongly believes that this was the case well into the sixteenth century.

Next to reflective criticism, literary madness offered the opportunity for biting satire. We have become accustomed to the cliché that "there are more lunatics outside the madhouse than inside." One of the first to say this was Thomas Tryon in his *Treatise of Dreams and Visions* of 1689. In his view, the mad voiced the thoughts and the fantasies which normal people repressed or at least disguised out of habit or calculation. At the same time, he judged, the cheating and cruelty of normal people were often worse than insanity. Tryon concluded: "The world is but a great *Bedlam*, where those that are *more mad*, lock up those that are *less*" (Feder: 155). This motif, and the use of madness for satire in general, returned with later writers, such as Jonathan Swift, Alexander Pope, and Laurence Sterne.

Apart from satirical passages, the literature of eighteenth-century England reveals a fascination with real madness in both its darker and its lighter forms. The latter were the relatively mild afflictions which were supposed to be widespread among elite groups. Melancholy still was a common term for these; contemporaries also spoke of "spleen" and "the English malady." The climate of the British isles was blamed for the depression or emotional disturbances from which many suffered. The fact that the inhabitants themselves accepted the term, English malady, indicates that this affliction was not simply valued negatively. In comparable circumstances the French spoke of *ennui*. Someone who is bored does not have to work. Words like melancholy were class specific, referring to the mild and almost exalted madness of the elite. Such afflictions were fashionable and some thought that they were particularly frequent among great minds.

Fascination with the darker side of madness constituted the interest in the real lunatic. He was locked up, troubled by delusions and hallucinations, or just wild and dirty. Ned Ward's portrait of the insane in the *London Bedlam* (about 1700) is illustrative:

We peeped into another room where a fellow was hard at work as if he's been treading mortar. "What is it, friend," said I, "thou art taking all this pains about?" He answered me thus, still continuing in action: "I am trampling down conscience under my feet, lest he should rise up and fly in my face. Have a care he doesn't fright thee, for he looks like the devil and is as fierce as a lion, but that I keep him muzzled. Therefore, get thee gone or I will set him upon thee." Then he fell a-clapping his hands, and cried, "Halloo, halloo, halloo, halloo, halloo," and thus we left him raving (Skultans: 44).

Upper class readers, semisecularized and ambivalent toward their own conscience, saw this feeling projected on the confined lunatic. With another crazy person Ward had to be a little more on his guard:

At last he counterfeits a sneeze, and shot such a mouthful of bread and cheese amongst us, that every spectator had some share of his kindness, which made us retreat; he calling after us Masters, Masters; some went back to hear what he had to say, and he had provided them a plentiful bowl of piss, which he cast very successfully amongst them, crying in a laugh, "I never give victuals, but I give drink, and you're welcome gentlemen" (Byrd: 18).

In this example insanity is the total contrast to the norms of civilized conduct. The lunatic is animal-like, wallowing in excrement and other filth.

The association of insanity with animal-like behavior is quite old. It is also present in the theme of the wild man or woodman, discussed in chapter 3. In addition to the motif of the "authentic" wild man, European literature contains stories of persons who take to the woods, temporarily imitating his behavior. Madness is involved here. The man who roams around in the forest does so out of insanity, usually caused by the loss of a relative or a jilted love. This insanity degrades humans to animals, although they do not automatically become hairy. Their condition is usually of a periodic nature. Such a bout of traveling through the woods in a state of madness does not damage their status. It happened to famous knights of romance, such as Tristan, Merlin, and Lancelot. The variations on the theme of the wild man testify to an interaction between elite and popular culture, so that our attention is drawn to the latter.

Popular Notions

Popular notions of insanity are not really in competition with those of the theoreticians. It is a question of a difference of emphasis. The principal effort of the authors on melancholy and bodily fluids is to explain how someone becomes insane. Vernacular words, on the other hand, rather describe how the insane behave; their function is labelling. With some reservations, a conclusion can be drawn from the various terms customary in the Netherlands since the fifteenth century. It looks as though, originally, the major dividing line ran between dangerous madmen and the harmless ones. Both types are mentioned in a fifteenth-century Utrecht source. In 1441 it was recorded that "there is a *gek*, named Lougen, going about the streets here and certain persons are used to robbing him of his clothes and letting him walk naked, to the embarrassment of good women and men." The magistrates forbade this, perhaps less out of compassion for Lougen than because of the embarrassment his treatment by the public caused. The word *gek*, still common in Dutch, is known also in Danish but not in most other Germanic languages; it originally referred to such a harmless person. A *gek's* conduct resembled that of the fool. Persons labelled as such often also had a physical defect, like a hump. The gek was a source of ridicule and amusement, as the quotation indicates. The fool, on the other hand, occupies a prominent place in popular culture. This points to an ambivalent attitude toward the harmless lunatic. After the fifteenth century those who were harmless were often called simpletons or the innocent. These terms can also be understood as derivatives from popular culture, with its association of princes of folly and child bishops. Crazy people and children were both innocent, in the sense of not being responsible for their actions. Dangerous ones were not responsible either, however. A dangerous madman is referred to in the Utrecht source in 1424: "Johan van Tyell, is out of his mind at times and no master over his senses and, in this state of insanity, he has induced fear and anxiety into the people and injured them with knives and other weapons . . ." (Weyde: 1). The magistrates proclaimed that anyone who slew Johan van Tyell—which God should prevent, of course—would be exempt from legal prosecution. Here we are confronted with a dangerous lunatic, one who has to be restrained by force at times. Contemporary Dutchmen frequently used the word *dol* in such a case. A *dol* person was aggressive and raging and his violence or the damage he caused made him a burden to those around him. He represents the second major type of madness in the preindustrial Netherlands.

Both major types can be found in seventeenth-century England too. Macdonald further distinguishes mild from severe cases which results in four "popular stereotypes of insanity." Also in his classification, aggressive lunacy stands out. Such a lunatic's violence was directed essentially at persons who ought to be dear to him, notably relatives. The destruction of one's property, like breaking windows or tearing one's clothes and walking naked through the streets belonged to this category as well. Thus, severely aggressive lunacy meant destroying—or the threatening to—that which is close and belongs to oneself: actions from which a person only seems to derive self-harm. The latter qualification is crucial, since aggressive behavior can also be labelled criminal. This is done when the deed is advantageous to the perpetrator. Even for the murder of a family member the motive can be revenge or the acquisition of an inheritance. Then the act can be understood, so that it is prosecuted as a crime. An act's incomprehensibility to the world around made it insane.

Macdonald lists fits and attacks as a serious form of harmless madness, either resembling delirious fever or accompanied by a torrent of words which do not seem to make sense. Those fits, often linked to fear of death and damnation, were therefore taken for a sign of the approaching end. The milder form of harmless madness mainly consisted of lethargy and a loss of sensation. This concerned persons who barely reacted to stimuli form their environment, without doing any other strange things. Emotional disturbances, delusions, and hallucinations, finally, constituted the fourth type of insanity in seventeenth-century England.

Demoniacs, Suicides, and Prophets

Although there was a degree of continuity to scientific and popular ideas, the image of madness changed, especially at the end of the preindustrial period. Ongoing secularization was the main driving force behind these changes. Two intimately related developments can be observed. First, the religious component in the image of madness declined and finally disappeared altogether. Supernatural explanations of human behavior became steadily more marginal and the association of madness with sin was no longer self-evident. Second, forms of conduct which until then had been interpreted exclusively in religious terms, increasingly tended to be redefined in terms of insanity. From the end of the seventeenth century, this tendency caused certain forms of religious fervor to be viewed as themselves manifestations of madness.

Around 1700 negative reactions to religious fervor began to be noted. The behavior and the ideas of numerous religious sects and individual preachers had provoked resistance for centuries. We have seen that the prophets of the Old Testament were sometimes called crazy. In preindustrial Europe, however, it was customary for a long time to express religious resentment in religious terms. Things that zealots disapproved of were called the work of the devil. Dance epidemics, often termed "collective psychoses" by twentieth-century authors, constitute an illustrative example. They appeared mainly in the fourteenth and fifteenth centuries. A group of people would start to dance and jump, invoking the names of Saint John or Saint Vitus. The effect was contagious and the participants were unable to stop. Some literally danced themselves to death, as the characters played by Jane Fonda and her partner almost did, although for other reasons, in the film *They Shoot Horses, Don't They*. Those who took a positive view of the dance believed that the participants were inspired by a saint. Their opponents claimed that the devil had taken possession of them or that their motives were sinful in some other way. Only an occasional skeptic suggested that madness might be involved. This became a more frequent reaction; the devil was no longer as obvious a candidate on whom to blame unpleasant situations and activities.

The concept of possession played a major role in this process of change. The secularization of madness was linked to the decline of exorcisms, described in chapter 1. Since the symptoms of possession— foaming at the mouth, wild gestures, weird talk—strongly resemble those of insanity, possession and insanity were associated in many minds for a long time. Nevertheless they were distinct phenomena in theory. Possession was also distinct from witchcraft. A witch had voluntarily concluded a pact with the devil, while the body of a demoniac had been taken by the devil against his or her will. Just like the madman, therefore, the demoniac was not responsible for his actions. The theoretical distinction, which was still valid around 1600, can be represented in the following scheme:

	Religious	Worldly
	Religious	Worldly
Not guilty	Possession	Insanity
Guilty	Witchcraft	Crime

It was crucial that this theoretical distinction was never consistently adhered to in practice. In the sixteenth and early in the seventeenth century, however, attempts to distinguish cases of possession from cases of insanity became more frequent, implying a modest beginning of secularization. In 1608, for example, a man was committed to the Utrecht madhouse upon the condition that, if the devil would tempt and fight with him, his relatives were to take care of him at their own risk. This must have been preceded by a debate about the causes of his behavior.

With the argument that Satan himself has an eye on madness, sixteenth-century authors attempted to explain the resemblances as well as to uphold the distinction. In principle, the devil might inflict all kind of troubles and diseases on humans, but he had a predilection for melancholy, mania, and epilepsy. Cause and consequence were mutually exchangeable, since, conversely, Satan felt most at home in the body of a melancholic person. This type of theory can be called semisecularized. In a similar vein, a connection was often supposed between insanity and sorcery or witchcraft. Sorcerers usually made their enemies ill, but sometimes insane for a change. At the beginning of the seventeenth century, 264 of Richard Napier's troubled clients thought that their condition originated from a magic spell.

The next phase in the secularization of madness involved changing attitudes toward suicide. Suicide might be linked to each of the four elements in the earlier scheme. The devil loved to persuade those whose bodies he took possession of to kill themselves. That happened to Apolonia Geisslbrecht, a thirty-year-old woman from Spalt near Nuremberg who had recently remarried, in 1582. With her new husband Apolonia had nothing but quarrels, leading her to attempt to hang and drown herself. After a few experiments, however, it was discovered that she was possessed by the devil. Witches sometimes killed themselves too, notably when they had been caught and elaborate tortures awaited them. The other two elements of the scheme are the ones most relevant to changes in the attitudes toward suicide. Insanity might bring about suicidal tendencies, but originally that conclusion was drawn rather infrequently. In sixteen out of fifty-four cases of suicide in the Middle Ages collected by Schmitt various forms of madness were involved. Originally, to kill oneself was primarily a crime, in a religious as well as a worldly sense.

In Christian thought a successful suicide was the ultimate sin, since by definition no repentance was possible. It originated out of desperation about one's own salvation in particular, and hence, involved doubt about God's mercy. The devil often tempted the desperate person to commit suicide. The most horrifying example was Judas, who hanged himself after throwing into the temple the silver coins he had obtained for Jesus's betrayal. We already met Judas as the prototype of the wicked Jew in popular literature. The association of Jew and suicide probably made the godless nature of the act all the more obvious to the populace. The general resentment was sealed by the laws of the secular authorities. Dead bodies could be criminally prosecuted. Because confiscation of goods which deprived relatives of their inheritance was a possibility in such trials, the would-be heirs frequently claimed that insanity was involved. Well into the seventeenth century, however, this claim was only accepted when other symptoms of insanity could be demonstrated as well.

The change came in the second half of the seventeenth and in the eighteenth century. Criminal prosecution of suicide gradually turned into a rarity. In Amsterdam the last trial, in which the dead body of the seventy-two-year-old sailor Michiel Straatsburg was indicted, took place in 1658. Elsewhere prosecution continued a little longer. Developments in England can be illustrated quantitatively. Every corpse discovered there was investigated by a coroner, after which a jury had to pronounce a judgment. If the person in question had taken his own life, the judgment was either "criminal suicide" or "out of his mind." The latter sentence became more and more frequent: from 7 to 30 percent in the middle of the seventeenth century to over 50 percent in the middle of the eighteenth. From about 1770 this was the only sentence pronounced. The conviction had arisen that suicide always involved madness. It was no longer an offense or a godless act but the ultimate consequence of melancholy or spleen. The fashionable character of these afflictions led to some acceptance of the act. Great names of the eighteenth century dealt with suicide. Enlightened philosophes such as Montesquieu and Voltaire gave a theoretical justification for the right to commit it, while the act itself was sentimentalized in the novels of Goethe and Rousseau. It continued, however, to be associated with insanity. Goethe declared that his *Werther* also painted a sickly youthful delusion but that he wished to leave that aspect to a physician.

In England the secularization of the image of madness generally proceeded at a fast pace. This was caused by specific developments related to socio-political antagonisms. Conflicts between religious movements had been quite intense in the first half of the seventeenth century, with immediate repercussions in the political arena. Religious minorities in particular fought the battle with supernatural help. The Anglicans, on the other hand, tended toward skepticism in this respect, gradually coming to deny possession and to consider everyone who claimed to be possessed as insane. The doctrine of the "cessation of miracles" gained ground in the Anglican church. Miracles, including any supernatural intervention in the course of affairs on earth, were supposed to have ceased happening after the age of the apostles. The implication of this belief is obvious: now whoever thought they had witnessed supernatural phenomena had to be mistaken. A number of Richard Napier's clients had seen apparitions, and he took some of these seriously. From the end of the seventeenth century, however, meetings with supernatural beings were denied as hallucinations or delusions by more and more people. Further, such delusions were now ranked with the more serious forms of madness. It is significant that Goodwin Wharton, a Whig member of Parliament from 1690 until his death in 1704, kept his adventures in other worlds a secret from others. In external appearance he was an average politician and a modest landowner. His rambles into the world of fairies, his conversations with angels, and the more than one-hundred pregnancies of his sixty-year-old mistress were only confided to his diary.

The English Revolution and the subsequent restoration of the monarchy had a catalytic effect. The disenchantment of the world gained a firmer hold among the orthodox establishment after 1660, which competed with the old religious sects and new movements such as Methodism. The established groups distrusted all forms of excessive and external religious zeal, which they collectively termed "enthusiasm." The new movements were characterized by great missionary fervor, expressed in mass meetings, and an impulsive spirituality, strongly contrasting with the intimate religious experience of the established groups. As a consequence, the established religions came to view excessive religious ardor per se as a form of insanity. The orthodox called the enthusiasts mad, who in their turn replied that they shared this charge with the prophets of the Old Testament. Some enthusiasts did in fact spend time in asylums. One was Christopher Smart. Having been previously locked up and released as "incurable," he spent four years, from 1759 to 1763, in a private institution in Bethnal Green. There he wrote *Jubilate Agno*, a millenarian work of poetry which sounds very strange indeed. It reflects Smart's conviction, which he was to proclaim later as a prophet, that he was a new Messiah called upon to reveal God's plan for the universe.

Dutch developments probably ran parallel to those in England. The leading groups in the Dutch Republic also tended to consider clamorous sects as politically dangerous and to adopt a skeptical attitude toward supernatural events. At the end of the seventeenth century there are two examples of religious enthusiasts who were labelled mad by some. One of them was a former burgomaster of Amsterdam, Koenraad van Beuningen, who retired from public life in 1684 to devote himself entirely to the kingdom of God. His fellows soon considered him insane, especially when he started to knock on neighbors' doors at night to warn them that the end was near. The other, Jan Rothe, already had a turbulent career as a prophet behind him when, in 1675, he accused William III of being a tyrant who let himself be worshipped as a God. He distributed pamphlets from a hiding place, but the city officials managed to arrest him after promising a reward of three-thousand guilders. If Rothe had not been related to patrician families, he might have ended on the scaffold. Partly to protect him, his relatives claimed that he was insane. Consequently, Rothe was merely confined to his home, while his brother-in-law, the magistrate Dirk Bas, was appointed as his guardian. The English minister Price had called him "a melancholic and insane person" in 1672 (Evenhuis: 186). Secularization is also reflected in the changing reactions to madness, which are dealt with next.

The Treatment of the Insane

The word, treatment, is preferred as a neutral, general term. It can include confinement as well as release, sympathy as well as indifference, mere custody as well as "cure." The question of which of these prevailed has to be answered here. Information is scarce; less is known about practice than about ideas. Archives of institutions from before 1800 are extant, but they have hardly been studied. A few forms of treatment in classical Athens were noted briefly in the previous section. Not much more is known about it. Our story begins in medieval Europe.

Pilgrimages

It is no surprise that the earliest reactions to madness were of a religious character. Like notions of insanity, its treatment was religiously colored for a long time. The spirituality of the elite and the populace in medieval Europe centered around the cult of saints. It has been explained in earlier chapters how a grave or another site associated with a saint was turned into a place of pilgrimage. There were all kind of reasons to go on pilgrimage. Some believers simply wished to do penance, while others had more concrete motives. Most saints had the reputation of specializing in particular fields. Saint Anthony, for example, is supposed even until our own day to help in finding lost objects. Other saints rescued people from various troubles. Those could be ordinary diseases but also possession, rabies, paralysis, or insanity.

Thus, a pilgrimage to a "madness saint" was one of the possible ways to get rid of insanity. It is difficult to determine when this custom arose. Although a number of the shrines in question dated from before A.D. 1000, the sources from that early period do not say who exactly the pilgrims were. Many saints were accorded a specific function only later. The oldest information about insane pilgrims, usually in the form of tales about the cures wrought by the saints, dates from the thirteenth century. The rituals which were customary at the shrines from the later Middle Ages onward were not recorded until the seventeenth century, when, in fact, they had been purged following Protestant criticism. Madness saints remained popular in Catholic regions after the period of the Reformation.

One of the most notorious madness saints was Saint Dimpna, who was worshipped in Geel in Belgium. Originally she had nothing to do with madness. Geel became a place of pilgrimage for the possessed and the insane, treated as one, in the second half of the fourteenth century. The zenith was reached in the seventeenth century. The arrival of so many pilgrims gave rise to the custom of lodging them in private homes. A number continued to live in Geel after finishing their pilgrimage. The place is well known for this until the present day. Lunatics live with private persons and they freely walk the streets. The seventeenth-century description of the shrine's ritual still speaks primarily of the possessed. They embark on a novena, nine days of religious contemplation. The ritual consists of seven items: (1) the pilgrims confess their sins and communicate; (2) they walk around the church three times and pass three times under the shrine containing Saint Dimpna's bones; (3) then the novena proper begins with a nine-day stay in the hospital belonging to the church, which they are not permitted to leave; (4) they attend mass there each day, drinking the water from the chalice in which the priest has washed his fingers; (5) they sleep with their clothes on for nine nights; (6) they make an offering to Dimpna consisting of their own weight in grain, which

(7) they have previously collected by begging. If a person has enough money, purchased grain is all right; "some unjustly think that this is less pleasing to God and Saint Dimpna." The ritual exemplifies the association of madness and sin: it is a form of expiation through which the participants hope to be freed from their affliction.

It is tempting to idealize the events at the shrine of madness saints and to claim that this was a golden age for the insane. Were they not walking around freely and wasn't their status of pilgrims that of pious believers on the way to a religious catharsis? To some extent this was true. Everyday reality, however, might be much more prosaic. First, the use of force was not uncommon; troublesome lunatics were not released. We hear of mad people whose families drove them to the shrine tied to a cart. Upon arrival some were tied to the altar; for others there were cells next to the church. Second, pilgrimages—and this holds true for all of them—brought material benefits to many. Grain for Saint Dimpna was of course food for the shrine and its administrators. Next, a host of laymen earned their living from the presence of pilgrims and their families. From an economic viewpoint, the shrine functioned like a modern tourist center. Tales about miraculous cures served as advertising brochures. Sometimes the advertisers were fraudulent, paying others to simulate insanity and cure. Although such practices were criticized, notably by humanists and Protestants, they were known and disapproved of before them.

Secular Forms of Treatment

Presumably not every lunatic went on pilgrimage, but little is known about other efforts at cure until the seventeenth century. It must not have been uncommon literally to beat insanity out of a person, but we do not know how often this happened. Thomas More tells about one case: a lunatic who had already stayed in Bedlam caused trouble to the inhabitants of the place where More was a magistrate. He had the nasty habit of disturbing mass with loud cries and lifting the skirts of kneeling women over their heads. More ordered the constables to whip the man, which made him come to his senses again and acknowledge his "faults." Hence, contemporaries saw this cure as a kind of conversion, which again reveals the religious and moral flavor. The whipping was a sort of rough exorcism. But whipping also belonged to the repertoire of ordinary punishments for delinquents. In early modern England some lawyers thought a plea of insanity in noncapital criminal cases useless, since it earned the suspect the same treatment which he sought to avoid. Nonetheless, the flogging of the insane is said to have been infrequent in England. It was only customary in the institutions of the eighteenth century. Flogging, to be sure, is not essentially different from modern forms of treatment like electroshock. Both methods are based on the hope that striking the body will affect the mind.

We may assume that few lunatics themselves requested a whipping. About physical cures undergone voluntarily before 1600 even less is known. Only a minority were able to afford the treatment of a specialist. The majority, as far as they opted for a physical cure, were obliged to rely on wandering quacks. In the Netherlands in the sixteenth and seventeenth centuries so-called stonecutters were active. They profited from the popular notion that insanity might be caused by a stone in one's head. This also could cause other ailments such as paralysis. We only know stonecutting from satirical prints about quackery. They picture the quack as a skillful magician (in the modern sense), who pretends to make an incision in the forehead and then triumphantly presents a stone to the credulous client. The frequency of those prints suggests that such operations were carried out in fact, but it remains unclear how the quacks succeeded in misleading their victims so blatantly.

And then there is the ship of fools. The motif is present in various literary works from the Rhineland around 1500, of which Sebastian Brant's *Narrenschiff* of 1494 is the best known. Foucault too thinks that in reality madmen were put on a boat together, sailing away as pilgrims in search of their lost reason. But proof from the Rhineland or elsewhere is lacking. Equally without proof, some authors have concluded from the motif of the wild man that lunatics were sometimes driven into the woods. It was indeed customary for urban governments to return individual, nonresident madmen to their place of birth. This happened in Bruges, for example. Sometimes those madmen were given pocket money to reach their destination; sometimes, when it had to be reached by river, they were put on a boat. This has nothing to do with the ship of fools, an allegorical theme which serves to criticize the follies and vanities of the sane world.

The Beginnings of Confinement

It is impossible to determine the percentage of lunatics who were subjected to these methods of treatment just described. In many cases, the community must have acquiesced, restricting itself to constant vigilance. If the madman was dangerous, his family might have locked him up at home. In an agrarian society with little geographic mobility most lunatics could be taken care of within their own community. As cities arose, problems increased. Some lunatics had no family in town; others could not be kept at home. The history of the confinement of the insane, then, begins with the emergence of cities.

At first they were not committed to separate institutions. Hospitals were the first institutions which occasionally admitted the insane. Unlike modern hospitals, they did not take care of only the sick. The homeless, poor travelers, the aged, and other needy persons also found a shelter in hospitals. In 1270 the court of Norwich determined that a man who had killed his wife and children was insane and he was committed to a hospital. A century later, the records of several Italian towns refer to madmen held in hospitals. Six persons staying in St. Mary of Bethlehem in London in 1403 were termed insane. This hospital evolved to become England's first madhouse, its name popularized into Bedlam. At the end of the Middle Ages monastic orders, such as the Holy Spirit and a little later the Cell brothers, devoted themselves to the founding of hospitals, a number of which eventually were reserved for the insane.

Hospitals as such were not closed institutions, and it is unknown whether the insane were kept in locked rooms. For relatively quiet lunatics, this may have been unnecessary. Unambiguous examples of confinement, however, are also known from the later Middle Ages. Ample information is available for northern Germany. In Hamburg it was recorded in 1376 that lunatics were kept in two towers of the ramparts. In one of them criminals were confined as well, although in a separate room. In Braunschweig in 1390 there is talk of cells near the city gates. Those cells, called by the local name of *dor(d)enkisten*, were common in the region. Often they appear to have been cages with windows on the street side. This arrangement offered passers-by the opportunity to make fun of the insane, as with animals in a zoo, but it also enabled the inmates to beg. In 1479 an inhabitant of Lübeck was recorded as having made a gift to the "poor mad people, sitting in front of the doors and gates in the *dordenkisten*" (Kirchhoff: 27). Ridicule and charity were both possible responses by the public. Insane members of richer families in Lübeck had separate rooms available in the city towers. Those locked up were usually referred to as *dol*, hence dangerous lunatics. Confinement in cells comparable to dorenkisten, at the city gates or at market squares, seems to have been practiced in other countries too. We note again that a golden age for the insane has never existed.

Hospitals were not institutions especially intended for the insane (except for those which later specialized), while the cells and cages do not deserve the name of institution. The earliest separate institutions, the first madhouses, emerged before 1500. Psychiatrists who write history consider this as a great achievement and disagree over exactly where and when the first madhouse was founded. A number of authors hold that it was the hospital of Our Lady of the Innocents, founded by Father Jofré at Valencia around 1410. It was supposed to have been intended exclusively for the insane, but it is quite uncertain whether that was true at its foundation. Let us first consider the Netherlands, then, where the information is less ambiguous.

The first Dutch madhouse was founded at Den Bosch in 1442, financed by a bequest from Reinier van Arkel. Its charter explains that the house is meant for persons who "are insane and are not masters over their senses and of necessity have to be kept constrained and under lock (Rooij: 91). Twenty years later Utrecht got the second Dutch madhouse, which was also made possible by a bequest, given by Willem Arntsz, a nobleman who had held office in the town. The charter is dated 1461, stating that the house is to admit six "poor, miserable, mad and raging people, who are in need of being kept constrained or under lock" (Weyde: 1). Both quotations contain the words constrained and locked, which indicate that these institutions were meant primarily for wild, dangerous lunatics. Indeed, in the northern Netherlands the word *dolhuis* was to become customary. Only later did these institutions begin to admit the simple-minded or the innocent.

The earliest madhouses belonged to the same category as hospitals and orphanages. Although a stay in one was unmistakably a form of confinement, they were founded as charitable institutions. The Utrecht records speak of a "work of charity." Willem Arntsz had promised to make his bequest in 1455 on the occasion of an amnesty for the political party to which he belonged. At the end of the fifteenth and in the course of the sixteenth century, however, a change of attitude took place in Europe leading to a more repressive treatment of various groups exhibiting deviant behavior (more about this in the next chapter). As a consequence, madhouses drifted away from the category of charitable institutions. We find the first signs of stigmatization in an association with the plague. The Utrecht madhouse was ordered to admit sufferers from the plague, who had long been treated as outcasts, during epidemics. The Amsterdam pesthouse had separate cells for the insane until the madhouse was opened in 1562, again following a bequest. Rotterdam built a new pest- and madhouse in 1599. From the middle of the seventeenth century plague did not return to the Netherlands, so that these institutions became pure madhouses again. Leprosy, which also carried a stigma, had earlier become infrequent. Around 1600 Amsterdam kept the simple insane in the leprosarium. In a number of German towns in the sixteenth and seventeenth centuries, empty leprosaria as well as pesthouses were turned into madhouses.

On a European scale, it is difficult to determine the exact chronology of what has been described, notably by Foucault, as expulsion and stigmatization of the insane. Certainly, the roots of this attitude date back to an early age. How, for example, are we to interpret the fact that a number of times in the middle of the fourteenth century the executioner was ordered to take a madman to the leprosarium in Bruges? And what about the placing of the insane next to criminals in Hamburg a few decades later? But the association of insanity and crime did not become common until the seventeenth century. In England, where Bedlam was the only madhouse until the middle of the century, local magistrates before then sometimes committed lunatics to houses of correction. That happened occasionally in the Netherlands too. France knew so-called hôpitaux généraux with wards for the insane, delinquents, and other deviants since about 1660. In eighteenth-century Germany the combination of a prison and a madhouse was extremely common. Upon the basis principally of such associations, historians have concluded that the insane were stigmatized. We should not imagine, however, that all madmen were locked up. Many of the vagabonds roaming through seventeenth-century England were a bit weird, or acted that way to raise sympathy. They were called Tom O'Bedlams because they had stayed in Bedlam, or said they had.

Madhouses and their Inmates. Not only did a stay in a madhouse have stigmatizing impact, it was also usually unpleasant. Most historians think that these institutions served only for custody and that the inmates were left largely to themselves. This opinion is generally correct. The few authors who claim the opposite come up with scarcely any proof. Madhouses were prisons, just like the institutions where beggars and thieves were confined, and contemporaries made no secret of this. Bedlam's inmates were referred to as prisoners in the second half of the sixteenth century. In a document of 1603 the cells in the Utrecht madhouse are called jails. The terminology of incarceration was apparently so common that the magistrates of Maastricht decided to "confine" a lunatic at Geel in 1747 and again in 1752. In addition to the mere fact that the inmates could not leave a madhouse, according to the prevailing stereotype all inmates were chained. This stereotype is based on little systematic research. In all probability, not all confined lunatics were chained all the time. But it was certainly not uncommon, as the cited passages from the charters of the Utrecht and Den Bosch institutions indicate. The accounts of the latter madhouse over the years 1471–1555 reveal orders for handcuffs, chains, belts, and strait chairs. In the seventeenth century the personnel of the madhouse at Bruges used handcuffs, strait jackets, and masks to prevent biting. The use of instruments of force to bridle the raging is a recurrent feature of the history of institutions until our own time. The so-called liberation of the insane by Pinel around 1800 is a myth created afterwards for propaganda purposes. Today, admittedly, the use of drugs has decreased dependency on conspicuous methods.

Madness was a source of amusement and ridicule from the age of the dorenkisten (cells) on. While the inmates were not allowed to leave the madhouse, visitors were allowed to enter it. Historians consider this custom annoying to lunatics, whose actual experience remains unknown, however. Ned Ward's descriptions, quoted in the previous section, suggest that to the contrary, at least some lunatics could amuse themselves with the visitors. The interest in Bedlam must have been huge. In 1657 the administrators, finding themselves unable to handle such large crowds, decided to close on Sundays. In the Netherlands visits to the insane appear to have been made on special days only; at least there were larger crowds then. At Den Bosch this happened at carnival time. On the day preceding Shrove Tuesday the staff treated the insane to warm pies; many people found this worth watching. Utrecht had its "madhouse fair" on Easter Monday and the Tuesday after. For a small sum of money visitors were admitted into the madhouse; often there were cake stalls in the hall.

Opposition to the display of lunatics existed already in the seventeenth century. In 1653 the Utrecht court sought to abolish the madhouse fair; its arguments were not recorded, but the regents of the house could not spare the income. In England Thomas Tryon, whom we met as a satirical writer, called for closing of Bedlam to visitors. He found the exhibition of the insane an inhumane show that only served the idle curiosity of youths and drunks. Bedlam was eventually barred to visitors in 1770. Opposition in the Netherlands increased from the middle of the eighteenth century. In 1748 the regents of the Den Bosch madhouse decided no longer to admit the public on the Monday before Shrove Tuesday. In recent years, they said, visitors had teased lunatics so much that they had become angry and could not be silenced for several days. This might deter rich families from taking the insane to the madhouse, decreasing its income. Besides, most visitors were soldiers and disorderly boys who slipped in without paying. Thus, the arguments were largely of a financial nature. In Utrecht the provincial synod of the Reformed church called for abolition of the madhouse fair in 1757, arguing that it was a residue from papist times. In 1783 they added that sympathy instead of mockery was the proper way to treat the insane. The prohibitions cited were not put into effect consistently. Visits were possible in Utrecht as well as Den Bosch as late as the beginning of the nineteenth century. A preliminary conclusion can be drawn from this: the emergence of madhouses from the fifteenth century onward brought a relative seclusion of the insane. Madness obtained a space of its own. Until the beginning of the nineteenth century, however, this seclusion was only partial. The public could come to watch the insane. Only after 1800 were the institutions closed to all spectators from outside.

The remark of the Den Bosch regents in 1748 suggests that lunatics from relatively wealthy families were also confined in madhouses. They were probably committed to separate wards with a milder regime. At least this was customary in Utrecht. In the eighteenth century, however, elite families often judged a stay in a madhouse beneath their dignity, although some still had members whom it was thought necessary to confine. In the Netherlands this could be done in so-called beterhuizen (houses for improvement). These institutions did not only have the insane as inmates. Their principal function was to detain drunks and other persons whose conduct was morally reprehensible. Thus, among the upper classes, madness no longer had an institution of its own. Beterhuizen had a relatively mild regime and did not admit visitors. This means that the seclusion of the insane and other deviants was more complete there.

There has been scarcely any quantitative study of the institutional experience of lunatics before 1800. A study of the hospital of St. Julian in Bruges is valuable. Although the author did not quantify his data, he presented them in such a fashion that they have been computerized. They apply to 595 committals from the period 1600–1795. The majority of those confined consisted of women, but their overrepresentation only dates from the eighteenth century, when they made up 65 percent of the total. In the seventeenth century the ratio was practically 1:1. The ages of the confined ranged from thirteen to eighty-seven years. In slightly over half of the cases the inmates' financial situation was indicated. The percentage of those called poor declined from 40 in the seventeenth century to 25 in the eighteenth. The length of a stay also varied strongly: 42 percent stayed in the madhouse for a year; 31 percent longer than ten and 18 percent longer than twenty years. A number of the insane had previously been committed somewhere else. This was the case with 16 percent in the seventeenth century and 48 percent in the eighteenth. In the latter period the previous committal had usually been in a private institution. Forty-six percent of those committed are recorded to have died in the madhouse, but in this case registration may not be complete. Finally, the type of insanity is alluded to in 161 cases. Those indications are not very clear, but they allow the conclusion that widely varying types were represented.

To what extent these data are representative for western Europe in the seventeenth and eighteenth centuries remains to be investigated. In any case, these figures cannot make us hear the voice of the inmates themselves. It is rarely heard at all, but in the seventeenth century there is a remarkable exception in the form of a work of poetry, written during a stay in Bedlam. *Lucida Intervalla* by James Carkesse was published in 1679. In one of his poems Carkesse defies Dr. Thomas Allen, proclaiming that his vomiting treatment would not succeed in killing the muses. He recommends the doctor take his own powder, from which he will surely die:

> What Homer, our great grandfather, did vomit,
> We licking up, turn sucking poets from it.
> Doctor, if this be my fate, when I spue,
> That lapping curs rise, all lampooning you.
> Your physick you must save, and past all hope,
> With *crocus metallorum* buy a rope (Feder: 157).

Medical Treatment?

Carkesse's poem describes a doctor attempting all kind of physical methods of treatment in Bedlam. In addition to induced vomiting, Carkesse mentions blood letting and purging, while he also associates the doctor with beatings, chains, and confinement in dark cells. Obviously, he did not like Dr. Allen. Bedlam had a medical administrator, Dr. Helkiah Crooke, as early as 1619. Crooke lived up to this name by financial malversations, which led to his dismissal in 1634. An additional charge was that he was seldom present in the institution and cured no one. Does this mean that physicians occupied themselves with the insane or, at least, were supposed to? Possibly England was a little precocious in this respect. On the other hand, it saw the rise of private madhouses after the middle of the seventeenth century; the majority of their proprietors were not medical specialists until 1800. In the Parisian *hôpital général* the insane were not subjected to treatment, but in the eighteenth century they were not admitted until a six-week cure in the *Hôtel-Dieu* had failed twice.

There is no sign that there was any medical intervention in Dutch madhouses. In Utrecht barber-surgeons visited the institution from the end of the sixteenth century, but their tasks consisted of treating physical ailments and shaving the insane. As late as the beginning of the nineteenth century the administrators refused admittance to a woman with the argument that she was suffering from melancholy and hence needed medical treatment. Surgeons in Den Bosch also restricted themselves to physical ailments. On one occasion a surgeon was called when a lunatic bit another inmate's leg. The administrators of the madhouse decided for themselves whether someone was fit to be released. In 1748 and 1760 they determined that a doctor was needed if it happened "that the insane are infected with some disease or other trouble" (Rooij: 282). The illness-model for insanity was obviously absent. Still, it arose in the Netherlands in the eighteenth century, as appears from petitions for confinement in beterhuizen. Originally it was the family itself who, as a rule, testified to the court that a member was insane; in cases of a petition for a prolonged stay the institution's manager often provided information. In the course of the eighteenth century, however, doctors' reports increased in frequency. Those declarations confirm that physicians occupied themselves with the insane, but we can also infer from them that no medical treatment was given in beterhuizen.

Not every lunatic was confined, of course. In the early modern period this was the fate primarily of more serious cases. Did milder cases receive any form of medical treatment? There is information about this in the notes made by Richard Napier from 1597 to 1642, which have been analyzed by Macdonald. Napier was one of the few practitioners who was not a quack and whose fees were within the reach of people of modest social status. The majority of his clients had physical complaints, but some two-thousand persons went to see him or were taken to him for mental or emotional disturbances. It is difficult to define Napier's position. He practiced astrology and had a perfect knowledge of the kabala. He was influenced by hermeticism and the theory of natural magic. At the same time, however, he was an Anglican clergyman with a solid reputation as a conservative and pious theologian. The methods of treatment he applied to clients with nonphysical complaints reflect this diversity of background. Astrology primarily served to obtain a diagnosis. Physiological forms of treatment might follow, such as purging, laxatives, blood letting, or prescribing various herbs and concoctions. Napier prescribed opiates as sedatives in cases of insomnia or fury. In addition to these physiological methods, he attempted to influence behavior. Melancholic persons received practical advice like "always choose merry company," "go to pleasant places," or "avoid somber thoughts." Persons who were psychologically troubled were advised to go to church regularly, since good Christian behavior would ultimately lead to normality. Astrology was also Napier's guide in determining whether sorcery had caused madness. At times he called upon the archangel Raphael in such cases. At a séance in 1619 Raphael confirmed that a spell had been cast upon five clients and predicted that two would recover. A little later Napier concluded that Raphael had been partly wrong, since one died.

The question is whether Napier should be defined as a physician and his treatment as therapy. One of the terms Macdonald uses for him is "healer." Originally, to heal meant to make someone "whole" again; unlike "cure" the word had religious and moral connotations. Many societies know the healer, who is at the same time a priest and a practitioner of medicine. He or she concentrates on diseases as well as problems of life. As long as religious and biological views of people were inextricably interwoven, there was a place for healers in Europe too. Napier was one, as were many of the "wise women." The secularization which set in from the middle of the seventeenth century made the religious component disappear, so that when the healer still existed, he became a physician. In the treatment of madness, however, he inherited the life problems which were henceforth increasingly viewed as illnesses.

Conclusion

Two long-term processes in the mental realm, privatization and secularization, are reflected in the developments regarding insanity. The first manifested itself notably in the emergence of madhouses. Madness partly disappeared from public life, acquiring its secluded space. This seclusion cannot be dated in an exact period but was present from the fifteenth century on. For a long time, however, madness remained semipublic, since the institutions admitted spectators. The acceleration in the process of privatization around 1800 put an end to this semi-openness.

Secularization is manifest in several ways. The practice of pilgrimage moved to the periphery, and interpretations of conduct in terms of possession declined in favor of insanity. Secularization is reflected most markedly in the rise of the illness-model. Biological explanations of behavior and a medical treatment of insanity were not absent from preindustrial Europe, but they were inextricably linked to a religious-moral approach. As madness and religion were separated, madness became the domain of physicians and the illness-model emerged.

7 THE BODY INJURED: Violence and Physical Suffering in Daily Life

In previous chapters we met various examples of violence: fights between the inhabitants of neighboring villages; men who beat their wives and vice versa; Jews murdered during the first Crusade; the self-chastisement of the flagellants; witches burned at the stake; madmen in chains. Aggressiveness and coercion were present in preindustrial Europe at all levels of life. But violence and the threat of it loom large in our society too. We observe foul play at sport's grounds, are confronted with mugging in the cities, and possibly fear the use of nuclear weapons. And yet the argument that everything has remained the same would sound strange in this book. As it happens, it would not be true. The nature of violence as well as the attitudes toward it have changed considerably in the course of the centuries. As these developments are related to the others surveyed here, they need to be discussed.

In today's parlance, violence has become a label pinned on almost any act that is found objectionable. We speak of verbal violence, sexual violence, and the structural violence which affects us indirectly. In these pages the focus is restricted to those forms which to a lesser or greater extent imply an encroachment upon the body's physical integrity. The three notions in the subtitle of this chapter are a guide. A person's body is often injured against his will; the word violence has this primary connotation. But sometimes people voluntarily risk the integrity of their bodies, in sports for example. The notion of physical suffering, therefore, is necessary too. Still another form of violence concerns the physical treatment legally imposed as punishment on delinquents. The notion of daily life, finally, has its function too. Violence at special moments, in particular the massive and collective violence of wars, revolutions and riots, is not discussed here. Enough has already been written about such violence.

There is no point in analyzing elements from previous chapters for a second time, except for a few themes which have been studied more systematically over time. Data on the treatment of criminals, our major theme, are abundant. Topics such as feuds and duels, crimes of violence, sports contests, and the tormenting of animals comprise the first section. The second section takes up the major theme with an analysis of scaffold punishments: their application, their ritual character, and their eventual disappearance. The last section discusses the rise of a new method for dealing with criminals: the prison, which had already appeared by the end of the sixteenth century but did not become the major penal institution until the nineteenth.

Violence in Preindustrial History

Among most animal species aggression, once prompted by external stimuli, manifests itself directly, responding to biologically inherent internal stimuli. Humans have usually learned to some degree to fit their violent inclinations into a pattern, which will vary according to the character of a given society. It may be simple or complex, ritual or instrumental; in each instance it will tell us something about the mental constitution of the people and the way it is socially formed. In the earliest societies, about which we have hardly any information, the pattern of violence was probably a function of the quest for food. Unlike most other species, humans from an early time had the advantage over other creatures which wanted to eat them. The necessity to find food for themselves, however, remained urgent. It forced some groups of people to cooperate but others to become hostile. Collins claims that in many tribal societies, there is no basic difference between hunting animals for food and the war hunt aimed at human foes. As soon as the signal for attack has been given, aggressive emotions may have relatively free rein. Human opponents are also equated to animals with whom there is practically no identification.

Feuds and Codes

The preindustrial society under discussion had already passed this stage. In agrarian Europe violence was never exclusively a question of allowing aggressive emotions free play. Violence was always ritualized. No matter how many deaths might result, miniwars between the lords of neighboring estates and vendettas between rival families had their own codes. The capacity for identification was greater than in tribal societies. Paradoxically, this manifested itself most clearly in the torture and maiming of enemies; someone who deliberately inflicts suffering on another had to be capable of sharing his feelings to a certain extent. In order to derive satisfaction from causing pain, he must himself know how it feels. Obviously this implies only a slight identification with the victim.

Still another characteristic of European agrarian societies around A.D. 1000 affected the experience of violence. These societies were more differentiated than the tribal world. One group, whom we may call simply "the knights," enjoyed a virtual monopoly on carrying weapons; they were specialists in violence. Ordinary peasants, whether serfs or free, might engage in fighting, but it was very different because they did not use weapons. Next there was the clergy. Clerics traditionally opposed the knightly warrior ethos and attempted to curb the aggressiveness they found in society. In particular they called upon supernatural forces in the struggle against feuds. In eleventh-century Flanders monks at various places managed to make peace among embattled knights by coming with the bones of Saint Ursmar. In one episode near Strazeele they carried the relics in a ceremonial procession encircling the scene of a battle among hostile ruffians, most of whom were thereupon reconciled. A few who refused fled, all to meet death in the next three months.

Already in the early Middle Ages, then, violence could not be employed without restraint. But this should not blind us to the fact that medieval society was without doubt much more violent than ours. Until the beginning of the sixteenth century group solidarity expressed in fighting, injuries, and even slayings was characteristic of all social classes from high to low. Burghers were involved no less than knights. The vendettas in the Italian cities, immortalized in the legend of Romeo and Juliet, are well known. Conflicts and party struggles in the urbanized Netherlands often became bloody too. Even the small village of Montaillou in France, where neither nobles nor burghers lived, was divided around 1300 into two coalitions of families who engaged in a sometimes bloody struggle. The dominant Clergues were supported by various other houses. Their position was challenged by the Liziers and the Azémas, of inferior lineage but still determined to come out on top. The antagonism between Catholics and Cathars played a role in this factional struggle, but it did not run exactly parallel to the family rivalry. In the end the determination of the less powerful faction was insufficient, and they went under. Raymond Lizier's body was found outside the village, murdered by unknown persons, probably at the order of the Clergues. Then, the victors, although themselves secretly embracing Catharism, marshalled their connections to have Pierre Azéma imprisoned by the Inquisition.

The authorities repeatedly tried to suppress these feuds, which remained customary for a long time. Florentine magistrates in the fourteenth century, for example, ruled that vendettas could only be practiced by the heads of families and then only under special conditions. In all other cases, the participants would be considered ordinary violent offenders and murderers, not as lawful defenders of their honor. For centuries, however, the authorities were relatively powerless in this respect. It was not until larger and stronger states emerged and cities became hierarchical units that the opportunities and the impulse to settle personal scores with arms in hand declined. This development did not take place at the same time everywhere. In certain areas, such as Sicily, the state's power is relatively limited even today and consequently the readiness to engage in vendettas is still strong. This relationship, discussed in chapter 1, needs no further explanation.

It is impossible to quantify the level of violence in all of Europe until the sixteenth century, but two nonstatistical observations relevant to mentalities may be made. First, the threshold of violence was lower than it is today. People were quicker and readier to engage in violent action. Second, aggressive behavior and the infliction of pain were tolerated to a greater extent. Bystanders were eager spectators in serious fights and were indifferent when servants, children, or thieves were punished. Several investigators of medieval England have observed that there were few restraints on the use of violence. People would insult each other for minor reasons, and the person insulted immediately responded with a physical assault. The number of murders within families was relatively low. Most perpetrators of homicides were neighbors, friends, or total strangers who had met accidentally. This suggests that the causes lay in suddenly infuriated passion rather than in long pent-up tensions. We get a view of this form of passion at the beginning of the sixteenth century and in another country in the autobiography of the artist Benvenuto Cellini. Unconcealed competitiveness and envy of the work of colleagues is difficult to imagine for us now. Cellini and the silversmith Lucagnolo, despising each other's work, entered into a contest: would the latter's bowl make more money than the former's ornament? Both started to work with grim faces and a derogatory smile. Artistic competition was not the only thing to heat up emotions. In Rome, at another time, a decorative jar made for a Spanish bishop was brought back to Cellini for repair. When a servant of the bishop came to get it at night, Cellini first refused to hand it over, since it had not been paid for. The servant immediately drew his sword, but when the artist did the same, he hesitated and withdrew. He later returned with a group of compatriots. A big fight ensued in which Cellini's neighbors eagerly participated, calling the Spaniards converted Jews not worthy of trust.

Violence Domesticated

English medieval sources are the only ones that allow us to draw valid conclusions about the level of violence in statistical terms. A graph has been constructed for England, showing the trend in the number of homicides from the thirteenth to the twentieth century. Although based on fragmentary data, it indicates that there were twenty homicides per one hundred thousand inhabitants in the thirteenth century; the number declined to thirteen or fourteen around 1500; it went even lower in the sixteenth and seventeenth centuries, reaching about five at the beginning of the eighteenth. Thereafter, the decreasing trend continues, although slightly. Nonmortal violence followed this trend. From his elaborate analysis of criminal trials, not only for murder or homicide but also for fighting, injuries and threats, Beattie concludes that English society grew less violent in the second half of the eighteenth century.

The taming of aggressive impulses in the course of the preindustrial period is unmistakable. Comparable developments probably took place on the European continent. French historians claim that criminality in the course of the seventeenth and eighteenth centuries came to consist of less violence and more theft. At the beginning of this period violent offenses predominated, while crimes against property did so at its end. This thesis can be contested with regard to thefts, but this need not concern us. The level of violence in France seems to have declined in fact between 1600 and 1800, although certainly not uniformly and at the same pace in all regions. In addition, the ritual violence of the young, formerly tolerated, was increasingly criminalized. In Sweden, too, the level of violent offenses declined in the course of the early modern period. To the extent this has been investigated in the Netherlands, a comparable trend is visible. The majority of the population of seventeenth-century Amsterdam carried a knife as a matter of course. When someone drew a knife during a fight in a tavern, the others immediately did the same. This points to a readiness for physical attack which was still relatively great. It is harder to tell from the Dutch statistical evidence just when this readiness eventually became smaller. Amsterdam witnessed a sharp decline in the number of those prosecuted from 1700 onward, but all types of offenses were involved. Offenders themselves often became more careful in their conduct. At the end of the eighteenth century many, although by no means all, of the robber bands operating in the Dutch Republic ordinarily employed violence in a selective way, not haphazardly. The gang known as the Great Dutch Band relied on informers who carefully sized up the situations in which it operated, so that victims seldom lost their lives.

Developments with respect to criminal violence did not coincide throughout Europe. The Mediterranean countries in particular maintained a high level of homicides and crimes causing injury for a long time. The figure for violence only started to decline in these lands in the twentieth century. Still another aspect of crime, the counter-violence of the victims, also reflected the attitude toward violence. Persons threatened with a knife today usually hand over their purse; many carry insurance against burglary. In earlier centuries the situation was different. Cases have been reported from eighteenth-century France of peasants who were robbed on their way to the market pursuing their assailants for hours and finally recovering their possessions by force. This is the reverse of our modern preferences: keeping their property was worth more to these peasants than avoiding injury, although probably not more than staying alive.

The history of dueling provides a concrete illustration of the taming of violence. Duels were practiced only during a period extending from the sixteenth to the nineteenth century. Bloody and even deadly, they were nonetheless a stylized form of violence. The ritualization of personal combat which had already taken place was further developed in the duel. In addition to vendettas, medieval nobles had fought their conflicts in three other ways: official judicial combats in person or by means of professional champions, or tournaments. A tournament of course was a sporting event, but it might quickly resemble an armed struggle, whether or not because of latent tensions. These three types of knightly combat disappeared, however, around 1500, their place taken by the formal duel. In most countries this shift was only completed after a pause in which almost nothing seemed to happen in this field. That is another warning against the idea of a unilinear development. The formal duel was conceived in Renaissance Italy, but it became a tradition particularly in France. It appeared in England in the course of the sixteenth century and in Germany in the seventeenth.

Formalization made the duel into a restrained and courteous event in the eyes of the participants. It began with the challenge by the party who considered himself irreparably insulted. Time and place were agreed upon and the weapons chosen. The participants preferred an uninhabited area with the first beams of sunrise or in the twilight, because of the illegality the affair soon acquired. The sword, the aristocratic weapon, was originally preferred; at a later period pistols were frequently used. Each party brought one or more seconds and a surgeon. In theory, one of the seconds' tasks was to convince the principals, after one or more blows or shots, that they had received enough satisfaction or to reconcile them. This did not always work out in practice. Notably in the sixteenth century, duels frequently resulted in casualties. The period around 1600 constituted the heyday of the duel, at least in France and England. In both countries the last peak came at the middle of the seventeenth century.

Criminalization and repression by the government and an ideological campaign by the church were the most important counterforces. The *Parlement* of Paris made duelling into a crime in 1599 by including it into the category of *lèse-majesté*. In 1627 the first aristocrat was executed, the count of Bouteville, who had engaged in no less than twenty-two duels between the ages of fifteen and twenty-eight. In 1651 a minority among the French aristocracy founded a brotherhood, whose members pledged themselves to renounce duelling. Later this attitude became common among the majority of the nobility. Nobles, however, were never the only duel fighters. Those who bore arms professionally were also inclined to use them in this way and, in the eighteenth century, the duel became characteristic of the world of the military. It has never been customary among the bourgeoisie; apparently, it was a stranger to the commercial mentality from the start. La Bruyère, voicing the opinions of the French bourgeoisie, called duels faddish and irrational. The strong bourgeois influence in the Dutch Republic perhaps explains why there was little heard of duels there. Soldiers and students were the principal culprits. In Germany too students were described as frequent duel fighters, and they continued the duel into the twentieth century. In most western European countries, however, its frequency sharply declined in the second half of the nineteenth century.

In addition to this official duel, there was an unofficial one, which can be considered an element of popular culture. Some information comes from England in the first half of the eighteenth century. Rather than choosing a weapon, the participants boxed. It was neither a sport contest nor a spontaneous fight, but a regulated combat designed to settle a conflict honorably. Although this popular duel did not usually lead to casualties, there were exceptions. In 1742 William Gray's opponent never rose again. Both men had quarrelled in a Surrey inn and they had decided to settle the matter at night in the courtyard, which the innkeeper lit with a candle.

The official duel was characteristic of a transitional period, in which nobles were no longer inclined toward savage assault, but still clung to a show of independence toward everyone, even the king. It was no coincidence that the theory of the duel was especially developed in sixteenth-century Italy. A duel, the protagonists said, only took place among equals. By definition, a person's honor could not be hurt by someone of lower status. Conversely, when a non-aristocratic soldier challenged a person of higher status, the confrontation could not take place unless the latter agreed, temporarily descending to the level of the challenger. In the cities of the Renaissance a high-ranking nobleman might find himself under a ruler whom he considered in fact only a commoner. Girolamo Muzio gave voice to this attitude. A poor or a rich man can proclaim himself as my lord, he said, but he cannot give orders to make me good or bad. This can be contrasted with the statement of the English chancellor Francis Bacon in the seventeenth century: "The fountaine of honour is the king, and his aspect, and the accesse to his person continueth honour in life, and to be banished from his presence is one of the greatest eclipses of honour that can bee" (Billacois: 348). The change of mentality implicit in this quotation was enforced in France by Louis XIV. He redefined the "point of honor" as "pleasing the king." English authors who wrote against the duel in the eighteenth century also aimed their attack primarily at the point of honor. A true sense of honor, they asserted, was incompatible with exercising violence.

A special code of honor was therefore central. In eighteenth-century England most challengers felt insulted because they had been called a liar. For France during the period 1560–1659, the following list of reported causes for a duel can be given: women (twenty times), membership of a rival family (ten times), competition for offices (seven times), because of an inheritance (seven times), and problems with precedence (six times). Knowledge of the causes of duels does not answer the question of why a violation of one's honor had to be negated by physical means. We can build an explanation upon Anton Blok's historical-anthropological analysis. Blok notes that the traditional code of honor, upheld in some Mediterranean regions until our day, was strongly interwoven with bodily and animal symbolism. The horns attributed to a cuckolded husband originally represented the horns of a billy goat, which allows other males to associate with she goats. By contrast, the reputation of a man of honor was linked to more aggressive animals. He is able to protect the women of his family, to keep down other men, thus commanding respect and showing that he has "balls." Such a direct linkage with animals and the body was already absent in the mentality of sixteenth-century noblemen in more northerly regions, but for them too honor was still strongly tied to the physical person. A violation of this honor could therefore only be revenged by violence, showing who could ultimately command the greatest respect.

From the end of the seventeenth century the notion of honor began to change in large parts of Europe. Honor was associated less and less with someone's outer appearance and his capacity to protect his followers physically. The concept was spiritualized; this was one of the things which French and English opponents of the duel sought to express verbally. In absolutist states service to the king became the greatest honor. In consequence the notion of honor in democratic states was robbed of its status connotations and linked to ideas about virtue. Thus the disappearance of the duel was not only a result of changing attitudes toward violence but also of the spiritualization of the concept of honor. These two changes of mentality, however, were interrelated. Both had to do with a decreasing importance of physical bravery, which was caused in its turn by the rise of stable and pacified states.

The spiritualization of the concept of honor also affected the practice of suicide. According to several authors, its frequency is inversely related to that of homicides. They argue that aggression is directed inward in one case and outward in the other. It remains to be seen whether the negative correlation is really strong. In any case, the knightly ethos was incompatible with acceptance of suicide. Many of the early homicides, by contrast, originated from insults to a person's honor and the necessity to command respect. The romanticization and slight acceptance of suicide which set in from the late eighteenth century would have been impossible without changes in the notion of honor. In a world where a violation of one's sense of honor could no longer be made good by physical attack, suicide became less shameful.

Sportive Recreations and the Fate of Animals

The history of various pastimes illustrates the changes in the experience of violence. A number of our contemporary sports are derived from preindustrial forms of recreation. Since many of these sports also have their origins in England, English pastimes are of special importance. The word, sport, was already used in England in the early modern period. People on the Continent adopted it in the nineteenth century to describe what they saw as a new type of recreation, less rough and more bound by rules. The preindustrial sports can be included in the lesser tradition, but persons from the elite played along at least until 1700. In England members of the gentry were reported to be enthusiastic football players well into the eighteenth century. Their descriptions of the game are therefore of a realistic nature, lacking a moralizing flavor. Wealthy burghers held themselves aloof from the traditional sports more strongly. Among the worldly elites they were in the lead in the change of mentalities which we shall discuss.

Football was the collective name for almost all team sports in England before about 1840. The oldest references date from the fourteenth century. But we would have a hard time to recognize it as any game known to us today. According to some authors, the name merely indicated that the players were not on horseback; for the rest, various kinds of play activities could be meant. The major differences between preindustrial and modern football can all be derived from the regulation and formal organization highly characteristic of today's sports. Anything like a national competition was unknown until the middle of the nineteenth century. In each village or small town two groups played against each other once or a few times a year. Each locality used different rules. Sometimes the teams were restricted in size, sometimes the number of participants was unlimited. There was seldom a specific playground. The participants used an open field or they played in the middle of the town. The audience was small; if someone came to watch, he was expected to participate. There were no fixed hours either. Derby's Shrove Tuesday match lasted well into the evening. Sometimes the players deliberately hid the ball until dark, smuggling it onward under a shirt or petticoat. Variants of the game had their own degree of toughness. Local traditions in East Anglia distinguished "rough play" from "civil play." In the first variant boxing was allowed as a technique, in the second only wrestling and kicking.

That leads us to the aspect which is most important in the context of this chapter: the freedom to inflict physical injury upon opponents. These games were also rituals, as is apparent from their association with the calendar of holidays. But this did not prevent them from being more violent than ours, as evidenced by the example from East Anglia. The "freemen marblers" of Corf Castle in Dorset even had a special fund for accidents. Each man married during the previous year put a shilling into a box from which, if a player was killed, an apprentice would be paid for the service of his widow. Of course no one liked to see players dragged away dead, but apparently, this was an accepted risk. Torn clothes, wounds, and broken bones must have been more usual. A few individuals would take the opportunity to strike at a neighbor against whom they had a grudge, even if he did not have the ball. In some cases, women were also mentioned as players. Games of this type, descriptions of which date mostly from the seventeenth and eighteenth centuries, can be called mock battles. The life of the players was not directly at stake, nor was inflicting injury the primary aim, but the character of the game and the acceptance of violence inherent in it still made physical injuries quite frequent.

The traditional sports disappeared or were reorganized in the course of the nineteenth century. Codification of rules led to a differentiation into soccer, rugby, and eventually still other sports. In the same period games with animals became subject to prohibition. Those games are merely a part of the rich but largely uninvestigated history of the relationships between humans and animals, but they touch directly on the theme of this chapter. Not all of the original animal sports were bloody affairs. Horse racing was very popular among the gentry in eighteenth-century England. A hundred years earlier aristocratic visitors were among the crowds watching cock fights and duels between a bull and a few wild dogs. In such games the audience enjoyed watching the animals they incited kill each other. Pastimes in which animals were tormented also occurred outside England. An Amsterdam ordinance of 1689 repeats a prohibition against walking large dogs in the street, adding that it was also forbidden to "organize a bear, bull or other fight against such dogs, bulldogs or foxes in this town or its jurisdiction" (*Municipal Archives, Amsterdam, Charter Book Q*, fo. 179). The servants of the prosecutor and the almshouse provosts were ordered to beat these dogs to death. The magistrates were therefore not moved by pity. This prohibition probably originated in a concern for public order in the crowded city. Spanish bull fights, which are still well known today, involved a struggle between a man and an animal, but an unequal one. In the sixteenth and seventeenth centuries, bull fights were less stylized than today. The court and the nobility in Spain formed an enthusiastic audience in this period. With the accession of the Bourbons in 1715 the game lost the court's favor, but a reaction came at the end of the eighteenth century. Reformers developed a new style in which the emphasis lay on the agility of the toreador rather than on butchering the bull. The spectacle was again shared by elite and populace together.

In one way or the other, cats suffered most, despite or perhaps even due to a certain ambivalence toward them. We saw in chapter 3 how they played a central role in all kind of magical customs. They were among the first species to be kept as pets; the habit arose in England in the sixteenth century. The sexual symbolism with which also we endow the word "pussy" was not unknown in preindustrial Europe. But sometimes the tormenting and killing of cats were precisely among the most pleasant pastimes which people could imagine. Three examples may be given.

In sixteenth-century Paris the festivities of St. John's Day culminated into the burning alive of stray cats. Tied in a sack or basket they were lowered into the pyre, which was sometimes lit by the king or the dauphin in person. Almost identical ceremonies were performed in other French cities, such as Metz where the tradition was maintained until about 1770. Hence, the Paris journeymen printers who played a game upon cats a few decades earlier were not alone. They managed to pull a trick on their boss and his wife, keeping them awake at night with mimicked meowing. It ended with a ritual massacre of all the cats they could lay hands on, complete with a mock execution. The journeymen considered this the most hilarious episode in their entire career. It would lead us too far to deal at length with the symbolism inherent in the event; it is sufficient to conclude that the act also expressed indifference to the suffering of animals. The third example comes from the Netherlands. In the second half of the eighteenth century the popular writer Le Francq van Berkhey described some popular recreations; among them was cat clubbing. The organizers put a cat in a barrel and hung the barrel in a tree. From a distance the village youths in turns threw a piece of wood, so that the barrel would finally fall apart. The winner was the one whose throw saw the cat either jumping out of the barrel or falling to the ground with it unconscious or dead.

The description of cat clubbing leads us to the theme of resistance to several of the pastimes just reviewed. Le Francq van Berkhey adds that "nowadays a ball is often put in the barrel instead of a cat." Voices had apparently been raised in his time against the tormenting of animals, but he says nothing more about it. More information on this point is available for England. Already at the beginning of the seventeenth century notably the Puritans attacked blood sports. They even condemned watching fights between animals, since their wildness was a consequence of mankind's fall; to enjoy the spectacle was sinful. The protest of this religious minority did not catch on at the time; especially among court circles, who defended traditional sports. Later, however, a growing sensitivity developed among the bourgeoisie and parts of the aristocracy, culminating into a rejection of animal-tormenting pastimes in the eighteenth century. Next, games between people also came under fire from the reformers. Traditional football had been attacked from the beginning, but in the fourteenth century it had been argued that it distracted from the sport of archery, which was much more useful for the country's defense. In the course of the eighteenth century the violent character of football was a reason for some to urge its abolition, considering it dangerous, irrational, and useless.

As we know, football all but disappeared, but then, in the middle of the nineteenth century it was reorganized and bound by strict rules so that it began to look like the game (called soccer by Americans) we know now. Once perfectly normal techniques for taking the ball from an opponent are now serious fouls. The inherent change of mentality is plain. Pastimes with animals, on the other hand, rather than being reformed in the nineteenth century, were legally prohibited and suppressed. Those developments are beyond the chronological framework of this book and hence they are merely noted. It has to be added that this change was not simultaneous throughout Europe. The persistence of bull fighting, despite its new style, unmistakably testifies to this. Neither did those developments involve all animals and every circumstance. Vivisection, for example, and the attitudes toward harmful insects testify to this in our time.

To conclude, sport violence and the tormenting of animals remained uncriticized for a longer time than the aristocratic duel. This need not surprise us. Duels were more deadly on the average than sports contests and the victims were human and often of high rank. Hence, duels were treated in principle as a more serious type of violence. All these developments together provide a picture of the complex process of the taming of violence. An increase in the capacity for identification played an important role. Vendettas, duels, and escalating village quarrels took place among people from each other's immediate surroundings, in principle equals. Their restriction meant that the internal identification within groups increased. It hurt to hurt those near to you. But the identification with groups of outsiders also increased, as we will see in the next section. Animals were a special kind of outsider and, in due course, some people could feel empathy with them too.

Heyday and Decline of Scaffold Punishments

Two types of attitudes that may be involved when violence is practiced, seen, and accepted are often distinguished, although in distinct terms. Here they are called vindictiveness and indifference. The first concept has to be interpreted broadly: vindictiveness refers to a conscious intention to hurt someone, regardless of who actually does the injury. In the case of indifference, the victim is harmed for other reasons than those stated, but the pain suffered fails to bother those who inflict it or observe it. Both attitudes can be present in a given situation. This holds true for most of the examples noted in the previous section, as well as for public executions. Magistrates largely acted out of vindictiveness, although it was regulated by law; judges thought that the culprits deserved their suffering. Vindictiveness may also be dominant among the victims of a crime and their relatives and immediate neighbors. The executioner, on the other hand, merely followed orders and primarily displayed indifference, the attitude that in the long run prevailed among the overwhelming majority of spectators at public performances of corporal and capital punishment in preindustrial Europe. It was precisely this indifference that was subject to a process of change at the end of the preindustrial period. Some groups turned against this attitude and attempted to influence others.

Awesome Ceremonies

Let us begin with the ritual which accompanied public executions in Amsterdam, as it was described between 1650 and 1670 by magistrate Hans Bontemantel. The scaffold was erected in front of the town hall at Dam square one to four times a year. A dozen or more offenders were usually subjected to a flogging, and then some also to a more serious penalty such as branding. One or two death sentences would also be carried out, depending on what trials had been held in the preceding period. A public execution was not just one event out of many, it was a ceremony in which the judges themselves played a major role. It was unmistakably ritualization of violence, with the magistrates consciously instituting it as a theatrical spectacle.

The execution usually took place on a Saturday. On Friday night the prosecutor and two judges visited those condemned to death in the courtyard of the town hall, where those on trial were jailed. The bailiff called upon them to prepare to die. When he finished, a preacher and an assistant especially charged with consoling the dying ministered

to the prisoners. On Saturday morning, prosecutor, judges and burgomasters arrived at the town hall dressed in their "blood robes" and
"blood sashes." Since those robes were black, their name only can
have referred to what was about to happen. Inside the town hall a
prayer by those present began the ceremony. Then the death sentences
were read for the first time. When this had been done, the prosecutor
asked all the judges and burgomasters in turn whether it was the
proper time to exercise justice according to the town's ancient custom.
When the answers had been given, the judges, instructed by the burgomasters, declared the culprits to be "children of death." The mode
of the death penalty was formally established next, again on the in-
struction of the burgomasters. Then the secretary recited the confirmed verdicts. The culprits were led to the court room, where they
were awaited by those sentenced to lesser punishments. The bell was
tolled and the rod of justice put out the window. The magistrates took
seats in the windows of the gallery, where they had a view of the scaffold and the spectators. The secretary then read aloud the sentences of
those condemned to corporal punishment. With the preacher and the
convicted men and women, the magistrates returned to the court
room once more to say a prayer. When they again took their seats, the
actual execution began. It was an anticlimax to some extent, since the
hangman carried out the death penalties first and then proceeded with
the lesser punishments, which offered the spectators an opportunity
to count the lashes; the number for each offender was determined by
the prosecutor on the spot. When it was all over, the magistrates withdrew and the rod of justice was taken in.

In other towns and villages in the Netherlands and elsewhere, a
similar type of ritual was performed, although with local variations.
In Amsterdam the cells of the condemned were in the basement of the
town hall so that they did not have to go into the street. Elsewhere they
went from jail to the place of execution in a ceremonial procession,
together with the judges, the hangman, and a minister or priest. That
was the procedure in Groningen and Utrecht in the Netherlands as
well as in large metropolises such as London, Paris, and Seville. In
Seville the culprit usually rode a donkey. The religious element in the
execution was somewhat more prominent in Catholic countries. For
example, the condemned was required to seek forgiveness in front of
the church, carrying a burning candle. In German Protestant districts
school children sang songs of death. Despite these variations, executions were essentially similar everywhere; they were public rituals,
staged so as to make the deepest impression upon the spectators.
Along with the theme of deserved punishment, the motifs of repen-

tance and justice were prominent. The formal participation of the magistrates made it all official.

For the historian of mentalities, the ritual context in which the corporal and capital punishment was performed is what really matters. We may consider this as part of the system of repression. Repression is distinct from punishment in a strictly juridical sense; it consists of all means which ruling groups employ to keep the population in line. Staging executions belongs to this just as much as prosecution policy, methods of interrogation, and the responses to noncriminal deviant behavior. Changes in mentality are reflected in the changing modes of repression. Yet we cannot take the severity or mildness of repression in all societies as an indication of its attitude toward violence. An institutionalized repression only develops with the rise of a stronger state authority. Feuds, dealt with in the previous section, were a form of private justice. With the emergence of more stable states and hierarchical cities, justice administered from above definitively took the place of vendettas. Judicial torture for those suspected of a serious crime who denied their guilt, which had been well established in the sixteenth century, also played a part in this new penal system. From then until at least the end of the nineteenth century, changing modes of repression can be taken as an indicator for changes in the experience of violence.

Modes of repression changed on two fronts from the sixteenth to the nineteenth century. Two major elements which originally had characterized the preindustrial system of repression as contrasted with that of today and which we saw in the Amsterdam ceremonial, gradually declined. Compared with our own time, repression was more strongly directed at the body and it had a more public character. But publicity and the body as target did not play an equally prominent role in preindustrial repression until the end. Their decline was implied in various changes from the sixteenth century onward. Let us first consider a few examples of the two elements and then review the changes.

The execution ceremony also served to underline the power of the rulers, in a period when the authority of government, although established, was not fully consolidated and bureaucratized. Violence by governments was made visible, but in a ritual form and certainly not as naked oppression. The spectacle of justice and repentance was also meant to remove some of the ugliness of the event, making it quite distinct from unbridled vindictiveness. The magistrates took great pains to organize a "beautiful execution." The condemned had to acknowledge the enormity of their crimes and the justice of their punishment. Before being led to the scaffold, those about to be whipped or branded kneeled down in front of the judges to thank them for their mildness. Those to be hanged or beheaded were expected to display repentance and to approach eternity with a clean conscience. When a culprit in a capital crime was not repentant, the judges had a clergyman try to persuade him at length until he gave in. Of course this did not always work, but the majority of those executed ultimately conformed to these religious expectations.

In some countries a speech delivered by the condemned from the scaffold provided the climax of the morality play. This was true notably of English culprits, who spoke with the rope already around their neck. John Marketman of West Ham, Essex, while drunk had murdered his wife out of jealousy in 1680. At the place of execution after the sermon he addressed himself to the public, reviewing his entire life. Even as a child he had been disobedient to his parents; as a young man he had desecrated the sabbath and committed all kinds of debauchery. Everything grew worse during his marriage. Now he asked forgiveness from God, hoping that each onlooker would pray with him. Then the hangman did his job. Sharpe analyzes a number of such speeches, concluding that they all followed a stereotypical pattern. Vices in earliest youth inevitably led to a great misdeed or a criminal existence. For the public the lesson was plain. In the Netherlands such speeches by the condemned were not permitted. The condemned expressed their repentance silently or kept on praying while their bones were broken, as the notorious murderess Hendrina Wouters did in 1746. Sometimes the Amsterdam prosecutor spoke to the offender the evening before the execution. He did so in 1766 with Jean Hubain, a Swiss atheist about to be broken on the wheel for robbery with murder. Hubain was not repentant, but the prosecutor still managed to speak edifying words:

Jean Hubain, the reason why I let you appear at this spot is to tell you openly that you are going to die because of committed and confessed crimes. . . . With such awesome ceremonies as this it is my habit to give an admonition to those condemned to death. . . . But in what way shall I admonish you, miserable Hubain, who has already been shown the road to salvation by so many of our ministers but who still persists in blasphemously mocking God and religion. . . . I speak to you . . . as a friendly advisor: lie down at God's throne of grace . . . , in order that tomorrow, when you raise your eyes in an awesome eternity, you may not find yourself in a place where you, worm, will never die but be tormented eternally (Spierenburg: 62).

Visible Examples.   Thus, the ceremony of justice served to confirm the power of the authorities and to underline the justice of punishment. The execution had an exemplary function. The fact that a display of violence could be taken as a positive example demonstrates once more that violence was largely acceptable to many people. This exemplary function is manifest more clearly still in some forms of punishment in which the aim was not at all to inflict physical suffering. Symbolism was a feature of repression at various levels. It could indeed be an element in punishments which were directed at the body, as when a knife fighter received a cut on his cheek, for example, or was flogged with a knife above his head. Some offenders, on the other hand, were merely exposed at the scaffold together with an object illustrating their crime or a note attached to their chest indicating the nature of the act. A third form of symbolism consisted of punishment in effigy. When a fugitive suspected of a serious crime was condemned in absentia, his sentence might contain such a clause. That was notably the case in France. The *parlements* ordered the courts to have an accurate effigy made of the culprit. Depending on the sentence, it was burned, hanged, or publicly damaged in another way. The fourth type, finally, involves the purest form of symbolism. Some culprits were subjected to a mimicry of corporal or capital punishment. Pregnant women, for example, were spared whipping because the unborn child was innocent. The hangman instead placed them on the scaffold with rods around their neck. In the Netherlands a mock beheading was not uncommon. This was a sentence that was imposed, for example, on knife fighters who had stabbed someone but who could not be held responsible unequivocally as causing the death. The perpetrators were blindfolded and had to kneel in a pile of sand by the scaffold; the executioner then swung his sword over their head. The idea behind the last two types is easily discovered. Where a physical punishment was impossible for whatever reason, but where guilt was still involved, the infliction of pain had to be enacted.

Even cadavers could fulfill an exemplary function. Towns and villages throughout Europe had a gallows field or gallows mountain where the corpses of some of those executed were exposed. The hanged dangled from the rope again, and those whose bones had been broken sat on a wheel, sometimes in a sort of harness to keep them upright and, hence, visible. This dishonor was an extra punishment for criminals on whom it was imposed. In chapter 5 we saw the importance of a decent funeral to everyone. Those exposed in a gallows field were not only deprived of a funeral, but their bodies remained outside the walls as well. In Amsterdam the corpses of 214 of the 390 capital offenders between 1650 and 1750 were taken to the gallows field. It was situated at the other side of IJe River, down which all incoming ships passed on the way to port. Exposure of the body was uncommon only in England. There the great fear of those condemned to death was to end up in the anatomy room.

For a long time the reactions of spectators confirmed that the spectacle of public suffering and pain was taken as a matter of course by almost everyone. As far as these reactions can be ascertained, they do not testify to any empathy with those punished or revulsion against what was done. Pity only occurred in special cases. The populace did not consider offenses such as smuggling as crimes and, hence, considered punishment of smugglers as unjust. Executions following riots were hazardous enterprises for the authorities because the majority of the populace sympathized with the rebels. In such cases, they identified to a high degree with the victims on the scaffold, and, where identification is present, spectators feel the pain too and disapprove of what they see. Scaffold punishments for thieves, burglars, murderers, and hooligans, on the other hand, failed to draw the majority of the onlookers into anything but unfeeling comment. They watched silently or bet on whether an offender would scream from pain during his flogging. Indifference prevailed in those cases, just as with spectators at cock or bullfights. The audience had no personal grudge against the condemned; they assembled simply for the sensation of the spectacle.

The Privatization of Repression

The two characteristic elements of preindustrial repression began to decline from about 1600. Publicity and corporal punishment became less prominent. Obviously these changes were a manifestation of privatization. They were dramatic in degree at first, but the penal system was altered considerably between 1770 and 1870.

The early changes can be traced especially in the Netherlands. In the course of the sixteenth century executions began to be performed at fixed places, which had not been the case previously. Medieval offenders were frequently whipped while led through the streets. A Rotterdam sentence of 1500 stipulated that the condemned was to be flogged while carried through the town on a cart. Even when an offender was not paraded through the streets, the location of the punishment could vary. In Amsterdam at the beginning of the sixteenth century, executions took place at Dam Square and at the "Reguliers," and St. Anthony gates. Such customs had disappeared by the beginning of the seventeenth century, when punishment was restricted to a single location. Another change concerned the declining role of the public as spectators at the pillory. During the Middle Ages they were encouraged to throw rotten fruit, dung, and stones at the offenders exposed on the pillory. In some districts, especially in England, this was still done in the eighteenth century, but Amsterdam was already more sober in this respect in the seventeenth century. Throwing objects at a culprit on the pillory was forbidden or discouraged.

An unambiguous development consisted in the disappearance of visible mutilation. Some corporal penalties which have become horrible to us, such as blinding and cutting off hands or ears, were no longer practiced. This development took place throughout western Europe, although at different points in time. In Amsterdam such punishments were applied in the first half of the seventeenth century at the latest. Branding continued to be practiced, but henceforth the scar was made only on the offender's back, so that it remained hidden from public view. Thus, a serious form of corporal punishment disappeared from daily experience.

The shift from stone to wooden scaffolds was probably restricted to the Dutch Republic. This took place in the course of the seventeenth century and meant a further decrease in visible repression. Stone scaffolds were permanent, annexed to the town hall or standing in an open space, with gallows and wheel always present. Passers-by were reminded of justice by them at all times, while wooden scaffolds allowed such remembrance to fade. They were erected on the day preceding the execution and quickly dismantled afterwards. In the intervening periods, planks and other parts lay in store. The poet Constantin Huygens, expressing the mentality which lay at the root of this new custom, protested against the practice of the Court of Holland in maintaining its stone scaffold at The Hague; it was, he said, the most villainous of all constructions. The gallows and wheel were horrible to see, especially in this handsome part of town where so many gentlemen lived and foreign envoys passed by. Huygens proposed that the stone scaffold be replaced with a statue of Justitia and a fountain be constructed. Fountains were a favorite motif. As we have seen, a fountain was built a century later in Paris on the place of the demolished Cemetery of the Innocents. Huygens did not live to see his wish for The Hague come true. The Court of Holland only replaced its stone scaffold with a wooden one in 1720. But Huygens's campaign does show that a certain sensitivity toward the system of corporal and capital punishments had taken hold of the elites already by the end of the seventeenth century.

This sensitivity really broke through a century later. The privatization of repression accelerated from the 1770s. Opposition to judicial torture was one of its earliest expressions. Voices had always been raised against torture, but in this period they grew louder and more emotional in tone. This caused even its defenders to begin to excuse themselves for their supposed lack of empathy. The Viennese jurist Von Sonnenfels, arguing for abolition of torture, opened his book with the statement that he would not take the easy way by evoking the helpless cries of the victims and calling upon the readers' feelings. This would be sufficient to convince them, but he wished to win them over to his point of view with intellectual arguments as well. Austria was one of the first countries to abolish judicial torture. Others followed, including the Netherlands in 1795–1798.

Around the same time revulsion against the exposure of cadavers increased. In this case, the relationship with changes in the experience of death is obvious. The fundamental characteristics, familiarity and publicity, had disappeared in the course of the eighteenth century and the ancient churchyard cemeteries had been closed. It therefore comes as no surprise that the sight of the corpses of criminals became repulsive too. A custom which raises aversion cannot fulfill an exemplary function. In the Netherlands the custom was abolished directly after the Batavian Revolution of 1795, with the argument that it was a relic from barbarous times. Gallows which had been used for that purpose in Bavaria were sold as old wood to the highest bidders between 1805 and 1814. Although this development was directly related to the concealment of death, it also meant a new step in the privatization of repression.

Finally, executions themselves fell into disfavor. At the end of the eighteenth century more and more spectators from the upper and middle classes found the spectacle unpleasant. In 1773 an anonymous citizen of Amsterdam wrote that he trembled and grew ice cold at every step those about to be hanged took up the ladder. He looked around and to his relief saw horror in the eyes of numerous other spectators. Well into the nineteenth century, such feelings were subordinated to the idea that scaffold punishment was nonetheless necessary. As late as 1838 a pamphlet called upon the Amsterdam populace to watch the public imposition of a number of corporal penalties, but its tone was different. The scaffold was now called a stage of sorrow and the proper attitude was to show compassion for the condemned, who were once as innocent as the spectators. The idea that offenders undergoing punishment had once been innocent lambs is diametrically opposed to the view, expressed earlier in English execution speeches, that they were destined from youth on to take the wrong road.

Sensitivity toward the proceedings on the scaffold became common among the elite in the nineteenth century. Despite this, they usually considered offenders as dangerous criminals who had to be taken into custody. The conclusion is that interhuman identification had increased. The spectators who expressed their horror at the event even imagined themselves in the shoes of the guilty and shared their pain. The indifference toward the suffering inflicted upon those second-class persons had declined, just as the indifference toward animal suffering had. Political decisions in the nineteenth century did not, however, automatically follow upon the increase in sensibilities. Yet the change of mentalities involved was the most important background to the eventual disappearance of public executions. Around the middle of the century most corporal penalties were abolished or, as with flogging in England, no longer imposed publicly. Capital punishment was moved from the scaffold to a room within the prison. This shift occurred in western Europe between 1850 and 1870, except for France where it had to wait until 1939. The Netherlands were one of the few countries to abolish the death penalty altogether. The last public execution there took place at Maastricht in 1860. This concluded the privatization of repression. Punishments directed primarily at the offender's body had disappeared or were imposed indoors. But repression was also subject to change at other fronts. This is discussed in the next section.

The Coming of the Prison

Scaffold punishments were never the only penalties, nor was their ceremonial imposition the only means of repression. Often they merely affected a minority of offenders. However, they were counted as the pearl in the crown of repression, from which all other penal measures derived their luster. The entire penal system, in fact, was pervaded by the elements of publicity and bodily punishment. We already saw this with respect to the latter. Although the pillory was not corporal penalty in the strict sense, those standing in it could be severely harassed by onlookers. To cause pain was the essence of torture, which was not punishment as such at all but a form of intensive examination. Physical discipline in prison workhouses is discussed later. In a similar vein, a measure of publicity was characteristic of various punishments which were not public in the strict sense. In this connection, prison workhouses should be mentioned again. Public banishment was employed until the beginning of the seventeenth century: a court attendant led the condemned out of town while drums were beaten or bells tolled. On their way from jail to ship, French and Spanish galley slaves were taken to the market square in every town they passed, where the inhabitants watched them groan and rattle their chains. As the two characteristics were present at several levels, the privatization of repression was manifest at all those levels too. There is sufficient reason, then, to take another look at the penal system, but an elaborate overview would be too much here. The focus will be on the emergence of prison workhouses, the precursors of modern penitentiaries, because this will complete our view of the privatization of repression.

There is a second reason to pay attention to prison workhouses. Their rise reflects still another change of mentality, which ought to be discussed in this book. It concerns a shift in the attitudes toward the poor in general and beggars and vagrants in particular. A more secularized view of poverty appeared, which, among other things, led to the confinement of those found to be reluctant to work. This change of mentality, culminating in the creation of prisons, is dealt with first. Next, the inclusion of prisons into the system of repression and their evolution as institutions of criminal justice are discussed.

From Charity to Suspicion

Prison workhouses were not the oldest institutions for confinement. The earlier appearance of madhouses was discussed in the previous chapter. Jails had existed for a long time, but they primarily served to detain debtors or suspects during trial. Condemned persons had sometimes been committed to medieval dungeons, but these places were not really equipped for long stays. Furthermore, some residents of monasteries remained in them more or less against their will. The prison workhouses which appeared around 1600 were, however, the first buildings established with the explicit purpose of subjecting undesirables to discipline. This was the new element. First, we have to ask who those undesirables were and why they ought to have been disciplined.

The magistrates of late medieval towns were confronted at times with the problem of how to deal with the multitude of nonnative beggars roaming through the streets. They probably played on occasion with the thought of driving them away, especially when rumors of the plague were circulating. But what should they do if a vagrant declared that he had come to pray at a shrine situated in the town? Pious pilgrims did not deserve to be expelled. This conclusion implies the force of the traditional attitude toward beggars and other poor people. This attitude had a strongly religious flavor. The poor in general and beggars and vagrants, usually denoted together as marginals, in particular, were seen as imitators of Christ. No wonder that many monks begged out of conviction. It was not only those who voluntarily gave up their property who followed in Jesus's footsteps. One who had never possessed anything at all was like him too and deserved alms. Although no beggar was overloaded with pious gifts, charity was hardly conditional. Almsgiving was a Christian duty, so that far from inquiring into the situation of the receiver, one should be happy at his presence. The poor provided the rich with an opportunity to be charitable and thus to earn heaven. In this way, all had their proper place in an order that would be pleasing to God.

There were already signs in the fourteenth and fifteenth centuries that this traditional attitude was starting to crumble. Urban rulers were inclined to believe that there were thieves and troublemakers among the strangers coming from outside. Not everyone would have embarked upon his journey with legitimate purposes. This was the heyday of pilgrimages, as we saw in the previous chapter. A number of pilgrims travelled great distances from England or the Netherlands to Santiago de Compostela or Rome. It was said that many pilgrims were scoundrels only pretending to be on their journey for pious purposes. At one moment, they would hold out their hand while wearing a penitential garment, while at another they were picking pockets or looking for a sexual adventure. Thus, pilgrims and suspected persons were to some extent associated. The magistrates reinforced this association by obliging some undesirables to undertake a pilgrimage. In the fourteenth and fifteenth centuries many Dutch courts sentenced offenders to go on pilgrimage to a faraway place. On their return they had to show a certificate to prove that they had completed the journey.

Nonetheless, the religious and benevolent attitude toward marginal persons and the poor continued to be dominant in this period. The attitude characterized by suspicions remained subordinate. The shift that happened from about 1500 meant that the less benevolent attitude became the dominant one. A few authors, among them Sebastian Brant, began to talk critically of vagabonds and argued that not every beggar deserved alms. Urban magistrates increasingly felt themselves responsible only for the poor who were citizens or at least residents. A reorganization of poor relief was carried through in many European towns in the first half of the sixteenth century. The secular authorities tightened their supervision and made charity dependent, in principle, on having roots in the town. No one cared about strangers who were sent back to their place of birth.

The increased control of the secular authorities over poor relief indicates that the new attitude was less religiously inspired. This should not be misunderstood. Society in general and the system of repression in particular were still pervaded with religion, as shown in the previous section. But the poor were no longer the image of Christ. Poverty was now seen as a curse, and marginal persons as a threat to public order. The established residents started to distinguish between the poor who deserved charity and those who did not. In principle, everyone who had a healthy body and still begged belonged to the second category, and could be hunted down and banished.

The Reformation coincided with this shift. Some authors claim that the new ideas about poverty were put forward by Protestants in particular. To a certain extent, Protestantism, which rejected the cult of saints and pilgrimages as well, did accelerate the shift. Both Luther and Calvin denied that charitable gifts could enhance one's chance for salvation. Last of all, the first prisons were opened in Protestant districts. But the shift was certainly not caused by the Reformation, since the new ideas had been present embryonically in the preceding centuries. The reorganization of poor relief took place in Catholic as well as Protestant regions; this also holds true for brief experiments with the imprisonment of beggars tried at various places from the end of the fifteenth century. Representatives of the Counter Reformation spoke very critically of marginal persons. Although in Protestant thinking almsgivers derived no benefit from their act, Protestants still considered charity as pleasing to God. Thus, the shift in attitudes toward poverty was largely independent from the course taken by the struggle between the religions. It was primarily a manifestation of secularization, that is, a small move in the direction of a slightly more secularized view of the world. People who had been previously treated in strictly religious terms were now dealt with in a more worldly way.

Forced Labor

The rise of imprisonment sealed the transformation. The novelty of prison workhouses lay in an approach to marginal persons which was both positive and more repressive. Instead of being banished, beggars and vagabonds were put to work. The argument was that persons who were not entitled to relief but still begged were in fact lazy and should be compelled to work. Forced labor would punish the unwilling and at the same time accustom them to a less dissolute life. The oldest Dutch institution, opened at Amsterdam in 1596, kept its prisoners busy rasping wood. They pulverized redwood logs with heavy saws, producing a dye-stuff. The institution was therefore called the rasphouse. A special team of provosts who hunted down and arrested beggars supplied it with inmate laborers.

The Amsterdam rasphouse was the first on the European continent, although prisons had already been established in English towns by the middle of the sixteenth century. Other places in the Dutch Republic soon followed the example of Amsterdam. Prison workhouses or comparable institutions were opened in several parts of Europe, such as the southern Netherlands (Belgium), France, and Germany, in the course of the seventeenth century. The system was essentially the same everywhere. Begging was prohibited, since all the deserving poor were presumed to be getting support. Special officials were charged with the seizure of foreign vagrants and others who disregarded the ban on begging. Those arrested were subjected to a term at forced labor.

The change of mentality just reviewed illustrates once more that in history we are seldom dealing with unilinear developments. The evolution of repression did not involve a progressively milder treatment of all deviants or outsiders. Originally marginal persons were hardly seen as potential victims of repression. Their status and that of other poor people declined sharply during the sixteenth century; from imitators of Christ they became work-shy troublemakers. Groups who had been tolerated previously were henceforth prosecuted as deviant outsiders. Viewed from that angle, repression was intensified. The new ideas were not accepted by everybody, however. The most convincing proof that traditional charity lived on was resistance to the officials charged with catching beggars, who were attacked by people in the streets, who tried to snatch away their victims. Amsterdam ordinances repeatedly warned against this offense and sometimes the attackers themselves were arrested and condemned. It is difficult to trace their social background. Such resistance has also been demonstrated elsewhere, in Lyon and some German towns for example, well into the eighteenth century.

Prison workhouses were never exclusively meant for beggars and vagabonds, although the problems the authorities faced with them did constitute the main immediate cause for their creation and later for a number of reopenings in the Dutch Republic around 1660. Thus, the Estates of Friesland declared in 1654: "Because of complaints from several quarters reporting that the inhabitants of this country are considerably troubled by vagabonds and idle and lazy beggars [we] have resolved that a prison workhouse will be re-established at Leeuwarden." Burgomasters and the Council of Utrecht, however, said something different in 1661: "Learning that youth is often tempted into idleness and other irregularities by the rogues here . . . , that also aged persons (even those who enjoy relief) often lead a dissolute life in drunkenness, quarrelling, cursing and swearing and brawls coming thereof, [we] have ordered, in order to prevent this, that the prison workhouse be re-opened" (Spierenburg ed.: 34–35). These moralistic considerations point at another motive which played a role at the beginning of the prison movement. The institutions were also meant for residents guilty of undesirable conduct. They might be men or women dependent upon the assistance given by the supervisors of the poor who showed themselves unworthy of support because of alcoholism, licentiousness, or other vices. They might also be persons from wealthier families, children who were hard to educate and recurrently ran away from home, for example. At the request of their families they were committed to prison until they reformed.

Criminal Prisons

These offenders were not imprisoned as a result of a criminal trial. No matter how worried the educators, spouses, or guardians might be, none of the vices mentioned were unlawful. In a strict sense, beggars did count as offenders, since they were engaged in a forbidden activity, but they were rarely seen as real criminals. They were not usually tried after their arrest, but were summarily committed to the prison workhouse. Originally, then, prison workhouses were not meant for criminals, but in most places they were eventually admitted to them in large numbers. The Amsterdam judges thought a spell in the rasphouse was fit treatment for young thieves; it was hoped they would return to proper conduct afterwards. The magistrates at Haarlem sentenced a few dozen delinquents to a stay in the town's prison workhouse during the first years after its foundation. Elsewhere this development proceeded more slowly. As the seventeenth century progressed, however, sentences to prison became ever more common. Within Europe, the Netherlands took the lead in this development; other countries followed in the eighteenth century. Forced-labor institutions certainly became criminal prisons when persons who had been in the hands of the executioner were kept there too. It became a common practice to subject offenders both to a corporal punishment on the scaffold and to a term of forced labor afterwards. Judges in the Dutch Republic and in Germany regularly pronounced such sentences around 1700.

The history of prison workhouses in the seventeenth and eighteenth centuries has many facets, but here we restrict ourselves to what is relevant to the privatization of repression. When the institutions had become criminal prisons, a new option for keeping criminals in line was available to courts. It may be debated whether this option immediately constituted an alternative to scaffold punishments. Individual culprits who endured a whipping first and were forced to work next may have felt it was additional punishment. The scaffold continued to set the tone for some time, but the notorious institution of the prison had already appeared on the scene. From then on forced labor in prison workhouses was a conspicuous part of the penal system as a whole. These institutions attracted many spectators. Visitors flocked to them in Amsterdam, which soon boasted a spinhouse next to its rasphouse and, a little later, a workhouse for minor offenders. The rise of imprisonment certainly meant an important change in the penal system.

The reference to visitors is a crucial one. Whoever paid a small sum was allowed inside to watch the inmates at their toil. They could see for themselves whether the red dust really made the rasphouse rogues look like Indians and whether the prostitutes in the spinhouse were as impertinent as was said. It was no different from the situation in madhouses. A part of penal practice was confined to a definite space, just as madness was, but seclusion was far from complete. The rise of imprisonment implied a contribution to the retreat of publicity in repression, but only to a limited extent. Prisons would not cease to admit curious visitors until the nineteenth century.

Developments ran parallel with respect to the degree of violence in the system of repression. Imprisonment was not primarily aimed at inflicting pain; in principle, the penalty consisted of forced labor and the loss of personal freedom. As a secondary element, however, physical chastisement certainly played a part. What did one do when a prisoner refused to work? He could be put on bread and water or confined in a dark cell, but a beating came to mind first. Along with refusal to work, undisciplined behavior could take various other forms, such as trying to escape. In these cases physical discipline was customary in every European prison. In some places the wardens handed out punishment immediately, flogging the prisoners in what was called their welcome.

An Amsterdam example demonstrates in a nutshell the link between publicity, corporal punishment, and the prison workhouse. It began with a trial against the guard at a gambling den who had injured a deputy of the prosecutor. The judges condemned him to a combination of scaffold punishment and imprisonment: a whipping, branding with a red-hot sword, and a term of twelve years in the rasphouse. The day of punishment was 24 January 1767. The guard did not utter one scream as he was receiving sixty lashes and the sword touched his back twice. He was back in the rasphouse in the afternoon, and a number of spectators went there directly from Dam Square to see him once more. He had the reputation for toughness. In the rasphouse he declared that rather than staying for twelve years, he preferred another whipping and branding. He showed his ravaged back to every visitor who offered a small coin to see it.

Physical discipline remained associated with prisons for a longer time than their openness and it has not disappeared entirely nowadays. But this form of physical treatment was concealed when prisons were closed to paying visitors during the first half of the nineteenth century. Simultaneously, imprisonment became more frequent as a penalty; this development took place in most European countries. All this formed part of the acceleration in the privatization of repression discussed in the previous section. When scaffold punishment disappeared, the prisons took over. But this shift had known a long prehistory.

Violence Concealed

Thus, violent encroachment upon the body was held within limits in the course of the preindustrial period. This fact was a reflection of several interrelated developments in the realm of mentalities. Increasing interhuman identification was especially crucial. It enabled people to imagine themselves in the shoes of others more often and more strongly. As a result, many forms of violence and the infliction of pain gradually became unacceptable. Physical retaliation became less frequent, games with animals were restricted, corporal penalties abolished, and sports reformed. Not all forms of violence disappeared, however. Just as in other areas of life, imposing restrictions often meant hiding and covering up, that is, privatization. Privatization was particularly visible in the field of repression. It gradually lost its public character, with the scaffold disappearing and the prison largely taking its place. Violent punishment did not completely become a

thing of the past, but henceforth it was practiced indoors. Secularization, finally, did not play a major part as it did in the case of madness.
Only the shift in attitudes toward marginal persons and the poor was
related to it, but it seems that this shift was quite separate from the
other developments in the area of mentalities that we have discussed.

In turn, these developments in the realm of mentalities were not autonomous. They were linked to social processes, especially but not exclusively to processes of state formation. The rise of states implied a
certain monopolization of violence which eventually favored an increase in sensitivity. Rulers first wiped out feuds and later restricted
duelling. At the same time, they made it clear that the monopoly of
violence belonged to them. This was a major function of scaffold punishments, which took the place of personal justice in the form of
feuds. When states became more stable and bureaucratic in the nineteenth century, the privatization of repression was reinforced. The
authorities could do without such visible modes of repression.
Obviously, this remained a matter of degree. Today there are those
who contest the state monopoly upon violence, to whom the authorities respond with counter-violence.

A series of intriguing parallels concludes this chapter. The treatment of criminals and of the insane shares a common element in each
successive period. In the fourteenth and fifteenth centuries it was pilgrimage. A journey to a shrine was imposed on some offenders as a
punishment, while this was the heyday of madness saints. Floggings
were common in various periods, both as a penalty for criminals and
to beat insanity out of a person. In early modern times the parallel is
almost complete. Criminals as well as the mad were locked away in
institutions to which visitors were admitted. The parallels continue
after the period covered by this book. In the nineteenth century both
criminals and mad persons ended up in closed institutions; while
doctors began to cure the insane, criminals were often also viewed as
sick. In the twentieth century, finally, electricity is the common element, in the form of electroshock treatment and the electric chair.

FAMILY AND
COMMUNITY II

8   FAMILY LIFE: Bonds Between Men and Women, Parents and Children

Now we return to the subject of family and community with the emphasis this time on developments during the final centuries of the preindustrial period and the transition to an industrial society. A pattern of long-term change was presented at the beginning of chapter 2. The phrase "from the house to the nuclear family" neatly summarized overall development. Originally, the primary group of parents and children played a relatively minor role in the outlook and experience of individual people. It was different from at least the sixteenth century onward. Whenever there is discussion of the family in chapters 8 and 9, as a rule, the nuclear group is meant.

There is something odd in the historiography of family life. Until about 1980 most historians claimed that marriages were arranged regardless of the prospective partners, after which spouses lived separate lives and treated their children without affection. Or, more precisely, this situation presumably prevailed until changes set in, usually during the last centuries of the preindustrial period. From about 1980 most historians claimed the opposite. Family life was said to have been affectionate already at an early date and hardly any significant changes ever took place in this field. When disagreement is that intense, the controversy cannot be ignored, and the arguments of several authors have to be reviewed more elaborately than in the preceding pages. This chapter deals with the most controversial themes. It discusses the common life of men and women in marriage and relations between parents and children, especially the treatment of infants. Other subjects related to the family, such as sexuality and the status of adolescents, are dealt with in the last chapter.

Conjugal Life

Men's views of women and vice versa and the nature of their mutual relationships constitute a broader subject than that of conjugal life alone. Within the history of mentalities, however, most research in which women-men relations are central has been done on themes such as marriage, choice of partner, and courtship. A few studies pay attention to the position of nuns in the Middle Ages and in Catholic countries after the Reformation, or to Beguines and other women living outside family bonds. But these studies are not sufficiently numerous to allow sound conclusions about trends or developments. That is why the emphasis here lies on the nuclear family.

How the church and the emerging states took a stand against kinship groups was described earlier. Church leaders demanded the exclusive authority to solemnize marriages, while secular rulers especially tried to curb the armed power of kinship networks. Thus, during the early preindustrial period, church and state considered families as anything but pillars to build upon. This changed from the beginning of the sixteenth century, when the conflict was more or less settled. Ecclesiastical agencies legitimated marriages and registered them in the name of the secular authorities. Only in the Dutch Republic was a civil marriage possible. Once kinship networks had been pushed back as a factor of power, attention shifted from them to the nuclear family. To the secular authorities, the compliance of family members with the decisions of their family head was a model for the obedience their subjects owed them. Ecclesiastical authors considered the ideal family as the kernel of the order God desired for the world. Only from the beginning of the sixteenth century did moralists begin to dwell upon a theme they would cherish until our day: the family as the cornerstone of society.

Reformation and Counter Reformation

To a certain extent the sixteenth century brought about a separation between Catholic and Protestant views of marriage. The ideas of the Reformation deviated from the Catholic tradition on at least three points. The first involved a major reorientation of Christian thought: virginity descended from its throne. Protestants denied that the virginal state deserved preference and recommended marriage for everyone. They abolished clerical celibacy and closed monasteries and convents, which for so long had been models of cohabitation outside family bonds. Martin Luther personally set an example by marrying a former nun. Lutherans in particular considered the closing of convents as a liberation of the women who had lived in them. They encouraged ex-nuns to publish their stories: how they had entered the convent as ignorant young girls and how badly they had been treated. Katherine von Bora, Luther's wife, was said to have been smuggled out of the convent together with eleven other women in herring barrels by the fish dealer Leonhard Koppe. In reality there were also nuns who resisted their "liberation" tooth and nail. The other side of the coin in Protestant thinking consisted of a revaluation of marriage. It was no longer just a remedy against lust; the conjugal state was now seen as intrinsically good. In addition to procreation, the mutual comfort spouses provided each other was an important goal of marriage. First of all this meant that Protestants dropped the long-standing suspicious attitude toward conjugal sexuality, viewing it much less as a necessary evil. Extramarital sexuality, on the other hand, remained as sinful as it was in the eyes of Catholics. Indeed, Protestants represented celibacy as a cheap excuse for clandestinely living a promiscuous life.

The indissolubility of marriage was a second point on which the Reformation brought change. Canon law only knew the possibility of nullification, as in the impotence suits, but not of divorce. In theory, nullification meant that it was established that the goals of marriage had not been met so that there never had been a real marriage. Lutherans as well as Calvinists, on the other hand, were usually prepared to grant a divorce to the non-guilty party in cases of adultery and malicious abandonment. The other partner's sin had put an end to the union. Protestant rulers usually adopted these positions. In the Dutch Republic and other countries both of these conditions counted as legal grounds for divorce. The third point concerns parental agreement. Protestants rejected the canon law rule that marriage is only made by mutual consent, demanding the formal consent of the parents as well.

In practice, however, Protestant and Catholic ideas about marriage converged to a greater extent in the early modern period than is apparent at first sight. Although Catholics maintained their ancient doctrine regarding weddings, they still emphasized the desirability of parental agreement. They could do so more readily because the conflict over the leading role in the ceremony was over. The obligation to publish the banns three times, proclaimed at the Council of Trent also served to prevent unions not desired by the parents. Protestant authorities adopted this custom. Thus, the early modern period witnessed a reconfirmation by the representatives of the church of parental authority over the choice of partners. How this worked out in practice will be discussed. The right to divorce, on the other hand, continued to differentiate Protestant from Catholic regions, but few people made use of it. In cases of adultery, ministers or elders first tried to reconcile the couple. Separation was more frequent than full divorce among Protestants as well as Catholics. That too will be treated.

Neither did the reorientation of Christian thought, finally, lead to a strong divergence of ideas. Obviously, the Catholic church maintained clerical celibacy and kept its monastic orders, among them several newly founded in the sixteenth century. Polemical writers from both sides underlined these differences. But on this point no less than on others, representatives of the Counter Reformation tried to take the wind out of the sails of Protestant critics. They stressed that monastic life implied a calling and that whoever was unfit for it should not embark upon it at all. More important still, Catholics in fact arrived at a revaluation of the conjugal state too. The first signs were visible already in the later Middle Ages, when clerics sang the praise of the ideal marriage. As early as the thirteenth century the English Franciscan Bartholomeus Anglicus wrote that the ideal spouse so loved his wife that he would thrust himself into all kinds of danger for her; he was as diligent and careful for her as he was for himself and advised her if she had done anything wrong. In the Netherlands two centuries later it was the Roermond Carthusian monk Dionysius who wrote a work entitled "The Praiseworthy Life of the Married." Around the same time the Bamberg canon Albrecht von Eyb expressed the same thought:

What could be happier than the name of father, mother and children [there was as yet no word for the nuclear family], where the children hang on their parents' arms and exchange many sweet kisses with them and where husband and wife are so drawn to one another by love and choice and experience such friendship between themselves that what one wants, the other also chooses and what one says, the other maintains in silence as if he had said it himself; where all good and evil is held in common, the good all the happier, the adversity all the lighter, because shared by two. Such and other matters praise and extol holy and worthy matrimony (Ozment: 187).

After 1500 Catholic moralists elaborated on this positive view of conjugal life. A relatively new object of veneration, the Holy Family, became the model for the ideal union. The peaceful bonds between Jesus and his earthly parents were held up as an example to all the faithful. Stress was on their pious mutual concern rather than on the unique virginal state of all three. The rise of the cult of the Holy Family had not been possible without the revaluation of Joseph. For a long time he had enjoyed an ambiguous status. He merely counted as Jesus's foster parent, while the populace could not quite accept the idea that there had been no natural father. They considered Joseph as a sort of cheated husband, "the holy cuckold." Especially in late medieval popular plays he was portrayed as an old man with a grey beard, leaning on a stick, and probably impotent. A significant motif is that of Saint Joseph's charivari, represented on many pictures of the Madonna's wedding ceremony in fifteenth-century Italy. The young men threaten the aged bridegroom or even beat him for taking away a marriageable virgin. Clerics tolerated this motif as long as the church was pictured as the location of the ceremony. From the sixteenth century, however, they opposed it. The ensuing revaluation was expressed in Italy, among other things, in the giving of names. In the fifteenth century practically no Italian was called Giuseppe, while this had become a common name by the eighteenth century. Elsewhere in Europe too after 1500 representatives of the church started to emphasize that it was an insult to picture Joseph as a cuckold and that in any case he had not been that old at the time of his wedding.

The new family ethic is reflected in the marital advice of religiously inspired authors in Catholic and Protestant countries. In England no change of tone is apparent in works published directly after the Reformation as compared with the period immediately preceding. Every author stresses, on the one hand, that marriage is a partnership based on affection and domesticity and, on the other, that the husband rules. The partners should be joined in mutual agreement and preferably be each other's equal in age and social status. Two late sixteenth-century authors, Dod and Cleaver, view the ideal properties of spouses as complementary, with the man playing an active role each time and the woman a passive one. He travels and seeks a living, while she keeps the house in order; he concerns himself with all kind of business, while she is alone and withdrawn; he is a clever speaker and she takes pride in her silence. In Germany the Lutheran writers of *Ehespiegeln* and *Haustafeln* offer comparable advice. Conjugal life, they state, brings many economic and psychological worries with it, but God has instituted this bond for human benefit and the balance will certainly be positive. The husband rules his family as God rules the world, but he ought to respect his wife. French Catholic moralists in the sixteenth century distinguish between love from desire and disinterested love.

The latter is based on affection and characterizes the ideal shared life of wife and husband. In the view of these Catholic writers too, the man clearly rules. A woman who does not follow her husband's orders or attempts to acquire authority over the household, Benedicti says in 1584, commits a sin.

Thus, sixteenth-century moralists proclaimed a similar message throughout western Europe. A heightened emphasis on affection was accompanied by a still quite strong sense of patriarchalism. Of course there were differences of accent. Lutherans, for example, also were inclined to condone a possible abuse of patriarchal authority. Although they obliged husbands to rule moderately, their wives were ordered to obey nonetheless even if they were treated with great severity. The subjection of women to unreasonable husbands formed part of the punishment they had inherited from Eve. The labors of child bearing were another part. These beliefs lead some historians to speak of a reinforcement of patriarchy in the sixteenth century. But we should not forget that it involved a micropatriarchy. The reinforcement was also a consequence of the decreased influence of wider kinship groups and surrogate fathers, resulting in greater emphasis on the position of head of a single household. Other authors think that the increased emphasis on conjugal affection and fidelity was related to the rise of the bourgeoisie. But the new family ethic was not specifically bourgeois. Rather, we should take the increase in state power into consideration. As a rule, the new ethic was approved by the secular authorities; at least they found it suitable for their subjects. As was to be expected, they left preaching to the clergy. Processes of state formation and the stabilization of church control over marriage tamed patriarchy; when that had been accomplished, the nuclear family was considered as a pillar of support for an authority viewed as benevolently paternalistic.

Wedding Celebrations

With ideology explained, it is time to shift focus to practice. In addition to what has been said about it in chapter 2, wedding ritual deserves some attention. The obligation to register a marriage had pinned down weddings to a single moment in time. Yet the idea that a series of events constitutes a marriage had not disappeared from consciousness. The ceremony in the church, or possibly civil marriage in the Dutch Republic formed the climax. After that, the wedding celebration was the most suitable occasion to display the union to relatives, friends, and neighbors.

Betrothal remained an important event in particular among the elite. It was then that the partners gave their consent and the parents from both sides expressed their agreement. In sixteenth-century England the betrothal was confirmed in a public celebration; many considered it the actual beginning of marriage. Uncertainty as to the moment when a marriage had to be considered legal and irrevocable prevailed throughout Europe among various groups. It was manifest in Holland in a celebrated lawsuit in 1599. Floris and Lysbet promised to share happiness and adversity in the parish church of a Rijnland village, where the minister joined them in matrimony in the presence of relatives from both sides. On their way home, however, their boat capsized and the couple perished pitifully. The two families, fraternally joined in church only a little while before, soon became bitter contestants. Since the rich bridegroom had not demanded a marriage settlement, the other party took its chance in court. Floris's family advanced the argument that no irrevocable conjugal bond had been established because the sexual consummation had not yet taken place. Obviously, this claim served to deny Lysbet's family a portion of the inheritance, but it must have been based on existing beliefs. The High Council decided that the ecclesiastical ceremony had brought about a marriage with all resulting rights.

In addition to this surviving character as a process, weddings remained public events. In villages and neighborhoods the involvement of the community continued to have the function of legitimizing a marriage. We observe this in sixteenth-century Augsburg. The neighbors accompanied the couple in a procession to church and from there to their new home. They danced and made music with flutes and drums. When a witness declared to have watched this procession, it was proof of the existence of a marriage. Sometimes the neighbors were given soup on the morning of the wedding. During the previous evening the prospective bridegroom went out with bachelors and married men. Often they were his workmates, and the drinking bout sealed his formal admittance into a guild. When they had finished their round, the men gave a serenade at the home of the prospective bride, who stayed there in the company of other women. The allocation of roles was plain again: the men go out and the women stay at home. The wedding ritual was also replete with sexual symbolism. The reformers, however, opposed this worldly ritual. They considered that noise and wild dances violated the dignity of the ecclesiastical ceremony, and they also disapproved of the morning provision of soup, probably because it stimulated all too great merriment on the way to church.

Catholic clergymen in France also opposed popular ritual, using the same arguments. Consequently, the early modern period witnessed a gradual separation of this ritual from the ecclesiastical ceremony. The neighbors still walked in procession with the couple, but they stopped making noise as they approached the church. A separation of ceremonies also occurred in England. During the solemnity in church those present impatiently waited for the end, when the blessing of the ring and the bridegroom's gift to the bride were to follow, which to them were the most essential events. Gillis emphasizes that worldly ritual grew more important precisely as a consequence of the ecclesiastical urge to purify the ceremony. Weddings were now celebrated with heavy drinking in a tavern, where previously only a small beer had been served in church.

Various reasons why the public character of a wedding celebration was sometimes ignored are reported for England. A minority of both poor and rich spurned the public ceremony. In England it was still possible to marry clandestinely, without publishing the banns. To some of the poor this was their only opportunity, since their own vicar, urged by respectable parishioners, simply refused to proclaim the banns out of fear that the couple would end up on the relief rolls. Other clandestine wedding candidates of low birth were sailors or migrant workers, people who were hardly rooted in a community. They looked for a quick and cheap union, as was possible in a London prison chapel. The rich had the opportunity to pay for a wedding outside the place where they lived. Distinguished residents increasingly used it in order to avoid a wedding celebration in the presence of the entire community. To them the conclusion of a marriage was a private event at which they tolerated only a few relatives and acquaintances. A legal change in the middle of the eighteenth century put an end to clandestine marriages, but not to the sale of licenses to wed outside one's place of residence. Anyone desiring a clandestine marriage after that date had to leave England, for example, to go to Gretna Green in Scotland. The majority who travelled to Gretna Green desired a cheap union; apparently, the journey was less expensive than a wedding celebration. The minority were partners from the upper classes ignoring the will of their parents. In the Dutch Republic too the number of citizens desiring to celebrate a wedding in silence increased in the eighteenth century.

Hierarchy

To conclude, there were two developments with respect to weddings in the early modern period. First, ecclesiastical ritual was purified so that the secular ritual became autonomous. Next, a number of distinguished members of the village or neighborhood community began to separate themselves from the secular ritual. Our next inquiry is into possible symptoms of a decline of the hierarchical character of marriage. In this case we have to consider physical violence between men and women.

A clear case of dominance of men over women outside marriage is offered by the ritual gang-rapes committed by groups of youths. Our information comes from France around 1500, but perhaps the phenomenon was known in other countries too. About four-fifths of the rapes reported from this period were collective, following a more or less identical scenario. Male bachelors from eighteen to twenty-five years approached the victim in her home at night. They yelled obscene words under the window, invaded the house, and each in his turn beat and raped the woman. When they had finished, they forced her to take some money. The perpetrators were male domestics, apprentices, journeymen, or seasonal workers. The victims were always women suspected of a dubious way of life, based on fact or not. Often they were poor women or immigrants to the town or village. To be sure, they did not always live alone. In 1516 in a village in the Aube region, Jeanne Jacquet was with her mother and stepfather, who had to stand by powerless during the assault. In court the neighbors declared they had heard a beating but had been unable to see who or what was being beaten. In other cases the neighbors also pretended to have heard nothing despite the noise. It was a ritual, more or less tolerated by the community. According to a calculation for the town of Dijon, one of every two young men participated in such a rape at least once in his lifetime. This custom disappeared in the course of the sixteenth century.

Traditional notions about the uncleanliness of the female body constitute a related subject. The fact that some of them were already touched upon in previous chapters testifies to their deep roots. The idea, for example, that the womb is a sort of animal, traveling through a woman's body, was present among the ancient Greeks as well as central European peasants in the early modern period. The belief that menstrual blood was unclean was equally widespread. The custom of restoring the deflowered bride to cleanliness after the wedding night has already been discussed. Childbearing, finally, also brought impurity with it. Among the ancient Jews the ritual purification of the mother had to follow the birth of a son after forty days, which is plain from the celebration of Candlemas on February 2. If a woman gave birth to a daughter, her uncleanliness lasted twice as long. This purification ritual was adopted by the churches of preindustrial Europe, by the Anglican and the Catholic until the beginning of the twentieth century. This suggests that in Europe too it met popular needs. Taken as a whole, the ideas about the female body's impurity remained prevalent well into the nineteenth century.

The most common form of violent treatment of women by men, which was related more directly to conjugal life, consisted of the physical discipline expected from husbands. We have seen that moralists admonished women to be submissive and men to be mild but decisive. This could involve a beating if necessary. Such advice raises two questions which are hard to answer. First, in what situations was a woman held to have crossed the accepted boundaries so far that she deserved a beating, and did the criterion for judging this change in the course of the centuries? Second, how did this work out in the daily life of spouses? Precise answers are impossible to give but the data known so far contain some indications. Two of the marital cases judged by the episcopal courts of Troyes and Châlons in the second half of the fifteenth century are suggestive. The cobbler Jean de Lacourt and Jaquotte Godin were summoned because they had been betrothed in church but had undertaken no further steps. Jaquotte declared that she no longer desired to marry because Jean insulted and beat her and punched her on the nose. He replied that he had only wanted to enforce conjugal obedience. The judges annulled the betrothal, but they imposed a fine on Jaquotte for refusing to proceed with the marriage. Another couple had also been engaged for a long time and may have been living together already. The woman declared, "As soon as our banns are published, he will probably start to beat me, but I still intend to marry." Her solution met no favor: the wedding had to take place in church within fifty days.

There is more information from Amsterdam a century and a half later. The reformed consistory dealt with a number of cases of fights among spouses, but it did so, as always, only if the quarrel had caused a scandal within the church community. The overwhelming majority involved men who beat their wives. They frequently acted under the influence of alcohol or in other special circumstances. The wife of the gravedigger Jan Claesz blamed him for catching the clap in an adulterous affair, whereupon he struck her in anger. In such cases the church community clearly disapproved of male violence. Possibly they did so too when a husband's hands were loose following a reprimand which was proper in the eyes of the community. Dutch moralists such as Jacob Cats went further than their foreign contemporaries, arguing that a man ought never beat his wife. Roodenburg concludes that the inhabitants of Holland around 1600 disapproved of wife beating, but that the English, for example, were less troubled by it. It remains to be investigated whether this points to a peculiar tradition in Holland or if a development which would take place elsewhere had set in earlier there.

In any case, it cannot be a coincidence that the records from the west part of the Dutch Republic seldom refer to charivari. The data concerning charivari, in many parts of Europe, demonstrate that physical dominance of men over women was seen as normal far into the early modern period. On the other hand, the appearance of the donkey ride evidently reflected a sense of insecurity about patriarchal authority. And it was noted in chapter 3 that the neighbors occasionally protected the beaten women. There are examples in England as well as the Dutch Republic of intervention by the neighbors when they thought a quarrel among spouses was getting out of hand. The charivaris to which violent husbands were subjected constitute the best illustration. For England, Thompson's quantitative study provides an unambiguous picture. Man-beats-wife charivaris became more frequent in the course of the eighteenth century. In the nineteenth century, male harshness had become almost the only reason for charivari; folklorists thought that it had never served any other purpose. Men were still dominant in the nineteenth century, but a more moderate maintenance of their authority was expected. Thompson speaks of a transition from hierarchical to courteous patriarchy. In the neighborhoods of the bigger cities in the eighteenth century charivaris of whatever type were seldom organized. But in Paris and the Dutch towns, for example, a maltreated wife could commit her husband to prison for a while. To be sure, that was just one of the possible reasons for confining a relative.

We encounter a typical example of the changed relationships in a Welsh village at the beginning of the nineteenth century. A woman-beats-husband charivari was held there, but under adverse conditions. The village males had decided to mock the weakness of a tailor and the dominance his wife exerted over him. First they went through neighboring villages in a procession. The men welcomed them by ringing church bells, but the women stayed at home and laughed at the participants from the windows. In their own village the women had assembled at the tailor's house, shouting at the procession and scolding the organizers.

All these manifestations of the hierarchical character of marriage and its eventual decline primarily concern the populace. For the elite there is the evidence of modes of address. In so far as these concern the relations between spouses, however, they rather testify to changes in the area of intimacy than that of hierarchy. That is why they are treated next. Among the elite, internal status differences were always of more fundamental importance than those between an individual woman and her husband, so that the latter received less emphasis. A particular group, small but relevant to the history of the family, serves as a starting point for the analysis of conjugal life among the elite.

The Courtly Nobility

Status differences between spouses were only slight among the upper aristocracy in western Europe in the early modern period, even though family strategies remained crucially important throughout the Ancien Régime. Our first example is the French aristocracy, as far as they belonged to court circles, in the period 1650–1800.

Spouses in this group behaved toward each other in quite distant fashion, in our view. The evidence from internal architecture is suggestive. Husband and wife each had separate quarters, with private rooms to receive visitors. They frequently slept apart too. Furthermore, each had his or her own personal servants. This partial separation was carried over into social life. Circles of acquaintances only partly overlapped, so that they did not see each other very often. We hear of a man who declined to say goodbye to his wife when he departed for the court for two days because she was still asleep. Instead he left a message with one of her servants. Literary works, finally, confirm this picture. In Molière's plays, which were popular in court circles, a close family life was sneered at as utterly bourgeois. The marriages of aristocrats were primarily concluded as a function of dynastic interests.

On the other hand, this aloofness did not coincide with a strong male supremacy. In these circles, admittedly small in number, a near equality between men and women was realized perhaps for the first time in history. Both sexes played an equally important role in social life; neither one was subordinate to the other at court, in salons, and in social life generally. This may not look impressive, but we are talking of activities and places to which only the top stratum had access. Thus, men and women took part equally in the affairs valued most highly in that society. Sexual customs also testified to a relative balance. Aristocrats considered themselves largely unbound by the ecclesiastical and secular commandments which common mortals had to obey. The style they gave to their life was to them a voluntary act, as it had been for the elite of classical Athens. They continued the tradition of courtly extramarital relationships, in which a lover or mistress was the natural object of passion. That is why Saint-Simon blamed Louis XIV for showing "absolute insensitivity" at the death of his former mistress, Madame de Montespan, despite "such a passionate love of so many years." Madame de Maintenon, his new mistress, did cry. We can leave open the question of how sincere she was. What matters is that both sexes practically enjoyed an equal freedom in extramarital affairs. Aloofness within marriage went together with equality within and without.

An antagonism in French cultural life in the second half of the seventeenth century makes it clear that both aloofness and equality belonged together. In addition to the Parisian salons visited by court circles, there was the academy of Saint-Cyr, which was frequented by members of the ancient landed nobility excluded from the Paris gatherings. In the salons women played the leading role. Writers associated with the salons defended equal rights for women. By contrast, writers sympathizing with Saint-Cyr displayed an antifeminist attitude. At Saint-Cyr, the difference of rank between aristocracy and bourgeoisie was emphasized. Nevertheless the institution taught women thrift, sobriety, and home management—virtues which were later to comprise a bourgeois ethic.

Outside France the aristocratic pattern of conduct was imitated. An equal status for lovers and mistresses also prevailed among the top stratum in the Dutch Republic in the eighteenth century. Conjugal life among the nobility at the Viennese court resembled the French situation. Information from Italy deepens our understanding of the matter. An institutionalized form of extramarital conduct prevailed among the aristocracy of northern and central Italy in the eighteenth century. Next to their husbands, most married women had a second partner called *cavalier servente* or *cicisbeo*. Officially, the relationship between the cavalier and his lady had to stop short of being sexual. He might be termed a male companion. The married lady and her male companion went together to church, to the theater, and to other public events. Sometimes their relationship lasted for over twenty years. Who would become the bride's male companion was often arranged in the marriage contract, while the bridegroom already belonged to another lady. This institution disappeared between 1780 and 1820, a period in which family life among the Italian nobility was subject to rapid change.

The French and Italian developments put us on the right track. Several authors claim that conjugal life in preindustrial Europe felt the impact of what is called a homosocial way of life (a poorly chosen word linguistically speaking). It means that out of bed men were usually among men and women among women. People satisfied their desire for social relations with members of the same sex. Subsequently, it is a fundamental change when men and women begin to look for sociability with each other more often. This change was first visible among the elite. The Italian institution of the male companion was one of its manifestations. It belonged to a transitional period when men and women felt a greater need to do things together, but marriages were still concluded for dynastic interests. Italian spouses had not spent much time together before 1700. In France such matters were less institutionalized, but the situation seems comparable. Notably the salons, where men and women conversed together, met the need for "heterosocial intercourse."

Love and Calculation

The hardest problem in the history of marriage is to determine what the future partners expected from each other and what their mutual feelings were during their partnership, and to note the differences in successive centuries and among various social groups. On this point more than on any other, historians are diametrically opposed to each other. Let us begin with the statement that love and calculation, emotions and material interests, were not necessarily incompatible for preindustrial people. In practice they were intimately interwoven, which also meant mutual influence. The character of emotional life was determined partly by the role material interests played.

The first moment when the two interweaving motives surfaced was that of the choice of a partner or the beginning of courtship. It can be no surprise that the partners usually originated in the same social class. That is largely the case at the present time too. The question is whether inside this class a partner was preferred who could raise or maintain one's own social status or bring a material or social advantage in some other way. A number of historians answer this question affirmatively, at least for a period preceding an assumed romantic revolution. But matters are somewhat more complex. Whatever the argument, we have to distinguish first between elite and populace.

Let us start with the people. It was explained in chapter 2 that for the majority of the agrarian population and for urban artisans, the wedding coincided with obtaining economic independence. There were of course some who never reached economic independence. Consequently, whoever belonged to the underclass of marginal people without a fixed residence seldom bothered with formal marriage. Men and women lived together until they again took separate roads. Most youths from the groups just above them expected to get married once, but they postponed it until the prospects were bright. The fact that the average age at first marriage rose in periods of economic malaise proves this. Thus, for the majority, marriage unmistakably had a material base. The primary task for the couple was to manage together a farm or a household-workshop. Did this also mean that the choice of a partner was too important to be left to those directly involved?

Recent studies, largely concerning England, contain enough evidence for us to conclude that in the sixteenth and seventeenth centuries the choice of partners was relatively free among broader groups than was originally supposed. Not only did young men and women take the initiative themselves, but their parents or relatives put few obstacles in their way. Roger Lowe, for example, an apprentice in Lancashire, and his girlfriend Mary Naylor promised to be true to each other forever during a walk in June 1663. Nonetheless, Roger asked Ann Barrow, who was courted by Mary Naylor's brother, in October if he could take the latter's place when their relationship turned out not to be serious. Eventually, Roger married Emm Potter four years later. During all this courting there was no talk of any involvement of the respective families. Katherine Imber, a Wiltshire girl, did have a conflict with her parents. They chided her for not ending a courtship of which they disapproved, but she replied that they were wrong to put such pressure on her and that it would displease God if she rejected her suitor. More examples like this can be given. It is not surprising that many prospective couples from the lower and lower-middle classes made their own choice. In the later Middle Ages these groups had won freedom from intervention by surrogate fathers. The natural fathers did not always fill the void. It was often prevented by geographic mobility, partly caused by the system of life-cycle servants. Besides, in the towns, mortality was relatively high. Between 1598 and 1619 about half of the London brides born in the city had no father at the moment of their wedding. In villages, social differences were relatively small in the sixteenth and seventeenth centuries and hence the chances for misalliances few. This led to parental moderation.

On the European continent the situation was sometimes different. Peasants in the German region of Hohenlohe, for example, embraced Lutheranism all the more readily because it offered them the opportunity for greater control over their children's marriages. They were not well versed in doctrinal matters, but they easily found their way to the church courts in order to let their own choice of a partner for their offspring prevail. Generally, however, the observation that the initiative frequently lay with the future couple is valid for the Continent too. Certainly where little or no property was at stake, the question of who married whom lost its relevance to parents. When status differences were greater and more property was at stake, parental efforts increased. That is made clear by the opposite customs in two Swedish regions at the beginning of the nineteenth century. In the flat country of Skåne sharp contrasts existed between rich and poor peasants, while the wooded region of Dalarna almost exclusively counted small landowners. In Skåne the parents looked for suitable partners, practically by-passing the couple. The young people of Dalarna took the initiative themselves and the parents put few obstacles in their way. As it happens, social stratification in the countryside grew more complex throughout western Europe in the course of the early modern period. That can explain why Shorter, whose information concerns the agrarian population between 1750 and 1850, concludes that parental consent was a must almost everywhere. In the period Shorter studied, this situation was a recent development rather than, as he thinks, an ancient tradition.

There are more aspects to the choice of a partner than the mere question of whose opinion prevails. Even when young people enjoyed a relative freedom in this respect, their criteria did not necessarily deviate from those of their families. Ambitious young men and women must have taken the economic prospects of a particular union into consideration. But it is hard to accept that affective attraction was not at all involved. Macfarlane's view that the choice was based on personal attraction as well as economic necessity has much to commend it, but it is more difficult to determine how exactly the two motives were interwoven. It is harder still to analyze the power of attraction. A pious young man praised his fiancée's Christian piety, another her beauty, while a third primarily imagined her as a faultless housewife. Young women looked for a strong shoulder or a husband who had little desire to blow his own horn. Religious motives could also play a role in another way. Confessional minorities exhibited a strong tendency toward endogamy. This often led to a greater pressure from the family, this time not for economic reasons. In a country such as the Dutch Republic, with its many denominations, religious endogamy implied a considerable restriction on the choice of a partner. One restriction was sanctioned by law. Jews were not allowed to have sexual intercourse with Christians or to marry them, and a few interfaith couples indeed were given criminal sentences.

Almost every author agrees that arranged marriages were customary among the elite for a long time. The family's determination in this varied with the place the heir concerned took in the order of siblings. The betrothal of a noble heir or a merchant's son destined to take over his father's firm was arranged by the parents as a matter of course. An etching by Abraham Bosse pictures the negotiations about a marriage contract among the French bourgeoisie in 1633. In the left one sees both parental couples putting their cards on the table, while a notary writes down the result. In the right are the future partners fondling each other. Damon says: "I have to love no one but you." Sylvie says: "I want to live under your rule and die with you in mind." Thus, he promised monogamy and she submissiveness. In England too, marriages among the elite were arranged well into the seventeenth century. In both countries, however, this changed toward the end of the preindustrial period. Dutch patrician parents in the eighteenth century also left their children relatively free, but it is unknown to what extent this had been different in a previous period. Stone's analysis of the English situation is most extensive. During the second half of the seventeenth and in the eighteenth century there are indications, especially from personal documents, that the contractual character of marriage diminished. Within a range of possible candidates the choice of a partner became freer, dictated less strongly by family interests and more by the expectation of personal compatibility. Where parents often determined the choice at the beginning of the seventeenth century, they eventually kept no more than a veto, and toward 1800 this was only pronounced for candidates thought very unsuitable. Consequently, the elite steered a reverse course compared with the populace—from arranged marriages to a relatively free choice of partners.

Between the first contact with the future partner and the wedding, there came courtship. The relative freedom arising among the elite in the eighteenth century gave more room to romantic attitudes. Among the people, on the other hand, courtship retained a ritual character. It was supervised by the entire community, notably the peer group who shared the same age, rather than by the parents. Locally varying codes regulated the behavior of young men who were courting and young women who were courted. This also happened especially when the choice was relatively open and consequently several courtships in a row were more common. Future couples met each other under the probing eyes of those present at *veillées* in France or in *Spinnstuben* in Germany. In England the first of May was the day when new courtships were begun and old ones broken off. In the villages of Holland youths assembled at the beginning of a fair and agreed on who went with whom. During feasts and dances the societies of the young took care that everything was in order. Usually, an engaged couple only met in the company of others. The gossip circuit of the community as a whole served to correct errants. If two lovers wished to negotiate with each other, friends often made the necessary preparations. From the beginning of the nineteenth century, when the common life of villages and neighborhoods had started to decline, these forms of supervision disappeared.

Apart Again

Once concluded, a marriage was indissoluble according to prevalent opinion. A few exceptions have been mentioned already. Besides permanent separation, the partners could also split up temporarily, whether or not for legitimate reasons. It is worthwhile to review all possibilities. A temporary separation could be simply a consequence of the tasks the husband had to perform. Where men were often away from home, women usually had a relatively independent position. This can be observed from the Middle Ages. Noble ladies managed the estate when their husband fought a campaign or a crusade. Among the populace in the early modern period in areas where navigation or fishery were major sources of living men were often away from home. In those regions, the maritime provinces of the Dutch Republic for example, women enjoyed a more independent position than elsewhere. A formal separation was another way of being temporarily apart, but it was viewed as less desirable by the community. This may be considered temporary, since reconciliation was aimed at in principle, even though it could turn out to be definitive. Before 1700, to be sure, separations were pronounced only occasionally.

Abandonment or splitting up informally were probably more frequent. Some men ran away, whether or not in search of adventure. No doubt the most famous case is now that of Martin Guerre, a husband from the village of Artigat in southern France, whose position and identity were usurped by another, who was accepted by his wife. Women ran away less often, but they had another possibility to get rid of their husband. Records have been preserved notably in England about so-called wife sales. Held by a rope or a halter, the woman was led to the marketplace by her husband, who offered her to the highest bidder. He made a sales speech, praising her domestic qualities. She was well prepared to display them, he continued, with the aid of an occasional beating. The ceremony's degrading character for the woman compensated for the husband's humiliation, for the cards had almost always been laid in advance. The woman was bought by her lover for a small sum and went to live with him. The ceremony's publicity enabled the community to sanction the new union. Menefee correctly views this popular custom as a do-it-yourself divorce.

Legal divorces and nullifications remained a rarity. The only separation accepted as legitimate by all was the dissolution of a marriage by God through the death of one of the partners. As we know, at that time God struck at a younger age than now on the average. Mortality among young adults meant that many marriages were relatively brief. In particular the mortality of women during and shortly after childbirth was considerable; if a woman knew ten to fifteen other women, she would know one who had died in childbirth. The average duration of a marriage in the seventeenth century may be put at fifteen to twenty years, which leads some historians to view divorce, in its modern frequency, as a twentieth-century substitute. Many embarked upon a second union, men slightly more often than women. It is remarkable that this was usually arranged rather quickly. In Paris and its surroundings from the sixteenth to the beginning of the eighteenth century, most men remarried within a few months or even weeks, the women within a period of some months to two years. In a sample from seventeenth and eighteenth-century England 48 percent of the men remarried within a year and 37 percent of the women. This speed was functional considering on the economic character of marriage. A partner's death meant that a position in the household had become vacant and it was necessary to fill it again. Emotional considerations were subordinate, not absent. In other circumstances, remarriage offered an opportunity to some whose first union had been prearranged and impersonal to use the second to satisfy long-repressed wants.

Intimacy?

That leads us to the elusive problem of the mutual feelings of husband and wife during marriage. In spite of all uncertainties it can be maintained that, at least among the elite, major changes took place in the period from the middle of the seventeenth to the beginning of the nineteenth century. Those changes did not imply the grand shift from loveless to affectionate marriages imagined by some historians. It seems implausible that the prearranged unions from before the eighteenth century remained entirely without love. Nevertheless, a new romantic ideal emerged among the elite simultaneously with the greater freedom in the choice of a partner. For France Flandrin's research demonstrates that love and marriage were associated more strongly than ever in the eighteenth century, in literary works and in philosophic treatises. In Rousseau's novels and, for that matter, in Germany in those of Goethe, the romantic ideal muddled the boundaries of social classes. For England Lawrence Stone observed the rise of the companionate marriage among the elite. Let us review the indications for this change, as he presents them.

One of the proofs adduced by Stone is indirect. The number of separations increased, notably in cases of impossible husbands. He considers this an indicator for the rise of the companionate marriage, since the threshold of splitting up when the choice turns out to have been altogether wrong is crossed more easily in this type of union. Mitterauer also emphasizes that the vulnerability to crisis increases as personal affection is more central. Two caveats, however, should be added. Informal separation was common too, equally so in an earlier period. Second, Dutch research shows that the lower and middle groups were largely responsible for the eighteenth-century increase in the number of formal separations. Stone's other indications are more convincing. Among the English elite marriage for love was gradually seen as the norm after 1700, while the romantic ideal was upheld. This appears from the emergence of the honeymoon, for example. When the custom first arose in the eighteenth century, the couple travelled in the company of a third party; from the middle of the nineteenth century the couple was alone. An increase in education for women also fits into this picture. It originated from a desire to view one's wife as a companion, which also meant a partner in conversation. The strongest indication is the manner in which spouses addressed each other in their private correspondence. During the eighteenth century more and more couples ignored the formal modes of address which had been customary previously. They called each other by their first name or used private sweet words.

The changing modes of address allow us to broaden the discussion to include other countries. Barbagli's precise analysis of the developments among the Italian aristocracy, based on letters and other personal documents, constitutes a model. He distinguishes four periods: 1500–1700, 1700–1780, 1780–1820, and after 1820. In each period custom moved in the direction of a smaller social distance within the family; the relatively elaborate repertoire of Italian modes of address made it possible to distinguish multiple stages. Thus, sons and daughters before 1700 opened their letters with "my lord father" and they spoke to him using *Vostra Signoria*. Parents used *voi* when speaking to their children. After 1820 this became a mutual *tu*. We must now consider the forms of address among spouses. Equality always prevailed between them, since women addressed themselves to their husbands in the same way as their husbands addressed them. Familiarity, however, increased. In the first three of the periods mentioned spouses spoke to each other saying, respectively, *Vostra Signoria, voi*, and *tu*. The beginning of a letter was first "my lord husband," or "my lady wife," and then it became just husband or wife and, finally, the person's name. In other words, modes of address originally referred to the position a person held and later became more individual.

The changes in modes of address implied that the nuclear family grew less hierarchical as well as more intimate. As far as spouses were concerned, the latter aspect predominated. Research which is being conducted in the Netherlands suggests that men and women in the eighteenth-century patriciate also adopted more informal modes of address. As early as the 1690s the assertive wife of the Zeeland minister Laurens Hoogentoren insisted on calling her husband by his first name in daily intercourse. It has been mentioned that more informal modes of address became fashionable in England as well. This development clearly indicates that conjugal life among the European elite was transformed. The argument of some historians that it was merely a change in fashion without any further meaning has to be totally rejected. It is hard to imagine that fashion changed just by coincidence, causing the same feelings to be expressed differently. To the contrary, simultaneously with a change in feelings the need arose for more direct and individual modes of expression. The change in forms of address reflected the romanticization of marriage and the increasing intimacy of the family. Men and women among the elite discarded the homosocial pattern of life. The developments with regard to male

companions in Italy also point in this direction. A transitional situation like this did not arise, or only to a lesser extent, in other countries.
Both among the Italian elite, however, and among their peers in the
rest of western Europe men and women eventually began to spend
more time in each other's company.

Comparable developments occurred in the lower regions of society,
but at a later period. Among the peasant population the homosocial
pattern of married life manifested itself in the traditional allocation of
tasks within the household. Men's jobs and women's jobs were strictly
separated. Women marketed the poultry, tossed the hay, and took care
of the vegetable garden. Cleaning and cooking were their business too.
Men plowed, scythed, and fired the oven. In urban artisan's homes
most tasks were separate too, or alternatively, women worked for an
outside employer. The strict separation of tasks prevented the partners from imagining themselves in the other's role, which reinforced
aloofness rather than decreasing it. The homosocial world was lost in
the course of the nineteenth and twentieth centuries, partly as a consequence of the spread of wage work and economic differentiation.
Among the populace too, spouses and men and women in general began to spend more time in each other's company.

The View of Children

The historiography of childhood faces problems similar to those dealt
with in the previous section. We want to know about parents' feelings
for their children and the hierarchical character of their mutual relationships. This raises still another problem: how did adults view young
people? What was their idea of who a child or a youth was or ought to be?
Disagreement prevails among historians on these points too, so that we
have to assess their arguments. This section considers only young
people until about age twelve; adolescents receive separate treatment.
Since we are dealing with the family, we restrict ourselves to legitimate
offspring, starting with the question of why couples had children.

The Use of Children

In a sense children came by themselves. Men and women married,
fulfilled their conjugal duties, and children were the frequent result.
This series of events was to many a matter of course. They knew very
well that sexual intercourse was a necessary precondition for having a

baby, but, since they also knew that the one did not automatically follow upon the other, they viewed conception as an expression of God's will. As the Lord takes away children, so did he give them, and his ways are equally inscrutable in both cases. Still, this does not preclude that parents often reflected, consciously or unconsciously, about the value of the divine gift.

It would be unrealistic to maintain that children were always unwanted. Nobles longed for an heir, peasants for future assistance in the field, and merchants for a successor. Married women who failed to get pregnant for a long time were happy if their fertility was proven in the end, even by a daughter. Yet there are societies where the most drastic response to an unwanted divine gift, "return to sender," is practiced. From China, where the authorities recently allowed no more than one child per family, murders of girls after birth have been reported. Infanticide was also a feature of classical antiquity, notably of girls and disfigured children. According to some authors, this custom remained prevalent in Europe during the early Middle Ages. But the degree of acceptance of infanticide and the frequency with which it was applied cannot be ascertained. Christian doctrine forbade it in any case. Figures are only known for the early modern period. Few trials for infanticide were conducted then and the accused were almost always unmarried mothers. It is unlikely that many newborn infants were deliberately killed in preindustrial Europe. Abandonment was a less drastic way to dispose of children. In antiquity it was not uncommon for poor parents to leave their children at a place where they hoped someone would take them. When this happened, they were usually raised as slaves. The Christian church also disapproved of abandonment, but individual Christians continued nevertheless to practice it. At the end of the preindustrial period magistrates even designated special places where children could be left. Figures showing increasing or decreasing numbers of foundlings primarily reflect economic fluctuations.

It may be presumed that most children legitimately born in preindustrial Europe were in fact reared. What value was attached to those children? There is no lack of cases of great concern for children and protection offered by their parents, also at an early period. An incident cited by several authors occurred in Oxford in 1298:

On Friday last John Trivaler and Alice his wife were in a shop where they abode in the parish of St. Mary late at night, ready to go to bed and the said Alice fixed a lighted candle on the wall by the straw which lay in the said shop, so that the flame of the candle reached the straw before it was discovered and immediately the fire spread throughout the shop, so that the said John and

Alice scarce escaped without, forgetting that they were leaving the child behind them. And immediately when the said Alice remembered that her son was in the fire within, she lept back into the shop to seek him and immediately when she entered she was overcome by the greatness of the fire and choked (Rotberg/ Rabb: 38–39).

Although Alice paid for her heroic deed with her life, her first reaction to the discovery of the fire had been to run outside. Probably, this was John's and Alice's only child. Besides, few conclusions can be drawn from a single event.

Another possibility is to inquire into the economic value of children. The difficulty of propagandizing for birth control in modern countries such as India, for example, lies in the fact that parents feel more secure for their old age as they boast more children. It remains to be seen whether parents in seventeenth-century France or eighteenth-century Netherlands thought this way. The economic value of a child born on a farm with sufficient hands to till the soil is different from that of one born at a time and place where the existence of proto-industry makes it possible to capitalize on his labor power at a young age. The latter does presuppose that parents plan for an investment and that they have the material means to do so. Nowhere, in any case, did children make an economic contribution until their seventh or eighth year. From that age they were put to work, as they were on farms in sixteenth and seventeenth-century England, weeding, removing stones from the field, gathering wood, scaring birds, and caring for babies. We may still ask whether those contributions were profitable from an economic point of view. Such a question, however, is not essential. We should rather consider the cultural pattern of expectation analyzed by Macfarlane. It is the norm in many non-European societies for children to continue to contribute to their parents' subsistence for as long as the latter live. The flow of money and goods goes mainly upward. In preindustrial Europe, however, in one region earlier than in another, the opposite norm emerged under the influence of commercialization and geographic mobility. The flow of money and goods went mainly downward. Parents helped their children to get settled as economically independent persons and, thereafter, lacking any claim, they could expect no more than voluntary assistance from them. We may conclude that they accepted the Christian message according to which children are God-given and it is one's duty to care for and raise them.

This is not to say that numerous offspring were never felt as a burden. The practice of abandonment suggests the contrary. For feudal knights perhaps, it was a boon to have many descendants, since they could contribute to the house's defense. Such an advantage was absent for the majority of the population in the later preindustrial period. Also, there are no indications that an excessively great fertility endowed women with a higher status. Too many children, then, were rather a burden. Flandrin stresses the relatively high frequency of accidents with children as the victims in the early modern period. Although according to him, no deliberate neglect was involved, the attitude of adults was influenced nonetheless by a cultural norm implying a lesser degree of attentiveness and precaution than in the twentieth century. This attitude must have been most common in large families. Such families, to be sure, were not very numerous, due to the prevailing infant mortality.

Limiting the number of children was originally rarely heard of. The only contraceptive technique widely known and available to everybody was coitus interruptus, "Onan's sin" (Onan's heavy punishment was imposed for "murdering" the potential offspring of his deceased brother). According to most authors, this technique was not used by married couples on a noticeable scale until the late seventeenth or eighteenth centuries, when it is attested for England, France, and Italy, among other places. Among the Italian aristocracy the average number of children per family declined from about six in 1750 to slightly over three in 1800. Generally, such a decline was especially characteristic for the elite. A possible explanation is that with the rise of the companionate marriage men cared more for their wives, wishing to spare them the pain and risks of recurrent childbirths. Since coitus interruptus is a contraceptive method performed by the man, husbands can only be talked into it by their wives through a request or negotiation. Attitudes toward children, however, may have been involved too. In that case, limiting their number meant that the sense of their individuality had increased. Fewer children received more attention.

Little Adults?

From the material utility of children we jump to the image of childhood cherished by adults. The discussion is still dominated by Philippe Ariès's work, published in 1960 as one of the first studies in the field of family history. Ariès thinks that there was no *sentiment de l'enfance* (sense of childhood) until the beginning of the seventeenth century. He expressly does not argue that children were neglected, abandoned, or held in contempt. What he means is that adults were little aware of the characteristics which made children and youths distinct from them. A sense of this distinctiveness was supposedly on the rise from the seventeenth century, culminating in the great attention paid to children during the Enlightenment. Let us look at Ariès's picture of the original situation.

The originally prevalent image of childhood can be described simply as rather indiscriminate. Children were seen as a separate group of people with their own needs, forms of expression, and world of experience, to a much lesser extent than at present. They were largely defined in negative terms: as persons who exhibited some defects in comparison with grownups. Other historians call this the image of the little adult. In the eyes of contemporaries the most essential characteristics of a child were smaller stature and physical and social inability to perform certain tasks. By a few simple steps the little creatures became capable and responsible adults. Very young children were least valued. Boys and girls wore the same long dresses and the parents hardly looked after them. At a certain age, usually between four and seven, boys and girls changed to adult costumes. Their distinctness was recognized to the extent that they were allowed to play. Toys such as wooden horses, little windmills, and dolls can be observed from the fifteenth century. In daily life, the not too young children were hardly protected from the adult world.

Linda Pollock is Ariès's main critic. Correctly, she says that it is impossible to have no idea at all of the distinctness of children. Ariès's position is too extreme. Pollock's analysis of diaries and letters convincingly demonstrates that adults were aware of the various stages of biological growth and socialization young people went through or had to go through. Parents paid ample attention to such moments and situations as the crying of babies, weaning, teething, learning to walk, first words, play, sleeping problems, and the necessity to rear and educate children, and to introduce them to religion. This attention was also given in the sixteenth and the early seventeenth century, hence before the period when Ariès saw a sense of childhood gradually emerging. The astrologer John Dee (1527–1608) noted in his diary that he watched his three-year-old son Arthur play daddy and mummy with Mary Herbert, probably a neighbor girl. The distinctness of children was also acknowledged to some extent in the Middle Ages. Saints who displayed their holiness from early youth were consistently depicted as atypical, "old" children. They did the opposite of what normal children were supposed to do—studying instead of playing, and praying instead of listening to dirty tales. Oblates in early-medieval monasteries constituted a distinct group, the "order of children," until age fifteen. They were considered as separate and their status was lower than that of adults.

But the attention paid to stages of growth by diarists in an early period does not mean that attitudes toward young people before 1600 were exactly the same as in the eighteenth century. Other sources point to an evolution indeed. We can see the little adults for ourselves in the visual arts of the period. Painters, who often represented other subjects in a quite realistic manner, made children look like dwarfs. They resembled adults in everything except their height. They had the same clothes, bodily posture, and serious expression on their face. The little adult disappeared from the visual arts from the time when, according to Ariès, a sense of childhood emerged. Eighteenth-century painters represented children much more playfully and realistically. Pollock, citing a study by Fuller, claims that the old portraits looked as they did because patrons wanted their offspring pictured with a view toward the future. Children were important for what they would become and less for what they were. This tends to confirm Ariès's thesis: there was hardly a sense of the distinctness of children. Children as such had a low status, but it was raised toward the end of the preindustrial period.

There are more indications for a changing view of children. After 1700 the habit of giving successive siblings the same Christian name disappeared. Parents had done this earlier both in cases when the older son or daughter had died and when he or she was (still) alive. Their motive was often to secure the continuity of a name which was traditionally used in the family. A poor father explained to the Florentine census-takers why he had put his son of three at the head of the list, preceding five older children: "The previous Antonio died and I remade him" (Klapisch-Zuber: 100). The most plausible explanation for the disappearance of this custom is that it was related to a growing sense of the individuality of separate children.

Truly convincing evidence for changes in the conception of childhood lies in the extent to which young people were denied knowledge of matters adults found disturbing. Originally the inclination to do this was slight, but it increased from the middle of the seventeenth century. The worlds of the old and the young had been intermingled previously and children had literally seen everything. This observation clearly reveals that the process of privatization was still in an early stage in the sixteenth century. Openness toward children prevailed in numerous domains of life. Educators did not introduce them gradually and carefully into the adult world, but with their first lessons they were taught about the existence of war, death, profit-seeking, fraud, jealousy, and sex. There were moral lessons, phrased in the same manner and tone as those taught to adults. The example of medieval child saints made this clear. That dirty tales reached normal children was a matter of course. According to Strauss, the attitudes of Lutheran educators in sixteenth-century Germany were determined by traditional wisdom, which had little to do with the lives of real children. The preoccupations of adults were central and they never seemed to remember what it was like to be young. The late sixteenth-century Dutch schoolmaster Dirk Adriaansz Valcoogh wrote down a number of verses which he had his pupils of ten to twelve years rattle off. In them there was frequent talk of adultery and whoredom, along with the recurrent complaint that times were growing worse and drinking and vice were becoming ever more common.

As late as the seventeenth century Puritan parents in particular made obtrusive attempts to inculcate a sense of sin in quite young sons and daughters. All this changed in the eighteenth century. Hell and damnation became less frequent attributes of the religious education of children. Children began to be considered as creatures to whom grave concerns were unknown, so that they ought not be burdened with adult problems. The status of young people was raised; more attention was paid to them as a distinct social group. The invention of the jigsaw puzzle in 1762 sprang from a growing need to adapt teaching methods to the experiential world of children. The first jigsaw puzzles mainly showed geographic maps. Willingness to spend money on children for educational as well as recreative purposes increased. In England some 2400 titles of children's books published between 1750 and 1814 have been counted. In the Netherlands, too, more of these works appeared. One author congratulated his little readers in the preface for living in an age in which they had so much serious attention. The warding off of young people from the adult world did not proceed equally fast in all areas. Until the middle of the nineteenth century, for example, schoolmasters granted their pupils a day off to watch an execution.

The originally prevalent openness about life went with a strong parent-child hierarchy. Patriarchy was not only manifest between men and women but also in the relationship its name specifically suggests. We noted that the status of children and youths was lower than today. This is apparent from the tradition of the feast of fools, where they were one of the inferior groups allowed to rule for a day. In daily practice, discipline and obedience were expected from children. The frequency with which they were beaten constitutes another controversial point in historical research. Much depends on the interpretation of educational writings. Sixteenth-century Lutherans and seventeenth-century Puritans emphasized that children were undisciplined by nature, so that their will had to be broken, although some Lutherans had a different opinion. By contrast, educators in the eighteenth century assumed that children were good by nature; this was one reason why it was wrong to familiarize them with the world's wickedness at too early an age. How these theories were translated into the practice of education and discipline remains largely in the dark. Most schoolmasters did not shy from using the rod, but mothers were often inclined to complain to them about too severe discipline. An intriguing observation from English research is also relevant to this discussion: the figure for suicide among young people in the sixteenth and seventeenth centuries was relatively high. Children and adolescents frequently killed themselves to evade punishment for some fault. This is not to say that they primarily feared the physical element of punishment. In any case, physical chastisement of children by their parents was considered normal for a long time. In a study of criminal cases in the Court of Friesland, Huussen concludes that this was true until the beginning of the nineteenth century. The judges sentenced a number of youthful offenders to a whipping to be meted out by the father, mother, or a court servant.

A preliminary conclusion may be drawn that physical discipline of children was socially acceptable into the nineteenth century. If we link this to the prevalent view of young people, we observe that until about 1600 small psychic distance existed between parents and children, coinciding with great social distance. But the former started to increase in an earlier period than the latter declined.

Infant Mortality and the Mother's Breast

A number of historians claim that feelings toward sucklings in particular were characterized for a long time by a large measure of indifference. When a child died, the parents felt hardly any grief, thinking that the loss of one would no doubt be compensated by another birth. From this several authors conclude that a supposed low degree of affection was a reaction to the period's demographic realities. The high infant mortality made it imperative for parents to adopt an attitude of resignation. It made no sense to get attached to one's offspring too early, as only a few would reach maturity. Shorter, who also thinks that parents hardly cared for their children, is inclined to argue the other way around. He claims that the high infant mortality was not the cause but partly the consequence of neglect, especially the neglect

implicit in paid wet-nursing. The mother's breast, then, plays a crucial part in the argumentation of historians.

Other authors deny that parents have ever been indifferent to infants. Pollock claims that personal documents between 1500 and 1900
unequivocally testify to parental affection for children of any age and
to about an equal degree in each century. Thus, she denies an original
"dark period" as well as a possible development afterwards. Nevertheless, she observes that the tone in which parents wrote about their
children did become more emotional in the course of the period studied. Is it possible to solve the riddle of tenderness versus indifference
toward little children?

Contradictory expressions are easy to find in historical literature. In
fourteenth-century Montaillou, for example, Cathar mothers sometimes ignored the prescriptions of their faith in order to caress their
children. Sybille Pierre was concerned about her sick daughter, who
had been subjected to the ceremony of the dying so that she was
allowed no more milk. Sybille could not watch her in agony and
suckled her child, upsetting her husband. At about the same time in
another heretical environment, that of Saint Guinefort's devotees,
ritual obliged parents to leave their children unprotected in the
cold. Contradictions remain in the seventeenth century. Elisabeth
Charlotte, sister-in-law of Louis XIV, wrote that she cried for six
months over the death of her little son. This might point to a sensitivity restricted to the aristocratic top stratum were it not for similar
observations among the lower classes in England at the beginning of
the century. Richard Napier, the famous healer, treated a number
of mothers who had become severely troubled by the death of their
child. He considered maternal tenderness as a symptom of good psychological functioning. Contemporary English moralists also assumed that mothers normally harbored tender feelings. What some
historians interpret as a factual theory was a moral prescription: do
not get attached to your offspring too quickly, since you may easily
lose them again. The struggle with religious imperatives and emotions running counter is illustrated perfectly in a passage from the autobiography of Nehemiah Wallington, a Puritan artisan from London.
Ten years of childbirth eventually left him and his wife Grace with one
daughter. The first child who died was Elizabeth, in October 1625, a
few days before she would reach the age of three. Nehemiah "forgot
himself, broke all his promises to God and refused all comfort from
men." Grace, seven months pregnant with their second son, chided
him: "Husband, I am persuaded you offend God in grieving for this
child so much. Do but consider what a deal of grief and care we are rid

of and what abundance of joy she is gone into." For Elizabeth celebrated her wedding with Jesus. But the sorrowful father retorted: "Do you not grieve for this child?" Grace replied: "No, truly, husband, if you will believe me, I do as freely give it again unto God, as I did receive it of him" (Seaver: 87–88).

This example is intriguing because feelings of grief prevailed with the father while the mother kept strictly to a pious response. Usually it must have been the mothers who attached themselves most strongly to young children. Even those historians who plead the existence of deep affection in an early period admit that fathers remained relatively aloof. It cannot be a coincidence that the wicked stepmother constitutes a favorite motif in popular tales, while stepfathers are rarely heard of. This suggests that in the popular imagination mothers in particular felt strong bonds to their children—their own of course. Robert Cawdrey, a sixteenth-century English family moralist, thought that women neglected their duties toward stepchildren more often than men. A stepfather might occasionally tamper with an inheritance, but a lack of maternal care was experienced as more poignant sorrow.

The relationship between maternal suckling and affection toward children is more complex than originally supposed by historians. Already in the Middle Ages ecclesiastical authors opposed paid wet-nursing. One of their arguments was that if the wet-nurse led a sinful life, her milk would be corrupted. The amazing child saints noticed this indeed and refused the breast. A few of them, fed by their own mother, only agreed to suck when she had not engaged in sex. In the early modern period medical specialists as well as moralists expressed their disapproval of paid wet-nursing. Eucharius Rösslin, town physician of Frankfurt from 1506 to 1526, stated that mother's milk should be preferred at all times. When parents were compelled nevertheless to entrust their child to a wet-nurse, she had to meet at least six conditions. Among other things, she had to have a bright complexion, a strong neck, and firm breasts. In the Netherlands Jacob Cats presented a similar list of conditions, also as a second-best solution. In France at the end of the seventeenth century the family moralist Girard de Villethierry repeated the church's rejection of paid wet-nurses.

For an early period it is hard to tell how many parents entrusted their child to a wet-nurse. In fourteenth-century Ghent most rich citizens did so. Reliable figures from the early modern period are available for France. In the seventeenth century less than 10 percent of parental couples in the aristocracy and the office-holding nobility sent their children out to be nursed. This figure was between 5 and 15 percent for Paris as a whole in the same period. On the other hand, the custom was widespread in some of the smaller towns. Significantly, the eighteenth and nineteenth centuries were the heyday of wet-nursing for hire. The custom spread to broad groups in the urban population and consequently numerous rural mothers offered themselves as wet-nurses. In Italy too paid wet-nursing was more widespread in the eighteenth century than before or after. What earlier historians interpreted as an age-old custom was in fact a novelty in the eighteenth century, at least on such a large scale. Sussman says that the custom was neither traditional nor modern. He explains its great spread in eighteenth and nineteenth-century France in reference to the country's long drawn-out transition to an industrial society. The percentage of working married women was relatively high, especially among artisans and shopkeepers, who were the major clients of wet-nurses, next to 30 percent of unmarried mothers.

Yet the chances of survival for children suckled by their own mother were in fact higher. An estimation of the average mortality per 1000 infants at the end of the eighteenth century comes to the following figures: 180 to 200 when they got the mother's breast; 250 to 400 when the parents placed them with a wet-nurse, who usually took one child at a time; 650 to 900 for foundlings given to a wet-nurse who often suckled several at a time. Since a statistical awareness also started to arise in the eighteenth century, it is understandable that the propaganda for maternal breast-feeding was intensified. But the great campaign begun then was primarily waged for sentimental motives. Reformers stressed that within the intimate family mothers and babies belonged together more than anyone else. In the Dutch Republic, where elites were strongly oriented toward France in the eighteenth century, a writer such as Betje Wolff pleaded for increased maternal care. Family bonds received equal emphasis in the simultaneous campaign against swaddling. It had been customary for a long time to wrap babies in bandages so tight that they were hardly able to move. According to medical opinion, this made the step from the womb to the cradle less traumatic, helped the baby's limbs to grow straight, and protected it from dust and dirt in the environment. But it was difficult for the mother to cuddle her swaddled child. That is why reformers attacked the custom, and we may attribute its abolition to sentimental motives. Swaddling went out of vogue in England in the eighteenth century and elsewhere in Europe in the course of the nineteenth.

The campaign for maternal breast-feeding was less successful at first. Suckling one's baby became briefly fashionable among women in the French nobility and bourgeoisie in the 1760s and 1770s as a part of the Rousseau craze. Subsequently, women from those groups resorted to wet-nurses again, but they went to greater trouble than before to find a good one. From 1769 the French authorities established special offices for wet-nurses to which parents from the lower-middle classes could resort. Hence, in the short run, the campaign's most conspicuous result was an increase in the quality of paid wet-nursing. In the nineteenth century, however, French upper-class mothers either suckled their child themselves or they had a wet-nurse living in. Mothers in the Italian elite had changed from live-in wet-nurses to breast-feeding. Sussman and Barbagli both think that the rise of the private sphere and the closed family among the aristocracy and the bourgeoisie were influential. Parents desired to keep their children with them and so they at least took a wet-nurse into their home. But even the live-in nurse came to be seen as an intruder into the private sphere by many, obliging mothers to breast-feed their babies. In all this, concern for the health of infants played only a minor role. Throughout Europe, the most dramatic decline of child mortality did not take place until the end of the nineteenth century. Our conclusion may be that paying wet-nurses was originally a luxury mainly indulged in by a minority among the rich without any conscious neglect being involved. Precisely as the custom became more widespread, the need for a more intimate family life emerged among the elite, which gave maternal breast-feeding a new emotional significance.

The Childhood Sentiment and the Family

Intriguingly, one of the great propagandists of the family sentiment did not look after his own children. Rousseau had five children with his companion Thérèse, a woman of low social origins. He abandoned them all and took no trouble to conceal this fact: "Five children resulted from my liaison with the poor girl who lived with me, all of whom were put out as foundlings. I have not even kept a note of their dates of birth, so little did I expect to see them again. . . . All things considered I did what I thought was best for them." With Thérèse's family they would have met a fate "that would be infinitely worse for them" (Laslett et al. 1980: 259). Rousseau's opponents, such as Diderot and Grimm, who did not shy away from personal attacks, failed to chide him for this. That is one more proof that the childhood sentiment was a by-product of the rise of the intimate, closed family. Without it this sentiment was unknown still.

Although it is the judgment of many today that an emphasis on the maternal role imposes restrictions on women, a comment is called for when this is viewed historically. Overall power relations between women and men rather changed in favor of the former around 1800. Patriarchy continued to prevail in the nineteenth century, but in comparison to earlier periods, except perhaps for the days of the courtly nobility, it was mitigated somewhat. From the self-evident acceptance by twelfth-century daughters of a marriage partner their father had selected to the companionate marriage of the eighteenth century, there is a fragmented line in the direction of a slight increase in women's power, even if simultaneously they were excluded from some social positions. Viewed historically, the maternal role was an innovation. It cannot be said that women were burdened with a well-defined type of care in order that others might enjoy leisure; the care of children simply had received less emphasis previously. Domestic life was revaluated and, within it, attention to small children occupied a central place. This was the particular domain of mothers, which caused their position to be stronger than it had been before.

9 THE RISE OF THE PRIVATE SPHERE

This chapter forms a continuation of the previous one. Simultaneously, it is meant as a conclusion to the book as a whole, since the process of privatization is the major thread connecting its chapters. We pick it up once more. In chapters 5 through 7 privatization was manifest in the developments with respect to the human body. Death, insanity, and violent punishments were removed from the theater of life to more or less secluded spaces. Forms of privatization inherent in the developments regarding the family were anticipated in the previous chapter. In daily existence, people acquired a need for secluded spaces, creating them both in concrete form and in a symbolic sense. A theme still left to discuss is sexuality, related to the body as well as to marriage. Sexuality too was concealed and surrounded with restraints toward the end of the preindustrial period (the first section). Privatization was at work in the disintegration of the lesser tradition and the diminishing cohesion of village and neighborhood communities. This is the subject of the middle section, where the end of the witch persecutions and the decline of youth societies also get attention. In the final section, all threads spun in this chapter and the preceding one come together.

Sexuality Curbed

Ecclesiastical norms with respect to sexuality within and outside marriage have been discussed. For later centuries of the preindustrial period, we are somewhat better informed about the extent to which they were lived up to. Uncertainties remain considerable nonetheless. It is abundantly clear that ecclesiastical and secular morals were in strong agreement in the Victorian age. Here we are concerned about the possible tensions between the two in the preceding centuries. Catholic and Protestant moralists of that period in any case put great emphasis on the marriage ethic. A more tenacious offensive against all kinds of extramarital sexuality set in with the Reformation and Counter Reformation, together with the beginnings of opposition to elements from popular culture.

Bastards

During the preindustrial period male dominance still pervaded lay norms. The sexuality of women was controlled and curbed more severely than that of men. Many investigators point to the prevalence of the so-called double standard, which remained valid throughout the preindustrial period and has not disappeared entirely today. Men were allowed a greater freedom than women; adultery especially counted as a much more serious offense for women. Differences in social status, to be sure, complicated this pattern. When a peasant ceded his wife to a gentleman for a night, for example, the community could see no harm in it. Contemporaries justified the double standard in the case of adultery with the argument that only the escapades of women cast doubt upon the legitimacy of one's offspring. Of course this argument implies that male complicity in that dangerous situation was less burdened with guilt feelings. The double standard caused all women to be divided in principle into two categories: the virtuous and the public. Among the first category we find virginal daughters, faithful wives, and chaste widows. Prostitutes belonged to the second category, together with promiscuous or adulterous women or those suspect of dishonorable ways in any other sense. Women from this group were not under the rule and control of a father and hence they were outlaws of a kind; sometimes literally, as appears from the ritual rapes which took place until the sixteenth century.

The unmistakable problem which served as a justification for the double standard is also a statistical problem to present-day historians. If the husband of a woman of apparently irreproachable conduct is not the natural father of her child, how are we to know it? It was the rule in various countries that children born to married women were automatically recognized as legitimate and, consequently, the husband as the father. Where the law was different, a reliable statistical investigation into the frequency of the births of "cuckold children" would be a chimera. In circles where, by exception, the double standard did not exist, as among the French and Italian aristocracy in the eighteenth century, contemporaries occasionally expressed their doubts about the legitimacy of children. But even their knowledge did not rise above the level of suspicion. Following his analytical approach of the problem, Laslett distinguishes nine types of bastardy. In practice, statistical research mainly deals with the offspring of unmarried women.

The bastardy theme forms the most telling example of an attempt to infer attitudes from demographic data. The basic premise is that in a society knowing few and deficient contraceptive techniques, the frequency of illegitimate births is an indication for the frequency of extramarital sexual intercourse. Few figures are known for an early period. As far as the Middle Ages are concerned, it can only be said that the sources often refer to bastards, which is reported for fourteenth-century Ghent, for example. The church had managed to outlaw official concubinage, but nonetheless it remained common well into the sixteenth century for nobles and rich burghers to have children outside marriage. Those bastards, usually begotten with women of lower social standing, were raised in their father's home, or else the mother received an allowance for their upkeep. Their status still was primarily that of freeborn but second-class children. It was not until the early modern period that this inferiority of status became the stigma of illegitimacy. For this period a long-term graph of the percentage of bastard births in England has been constructed. These figures of course concern the entire population and not merely the elites. A small peak came at the end of the sixteenth century, after which a decline set in until a low point had been reached by the middle of the seventeenth century. The percentage then remained relatively low for a long time, but it rose very quickly to a high peak at the end of the eighteenth century. The chronological range of the series of figures available for other countries is more modest, but one interesting observation recurs in every region studied: the great increase toward 1800 was practically universal, although central Europe was later with this rise than western and northern Europe. In Rotterdam, for example, the illegitimacy ratio rose from 3.8 percent in 1775 to 6.6 percent in 1800. How can we explain this increase throughout Europe?

Did the people allow themselves greater sexual liberties (again)? Shorter thinks they did. He infers from the figures that notably the sexual activities of women broke loose from traditional restraints. The process of romanticization manifested itself also outside the conjugal bond, which caused extramarital pregnancies to increase in number. According to this thesis, bastards born in lower numbers in a preromantic period were the fruit of impulsive sex. The most important proof for this lies in the seasonality of illegitimate conceptions, which often took place in the months of the great festivals. That pattern has been observed, among others, in eighteenth-century Flanders and

Sweden, but it was entirely absent from England. Whether deliberate or impulsive sex was involved though, the implication of Shorter's thesis is that bastardy was always a result of activities in which the participants had taken the initiative without agreeing on any further bond.

Most historians deny this. They interpret illegitimate births in the context of courtship. The "courtship theory" explains the increase in bastardy toward 1800 through the following steps: (1) among the populace marriage still meant primarily an economic union; (2) engagements were broken off mainly when the prospects of economic independence were shattered; (3) in the economic crisis at the end of the eighteenth century more engagements ended than before; (4) in a number of these cases the girl was already pregnant. The implication of this theory is that even before the second half of the eighteenth century, bastard births were a result of disrupted courtships. Two other demographic observations valid for both periods make this thesis plausible: (1) on the average, unmarried mothers were about as old as the married ones having their first child; (2) marital and extramarital fertility correlate. In times and at places where few marriages were concluded and they were begun at an even older age, few bastards were born. Mitterauer presents a variant of the explanation mentioned for the rise around 1800. The illegitimacy ratio had always been highest in regions where so-called life-cycle servants abounded. The economic and demographic situation around 1800 made this group become especially numerous in the countryside. For one thing, the mortality of adolescents had sharply decreased as a consequence of the improved quality of food. In this way, Mitterauer even establishes a relationship between potatoes and bastards. His theory resembles the other one to the extent that both are looking for an explanation of illegitimacy in economic terms.

Thus, fluctuations in bastard births mainly tell us something about sexuality which, although extramarital, is still aimed at marriage. The major conclusion is that among the populace there were no objections to making love during courtship. This is also apparent from the much higher frequency of premarital pregnancies, considered as such by statisticians with a built-in margin of certainty when the first child is born within eight months after the wedding. That happened to one-fourth to one-third of the married couples in the Bavarian village of Unterfinning between 1670 and 1720, while a bastard was born only once in every five or ten years. Young people always viewed the first act of making love as a kind of transaction, in which the girl gave up her virginity in exchange for a definite offer from the other party: a marriage vow and, preferably, some economic capital. Unmarried mothers complained that they had believed in those promises and had been deceived. Such complaints could be heard all over Europe and were not merely an excuse to the community. Of the unmarried mothers questioned in Languedoc between 1715 and 1780, 45 percent replied they had given in because they had trusted the man's vow. The norm which allowed making love during courtship was a popular continuation of the ancient tradition according to which the establishment of a conjugal bond was a long drawn-out process with no single moment in time standing out. At least, that was the attitude of the agrarian population and the lowest groups in the towns. The community imposed a stricter ethic on "respectable" urban artisans in the early modern period. Especially in Germany the guilds guarded their reputation, declaring any member who had made love before his wedding infamous. In 1623, when the Bremen baker Berent Cappelmann had a son after twenty weeks of marriage, his guild fellows expelled him and nailed boards to his window. The parties were reconciled through mediation of the town senate; this body had to intervene anew in 1647, when the guilds refused admittance to Berent's son, calling him infamous too. In these matters, the magistrates appeared to be less radical than the guild.

The Chastity Offensive

Thus far, the analysis leaves the sexual life of those not (yet) contemplating a marriage undiscussed. Ecclesiastical moralists of the early modern period condemned a broader spectrum of sexually colored acts than only those which could lead to pregnancy. From the later Middle Ages the norms of the church were enforced by its own courts, while secular law also defined various forms of deviant sex as illegal. Judicial attention to forbidden sex varied strongly. Church courts in thirteenth-century England often imposed a whipping for adultery or fornication. In the fifteenth through seventeenth centuries they were usually satisfied with a public penance. The secular judges of seventeenth and eighteenth-century Amsterdam were not too much concerned about these two offenses, but they often tried prostitutes. Sodomy was punished by death in several countries. Generally, however, the chastity offensive of the early modern period was mainly waged by clergymen, who had to rely on their powers of persuasion.

As a major result of this offensive, the sexual imagination was removed from the public sphere. A relative openness with respect to sexuality and in related fields such as nudity had prevailed for a long time. It can be observed in medieval chronicles and sixteenth-century school books. We saw that children also shared in it. Six-year olds were admonished not to spend their money on whores. At the beginning of the seventeenth century, court ladies played sexual games with the young Louis XIII as a matter of course. Only when this openness was in decline at the end of the eighteenth century did pornography emerge as a genre. What was no longer allowed returned in a secretive manner. Originally openness was fully compatible with the norms regulating actual behavior. A statute in medieval Lübeck, for example, determined that the punishment for an adulterous man was to be led through town by his female accomplice holding the most implicated part of his body. We do not know whether this rule was ever applied. Actual punishment could take extreme forms though, as in the case of a nun and a servant of the convent in twelfth-century Yorkshire, who secretly met each night. When this was discovered, the other nuns forced her to chop off her lover's member and put it into her mouth. It should be added that the cleric who wrote this down thought they had gone too far. We find another curious mixture of openness and norm enforcement in the impotence suits already discussed. Especially those in sixteenth and seventeenth-century France, involving persons from the aristocracy or high Parisian circles, drew the public's attention. Many people were informed about them and wished to hear about new developments.

All this concerns special cases. The originally prevalent openness was expressed first of all in sexual imagination and symbolism in situations relating to marriage: during courtship and at wedding celebrations. The feasts and dances of the village youth and their collective meetings during the *veillées* or in the *Spinnstuben* were full of symbolism referring to the prospective conjugal union. Weddings were a time for busy speculation about the fertility of the first night of marriage and later. Relatives and neighbors often accompanied the couple to bed and they listened at the door until they were satisfied that matters proceeded as they should. With the Bremen guilds, who embraced such a strict ethic, this *bettsetzen* had still another aspect: two sworn masters first had to check the bride's virginity with their own hands. This inspection cost the bridegroom the sum of six marks. When an early birth of a child followed in spite of this, the inspectors themselves were expelled from the guild for neglecting their duties.

It was especially the plain symbolism at collective meetings, dances, and wedding celebrations which was repellent to the moralists. The chastity offensive begun in the sixteenth century by the Protestant and Catholic clergy implied a rejection of the openness just noted. German clerics condemned the encounters of boys and girls in the Spinnstuben. The magistrates satisfied them in so far as they issued ordinances from the seventeenth century restricting attendance to women or to brothers and sisters at most. Throughout Europe the moralists were successful sooner or later. According to Van Ussel, a process of increasing prudery can be observed from the seventeenth century. Rich farmers and established bourgeois, and others following them later, gradually began to consider even the sexual imagination directed at sex in marriage as indelicate. They wished this imagination to be concealed and the conjugal bedroom protected as a private domain. The events surrounding the chase of the garter in English villages are illustrative. The bride's garter symbolized the power of love and had to be conquered on her wedding day by the bachelors who stayed behind. In the sixteenth century this was done during the ceremony in church, where the most agile among them snatched the precious object. With the purging of the ecclesiastical celebration the custom changed into a run to the bride's home after the service. The winner had the right to take off the garter. In the course of time, this piece of clothing became a finely embroidered one for the occasion. But eventually, moralists found even this custom too permissive and around 1800 they tried to prohibit the run. They were supported by well-to-do families, who had come to consider the custom simply indecent. The daughters of rich or prudish farmers henceforth refused to lift their skirt. Some put a garter around their shoe, but the boys would not run for that: "Most surely, she must have ugly legs." The decline of community life put a definitive end to such customs.

Night Courting

Our attention has been drawn back constantly to sexuality with marriage in mind, so that it has to be directed at other subjects. The obvious course is to inquire into the sexual life of young bachelors. Conceding that biological maturity came at a later age then than at present, we are still left with a stage of life from that moment until the beginning of a steady courtship that took almost ten years. From the rarity of bastards some historians conclude that sex life during that stage was confined to the solitary habit. Ecclesiastical writers condemned masturbation from the early Middle Ages, although most permitted it for married women who had not reached orgasm after their partner had finished. But they did not push this condemnation. Physicians for their part considered occasional masturbation as beneficial to the health of men. This induced the French moralist Goffar to write in 1628 that doctors who recommended it for reasons of health themselves committed a grave sin. The solitary habit did not become an object of serious concern until the eighteenth century, when medical opinion turned around. Doctors began to consider masturbation to be as dangerous to a person's health as clerics thought it for his salvation. Especially in the nineteenth century this led to a veritable obsession against it among several groups in society.

It is unlikely, however, that the sex life of young bachelors in the early modern period remained confined to masturbation. Some entered into brief relationships during this stage of life. Did the low frequency of bastard births mean that young men and women seldom went all the way in such relationships? Fairchilds thinks it does. From her investigation of pregnancy declarations in eighteenth-century Provence it appears that "short-term encounters" accounted for no more than 5 to 9 percent of the number of extramarital pregnancies. In a third to a half of these cases, she claims, there are indications that rape was involved. A few caveats have to be added to this. First, the chances for pregnancy evidently increase with each coition, although not proportionately. Second, there are several forms of non-coital sex. Precisely those activities have resisted quantitative analysis up to now, since a valid indicator is lacking. This necessitates an interpretation of qualitative data.

The various interpretations focus upon a custom that was widespread at least in the countryside. Under the supervision of the peer group, a young man met his loved one at the window or the door of her home; often he was admitted into her bed as well. The general term for this is "night courting," but the words used by contemporaries often varied with the region, as they did in France. The English might also refer to it as "sitting up," while it was called *nachtvrijen* in the Netherlands, *Fensterln* in Germany, and *kiltgang* in Sweden. On the Wadden Islands of the Netherlands night courting remained customary well into the nineteenth century. The young men agreed in advance who was to visit whom and exchanged information about the cool reception to be expected from some girls and the eagerness of others. Often they went to farms in surrounding villages. Folklorists in various countries, who were the first to study this phenomenon around 1900, imagined that the lovers merely held each other's hand in bed, and a recent historian such as Shorter repeats their judgment. According to him, younger as well as older people had a relatively weak libido, due to hard work and bad health and nourishment. Others, who think their libido was strong enough, find it unlikely that the lovers became intimate during night courting and still managed to restrain themselves from consummation. Therefore, they conclude that in fact nothing happened.

Flandrin, however, explains how intimacy and avoidance of conception could go together. He distinguishes two models of sexuality. The conjugal model was oriented toward fertility, procreation, and coition. The youth model, on the other hand, centered around non-coital sex. Forms of intimacy-without-going-all-the-way, handed down from generation to generation, guaranteed a low frequency of extramarital pregnancies. Gillis implicitly joins this thesis, as he characterizes the life stage preceding steady courtship as one of "polygamous play." Clerics, however, saw nothing but unchastity in night courting. Growing opposition from the church caused the chain of tradition to be broken. Among young people themselves the non-coital model retreated to the margins of consciousness, which meant that henceforth, if they became intimate after all, they could only have the other model in mind. This leads Flandrin to an alternative explanation for the great rise in illegitimacy, yet based in part on an increase in the frequency of sexual intercourse without the prospect of marriage. The explanation implies a paradox: church opposition to night courting led, through a decline in the frequency of the habit and an intrusion of the coital model, to an increase in extramarital pregnancies. Rare passages in diaries from the period before 1700, written mostly by men from the upper reaches of society, confirm the existence of a non-coital model. In Samuel Pepys's diary, which is best known in this respect, there is constant mention of forms of sex that do not lead to pregnancy. For the peasant population we have Quaife's study of the prosecution of deviant sex in England in the first half of the seventeenth century. According to him, illegal sex and promiscuity were accepted by the community's public opinion. Many sinned once in a while, but only a few, who may have been denounced by neighbors with whom they had quarreled, ended up in court. Significantly, the majority of trials concerned non-coital sex.

The life of unmarried youths, then, was probably less sexless than someone like Shorter assumes. It is practically impossible, however, to determine the actual experience of sexuality. We may take for granted that in the non-coital model there was less talk of a transaction, the exchange of male pleasure for female security. In conjugal and prenuptial sexual intercourse, several historians believe that men had little concern for women's desires. A few caveats are again in order. A number of contemporaries claimed that it was precisely women who could be overwhelmed by sexual desire from time to time. According to the medical theory prevalent until about 1660, semen existed too in women as well as in men, and without a female orgasm no conception was possible. In Jane Sharp's manual for midwives, frequently reprinted in the eighteenth century, the mons veneris is called "mountain of pleasure." For the Netherlands there are examples of women taking the initiative toward prenuptial intercourse as well as of those who took pleasure in conjugal sexuality. The innkeeper's daughter with whom Wijnant van Velsen was taking a stroll in 1661, lay down on her back along the road, inviting him "to venture a playful journey with her" (Haks: 79–80). The autobiography of the seventeenth-century minister's widow Isabella de Moerloose is interesting too. She described her sex life with her late husband in positive terms, although she did not enjoy every variant. This minister, who had been a widower himself previously and already had children, practiced coitus interruptus.

Relationships of unequal status, finally, such as that between master and servant girl, are rightly considered a category apart by historians. Coition was common in such relationships. Most historians assume that these, whether steady or one-night stands, were based on coercion and domination on the part of the men of superior status, so that women drew little pleasure from them. A counterexample, the history of Giovanni and Lusanna, comes from an early period. Men in the Florentine patriciate took a younger wife from their own social group when they were well in their thirties and, before that time, they looked for love with women from the lower classes, married or not. That was how the long-standing affair between Giovanni and Lusanna in the middle of the fifteenth century began. The exceptional thing is that, when the inevitable moment had come, she was prepared to contest her lover's marriage in court. Eventually, she lost on appeal.

Prostitution

Two forms of deviant sex, prostitution and homosexuality, require separate attention. We start with the first. It was explained earlier that women were divided into two categories, with prostitutes not surprisingly belonging to those without honor. To a certain extent every woman not under patriarchal supervision was considered a sort of whore. It is no coincidence that French ritual rapists often forced their victims to take some money. In a country like Spain the belief was also widespread that there was nothing wrong in a man's incidental love-making with a "woman at large." If contacts were made more or less voluntarily on her part, he would still appreciate it when she accepted a small sum afterwards. Love that was paid for could never be sinful; such was the notion which the Inquisition attempted to suppress from the sixteenth century on. The association between being unattached, sexual availability, and financial transaction was a logical one to con-temporaries. Prostitution began where the rule of the fathers was no longer all-embracing. It is understandable, therefore, that the rising states, which took the place of families in other fields too, subse-quently started to deal with whores.

A rough sketch can be given of the development in the policies of the authorities throughout western Europe. In the agrarian society around A.D. 1000, where the rule of the fathers was omnipresent and geographic mobility almost unknown, references to prostitution are lacking. Such references first surface in the towns around 1200. They usually concern prohibitions upon public women from residing within the city walls or in respectable neighborhoods. A little later the magistrates assigned them to special districts. In Montpellier in 1285, for example, all whores were ordered to take up domicile in the "hot street." In the fourteenth and fifteenth centuries urban authorities themselves increasingly proceeded to establish brothels, although they sometimes leased them to a brothel-keeper. Under the influence of the reform movements of the sixteenth century, however, policies became more repressive in both Protestant and Catholic countries. The authorities closed brothels and declared prostitution a crime. Al-though it remained an offense in the seventeenth and eighteenth cen-turies, brothels were secretly allowed, especially in the bigger cities. In the nineteenth century, finally, the national governments in some countries again adopted a policy of regulation, arguing that it was better to control an ineradicable evil than permit it to thrive clandestinely.

We are well informed on the late medieval situation through Otis's study of Languedoc. She emphasizes the problem of the protection of whores from assault. Assignment to special districts also served this purpose. In the hot street of Montpellier it was expressly forbidden to molest the women or to chase them away. The house rules of fifteenth-century brothels obliged the clients to leave their weapons with the "abbot" upon entry. That the head of a brothel in the fifteenth century was called an abbot is interesting for more than one reason. It means that the terminology for the cohabitation of a group of dishonorable women was derived from its holy counterpart, the convent. It also means that this group, living outside family bonds, was subjected to a sort of second-class patriarchal control. This had not originally been the case. The earliest brothels in Languedoc were usually managed by women. The same situation prevailed in fourteenth-century Seville. Urban ordinances spoke of prostitution rooms in "false convents" headed by an abbess. In 1462 the prostitutes of Toulouse submitted a petition to the *parlement* in that town: they now had an abbot instead of an abbess but found him a common pimp who squeezed too much money out of them. Their complaint met no favor. Male supervision over prostitutes probably originated in the illegal circuit created by urban regulation. In a violent world, whoever lived as a whore alone and outside the special districts could not do without a protector; equally uprooted men were probably available for this role. Most of the illegal prostitutes arrested in fifteenth-century Florence also had a pimp. The brothels there had male keepers too.

For the early modern period we have two contrasting cities: Seville and Amsterdam. Seville had one official brothel at the beginning of the seventeenth century, now headed by three *padres*. These "fathers" were entitled to obedience from the women just as a husband was from his wife or her confessor from a nun. On Mary Magdalene's day, 22 July, a priest came to urge the women to convert, after which town officials proceeded with more mundane affairs such as fining a padre who had admitted too young a girl or another type of unauthorized whore. In most Catholic countries, permitting a limited number of brothels was accompanied by promoting conversions. Special houses of refuge were established for prostitutes who stopped working, but it was whispered that many women did not convert until they were too old for the job. The Protestant Dutch Republic did not know such houses of refuge. By contrast, prostitutes in seventeenth and eighteenth-century Amsterdam often ended up in the spinhouse, the women's prison. By this time they were usually recidivists; brothel-keepers more often suffered imprisonment at their first trial. Amsterdam brothels in that period were almost exclusively headed by women. This is also the case in Leiden. Possibly this is related to the more independent position of women in general in the Netherlands. The trials of prostitutes and their female supervisors followed irregularly conducted raids and are only the tip of the iceberg. In fact, prostitution was connived at in early modern Amsterdam. The magistrates were more severe toward women who practiced their trade alone in the streets. The latter constituted a vulnerable group, often consisting of women who had travelled to Amsterdam from other parts of the Republic, northwestern Germany, or Scandinavia in the hope of honest employment. In the early modern period we find this group in all major European cities.

Homosexuality

As we shift the focus to homosexual activities, terminology must be clarified first. Well into the nineteenth century, sodomy was the common name for sex between men, and it was linked to a definite set of ideas. We should remember that the ancient Greeks and Romans put few restrictions in the way of sex between men. It was an anathema, on the other hand, to Christian morality. Nonetheless, as some authors claim, a relative tolerance prevailed in practice well into the Middle Ages. In the later Middle Ages, repression is said to have increased. Urban magistrates in fifteenth-century Italy were so concerned about sodomy that it gave them an extra reason to promote prostitution. At the beginning of that century, Florence's rulers established a few brothels with the explicit aim of keeping men from homosexual behavior. It remains to be seen whether they were successful. In Florence and Venice a number of incorrigibles were crypto-sodomitical even as whore's visitors. The prostitutes they frequented cut their hair short and acted as young men in order to seduce their clients all the more. Some cross-dressed and were suspected of specializing in anal intercourse. As a result of the policy of the authorities, many Florentines at the end of the century thought that the city counted too many whores. The preacher Savonarola, who as far as chastity was concerned inveighed mainly against prostitution, indeed advised his fellow citizens not to worry too much about sodomy; it was less frequent than one might suppose from hearing the gossip in the street.

But in fact, an ambivalent attitude toward sodomy prevailed in Renaissance Italy. The complaints about its supposed great frequency were founded on an existing tradition. Some contemporaries, among them several great artists, glorified sodomy more or less covertly under the influence of the classical heritage. Ganymede, a young man from Greek mythology who had been the lover of Zeus, the supreme god, was presented in a favorable manner by Michelangelo, among others. Benvenuto Cellini was sentenced in absentia for sodomy, but his fellow citizens were later glad to pardon him. With the Reformation and Counter Reformation, this ambivalence gave way to unequivocal intolerance again. The remembrance of the Renaissance remained alive in Protestant countries. Protestant moralists thought sodomy a typically Catholic practice, one not unfamiliar to unmarried priests. In the Dutch Republic it was widely believed that the diplomats who came from the Mediterranean to negotiate peace at the congress of Utrecht in 1713, had introduced the habit in the country. In general, many Europeans believed that sodomy was indulged in principally at the courts of princes, where the status of those involved guaranteed impunity.

One of the basic issues in sodomy research concerns the development of a gay identity in the past and the exact timing of its emergence. According to the view of sodomy which prevailed in Christian Europe for a long time, it was merely one of the perversities a dissolute man might indulge in. It was thought unlikely that such perverts would restrict themselves to sex with other men. The life story of the Anglican bishop John Atherton, composed at the occasion of his hanging in 1640, says that from adultery through incest and rape he finally arrived at sodomy, the only charge actually brought against him. In this stereotypical cluster of images, sodomy could not be viewed separately from all kind of other "debauches." Moralists knew no homosexual identity, nor did the practitioners themselves. According to Bray, homosexual behavior was not uncommon among the populace of seventeenth-century England; among male domestic servants, for example, who often had to share a bed. In daily reality, the step from normal sex involving lads and lasses to that involving lads only was more natural than the one from all kinds of deviant sex to sodomy, as the moralists believed. The grotesqueness of this stereotype meant that the practitioners did not view their practices as sodomy.

For England and the Netherlands the appearance of a gay identity can be dated around 1700. A distinct subculture emerged in both countries at the end of the seventeenth century. London, for example, knew so-called molly houses, where gentlemen convened to have fun together. The popular name "molly" was given to a man who had an exclusive preference for other men. In Amsterdam the gallery under the town hall was a meeting place in the 1690s. Putting one's foot on another's was a signal that one belonged to "that sort of people." This subculture arose in the context of increased persecution, which caused the sense of identity to become stronger still. The enforcers of law in England started to raid molly houses from 1699 onward. In the Netherlands the prosecution of sodomy was intensified in the eighteenth century, first in Rotterdam and from 1730 in other towns as well. A few trials involved sailors from the ships of the Dutch West India Company, but more often those prosecuted were established residents. It appears from the interrogations that a thriving subculture had come into existence, with special meeting places and contact networks. In this period it became common to refer to someone as a sodomite, instead of one who practiced sodomy. Thus, a gay identity was in the making.

This was hardly so for women in preindustrial Europe. Lesbian activities were largely excluded from the mental world of men as well as women. The case of the seventeenth-century Italian nun Benedetta Carlini is illustrative. Her dossier, with an extensive report of lesbian behavior, is the oldest known so far. Benedetta enjoyed a special status as a prophetess, stigmatized (in the original meaning of the word) with Jesus's wounds. But she was unmasked as a fraud. The investigation into her activities revealed that she had an affair with a fellow sister. The two women lay on each other, provoked mutual orgasms, but did not use any artificial aid. Benedetta pretended that she was a male angel. Even to herself, her behavior was more comprehensible when she associated it with the model of heterosexual love.

The case of this Italian nun reveals the view of women and sex which prevailed in early modern Europe. To contemporaries from the elites, full-blown sex always involved penetration, as it had for the ancient Greeks and Romans. Young bachelors from the populace probably agreed with them, considering the non-coital model as a temporary preference. In case of sex between two women, this view led one of the partners to adopt a male identity, as Benedetta Carlini did and the prostitutes in her country had done earlier for quite different reasons. In the Dutch Republic in the seventeenth century, a few women were punished for having married another woman in men's clothes. The image of penetration also caused the community very quickly to suspect the use of an aid. The French writer Brantôme condemned the use of a *godemiche* (dildo) as extremely unnatural.

On the other hand, the prevalent view meant that some sexual acts between women were not disapproved of. In French court circles many thought lightly about the mutual caresses of women, even if these had a strongly physical character. Brantôme claimed that *donna con donna* was less dangerous than adultery, because a man did not lose his wife in that case. When women did something with each other, men viewed it as innocent play, which would only inculcate a greater desire for heterosexual love in the participants. The players themselves accepted this image and did not see lesbian activities as involving a specific preference. Medical opinion was in line with this. The physician Liébault advised that it might benefit conjugal love-making when the mistress had been warmed up by her maid in advance. In addition to sexual play, a tradition of romantic friendship between women existed in the early modern period. It was expressed, among other things, in literature. According to Faderman, women who were romantic friends shared all their feelings and emotions, but their relationships were never sexual and the community did not consider them as such. Yet there is some evidence suggesting that "modern" lesbian relationships occasionally developed in popular circles in the larger cities toward the end of the preindustrial period. The Amsterdam court prosecuted a number of women for same-sex intercourse in the 1790s. It began with a crime of passion in 1792. Bets Wiebes and Bartha Schuurman had been living together for several months when Bartha, thinking that Bets also had an affair with Catherina de Haan, stabbed Catherina to death out of jealousy. Apparently, this murder case alerted the judges to the activities of other women. Thus, a lesbian identity was in the making too, although to a lesser degree and at a later time than a gay identity.

The Disintegration of the Lesser Tradition

The offensive against all forms of deviant sexuality, launched mainly by clerics, in principle was directed at all social groups. But moralists were inclined to credit peasants and artisans with being particularly uncivilized. The chastity offensive formed part of a more encompassing attempt to transform the culture of the people. This was one of the reasons why the lesser tradition of village and neighborhood communities was eventually lost. This section probes its disintegration.

The decline of preindustrial popular culture was not only a result of conscious repression or attempts at reform. The weakening of the community bonds which had sustained it for so long was mainly caused by social and economic developments. They will be noted later. First, we remain in the realm of mentality. With the chastity offensive already discussed, the disenchantment of the world is the process left to review. Changing notions of religion, magic, and the cosmos among the elite influenced popular culture.

An End to Witchcraft Trials

The demise of witchcraft trials in Europe illustrates these changing notions. The end of the witch persecutions has been pinned down at various dates. The earliest is 1610; around that year they were stopped in the Dutch Republic and Spain, their enemy at that moment. In some of the regions with mass persecutions practically no more trials were conducted after the wave which began around 1630. From a European perspective, however, the end date has to be fixed at a later time. Following Norman Cohn, 1680 is opted for, so that the period of persecution covers exactly two centuries. The year 1680 is about the median of the end dates in the core areas. For seven districts in the Jura, years between 1661 and 1683 are mentioned as the last in which a criminal trial based on witchcraft doctrine was conducted. There were no significant differences between Calvinist, Catholic, and Lutheran territories on this point. The Jura was not the last in line. The last great panic in the European core areas occurred in 1697, with the Scottish village of Paisley as the scene. The court prosecuted twenty persons, seven of whom were hanged. In the eighteenth century only Poland witnessed a steady series of trials. Elsewhere in Europe they had become sporadic and executions were rarer still. The literature reveals few details about these eighteenth-century trials; they were probably concerned with harmful sorcery rather than witchcraft. Monter confirms this supposition for the Jura. Why did the attention the elite judges paid to witches dwindle from the end of the seventeenth century?

A possible answer is that they shrank from the effects of their own deeds, without starting to doubt the existence of witches. That is Midelfort's thesis. According to him, the witch hunt ceased from its internal dynamics. The crisis of confidence which came in the wake of the great panics turned into a general crisis of confidence regarding witchcraft trials as such. In the bishopric of Würzburg, for example, the bishop himself and his chancellor were accused in 1630. The bishop immediately ordered the trials to stop and had masses said for the innocent victims of justice. Such a sense of "what are we really doing" is supposed to have befallen all authorities eventually. Midelfort's explanation is attuned to the region he studied. The model of the crisis of confidence appears specific to the areas with great panics. Another theory, embraced in several variants by Trevor-Roper and Dupont-Bouchat, among others, is of a more general type. The witch hunt ended because attention was deflected to new scapegoats. Before 1480 these had been Jews and heretics. During the tranquil period between 1520 and 1560 they were religious opponents. Thereafter they were mainly marginal persons and sexual deviants, or Jews again. Such an alternation, however, can be demonstrated, if at all, only for witches and Jews, who were hardly persecuted between 1480 and 1680. Besides, this type of explanation raises more questions than it answers. Why is one group a suitable scapegoat in one period and another group in another period?

There was more involved than just a lack of self-confidence or an alternation of scapegoats. Such observations are primarily useful for explaining the end of individual persecutions. What we really have to explain is the structural ripeness for witch persecutions which characterized western European societies for two centuries. Why did it disappear? Whatever else it meant, the disappearance of this structural ripeness implied that the fear of the demonic sect diminished among the magistrates and that the hold which the belief in this company had gained over people's minds became weaker. Hence, an explanation for the demise of witchcraft trials has to begin with the rise of this fear. The obsession with the devil's works was already manifest in the period when Jews and heretics were persecuted and witchcraft doctrine was developed. The historians Bouwsma and Delumeau think that the period from the beginning of the fourteenth until the end of the seventeenth century was characterized by a heightened collective anxiety and feelings of insecurity among elite groups. Following their argument, we may put it this way: the coming of persecutions, first of Jews and heretics and later of witches, was related to the rise of this collective fear, while its demise ended the series of persecutions. It remains unexplained of course why anxiety increased and then disappeared again. Its disappearance was possibly related to changes in world outlook which brought a more optimistic view of nature and human capabilities.

It is important to note that when the elites stopped believing in witches, they did not fall back upon older magical notions. As far as this group was concerned, the demise of witchcraft trials coincided with an acceleration in the process of disenchantment of the world. In the Dutch Republic this can be traced unambiguously in criminal trials. Fortune tellers, soothsayers, popular exorcists, and magical healers remained active; when their activities raised commotion, they were often arrested. From the middle of the seventeenth century the judges steadfastly condemned them as frauds. Preferably they compelled the accused to acknowledge themselves that their practices were without effect. The Netherlands were a little precocious with this shift, but a similar approach became common later elsewhere in western Europe. The demise of witch persecutions coincided with the scientific revolution, which would eventually lead to a mechanical world outlook, but the one was not simply the consequence of the other. The scientific revolution on the one hand and the shift from belief in magic to the unmasking of sorcerers as frauds on the other were both a manifestation of a phase in the process of disenchantment of the world. The new beliefs were not to receive an ideological base until after 1700. The change at the end of the seventeenth century certainly did not imply that the elites turned less Christian. Scientists remained pious sons of the church. As far as witchcraft was concerned, the struggle was between conservative and innovative believers. To the conservatives the removal of one stone, no matter which, would shatter the foundation of the faith: without witches, no devil and without the devil, no Christianity. To more modern believers, such as the Dutch minister Balthasar Bekker, Christianity was compatible with a less blatant personification of evil. Bekker, to be sure, was heavily attacked by his colleagues, a sign that even in the Dutch Republic the ideological battle was not yet over at the end of the seventeenth century.

Civilizing Offensives

The attempts of secular rulers to define magical practices as fraud and those of ecclesiastical moralists to curb sexuality can be viewed as civilizing offensives, one at the cognitive and the other at the normative level. They made inroads into preindustrial popular culture. There has always been opposition to customs and beliefs from the lesser tradition; some of it was noted in chapter 3. Originally, however, the opposition was not very systematic. Individual reformers attacked various customs and beliefs in a selective manner. Let us review the successive phases of opposition.

Even before the Reformation, bishops and other church prelates began to object more vehemently to such customs as the feast of fools and the ass mass. Unanimity did not yet prevail in those circles, however. Around 1500 several Spanish ecclesiastical authors defended submission to an *obispillo* as a useful exercise in Christian humility. But eventually, clerics viewed such celebrations as a mere mockery of the church. They emphasized that the profane ought to be separated from the sacred. Dancing in church or riding a donkey was an insult to the dignity of the faith. The position the reformers took toward the lesser tradition was ambiguous at first. Luther's disciples turned elements from popular culture to propaganda uses, promoting antipapist carnivals. But Protestants rejected the cult of saints, considered most Catholic rites as idolatry, and in general favored soberness. This led to the abolition of saints' festivals, suspicion toward other forms of festivity and pleasure, and an attack on rituals seen as papist. Catholics reacted in their turn. They confirmed traditional articles of faith such as the existence of saints but defined the boundaries of orthodoxy more strictly and took a stand against anything viewed as an abuse. Only where they constituted a minority, as in the Dutch Republic, did they cling to their ancient traditions more indiscriminately. Generally, however, we may speak of a reform movement around 1600 which was sustained both by Catholics and Protestants, clergy and religiously inspired laymen.

As has been noted, this movement was split into a chastity offensive and an assault on superstition. The chastity offensive was not confined to the domain of sexuality. Reformers also opposed excessive banquets, theatrical performances, and dancing, forms of recreation that were also popular among the elites. The assault on superstition was directed at magical healing and several rituals considered pagan, among other things. Both battles were won only in part around 1600. The chastity offensive was not immediately successful because it was also aimed at the upper classes. They enjoyed dancing, for example. The secular elite in England revealed their appreciation of forms of popular culture which were under attack from the religious elite of Puritan reformers. There were examples of this in the Dutch Republic too. The assault on superstition was not successful because witchcraft was rife among the elites as well. In this way, a popular culture which at most should be called a little more sober and less exuberant, continued to exist in the seventeenth and eighteenth centuries. The triumph of Lent, as Burke calls it, was only partial.

Meanwhile another development set in which cannot be termed an offensive but was to have greater repercussions in the end. The elites distanced themselves from the customs, rituals, and festivities which for so long they had shared with the populace. Symbolically, the young Louis XIV still participated in the celebrations of the Parisian youth, but later the king completely withdrew into court etiquette. Louis's life course reflects the social process of the elites' withdrawal from popular culture. This development can be situated especially in the eighteenth century. The aristocracy and the upper bourgeoisie were alienated from the lesser tradition, which for them was no longer a second culture. Although this primarily induced them to avoid villages and neighborhoods, it also meant new support for the active opposition on the part of the clergy. This mainly concerned the normative level. The chastity offensive was received more favorably now by secular elite groups who had adopted more restrictive models of conduct themselves. They were no longer able to experience the innovative force of rude humor, grotesque mockery, and the exaltation of the body's lower parts. Henceforth, the aristocracy and the upper bourgeoisie considered popular culture as vulgar, in the pejorative sense as we use the word now. They equated it with the triad of food, sex, and violence: coarse manners in eating, exuberant love-making, and rude fighting. The withdrawal of the elites from popular culture had not yet run its course in the eighteenth century. Forms of patronage continued to exist, such as in England, in which the local gentry did not themselves participate in festivals but still gave their blessing to them.

Developments were more complicated at the cognitive level. First, the ambivalence which had been inherent in the assault on superstition faded away. Toward 1700 the secular elites as well as numerous clergymen were no longer convinced of the existence of witches so that they struggled against the magical beliefs of the populace in a more straightforward manner. After a brief span of time, however, the front was in disarray again. The combat of superstition received a new impulse in the eighteenth century under the influence of the Enlightenment so that some innovators were not members of the church. Enlightened authors also considered many rites of Catholics and Protestants as superstition. Chapter 5 described the rejection by French philosophes of the Catholic ceremony of death. Together with the witches, they relegated the devil, hell, and the church's mediating function to the past. Of course the established believers did not accept this view. They were now engaged in a struggle on two fronts. In England they took a stand against prophesy, popular rites considered superstitious, and the enthusiasm of the sects, on the one hand, and the spread of deist or even atheist convictions on the other. Civil servants in the southern Netherlands, representing the Austrian central government, started to combat popular notions and customs at the end of the eighteenth century. But their struggle was so interwoven with an attack at the power of the Catholic church, inspired by the Enlightenment, that the clergy united with the people in a conservative revolt against Austrian rule. In the nineteenth century, finally, clergy and lay elites in western Europe had a partial rapprochement. Under the influence of Victorian morality, bourgeois and religious reformers joined in a confrontation with popular culture.

In the eighteenth and nineteenth centuries, clergy and bourgeoisie were in the strongest agreement when it came to opposing such pastimes of the populace which they considered to lack seriousness. Employers and clerics denounced drinking in cabarets and pubs more strongly than before. In an earlier period such voices had not been so loud. Chavatte, a Lille worsted weaver at the end of the seventeenth century, despite his piety, could be found often in a tavern or cabaret. In the middle of the eighteenth century, the Parisian glazier Ménétra, who like Chavatte, wrote his autobiography, also frequented public drinking places. The opposition of moralists to inns and taverns was especially strong in England. Societies whose explicit aim was to keep artisans and peasants out of alehouses and the like were founded there from the 1690s. We may wonder whether the opposition by the clergy was partly a subconscious reaction to the fact that the tavern had superseded the parish church as the focal point of the community's social life in early modern England. Moralists and well-to-do citizens also opposed fairs and sports events because they provided an opportunity for licentious behavior and attracted vagabonds.

The main argument against all pastimes collectively was that too much spare time was disadvantageous to economic productivity. The civilizing offensives were in line with a long-term development in which people acquired a more abstract and methodical sense of time. This development, already begun in the later Middle Ages, was accelerated by the invention of mechanical clocks, which made possible a more punctual sense of time. The primary aim in the eighteenth and nineteenth centuries was to accustom wage workers to a regular labor schedule. Artisans, especially but not exclusively when they had their own shops, were used to working only when they thought it necessary, although there was a certain regularity even for them. It was the custom in some countries to extend the weekend when business seemed to permit it. English craftsmen spoke of Saint Monday, their German colleagues of Blue Monday. Wallington, a London artisan at the beginning of the seventeenth century, admitted that he often indulged in long chats on that day, but, as a Puritan, he always regretted it afterwards. Ménétra sometimes closed his shop on Monday morning to make the rounds with colleagues. The opposition to Saint Monday by magistrates and employers clearly set in before the Industrial Revolution. A Prussian edict of 1783 ordered the managers of hostels for traveling journeymen not to admit their guests before Monday evening. Success was not immediate. In England some groups continued to hold on to the free day until the beginning of the twentieth century. We may wonder whether the introduction of a free Saturday in the 1960s had the subconscious aim of avoiding a revival of Blue Monday.

The Decline of Community Life

Some of the checks upon traditional customs were by-products of some general developments in society. Commercialization, for example, ultimately led to a decline of popular art. Mass products took the place of the results of domestic craft. Traditional festivals were affected by economic developments too. More and more events were organized by employers, which caused the role of bachelor societies to diminish. Recreations such as the old game of football literally lost ground. The economic individualization in general and land enclosures in particular limited the opportunities for playing: a more complex infrastructure made playing inside the town more and more difficult. State formation also was involved in the decline of the lesser tradition. The central government in absolutist France increasingly curbed the autonomy of towns. As a result the sense of urban identity diminished, ultimately leading to a defunctionalization of local celebrations often dating back to the fourteenth century. Subsequently, the rise of national states entailed conforming and standardization of culture. A national culture emerged, modeled at that in the center and based on the national language. Popular rituals such as charivari retained strong ties with local language. Thus, popular culture turned into regional culture, which was less and less appealing to those who wished to rise in the world. The renunciation of popular habits became a way of social climbing.

An increase in social differentiation within villages and neighborhoods constituted another crucial development. Not only did aristocracy and higher bourgeoisie withdraw from popular culture, the people themselves became divided. The gulf between the richer farmers and the other villagers widened, while towns witnessed a comparable segregation of the well-to-do and simple craftsmen. Rich farmers and respectable citizens began to withdraw from community life. In England this development set in as early as the seventeenth century; previous chapters gave various examples. Social differentiation within villages led to a rearrangement of seating in parish churches. Families who had previously enjoyed a respectable status were impoverished and the newly rich, conscious of their contribution to the parish box, sought the best pews, wishing to distinguish themselves from poorer villagers. Elsewhere in western Europe such antagonisms arose mainly in the eighteenth century. In Leiden and The Hague, for example, the frequency of neighborhood festivals declined. Social differentiation also spread to villages on the Continent. The sons of richer peasants no longer participated in the activities of youth societies, which also came under the fire of moralists. When well-to-do members of the community were threatened with a charivari, which they now saw as an inroad into their private life, they called upon the forces of law and order to interfere.

The demise of youth societies was a major element in the decline of community life. They had usually been the active agents with festivals and charivaris. Youth societies and their disappearance also play an essential role in the historical debate about adolescence. Twentieth-century psychologists define puberty and adolescence as a transitional phase between childhood and adulthood, which may take a stormy course and be accompanied by conflicts at times. Ariès denies that such a stormy transitional phase existed in France before the modern period. For centuries, he claims, the transition to adulthood had been a matter of course, occurring at a relatively young age. It meant a rise in social status, not a psychological step. Among the elites, puberty emerged in the course of the seventeenth and eighteenth centuries under the influence of education. Ever larger numbers of adolescents from the bourgeoisie and the aristocracy received a lengthy education in boarding schools. In this way, a transitional period was created, which evolved into a psychological transformation-phase. Strauss supports Ariès's thesis, arguing that a similar development took place in the Lutheran areas of Germany.

It is precisely the existence of youth societies, however, which casts doubt on the universality of the original lack of a puberty phase. To young people from the elites, prolonged schooling may have entailed a psychological change, but young people from the popular classes, at least the males, had always acted as a group. Natalie Davis claims that adolescents therefore did form a category apart, coinciding with the group of apprentices, journeymen, and farm hands who often lived with their employers. This stage of life lasted until the servant married. Although some remained bachelors until a late age or for life, adolescents clearly set the tone among the group of servants and in the societies. We can only guess to what extent they formed a separate category from a psychological angle. Mitterauer emphasizes that the situation in preindustrial Europe at least was fundamentally different from that in many other societies. Other societies often featured a brief transition to adulthood, taking place as sexual maturity had been reached and accompanied by initiation rituals. Most people in preindustrial Europe took a big step in their youth twice. The first more or less coincided with sexual maturation. It consisted of entry into a youth society and the adoption of a paid job, often in another household. The next step was marriage and the formation of a household of one's own. Adolescence came in between, for men as well as for women, as a distinct phase in the course of life. The decline of community life, on which the societies had made such a large impact, and economic developments, eroding the institution of servanthood, caused this specific phase to become less recognizable. Apparently developments in this respect ran a reversed course among the populace compared with the elites. The theme of adolescence has taken us back into the bosom of the family. The next section pulls all these threads together.

The Triumph of the Family

As differentiated as the developments discussed in this chapter and the previous one are, for a large part they point in the same direction: the family occupied a more central place in European culture. The nuclear group is meant of course; it became a relatively intimate and closed entity, more than just a household. A few developments at the end of the preindustrial period mark the triumph of the family.

Words are important in this respect. It has been noted that the ancient Greeks and Romans had no word for the unit of parent(s) and child(ren), nor did the later western European languages. The Dutch language, among others, testifies to this. Middle Dutch knew the word *gesinde*, meaning suite, in particular the suite or entourage of a prince, who is lord and father over his court. In the sixteenth century the word stood for "persons in a house who are subject to its head": wife, children, apprentices, and servants. Next, people spoke of "a father and his *gezin*." It was only around 1800 that the father was seen as also belonging to the *gezin*, meaning nuclear family. By that time, then, it was finally possible to name the unit of parents and children. The Dutch language had gone through a rather pronounced development, which had parallels in other western European languages. In German in the course of the eighteenth century, the Romance word, family, superseded the word, house, to denote the closest relatives living there. The French and English continued to rely on the word, family, but it increasingly referred to the nuclear group. It remains to be seen whether the adoption of a distinct word in Dutch means that reflection about the nuclear family was strongest in the Netherlands. The need to name this unit, in any case, was felt throughout western Europe.

This need arose because the unit indeed became more nuclear. Apprentices, domestic servants, and boarders were excluded. As far as the first group is concerned, it has just been discussed. Because of the spread of wage work, in large manufactories and later in industrial factories, fewer and fewer young people spent their training period in a shop which was also a household. But it was not just a matter of economic change. Master artisans also introduced a separation of the living space from the working space around 1800. The living space was the domain of the family. It was a private area where apprentices and journeymen, mere wage workers who now contracted for a job, had no business. The boss was no longer a surrogate father. In the Netherlands, at least in Holland, this development set in at a rather early date. Already in the seventeenth century there were places where apprentices continued to live in their parental homes. In the eighteenth century the majority of domestic servants lived out as well.

A parallel and more unequivocal development involved the depersonalization of master-servant relations. Domestic personnel, male and female, had belonged to the household more closely than apprentices. Originally, the ties between masters and servants were highly personal, which did not mean that conflicts were unknown. To the contrary, the master acted like any father, rewarding his lads and maids but sometimes also chastising them. Sixteenth-century Lutheran family moralists recommended that a father of a household who took a new servant also inquire into the domestic's religious knowledge. In addition, he should see to it that his servant went to church to learn the catechism. Personal ties were not confined to the relationship of servants with their master. They often assisted in rearing children; a maid could become a nurse and vice versa. Maids who had stayed for a long time and had performed their service well sometimes received a trousseau from their surrogate father upon marriage. Of course this personal relationship did not mean that the ties binding a master and his domestic servants were as close as those he had with his own children.

The position of the house's personnel and the changes it underwent have been investigated for France in particular. The numbers of domestics were highest in the seventeenth and at the beginning of the eighteenth century, when aristocratic households boasted numerous lackeys, coach drivers, and kitchen maids; the rich bourgeoisie imitated the aristocracy to the best of their possibilities. Numbers declined in the course of the eighteenth century. Several authors date the process of depersonalization around this time. To the domestics themselves, the pocket money or wage may have been the thing most coveted from their master even before 1700, but in the course of the eighteenth century the relationship became more impersonal on his part too. Certain categories of personnel, such as lackeys and porters, had always been viewed as wage workers. Now this increasingly happened to other servants as well. Again, we are not just dealing with an economic development. Fathers, wishing to have personal intercourse only with their wife and children, excluded servants from family life. The interior architecture of houses became attuned to these new needs. More separate rooms were constructed in which the domestic personnel could stay when they were not required in the family's quarters. The less personal relationship also seems to have led to a decrease in the number of secret sexual affairs between maids and masters. These did not entirely become a thing of the past though; there are enough examples from the Dutch Republic in the eighteenth century. Finally, still another group of ambiguous status, boarders, was kept at a greater distance from family life. Although little research has been done outside France, it may be supposed that comparable developments took place in England and the Netherlands perhaps even somewhat earlier. Master-servant relationships changed from familial and paternalistic to impersonal and contractual.

Another group which deserves brief attention is the aged. The prevalent western European household pattern implied that few grandparents lived in the home of their married children. That did not preclude them from playing a role in family life. Research into the position of older people in the preindustrial period is still in its infancy. Most certainly, however, a golden age for the old, in which they were treated with great respect and their children took care of them as a matter of course, even if living at a distance, never existed. Our homes for the aged, for example, have old roots. From the later Middle Ages onward the aged were regularly committed to hospitals or boarding houses, although the percentage of those institutionalized was lower than today. It was mainly an urban phenomenon. In agrarian regions, the system of a transfer of the farm, especially widespread in Scandinavia and central Europe, determined the cultural definition of old age. After the transfer the old couple usually moved to a smaller house on the farm. Figures from Sweden and Finland at the beginning of the nineteenth century reveal that on the average peasants retired when they were in their fifties. Consequently, old age began then, which also means that preindustrial society counted a larger number of the aged than we would suspect looking at mortality figures.

Contemporaries from one and the same region had different appreciations of the status and influence accorded to the peasant and his wife after retirement. Transfer contracts were usually made, minutely summing up the farm work expected from the old couple and the recompense they were to get. One old couple in Scandinavia even had recorded how many cups of coffee a day they would be served. In Languedoc, where the former head and his wife did stay in the same farm house, detailed contracts were drawn up too, establishing the quantities of grain, wine, and clothing to be supplied. Such contracts demonstrate that the persons involved were not inclined to put their trust in verbal agreements. Another conclusion is that rural grandparents played a role in family life. Whether they lived separately or stayed in the house, they were a sort of superior domestic servant. This system did not really change, but due to increasing urbanization, ever fewer older people were involved. Looking at the group as a whole, then, the position of the aged was subject to change during the transition to an industrial society. Eventually, they became the granddads and grannies of today: persons whom the grandchildren visit but who are not part of daily family life.

Thus, from the end of the preindustrial period, more and more groups were excluded from family life. Distant relatives had never been part of it. The importance of the kinship network, however defined, decreased with the suppression of the blood feud in the later Middle Ages. Historians disagree on the influence left to this group. Throughout the early modern period, it is probable that kin seldom acted as a unit. There was a measure of mutual contact and support. Orphaned children were entrusted preferably to the care of relatives, and aunts frequently kept an eye on the behavior of stepmothers. People remembered who were distant kin and called a broad and undifferentiated group among them by the name of cousin. In his letters, the Dutch statesman John de Witt addressed fifty-four different persons in this way. But this group mattered little for the daily course of events within the family. Emotional identification with one's lineage was maintained most strongly and for the longest time among the aristocracy. The domestic life of aristocrats was also influenced by the peer group well into the eighteenth century. It is only for this top stratum, then, that the rise of a more closed family also entailed a diminishing influence of kin and peers on domestic affairs.

Among the populace the decline of community life was the counterpart to this development. From the later Middle Ages until the beginning of the nineteenth century, village and neighborhood communities had meddled with the family. The rise of the closed nuclear family among peasants and artisans and the decline of community life are two sides of the same coin. Those developments have been dealt with at length and are emphasized once more because of their fundamental importance. Consequently, the family also became more domesticated and enclosed among the populace during the transition to an industrial society, although somewhat later than among the elite.

In the wake of this relatively closed character, intimacy increased, again mainly among the elite. As an illustration, we may consider again the modes of address between family members in the Italian aristocracy, which became more informal. The crucial thing is that this held true for all family members, including the correspondence of siblings, for example. Before 1700 brothers and sisters had addressed each other using *Vostra Signoria*, and had opened their letters with something like "honored brother" or "sister." After 1780 they said *tu* to each other and used first names in letters. According to Barbagli, these changes mark the transition from a patriarchal to an intimate and conjugal family.

Thus, we are back to the long-term developments introduced at the beginning of chapter 2. The rule of the fathers first receded before a multiplicity of households and, subsequently, those households grew less hierarchical and mutual ties became more intimate. Partly under the influence of state formation processes and economic developments, an orientation on the house was gradually replaced by an orientation on the nuclear family. Henceforth, it was the emotional and psychological bonds which first of all kept a family together. The family was proclaimed a safe haven in the midst of the dangerous temptations in the surrounding world. Those developments are reflected most tellingly in the process of domestication. The family excluded neighbors, kin, apprentices, servants, and boarders and was affected less by activities in the village or neighborhood. Weddings and funerals lost their collective character. All these changes together constituted the most central element of privatization. The domestic family turned into a closed unit situated behind the scenes of public life.

In the field of affective and emotional ties, developments were somewhat more ambiguous. From the sixteenth century onward the majority of the population was exposed to a never-ceasing propaganda for an intimate and friendly, though not egalitarian, family life. The extent to which this change influenced actual practice is not sufficiently known. The hierarchical character of marriage, at least, seems to have diminished around 1800, and this must have had an effect on affective relationships. Among the elites the family came to occupy a central place in cultural life from the eighteenth century. It was allocated a role of its own, which had hardly been the case previously. Emotions were more thoroughly restrained in all kind of situations in the outside world, but within the family they could be and were expected to be expressed, sometimes even cultivated. The rise of the intimate family and the private sphere was the complement of the depersonalization and self-control which had come to characterize the relations between people in other areas of life.

BIBLIOGRAPHY

1

Blok, Anton. "Achter de coulissen." *De Gids* 140 (1977): 257–270.
Bijdragen en Mededelingen betreffende de Geschiedenis der Nederlanden 98,3 (1983) [special issue on the history of mentalities].

Corbin, Alain. *Le miasme et la jonquille: L'odorat et l'imaginaire social, 18e– 19e siècles.* Paris, 1982.

Ehalt, Hubert Ch. *Ausdrucksformen absolutistischer Herrschaft: Der Wiener Hof im 17. und 18. Jahrhundert.* München, 1980.
Elias, Norbert. *Die höfische Gesellschaft: Untersuchungen zur Soziologie des Königtums und der höfischen Aristokratie.* Neuwied-Berlin, 1969.
———. *Über den Prozess der Zivilisation: Soziogenetische und psycho-genetische Untersuchungen.* 2 volumes, Bern-München, 1969.

Frijhoff, Willem. "Impasses en beloften van de mentaliteitsgeschiedenis." *Tijdschrift voor Sociale Geschiedenis* 10 (1984): 406–437.

Gismondi, Michael A. "The gift of theory: A critique of the histoire des mentalités." *Social History* 10,2 (1985): 211–230.
Gleichmann, Peter R., Johan Goudsblom, and Hermann Korte, eds. *Human Figurations: Essays for Norbert Elias.* Amsterdam, 1977.
———. Johan Goudsblom en Herman Korte, eds. *Materialien zu Norbert Elias' Zivilisationstheorie.* Frankfurt a.M., 1979.
Goff, Jacques Le. "Les mentalités: Une histoire ambiguë." In Jacques Le Goff and Pierre Nora, eds. *Faire l'histoire, nouveaux objets,* III. Paris, 1974: 76– 94.

Huizinga, Johan. *Herfsttij der middeleeuwen.* Haarlem, 1919.
Hutton, Patrick H. "The history of mentalities: the new map of cultural history." *History and Theory* 20 (1981): 237–259.

Jong, Mayke de. "Claustrum versus saeculum: Opvoeding en affectbeheersing in een Karolingische kloostergemeenschap." *Symposion* 3 (1981): 46–65.

Ladurie, Emmanuel Le Roy. *Montaillou: Cathars and Catholics in a French village, 1294–1324.* Harmondsworth, 1980.

Mennell, Stephen. *All manners of food: Eating and taste in England and France from the middle ages to the present.* Oxford, 1985.

Romein, Jan. "De Europese geschiedenis als afwijking van het algemeen menselijk patroon." In Jan Romein. *In de ban van Prambanan: Indonesische voordrachten en indrukken.* Amsterdam, 1954: 23–57.

Spierenburg, Pieter. *Elites and etiquette: Mentality and social structure in the early modern Northern Netherlands*. Rotterdam: Centrum voor Maatschappijgeschiedenis, 9, 1981.

Stearns, Peter N. and Carol Z. Stearns. "Emotionology: Clarifying the history of emotions and emotional standards." *American Historical Review* 90,4 (1985): 813–836.

Vovelle, Michel. *Idéologies et mentalités*. Paris, 1982.

Weber, Max. *Gesammelte Aufsätze zur Religionssoziologie*, I. Tübingen, 1922.

Winckelmann, Johannes. "Die Herkunft von Max Webers Entzauberungs-Konzeption. *Kölner Zeitschrift für Soziologie und Sozialpsychologie* 32 (1980): 12–53.

2

Biller, P. P. A. "Birth control in the West in the 13th and early 14th centuries." *Past and Present* 94 (1982): 3–26.

Burguière, André. "Pour une typologie des formes d'organisation domestique de l'Europe moderne, 16e–19e siècles." *Annales ESC* 41 (1986): 639–655.

Charles, Lindsay and Lorna Duffin, eds. *Women and work in preindustrial England*. London, 1985.

Demyttenaere, Bert. "Vrouw en sexualiteit: Een aantal kerkideologische standpunten in de vroege middeleeuwen." *Tijdschrift voor Geschiedenis* 86 (1973): 236–261.

Duby, Georges. *Le chevalier, la femme et le prêtre: Le mariage dans la France féodale*. Paris, 1981.

Ennen, Edith. *Frauen im Mittelalter*. München, 1985.

Flandrin, Jean-Louis. *Un temps pour embrasser: Aux origines de la morale sexuelle Occidentale, 6e–11e siècle*. Paris, 1983.

Foucault, Michel. *Geschiedenis van de sexualiteit*. 3 volumes, Nijmegen, 1984.

Goody, Jack. *The development of the family and marriage in Europe*. Cambridge, 1983.

Hanawalt, Barbara A. *The ties that bound: Peasant families in medieval England*. New York-Oxford, 1986.

Hanawalt, Barbara A., ed. *Women and work in preindustrial Europe*. Bloomington, 1986.

Helmholz, Richard H. *Marriage litigation in medieval England*. Cambridge, 1974.

Herlihy, David. *Medieval households*. Cambridge: Mass.-London, 1985.

Herlihy, David and Christiane Klapisch-Zuber. *Les Toscans et leur familles. Une étude du Catasto Florentin de 1427*. Paris, 1978.

Humphreys, Sally C. *The family, women and death: Comparative studies*. London, 1983.

Jong, Mayke de. *Kind en klooster in de vroege middeleeuwen*. Amsterdam, 1986.

Kelly, Henry Ansgar. *Love and marriage in the age of Chaucer*. Ithaca-London, 1975.
Klapisch-Zuber, Christiane. *Women, family and ritual in Renaissance Italy*. Chicago-London, 1985.
Kuiper, Willem. "Over het slaan van vrouwen in de voorhoofse epiek." *Tijdschrift voor Sociale Geschiedenis* 35 (1984): 228–242.

Laslett, Peter. *Family life and illicit love in earlier generations: Essays in historical sociology*. Cambridge, 1977.
Laslett, Peter and Richard Wall, eds. *Household and family in past time*. Cambridge, 1972.

Mitterauer, Michael. *Grundtypen alteuropäischer Sozialformen: Haus und Gemeinde in vorindustriellen Gesellschaften*. Stuttgart, 1979.

Nicholas, David. *The domestic life of a medieval city: Women, children and the family in 14th-century Ghent*. Lincoln-London, 1985.
North, Tim. "Legerwite in the 13th and 14th centuries." *Past and Present* 111 (1986): 3–16.

Pernoud, Régine. *La femme au temps des cathédrales*. Paris, 1980.

Ross, Margaret Clunies. "Concubinage in Anglo-Saxon England." *Past and Present* 108 (1985): 3–34.
Rotberg, Robert I. and Theodore K. Rabb, eds. *Marriage and fertility*. Studies in Interdisciplinary History. Princeton, 1980.

Schilders, Ed. *De voorhuid van Jezus en andere Roomse wonderen*. Groningen, 1985.
Schröter, Michael. *Wo zwei zusammenkommen in rechter Ehe: Sozio- und psychogenetishe Studien über Eheschliessungsvorgänge vom 12. bis 15. Jahrhundert*. Frankfurt a.M., 1985.
Shahar, Shulamith. *Die Frau im Mittelalter*. s.l., 1983.
Sheehan, Michael M. "Choice of marriage partner in the middle ages." *Studies in Medieval and Renaissance History* (1978): 3–33.
———. "Marriage theory and practice in the conciliar legislation and diocesan statutes of medieval England." *Mediaeval Studies* 40 (1978): 408–460.

Tilly, Louise A., and Joan W. Scott. *Women, work and family*. New York, 1978.

Wall, Richard et al., eds. *Family forms in historic Europe*. Cambridge, 1983.

3

Babcock, Barbara A., ed. *The reversible world: Symbolic inversion in art and society*. Ithaca-London, 1978.

Bakhtin, Mikhail. *Rabelais and his world.* Cambridge: Mass.-London, 1968.

Baroja, Julio Caro. *Le carnaval.* Paris, 1979.

Bennassar, Bartolomé. *L'homme Espagnol: Attitudes et mentalités du 16e au 19e siècle.* Paris, 1975.

Bercé, Yves-Marie. *Fête et révolte: Des mentalités populaires du XVIe au XVIIIe siècle: Essai.* Paris, 1976.

Berg, G. C. J. J. van den, ed. *Staphorst en zijn gerichten: Verslag van een juridisch-antropologisch onderzoek.* Meppel-Amsterdam, 1980.

Bernheimer, Richard. *Wild men in the Middle Ages: A study in art, sentiment and demonology.* Cambridge: Mass., 1952.

Boiteux, Martine. "Carnaval annexé: Essai de lecture d'une fête Romaine." *Annales ESC* 32,2 (1977): 356–380.

Bollème, Geneviève. *Les almanachs populaires aux 17e et 18e siècles: Essai d'histoire sociale.* Paris-La Haye, 1969.

Bonnain-Moerdyk, Rolande and Donald Moerdyk. "A propos du charivari: discours bourgeois et coutumes populaires." *Annales ESC* 32,2 (1977): 381–398.

Bristol, Michael D. *Carnival and theater: Plebeian culture and the structure of authority in Renaissance England.* New York-London, 1985.

Burke, Peter. *Popular culture in early modern Europe.* New York, 1978.

Camporesi, Piero. *Le pain sauvage: L'imaginaire de la faim de la Renaissance au 18e siècle.* Paris, 1981.

Capp, Bernard. *Astrology and the popular press: English almanacs, 1500–1800.* London-Boston, 1979.

Darnton, Robert. *The great cat massacre and other episodes in French cultural history.* New York, 1984.

Davis, Natalie Zemon. *Society and culture in early modern France.* Stanford, 1975.

Dekker, Rudolf and Lotte van de Pol. *Daar was laatst een meisje loos: Nederlandse vrouwen als matrozen en soldaten. Een historisch onderzoek.* Baarn, 1981.

Delumeau, Jean, ed. *La mort des pays de cocagne: Comportements collectifs de la Renaissance à l'âge classique.* Paris, 1976.

Deursen, A. Th. van. *Het kopergeld van de gouden eeuw. II, Volkscultuur.* Assen-Amsterdam, 1978.

Driesen, Otto. *Der Ursprung des Harlekin: Ein kulturgeschichtliches Problem.* Berlin, 1904.

Dülmen, Richard van, ed. *Kultur der einfachen Leute: Bayerisches Volksleben vom 16. bis zum 19. Jahrhundert.* München, 1983.

Dülmen, Richard van and Norbert Schindler, eds. *Volkskultur: Zur Wiederentdeckung des vergessenen Alltags, 16.–20. Jahrhundert.* Frankfurt a.M., 1984.

Finucane, Ronald C. *Miracles and pilgrims: Popular beliefs in medieval England.* London, 1977.

Frijhoff, Willem. "Official and popular religion in Christianity: The late middle ages and early modern times, 13th–18th centuries." In Pieter Hendrik Vrijhof and Jacques Waardenburg, eds. *Official and popular religion: Analysis of a theme for religious studies.* Den Haag, 1979: 71–116.

Gaignebet, Claude and Marie-Claude Florentin. *Le carnaval: Essais de mythologie populaire.* Paris, 1974.

Ginzburg, Carlo. *The cheese and the worms: The cosmos of a 16th century miller.* Baltimore, 1980.
Goff, Jacques Le. *Time, work and culture in the middle ages.* Chicago-London, 1980.
Goff, Jacques Le and Jean-Claude Schmitt, eds. *Le charivari: Actes de la table ronde organisée à Paris.* Paris, 1981.
Greyerz, Kaspar von, ed. *Religion and society in early modern Europe, 1500–1800.* London, 1984.
Grinberg, Martine and Sam Kinser. "Les combats de carnaval et de carême: Trajets d'une métaphore." *Annales ESC* 38,1 (1983): 65–98.

Heers, Jacques. *Fêtes des fous et carnavals.* s.l., 1983.
Hill, Christopher. *The world turned upside down: Radical ideas during the English Revolution.* Harmondsworth, 1972.

Ingram, Martin. "Ridings, rough music and the 'reform of popular culture' in early modern England." *Past and Present* 105 (1984): 79–113.
Isherwood, Robert M. "Entertainment in the Parisian fairs in the eighteenth century." *Journal of Modern History* 53 (1981): 24–48.

Jacobs, Marc. "Charivari en volksgerichten: Sleutelfenomenen voor sociale geschiedenis." *TSG* 12,4 (1986): 365–392.

Kaplan, Steven L., ed. *Understanding popular culture: Europe from the middle ages to the 19th century.* Berlin, 1984.
Kunzle, David. *The early comic strip: Narrative strips and picture stories in the European broadsheet from c.1450 to 1825.* Berkeley, 1973.

Ladurie, Emmanuel Le Roy. *Carnival in Romans: A people's uprising at Romans, 1579–1580.* Harmondsworth, 1981.
Lottin, Alain. *Chavatte, ouvrier Lillois, un comtemporain de Louis XIV.* Paris, 1979.

Martin, Fred. "De liedjeszanger als massamedium: Straatzangers in de 18e en 19e eeuw." *Tijdschrift voor Geschiedenis* 97 (1984): 422–446.
Ménétra, Jacques-Louis. *Journal de ma vie.* Edited by Daniel Roche. Paris, 1982.
Mandrou, Robert. *De la culture populaire au 17e et 18e siècle: La bibliothèque bleue de Troyes.* s.l., 1975.
Muchembled, Robert. *Culture populaire et culture des élites dans la France moderne, 15e–18e siècles.* Paris, 1978.

Obelkevich, James, ed. *Religion and the people, 800–1700.* Chapel Hill: N.C., 1979.

Pellegrin, Nicole. *Les bachelleries: Organisations et fêtes de la jeunesse dans le Centre-Ouest, 15e–18e siècles.* Poitiers, 1982.
Propp, Vladimir. *Theory and history of folklore.* Edited with an introduction and notes by Anatoly Liberman. Minneapolis, 1984.

Reay, Barry, ed. *Popular culture in 17th-century England.* London-Sydney, 1985.
Rollison, David. "Property, ideology and popular culture in a Gloucestershire village, 1660–1740." *Past and Present* 93 (1981): 70–97.

Rooijakkers, Gerard and Theo van der Zee, eds. *Religieuze volkscultuur: De spanning tussen de voorgeschreven orde en de geleefde praktijk.* Nijmegen, 1986.

Russell, Jeffrey Burton. *Lucifer: The Devil in the Middle Ages.* Ithaca-London, 1984.

Sabean, David Warren. *Power in the Blood: Popular Culture and Village Discourse in Early Modern Germany.* Cambridge, 1984.

Sacks, David Harris. "The demise of the martyrs: The feasts of St. Clement and St. Katherine in Bristol, 1400–1600." *Social History* 11,2 (1986): 141–169.

Schmitt, Jean-Claude. *Le saint lévrier: Guinefort, guérisseur d'enfants depuis le 13e siècle.* Paris, 1979.

Schnapper, Antoine. "Persistance des géants." *Annales ESC* 41,1 (1986): 177–200.

Schulten, Paul G. G. M. *De Circumcellionen: Een sociaal-religieuze beweging in de late Oudheid.* Scheveningen, 1984.

Scribner, Bob. "Reformation, carnival and the world turned upside down." *Social History* 3,3 (1978): 303–328.

Scribner, R. W. *For the sake of simple folk: Popular propaganda for the German Reformation.* Cambridge, 1981.

Soriano, Marc. *Les contes de Perrault: Culture savante et traditions populaires.* Paris, 1968.

Spierenburg, Pieter. "De omgekeerde wereld: Over volkscultuur en hiërarchie in preïndustrieel Europa." *De Gids* 150 (1987): 696–708.

Spufford, Margaret. *Small books and pleasant histories: Popular fiction and its readership in 17th century England.* London, 1981.

Storch, Robert D., ed. *Popular culture and custom in nineteenth-century England.* London, 1982.

Thelander, Dorothy R. "Mother goose and her goslings: The France of Louis XIV as seen through the fairy tale." *Journal of Modern History* 54,3 (1982): 467–496.

Turner, Victor W. *The Ritual Process: Structure and Anti-Structure.* London, 1969.

Underdown, David. *Revel, riot and rebellion: Popular politics and culture in England, 1603–1660.* Oxford, 1985.

Zijderveld, Anton C. *Reality in a looking-glass: Rationality through an analysis of traditional folly.* London, 1982.

4

Anglo, Sydney, ed. *The damned art: Essays in the literature of witchcraft.* London, 1977.

Baroja, Julio Caro. *The world of the witches.* Chicago, 1964.

Beliën, Herman M. and Peter C. van der Eerden. *Satans trawanten: Heksen en heksenvervolging.* Haarlem, 1985.

Blécourt, Willem de and Marijke Gijswijt-Hofstra, eds. *Kwade mensen: Toverij in Nederland* Volkskundig, Bulletin 12. Amsterdam, 1986.

Bouwsma, William J. "Anxiety and the formation of early modern culture." In Barbara C. Malament, ed. *After the Reformation: Essays in honor of J. H. Hexter.* Manchester, 1980: 215–246.

Boyer, Paul and Stephen Nissenbaum. *Salem possessed: The social origins of witchcraft.* Camabridge: Mass.-London, 1974.

Castan, Yves. *Magie et sorcellerie à l'époque moderne.* Paris, 1979.

Cohen, Jeremy. *The friars and the Jews: The evolution of medieval anti-Judaism.* Ithaca-London, 1982.

Cohn, Norman. *Europe's inner demons: An enquiry inspired by the great witch hunt.* London, 1975.

Dasberg, Lena. *Untersuchungen über die Entwertung des Judenstatus im 11. Jahrhundert.* Den Haag, 1965.

Degn, Christian, Hartmut Lehmann, Dagmar Unverhau, eds. *Hexenprozesse: Deutsche und skandinavische Beiträge.* Neumünster, 1983.

Delumeau, Jean. *La peur en Occident (XIVe–XVIIIe siècles): Une cité assiégée.* s.l., 1978.

———. *Le péché et la peur: La culpabilisation en Occident (XIIIe–XVIIIe siècles).* Paris, 1983.

Demos, John Putnam. *Entertaining Satan: Witchcraft and the culture of early New England.* New York-Oxford, 1982.

Dresen-Coenders, Lène. *Het verbond van heks en duivel: Een waandenkbeeld aan het begin van de moderne tijd als symptoom van een veranderende situatie van de vrouw en als middel tot hervorming der zeden.* Baarn, 1983.

Dupont-Bouchat, Marie-Sylvie, Robert Muchembled, Willem Frijhoff. *Prophètes et sorcieres dans le Pays-Bas, XVIe–XVIIIe siècle.* Paris, 1978.

Frijhoff, Willem. "Satan en het magisch universum: Raakvlakken, wisselwerkingen, reminiscenties in Oost-Gelderland sedert de 16e eeuw." *Tijdschrift voor Geschiedenis* 97,3 (1984): 382–406.

Ginzburg, Carlo. *Les batailles nocturnes: Sorcellerie et rituels agraires en Frioul, XVIe–XVIIe siècle.* Lagrasse, 1980.

———. "Présomptions sur le sabbat." *Annales ESC* 39,2 (1984): 341–354.

Gijswijt-Hofstra, Marijke. "Bijdrage tot theorievorming over de 16e en 17e eeuwse Europese heksenvervolgingen." *Mens en Maatschappij* 47 (1972): 304–336.

Heikkinen, Antero. *Paholaisen liittolaiset: Noita-ja magiakäsityksiä ja-oikeudenkäyntejä Suomessa 1600-luvun jälkipuoliskolla (n. 1640–1712).* Helsinki, 1969 (with English summary).

Henningsen, Gustav. *The witches' advocate; Basque witchcraft and the Spanish inquisition (1609–1614).* Reno, Nevada, 1980.

Honegger, Claudia, ed. *Die Hexen der Neuzeit: Studien zur Sozialgeschichte eines kulturellen Deutungsmusters.* Frankfurt a.M., 1978.

Horsley, Richard A. "Who were the witches? The social roles of the accused in the European witch trials." *Journal of Interdisciplinary History* 9,4 (1979): 689–715.

Hughes, Muriel Joy. *Women healers in medieval life and literature.* New York, 1968.

Kamber, Peter. "La chasse aux sorciers et aux sorcières dans le Pays de Vaud: Aspects quantitatifs (1581–1620)." *Revue Historique Vaudoise* (1982): 21–33.

Kemperink, J. H. P. "Heksenprocessen te Amersfoort op het einde der 16e eeuw." *Tijdschrift voor Geschiedenis* 70 (1957): 218–230.

Kieckhefer, Richard. *European witch trials: Their foundations in popular and learned culture.* Berkeley-Los Angeles, 1976.

Klaits, Joseph. *Servants of Satan: The age of the witch hunts.* Bloomington, 1985.

Kruysdijk, Annemarie van. "Heksen in Gelderland." *Bijdragen en Mededelingen Gelre* 72 (1981): 47–67.

Larner, Christina. *Enemies of God: The witch-hunt in Scotland.* Baltimore, 1981.

———. *Witchcraft and religion: The politics of popular belief.* Oxford, 1984.

Macfarlane, Alan. *Witchcraft in Tudor and Stuart England: A regional and comparative study.* London, 1970.

Mandrou, Robert. *Magistrats et sorciers en France au XVIIe siècle: Une analyse de psychologie historique.* Paris, s.a.

Midelfort, H. C. Erik. *Witch hunting in Southwestern Germany, 1562–1684: The social and intellectual foundations.* Stanford, 1972.

Monter, E. William. *Witchcraft in France and Switzerland: The borderlands during the Reformation.* Ithaca-London, 1976.

Peters, Edward. *The magician, the witch and the law.* Hassocks, 1978.

Schormann, Gerhard. *Hexenprozesse in Nordwestdeutschland.* Hildesheim, 1977.

———. *Hexenprozesse in Deutschland.* Göttingen, 1981.

Soman, Alfred. "Het Parlement van Parijs en de Grote Heksenjacht (1565–1640). *Tijdschrift voor Criminologie* 20 (1978): 186–202.

Thomas, Keith. *Religion and the decline of magic: Studies in popular beliefs in 16th and 17th century England.* Harmondsworth, 1973.

Trachtenberg, Joshua. *The devil and the Jews: The medieval conception of the Jew and its relation to modern anti-Semitism.* New Haven-London, 1943.

Trevor-Roper, Hugh R. *The European witch-craze of the 16th and 17th centuries.* Harmondsworth, 1969.

Unverhau, Dagmar. "Kieler Hexen und Zauberer zur Zeit der grossen Verfolgung (1530–1676)." *Mitteilungen der Gesellschaft für Kieler Stadtgeschichte* 68,3/4 (1981): 41–96.

Walinski-Kiehl, Robert Stefan. *Prosecuting witches in early modern Germany, with special reference to the bishopric of Bamberg, 1595–1680.* Portsmouth, 1981.

Walker, Daniel Pickering. *Spiritual and demonic magic from Ficino to Campanella.* London, 1958.

5

Ariès, Philippe. *Western attitudes toward death from the middle ages to the present.* Baltimore-London, 1974.
——. *The hour of our death.* New York, 1981.
——. "Le purgatoire et la cosmologie de l'au-delà." *Annales ESC* 38,1 (1983): 151–157.

Banck, Geert A. et al., eds. *Gestalten van de dood: Studies over abortus, euthanasie, rouw, zelfmoord en doodstraf.* Baarn, 1980.
Blum, Paul Richard, ed. *Studien zur Thematik des Todes im 16. Jahrhundert.* Wolfenbüttel, 1983.
Boase, Thomas Sherrer Ross. *Death in the Middle Ages: Mortality, Judgment and Remembrance.* London, 1972.
Boer, Pim den. "Naar een geschiedenis van de dood: Mogelijkheden tot onderzoek naar de houding ten opzichte van de dode en de dood ten tijde van de Republiek." *Tijdschrift voor Geschiedenis* 89 (1976): 161–201.
Bosch, Dick van den. "De laatste eer aan de eerste stand: Aristocratische begrafenisrituelen in Limburg van de 18e tot de 20e eeuw." *Tijdschrift voor Sociale Geschiedenis* 18 (1980): 181–210.

Chartier, Roger. "Les arts de mourir, 1450–1600." *Annales ESC* 31,1 (1976): 51–75.
Chaunu, Pierre. *La morte à Paris: XVIe, XVIIe et XVIII siècles.* s.l., 1978.
Chiffoleau, Jacques. *La comptabilité de l'au-delà: Les hommes, la mort et la religion dans la région d'Avignon à la fin du moyen age, vers 1320-vers 1380.* Rome, 1980.
Cipolla, Carlo M. *Faith, reason and the plague in 17th-century Tuscany.* New York-London, 1979.
Cobb, Richard. *Death in Paris: The records of the Basse-Geôle de la Seine, October 1795–September 1801, Vendémiaire year IV-Fructidor year IX.* Oxford, 1978.
Corvisier, André. "La représentation de la société dans les danses des morts du 15e au 18e siècles." *Revue d'Histoire Moderne et Contemporaine* 16 (1969): 489–539.
Croix, Alain. "L'homme et son corps dans l'au-delà." In Arthur Imhof, ed. *Leib und Leben in der Geschichte der Neuzeit.* Berlin, 1983: 155–162.
Cruysse, Dirk van der. *La mort dans les mémoires de Saint-Simon: Clio au jardin de Thanatos.* Paris, 1981.

Dood en begraven, sterven en rouwen, 1700–1900 [exhibition catalogue, Utrecht, 1980].

Elias, Norbert. *Über die Einsamkeit der Sterbenden in unseren Tagen.* Frankfurt a.M., 1982.
Etlin, Richard A. *The Architecture of Death: The Transformation of the Cemetery in Eighteenth-Century Paris.* Cambridge: Mass.-London, 1984.

Favre, Robert. *La mort dans la littérature et la pansée fraçaises au siècle des Lumières.* Lyon, s.a.
Finucane, Ronald C. *Appearances of the Dead: A Cultural History of Ghosts.* London, 1982.

Franke, Herman. *De dood in het leven van alledag: Twee eeuwen rouwadvertenties en openbare strafvoltrekkingen in Nederland.* Den Haag, 1985.

Gittings, Clare. *Death, burial and the individual in early modern England.* London-Sydney, 1984.
Goff, Jacques Le. *La Naissance du Purgatoire.* Paris, 1981.

Klein, Luise. *Die Bereitung zum Sterben: Studien zu den frühen reformatorischen Sterbebüchern.* Göttingen, 1958.

Lebrun, François. *Les hommes et la mort en Anjou aux 17e et 18e siècles. Essai de démographie et de psychologie historiques.* Paris-La Haye, 1971.
Lenz, Rudolf, ed. *Leichenpredigten als Quelle historischer Wissenschaften.* 2 volumes. I, Köln-Wien, 1975; II, Marburg a.d. Lahn, 1979.
Lerner, Robert E. "The black death and Western European eschatological mentalities." *American Historical Review* 86 (1981): 533–552.
Lottin, Alain. "Les morts chassés de la cité: 'Lumières et Préjugés': les "émeutes" à Lille (1779) et à Cambrai (1786), lors du transfert des cimétières." *Revue du Nord* 60 (1978): 73–117.

MacManners, John. *Death and the Enlightenment: Changing attitudes to death among Christians and unbelievers in 18th-century France.* Oxford, 1985.

Roche, Daniel. "La mémoire de la mort." *Annales ESC* 31,1 (1976): 76–119.

Schmidt-Grave, Horst. *Leichenreden und Leichenpredigten Tübinger Professoren, 1550–1750. Untersuchungen zur biographischen Geschichtsschreibung in der frühle Neuzeit.* Tübingen, 1974.
Stannard, David E. *The Puritan way of death: A study in religion, culture and social change.* New York, 1977.
Sutto, Claude, ed. *Le sentiment de la mort au moyen âge.* Montréal, 1979.

Taylor, Jane H. M., ed. *Dies Illa: Death in the middle ages.* Liverpool, 1984.
Tenenti, Alberto. *Sens de la mort et amour de la vie: Renaissance en Italie et en France.* s.l., 1983.

Vovelle, Michel. *Piété baroque et déchristianisation en Provence au XVIIIe siècle: Les attitudes devant la mort d'après les clauses des testaments.* Paris, 1973.
———. *Mourir autrefois: Attitudes collectives devant la mort aux XVIIe et XVIIIe siècles.* s.l., 1974.
———. *La Mort et l'Occident de 1300 à nos jours.* Paris, 1983.

Whaley, J., ed. *Mirrors of mortality: Studies in the social history of death.* London, 1981.
Wilson, Stephen. "Death and the social historians." *Social History* 5,3 (1980): 435–451.

Ziegler, Philip. *The black death.* Harmondsworth, 1969.

6

Allderidge, Patricia. "Management and mismanagement at Bedlam, 1547–1633." In Charles Webster, ed. *Health, medicine and mortality in the 16th century*. Cambridge, 1979: 141–164.

Beek, H. H. *Waanzin in de middeleeuwen: Beeld van de gestoorde en bemoeinis met de zieke*. Nijkerk-Haarlem, 1969.
Binneveld, Hans. *Filantropie, repressie en medische zorg: Geschiedenis van de inrichtingspsychiatrie*. Deventer, 1985.
Breukink, H. "Overzicht van opvatting en behandeling van geesteszieken in oude tijden." *Nederlands tijdschrift voor geneeskunde* 65,1B (1921): 3076–3094; 65,2B (1921): 2805–2814; 66,2A (1922): 1076–1091.
Byrd, Max. *Visits to Bedlam: Madness and literature in the eighteenth century*. Columbia: S.C., 1974.

Cornips, J. *Bijdrage tot de geschiedenis van de krankzinnigenzorg te Maastricht*. Maastricht, 1952.

DePorte, Michael V. *Nightmares and hobbyhorses: Swift, Sterne and Augustan ideas of madness*. San Marino, 1974.

Ernst, Cécile. *Teufelaustreibungen: Die Praxis der katholischen Kirche im 16. und 17. Jahrhundert*. Bern, 1972.
Evenhuis, R. B. *Ook dat was Amsterdam*. III. Amsterdam, 1965.

Feder, Lillian. *Madness in literature*. Princeton, 1980.
Folie et déraison à la Renaissance: Colloque international tenu en novembre 1973 sous les auspices de la Fédération Internationale des Instituts et Sociétés pour l'Etude de la Renaissance. Brussels, 1976.
Foucault, Michel. *Folie et déraison: Histoire de la folie à l'age classique*. Paris, 1961.

Geldhof, J. *Pelgrims, dulle lieden en vondelingen te Brugge, 1275–1975: Zeven eeuwen geschiedenis van het Sint-Juliaansgasthuis en van de psychiatrische kliniek O.-L.-Vrouwe te Brugge-Sint Michiels*. Brugge, 1975.

Heyd, Michael. "The reaction to enthusiasm in the 17th century: towards an integrative approach." *Journal of Modern History* 53 (1981): 258–280.
Howells, John G. ed. *World History of psychiatry*. London, 1975.
Hunter, Richard and Ida Macalpine, eds. *Three hundred years of psychiatry 1535–1860: A history presented in selected English texts*. London, 1963.
Hut, L. J. et al., *De Willem Arntsz Stichting, 1461–1961*. Utrecht, 1961.

Jetter, Dieter. *Geschichte des Hospitals, I, Westdeutschland von den Anfängen bis 1850*. Wiesbaden, 1966.

Kirchhoff, Theodor. *Grundriss einer Geschichte der deutschen Irrenpflege*. Berlin, 1890.

Laing, Ronald D. *The politics of experience and the bird of paradise*. New York, 1967.

Leen, J. van der. *Geschiedenis van het pest- en dolhuis der gemeente Rotter-dam. s.l.*, 1934.

Lith, J. P. T. van der. *Geschiedenis van het krankzinnigengesticht te Utrecht, gedurende deszelfs 400-jarig bestaan.* Utrecht, 1863.

Macalpine, Ida and Richard Hunter. *George III and the mad-business.* London, 1969.

Macdonald, Michael. *Mystical Bedlam: Madness, anxiety and healing in 17th-century England.* Cambridge, 1981.

———. "Insanity and the realities of history in early modern England." *Psychological Medicine* 11 (1981): 11–25.

———. "The secularization of suicide in England, 1660–1800." *Past and Present* 111 (1986): 50–97.

Midelfort, H. C. Erik. "Madness and civilization in early modern Europe: A reappraisal of Michel Foucault." In Barbara C. Malament, ed. *After the Reformation: Essays in honor of J. H. Hexter.* Manchester, 1980: 247–265.

Parry-Jones, William Ll. *The trade in lunacy: A study of private madhouses in England in the eighteenth and nineteenth centuries.* London-Toronto, 1972.

Porter, Roy. "The diary of a madman, 17th-century style: Goodwin Wharton, MP and communer with the fairy world." *Psychological Medicine* 16 (1986): 503–513.

Rooij, Henri J. M. van. *Het Gesticht 'Reinier van Arkel' te 's-Hertogenbosch, het oudste krankzinnigengesticht in Nederland. s.l.*, 1928.

Rosen, George. *Madness in society: Chapters in the historical sociology of mental illness.* London, 1968.

Schmitt, Jean-Claude. "Le suicide au moyen age." *Annales ESC* 31,1 (1976): 3–28.

Schrenk, Martin. *Über den Umgang mit Geisteskranken. Die Entwicklung der psychiatrischen Therapie vom 'moralischen Regime' in England und Frankreich zu den 'psychischen Curmethoden' in Deutschland,* Berlin etc. 1973.

Simon, Bennett. *Mind and madness in ancient Greece: The classical roots of modern psychiatry.* Ithaca-London, 1978.

Skultans, Vieda. *English madness: Ideas on insanity, 1580–1890.* London, 1979.

Spierenburg, Pieter. "Financiën en familie-eer: Opsluiting en opgeslotenen op verzoek te Leiden, 1680–1805." In *Armoede en sociale spanning: Sociaal-historische studies over Leiden in de achttiende eeuw.* H. A. Diederiks et al. (red.), Hilversum, 1985: 117–135.

Szasz, Thomas S. *The myth of mental illness: Foundations of a theory of personal conduct. s.l.*, 1961.

———. *The manufacture of madness: A comparative study of the Inquisition and the mental health movement.* New York, 1970.

Trimbos, Kees. *Antipsychiatrie: Een overzicht.* Deventer, 1978.

Vandekerckhove, Lieven. *Van straffen gesproken: De bestraffing van zelfdoding in het oude Europa.* Tielt, 1985.

Walker, Daniel Pickering. *Unclean spirits: Possession and exorcism in France and England in the late sixteenth and early seventeenth centuries.* London, 1981.

Walker, Nigel. *Crime and insanity in England.* I, *The historical perspective.* Edinburgh, 1968.

Weyde, A. J. van der. *De behandeling der krankzinnigen in vroeger tijd te Utrecht.* Rede, Utrecht, 1931.

Zell, Michael. "Suicide in preindustrial England." *Social History* 11 (1986): 303–317.

7

Andrew, Donna T. "The code of honour and its critics: The opposition to duelling in England, 1700–1850." *Social History* 5 (1980): 409–434.

Beattie, John M. *Crime and the courts in England, 1660–1800.* Oxford, 1986.

Becker, Marvin B. "Changing patterns of violence and justice in 14th and 15th-century Florence." *Comparative Studies in Society and History* 18,3 (1976): 281–296.

Beier, A. L. *Masterless men: The vagrancy problem in England, 1560–1640.* London-New York, 1985.

Berkhey, Johannes le Francq van. *Natuurlijke historie van Holland.* III. Amsterdam, 1776.

Billacois, François. *Le duel dans la société française des 16e–17e siècles. Essai de psychosociologie historique.* Paris, 1986.

Blok, Anton. *The mafia of a Sicilian village, 1860–1960: A study of violent peasant entrepreneurs.* New York, 1974.

———. "Eer en de fysieke persoon." *Tijdschrift voor Sociale Geschiedenis* 18 (1980): 211–230.

Cameron, Iain A. *Crime and repression in the Auvergne and the Guyenne, 1720–1790.* Cambridge, 1981.

Castan, Nicole. *Justice et répression en Languedoc à l'époque des Lumières.* Paris, 1980.

Cellini, Benvenuto. *Het leven van -.* Amsterdam, 1982.

Chesnais, Jean-Claude. *Histoire de la violence en Occident de 1800 à nos jours.* Paris, 1981.

Cohen, Esther. "Law, folklore and animal lore." *Past and Present* 110 (1986): 6–37.

Collins, Randall. "Three faces of cruelty: Towards a comparative sociology of violence." *Theory and Society* 1 (1974): 415–440.

Delort, Robert. *Les animaux ont une histoire.* Paris, 1984.

Dunning, Eric and Kenneth Sheard. *Barbarians, gentlemen and players: A sociological study of the development of rugby football.* Oxford, 1979.

Egmond, Florike. *Banditisme in de Franse tijd: Profiel van de Grote Nederlandse Bende, 1790–1799.* s.l., 1986.

Faber, Sjoerd. *Strafrechtspleging en criminaliteit te Amsterdam, 1680–1811: De nieuwe menslievendheid.* Arnhem, 1983.
Farge, Arlette. *La vie fragile: Violence, pouvoirs et solidarités à Paris au 18e siècle.* Paris, 1986.
Foucault, Michel. *Surveiller et punir: Naissance de la prison.* Paris, 1975.

Given, James Buchanan. *Society and homicide in 13th-century England.* Stanford, 1977.
Gutton, Jean-Pierre. *La société et les pauvres en Europe, 16e–18e siècles.* s.l., 1974.

Hanawalt, Barbara. "Violent death in 14th and early 15th-century England." *Comparative Studies in Society and History* 18 (1976): 297–320.
Herwaarden, Jan van. *Opgelegde bedevaarten: Een studie over de praktijk van het opleggen van bedevaarten in de Nederlanden gedurende de late middeleeuwen.* Assen-Amsterdam, 1978.
Hufton, Olwen H. *The poor of eighteenth-century France, 1750–1789.* Oxford, 1974.

Jong, Mayke de. "Monniken, ridders en geweld in elfde eeuws Vlaanderen." *Sociologische Gids* 29 (1982): 279–295.

Linebaugh, Peter. "The Tyburn riot against the surgeons." In Douglas Hay et al., *Albion's fatal tree: Crime and society in 18th-century England.* New York, 1975: 65–117.

Malcolmson, Robert W. *Popular recreations in English society, 1700–1850.* Cambridge, 1973.
Martines, Lauro, ed. *Violence and civil disorder in Italian cities, 1200–1500.* Berkeley, 1972.
Muchembled, Robert. "Anthropologie de la violence dans la France moderne, 15e–18e siècle." *Revue de Synthèse* IVe série, nr. 1 (1987): 31–55.

Österberg, Eva. "Violence among peasants: Comparative perspectives on 16th and 17th-century Sweden." In Göran Rystad, ed. *Europe and Scandinavia: Aspects of the process of integration in the 17th century.* Lund, 1983: 257–275.

Peters, Edward. *Torture.* Oxford, 1985.
Pike, Ruth. *Penal servitude in early modern Spain.* Madison, 1983.
Pleij, Herman. *Het gilde van de blauwe schuit: Literatuur, volksfeest en burgermoraal in de late middeleeuwen.* Amsterdam, 1979.

Scherpner, Hans. *Theorie der Fürsorge.* Hanna Scherpner, ed. Göttingen, 1962.
Sharpe, James A. "Last dying speeches: Religion, ideology and public execution in 17th-century England." *Past and Present* 107 (1985): 144–167.
Soly, Hugo. "Economische ontwikkeling en sociale politiek in Europa tijdens de overgang van middeleeuwen naar nieuwe tijden." *Tijdschrift voor Geschiedenis* 88 (1975): 584–597.
Spierenburg, Pieter. *The spectacle of suffering: Executions and the evolution of repression: from a preindustrial metropolis to the European experience.* Cambridge, 1984.
Spierenburg, Pieter, ed. *The emergence of carceral institutions: Prisons, gal-*

leys and lunatic asylums, 1550–1900. Rotterdam: Centrum voor Maatschappijgeschiedenis 12, 1984.

Stekl, Hannes. *Österreichs Zucht- und Arbeitshäuser, 1671–1920: Institutionen zwischen Fürsorge und Strafvollzug.* Wien, 1978.

Stone, Lawrence. "Interpersonal violence in English society, 1300–1980." *Past and Present* 101 (1983): 22–33.

Thomas, Keith. *Man and the natural world: A history of the modern sensibility.* New York, 1983.

Turner, James. *Animals, pain and humanity in the Victorian mind: Reckoning with the beast.* Baltimore-London, 1980.

Weel, A. J. van. "De wetgeving tegen het duelleren in de Republiek der Verenigde Nederlanden." *Nederlands Archievenblad* 81 (1977): 282–296.

8

Anderson, Michael. *Approaches to the history of the Western family, 1500–1914.* London, 1980.

Ariès, Philippe. *L'enfant et la vie familiale sous l'Ancien Régime.* Paris, 1960.

Barbagli, Marzio. *Sotto lo stesso tetto: Mutamenti della famiglia in Italia dal XV al XX secolo.* Bologna, 1984.

Boswell, John Eastburn. "Expositio and oblatio: The abandonment of children and the Ancient and Medieval family." *American Historical Review* 89 (1984): 10–33.

Bulst, Neithard et al., eds. *Familie zwischen Tradition und Moderne: Studien zur Geschichte der Familie in Deutschland und Frankreich vom 16. bis zum 20. Jahrhundert.* Göttingen, 1981.

Claverie, Elisabeth and Pierre Lamaison. *L'impossible mariage: Violence et parenté en Gévaudan, 17e, 18e et 19e siècles.* Paris, 1982.

Darrow, Margaret H. "Popular concepts of marital choice in 18th-century France." *Journal of Social History* 19 (1985): 261–272.

Davis, Natalie Zemon. *The return of Martin Guerre.* Cambridge: Mass.-London, 1983.

Demause, Lloyd, ed. *The history of childhood.* s.l., 1974.

Dupâquier, Jacques. *La population rurale du Bassin Parisien à l'époque de Louis XIV.* Paris-Lille, 1979.

Fauve-Chamoux, Antoinette. "Innovation et comportement parental en milieu urbain, 15e–19e siècles." *Annales ESC* 40,5 (1985): 1023–1039.

Flandrin, Jean-Louis. *Les amours paysannes: Amour et sexualité dans les campagnes de l'ancienne France, 16e–19e siècle.* Paris, 1975.

———. *Families in former times: Kinship, household and sexuality.* Cambridge, 1979.

———. *Le sexe et l'Occident: Evolution des attitudes et des comportements.* Paris, 1981.

Forster, Robert and Orest Ranum, eds. *Family and society: Selections from the Annales.* Baltimore-London, 1976.
———. *Ritual, religion and the sacred: Selections from the Annales, Vol. 7.* Baltimore-London, 1982.

Gillis, John R. *For better, for worse: British marriages, 1600 to the present.* New York-Oxford, 1985.
Greven, Philip. *The protestant temperament: Patterns of child-rearing, religious experience and the self in early America.* New York, 1977.

Haks, Donald. *Huwelijk en gezin in Holland in de 17e en 18e eeuw.* Assen, 1982.
Houlbrooke, Ralph A. *The English family, 1450–1700.* London-New York, 1984.
Hunt, David. *Parents and children in history: The psychology of family life in early modern France.* New York-London, 1970.
Huussen, Arend H., jr. *De codificatie van het Nederlandse huwelijksrecht, 1795–1838.* Amsterdam, 1975.
———. "Het kind in Friesland tijdens de 18e en 19e eeuw: Gezinshistorische en strafrechtshistorische aspecten." *Tijdschrift voor Geschiedenis* 94 (1981): 391–411.

Imhof, Arthur E. *Säuglingssterblichkeit im europäischen Kontext, 17.-20. Jahrhundert. Überlegungen zu einem Buch von Anders Brandström* (Demographic Data Base Newsletter 2). Umeå, 1984.

Joor, Johan. "Echtscheiding en scheiding van tafel en bed in Alkmaar in de periode 1700–1810." *Tijdschrift voor Sociale Geschiedenis* 11,3 (1985): 197–230.

Kooy, G. A., ed. *Gezinsgeschiedenis: Vier eeuwen gezin in Nederland.* Assen-Maastricht, 1985.

Löfgren, Orvar. "Family and household among Scandinavian peasants: An exploratory essay." *Ethnologia Scandinavica* (1974): 17–52.
Lougee, Carolyn C. *Le paradis des femmes: Women, salons and social stratification in seventeenth-century France.* Princeton, 1976.

Macfarlane, Alan. *Marriage and love in England, 1300–1840.* Oxford, 1986.
Medick, Hans and David Sabean, eds. *Emotionen und materielle Interessen: Sozialanthropologische und historische Beiträge zur Familienforschung.* Göttingen, 1984.
Menefee, Samuel Pyeatt. *Wives for sale: An ethnographic study of British popular divorce.* Oxford, 1981.
Mitterauer, Michael and Reinhard Sieder. *Vom Patriarchat zur Partnerschaft: Zum Strukturwandel der Familie.* München, 1977.

Outhwaite, R. B., ed. *Marriage and society: Studies in the social history of marriage.* London, 1981.
Ozment, Steven. *When fathers ruled: Family life in Reformation Europe.* Cambridge: Mass.-London, 1983.

Peeters, Henricus Franciscus Maria. *Kind en jeugdige in het begin van de moderne tijd, ca. 1500–ca. 1650.* Hilversum-Antwerpen, 1966.

Pfalz, Liselotte von der. *A woman's life in the court of the Sun King: Letters of -, 1652–1722.* Translated and introduced by Elborg Forster. Baltimore-London, 1984.

Pleij, Herman. "Jozef als pantoffelheld: Opmerkingen over de relatie tussen literatuur en mentaliteit in de late middeleeuwen." *Symposion* 3 (1981): 66–81.

Plumb, J. H. "The new world of children in 18th-century England." *Past and Present* 67 (1975): 64–95.

Pollock, Linda A. *Forgotten children: Parent-child relations from 1500 to 1900.* Cambridge, 1983.

Robisheaux, Thomas. "Peasants and pastors: Rural youth control and the Reformation in Hohenlohe, 1540–1680." *Social History* 6 (1981): 281–300.

Roodenburg, Herman. "Beating spouses: Marital violence and the consistory of the Reformed Church of Amsterdam, 1579–1630" [contribution to the second International Conference on the History of Crime and Criminal Justice,] Maastricht, 1984.

Roper, Lyndal. "'Going to church and street.' Weddings in Reformation Augsburg." *Past and Present* 106 (1985): 62–101.

Seaver, Paul S. *Wallington's world: A puritan artisan in 17th-century London.* Stanford, 1985.

Shorter, Edward. *The making of the modern family.* Glasgow, 1977.

——. *A history of women's bodies.* New York, 1982.

Spierenburg, Pieter. "Het gezinsideaal in kinderboeken rond 1800." In *Leeskabinet. Grepen uit de geschiedenis en de boekerij van het Rotterdamsch Leeskabinet, 1859–1984.* Leiden, 1984: 50–63.

Stone, Lawrence. *The family, sex and marriage in England, 1500–1800.* New York, 1977.

——. "Family history in the 1980's: Past achievements and future trends." *Journal of Interdisciplinary History* 12 (1981): 51–87.

Strauss, Gerald. *Luther's house of learning: Indoctrination of the young in the German Reformation.* Baltimore-London, 1978.

Sussman, George D. *Selling mother's milk: The wet-nursing business in France, 1715–1914.* Urbana: Ill., 1982.

Thompson, E. P. "'Rough Music': Le Charivari Anglais." *Annales ESC* 27 (1972): 285–312.

Trumbach, Randolph. *The rise of the egalitarian family: Aristocratic kinship and domestic relations in 18th-century England.* New York, 1978.

Tijdschrift voor Geschiedenis 94,3 (1981) [special issue about children's history].

Vandenbroeke, Chr. "Karakteristieken van het huwelijks- en voortplantingspatroon in Vlaanderen en Brabant, 17e–19e eeuw." *Tijdschrift voor Sociale Geschiedenis* 5 (1976): 107–145.

Weinstein, Donald and Rudolph M. Bell. *Saints and society: The two worlds of Western Christendom, 1000–1700.* Chicago-London, 1982.

Wheaton, Robert and Tamara K. Hareven, eds. *Family and sexuality in French history.* Philadelphia, 1980.

Wilson, Stephen. "The myth of motherhood a myth: The historical view of European child-rearing." *Social History* 9 (1984): 181–198.

Wrightson, Keith. *English society, 1580–1680.* New Brunswick: N.J., 1982.

9

Ariès, Philippe and André Béjin, eds. *Western sexuality: Practice and precept in past and present times.* Oxford, 1985.

Beauroy, Jacques et. al., eds. *The wolf and the lamb: Popular culture in France from the Old Regime to the 20th century.* Saratoga: Cal., 1977.

Boerdam, Christi. "Ongehuwd moederschap als sociaal verschijnsel. Casus: Rotterdam op het einde van de 18e eeuw." *Tijdschrift voor Geschiedenis* 98,2 (1985): 157–175.

Boswell, John. *Christianity, social tolerance and homosexuality: Gay people in Western Europe from the beginning of the Christian era to the 14th century.* Chicago-London, 1980.

Boucé, Paul-Gabriel, ed. *Sexuality in 18th-century Britain.* Manchester, 1982.

Bray, Alan. *Homosexuality in Renaissance England.* London, 1982.

Brown, Judith C. *Immodest acts: The life of a lesbian nun in Renaissance Italy.* New York-Oxford, 1986.

Brucker, Gene. *Giovanni and Lusanna: Love and marriage in Renaissance Florence.* London, 1986.

Castan, Yves. *Honnêteté et relations sociales en Languedoc, 1715–1780.* Paris, 1974.

Cipolla, Carlo M. *Clocks and culture, 1300–1700.* London, 1967.

Clark, Peter. *The English alehouse: A social history, 1200–1830.* London-New York, 1983.

Constable, Giles. "Aelred of Rievaulx and the nun of Watton: An episode in the early history of the Gilbertine order." In Derek Baker, ed. *Medieval women. Dedicated and presented to professor Rosalind M. T. Hill on the occasion of her 70th birthday.* Oxford, 1978: 205–262.

Cressy, David. "Kinship and kin interaction in early modern England." *Past and Present* 113 (1986): 38–69.

Darmon, Pierre. *Le tribunal de l'impuissance: Virilité et défaillances conjugales dans l'Ancienne France.* Paris, 1979.

———. *Le mythe de la procréation à l'age baroque.* Paris, 1981.

Dekker, Rudolf and Herman Roodenburg. "Humor in de 17e eeuw: Opvoeding, huwelijk en seksualiteit in de moppen van Aernout van Overbeke, 1632–1674." *Tijdschrift voor Sociale Gieschiedenis* 35 (1984): 243–266.

Easlea, Brian. *Witch hunting, magic and the new philosophy: An introduction to debates of the Scientific Revolution.* Brighton-Atlantic Highlands, 1980.

Faderman, Lillian. *Surpassing the love of men: Romantic friendship and love between women from the Renaissance to the present.* New York, 1981.

Fairchilds, Cissie. *Domestic enemies: Servants and their masters in Old Regime, France.* Baltimore-London, 1984.

Goodich, Michael. *The unmentionable vice: Homosexuality in the later medieval period.* Santa Barbara-Oxford, 1979.

Gutton, Jean-Pierre. *Domestiques et serviteurs dans la France de l'Ancien Régime.* Paris, 1981.

Gyssels, Marie Claire. "Het voorechtelijk seksueel gedrag in Vlaanderen, 1700–1880." *Tijdschrift voor Sociale Geschiedenis* 33 (1984): 71–104.

Hagstrum, Jean. *Sex and sensibility: Ideal and erotic love from Milton to Mozart.* Chicago-London, 1980.

Konrad, Helmut, ed. *Der alte Mensch in der Geschichte.* Wien, 1982.

Landes, David S. *Revolution in time: Clocks and the making of the modern world.* Cambridge: Mass.-London, 1983.
Laslett, Peter, Karla Oosterveen, Richard M. Smith, eds. *Bastardy and its comparative history.* London, 1980.

Mars, Leonard. "What was Onan's crime?" *Comparative Studies in Society and History* 26 (1984): 429–439.
Maza, Sarah C. *Servants and masters in 18th-century France: The uses of loyalty.* Princeton, 1983.
Medick, Hans. "Spinnstuben auf dem Dorf: Jugendliche Sexualkultur und Feierabendbrauch in der ländlichen Gesellschaft der frühen Neuzeit." In Gerhard Huck, ed. *Sozialgeschichte der Freizeit.* Wuppertal, 1980: 19–49.
Meer, Theo van der. *De wesentlijcke sonde van sodomie en andere vuyligheden: Sodomietenvervolgingen in Amsterdam, 1730–1811.* Amsterdam, 1984.
Mitterauer, Michael. *Ledige Mütter: Zur Geschichte illegitimer Geburten in Europa.* München, 1983.
———. "Gesindedienst und Jugendphase im europäischen Vergleich." *Geschichte und Gesellschaft* 11 (1985): 177–204.
Monter, William. *Ritual, myth and magic in early modern Europe.* Brighton, 1983.
Murphy, Terence R. "Woful childe of parents rage: Suicide of children and adolescents in early modern England, 1507–1710." *Sixteenth-Century Journal* 17 (1986): 259–270.

Noordam, Dirk Jaap. "Prostitutie in Leiden in de 18e eeuw." In Dick E. H. de Boer, ed. *Leidse facetten: Tien studies over Leidse geschiedenis.* s.l., 1982: 65–102.

Otis, Leah Lydia. *Prostitution in medieval society: The history of an urban institution in Languedoc.* Chicago-London, 1985.

Perry, Mary Elizabeth. "Deviant insiders: Legalized prostitutes and a consciousness of women in early modern Seville." *Comparative Studies in Society and History* 27 (1985): 138–158.

Quaife, G. R. *Wanton wenches and wayward wives: Peasants and illicit sex in early seventeenth-century England.* London, 1979.

Roodenburg, Herman. "De autobiografie van Isabella de Moerloose: Sex, opvoeding en volksgeloof in de 17e eeuw." *Tijdschrift voor Sociale Geschiedenis* 32 (1983): 311–342.
Ruggiero, Guido. *The boundaries of eros: Sex crime and sexuality in Renaissance Venice.* Oxford, 1985.

Solé, Jacques. *L'amour en Occident à l'époque moderne.* Paris, 1976.

Stearns, Peter N., ed. *Old age in preindustrial society.* New York-London, 1982.
Sterk, Hans. "Buitenechtelijke geboorten in Utrecht, 1775–1825: Een historisch-demografisch onderzoek." *Tijdschrift voor Sociale Geschiedenis* 13,1 (1987): 1–32.

Thomas, Keith. *Age and authority in early modern England. Raleigh lecture on history.* London, 1976.
Thompson, E. P. "Time, work-discipline and industrial capitalism." *Past and Present* 38 (1967): 56–97.
Trexler, Richard C. "La prostitution Florentine au 15e siècle: Patronages et cleintèles." *Annales ESC* 36 (1981): 983–1015.

Ussel, J. M. W. van. "Sociogenese en evolutie van het probleem der seksuele propaedeuse tussen de 16e en de 18e eeuw." vooral in Frankrijk en Duitsland, 2 volumes. Gent, 1967.

Wissell, Rudolf. *Des alten Handwerks Recht und Gewohnheit.* Ernst Schraepler, ed. I. Berlin, 1971.
Wrightson, Keith and David Levine. *Poverty and piety in an English village: Terling, 1525–1700.* New York, 1979.

Yeo, Eileen and Stephen Yeo, eds. *Popular culture and class conflict, 1590–1914.* Brighton-Atlantic Highlands: N.J., 1981.

INDEX